John G. Morris

Synopsis of the described Lepidoptera of North America, Part 1

Diurnal and Crepuscular Lepidoptera

John G. Morris

Synopsis of the described Lepidoptera of North America, Part 1
Diurnal and Crepuscular Lepidoptera

ISBN/EAN: 9783741192319

Manufactured in Europe, USA, Canada, Australia, Japa

Cover: Foto ©Thomas Meinert / pixelio.de

Manufactured and distributed by brebook publishing software
(www.brebook.com)

John G. Morris

Synopsis of the described Lepidoptera of North America, Part 1

SMITHSONIAN MISCELLANEOUS COLLECTIONS.

SYNOPSIS

OF THE DESCRIBED

LEPIDOPTERA

OF

NORTH AMERICA.

Part I.—DIURNAL AND CREPUSCULAR LEPIDOPTERA.

COMPILED FOR THE SMITHSONIAN INSTITUTION

BY

JOHN G. MORRIS.

WASHINGTON:
SMITHSONIAN INSTITUTION.
FEBRUARY, 1862.

ADVERTISEMENT.

The present "Synopsis of North American Lepidoptera" has been compiled by the Rev. Dr. J. G. Morris, of Baltimore, at the request of the Institution, to serve as a companion to the Catalogue published in 1860. The work is necessarily incomplete, claiming to be nothing more than a compilation of the published descriptions of the species of the same order; but its publication has been earnestly urged, as tending to facilitate a knowledge of an order of insects of great economical importance.

Dr. Clemens, of Easton, Pa., has made a number of important additions and corrections while the work was passing through the press, besides furnishing an original Appendix.

The Institution is also under obligations to Dr. J. L. Leconte, Prof. S. S. Haldeman, Mr. W. H. Edwards, and Dr. B. Clemens, for assistance in correcting the proofs of the work.

JOSEPH HENRY,
Secretary S. I.

Smithsonian Institution,
Washington, February, 1862.

PREFACE.

It is a gratifying fact that the science of entomology is making rapid progress in our country, and that so much has already been accomplished by industrious students. There is an increasing demand for books on this subject, but as yet none has been published professing to describe all the species of any one order of our insects. Admirable monographs of some families and genera of Coleoptera have been published by Dr. Leconte and others, and of our Sphingidæ by Drs. Harris and Clemens. Other entomologists, as Say, Melsheimer, Peale, Fitch, Ziegler, Haldeman, Uhler, and a few others, have contributed essentially to the discrimination of the species of various orders, but thus far no more comprehensive work has been attempted. Dr. Harris's invaluable book on the insects of New England injurious to vegetation, approaches the nearest to such a work of any that have appeared in our country. The splendid and costly volume of Boisduval and Leconte on our diurnal butterflies, published in Paris, 1833, has never been finished, and contains but twenty-one genera and ninety-three species. Foreign naturalists have described hundreds of our species, but their descriptions are scattered through a number of journals and other works not easily accessible to the American student.

I have attempted in this work to bring together in as narrow a compass as possible all our described Lepidoptera, embracing the Rhopalocera and the first two tribes of the Heterocera. Thus all our known diurnals, Sphinges and Bombyces, are included, down to the Noctuidæ proper. The latter will probably be taken up at some future time. I have collected the descriptions from many different authors, to whom due credit is given, but I have omitted some of the references to books, having given them in full in my catalogue

of North American Lepidoptera, published by the Smithsonian
Institution, which students will, of course, consult, if they desire
to know the literature of the species. For the same reason, I
have also omitted the list of abbreviations.

With the generous permission of Dr. Clemens, of Easton, Pa.,
I have incorporated nearly the whole of his admirable synopsis of
North American Sphingidæ, published in the Journal of the Academy of Natural Sciences, Philadelphia, 1859, only omitting some
minor details and the references to other authors. I have also
added his descriptions of Arctiidae, published in the Proceedings
of the Philadelphia Academy for Nov., 1859. He has himself
furnished an appendix containing many new and original views in
regard to the classification of our Lepidoptera, with descriptions
of genera and species.

In a supplement will be found a notice of such species as have
come to my notice up to the present date, principally from the
publications of Mr. S. H. Scudder and Mr. Edwards. The
latter gentleman has also supplied some important rectifications of
synonymy.

I have inserted descriptions of what are deemed by some to be
distinct species, but which are regarded by others as mere varieties,
in order to give their authors an opportunity of being heard, and
that readers may conveniently compare them.

As regards the classification, I have chiefly adopted that of Dr.
Herrich-Schaeffer, of Ratisbon, with some modifications of Walker,
of the British Museum. No doubt, changes will hereafter be
found necessary.

J. G. MORRIS.

BALTIMORE, December, 1861.

TABLE OF CONTENTS.

INTRODUCTION.

(FROM THE GERMAN OF V. HEINEMANN [*])

BUTTERFLIES are insects having six feet and membranous wings covered with minute scales. They undergo a perfect transformation; the caterpillar or larva, furnished with ten to eighteen feet, is hatched from the egg, and after various moulting, is changed into the pupa, from which after a longer or shorter period, the perfect butterfly comes forth. It performs its destined office, the female deposits her eggs and dies.

The butterfly consists of the body and members; the former is

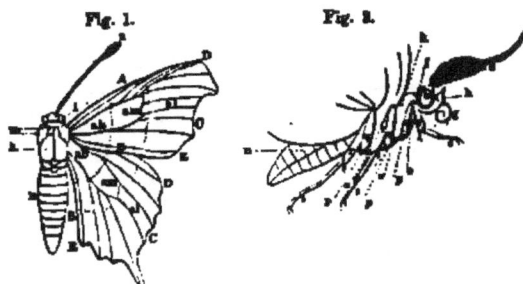

Fig. 1.　　　　Fig. 2.

composed of head, thorax, and abdomen; the members are the feet and wings.

[*] Die Schmetterlinge Deutschlands und der Schweiz. Systematisch bearbeitet von H. v. Heinemann. Braunschweig. 1859. F. Vieweg und Sohn.

HEAD, *caput.* Figs. 3 to 7.

Fig. 3.   Fig. 4.

The head is located in front of the thorax and separated from it,
in most instances, by a very indistinct segment. On both sides
are situated the large globular reticulated eyes, *oculi*, b; between
them and above is the *vertex*, c; in front is the *frons*, d; and below at the end is the mouth, *os*. The orbits of the eyes, *orbita*, fig.
4, e, are often distinguished by color and the character of the
scales. Between the *vertex* and *frons* are the feelers, *antennæ*, a,
near the eyes, behind them at the *orbita*, or at a little distance from
them in many species, are two small, round, smooth elevations,
which are called simple eyes, *oculli*, f.

The parts of the mouth are but little developed in butterflies.
The proboscis or tongue, *lingua*, g, is composed of the two lower
jaws (*maxillæ*) grown together as a double tube and usually separated only at the end, and which, for the most part, is corneous and
spiral. It is seldom absent, or consists only of two slender, soft
threads. Under the tongue are placed the two *palpi*, h, which are
three jointed; above these in many nocturnal moths there are in
addition two *palpuli*, figs. 5 and 6, i. The *palpi* are of various

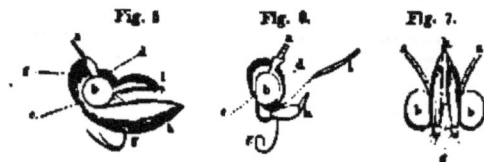

Fig. 5.   Fig. 6.   Fig. 7.

form and size, sometimes scarcely visible, sometimes as long as the
head and thorax together; the scales on the *palpi* are also of various density; the second joint is usually the longest and most
densely scaled, the terminal joint is, for the most part, slender and
pointed, frequently setaceous.

The feelers (*antennæ*) vary also in length; sometimes not exceeding the breadth of the head, and sometimes much longer than the length of the body.   They are *filiform* (thread-like) when the shaft is of equal thickness throughout the length, fig. 8; *setiform* (bristle shaped), when it becomes thinner towards the point, fig. 9; *fusiform* (spindle shaped), when it is thickest in the middle and thin at the root and point, fig. 10; *clavate* (club form), fig. 1, a, when it gradually thickens towards the summit, and *capitate* (knob form), fig. 11, when it suddenly enlarges at the end.

Fig. 8. 9.   10. 11.

With regard to their covering, the antennæ are either naked, or finely or compactly ciliated, fig. 12, or furnished with two single hairs on each segment, fig. 13, or tufted, fig. 14.

Fig. 12.   Fig. 13.   Fig. 14.

The processes of the antennæ are either in the form of obtuse *pyramidal* teeth, fig. 15, or serrate, fig. 16, or pectinate, fig. 18.

Fig. 15.   Fig. 16.   Fig. 17.   Fig. 18.

A comb-like or pectinate process from the under side of the antennæ is called *lamellate*, fig. 17. Frequently the processes themselves are ciliated, the pectinations equal on both sides, and the pyramidal teeth usually furnished at their summit with short cilia.

THORAX. Figs. 1, 2, k.

Fig. 1.   Fig. 2k.

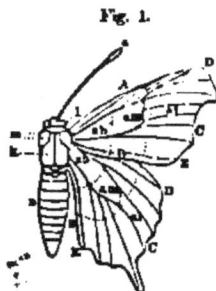
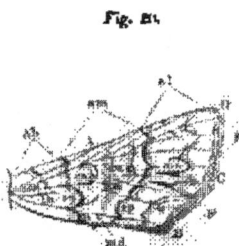

The thorax in front, bears the head; behind, the abdomen; beneath, the legs, and on the sides, the wings; the fore part, *collare*, l, and the shoulder-covers, *scapulæ*, m, which cover the roots of the wings, are often prominent. Besides this, the scales above often form peculiar elevations.

ABDOMEN. Figs. 1, 2, n.

This consists of six to seven rings, the segments of which are for the most part discernible under the scales. These segments often have above, or on the sides or behind, tufts of hair.

LEGS, *pedes*. Figs. 2, 18.

There are three pairs of legs, *pedes antici*, A, *pedes medii*, B, and *pedes postici*, C. They are composed of the *coxa*, by means of which the leg is inserted into the body, o, the *trochanter*, p, which unites the *coxa* and the *femur*, q; the *tibia*, r, and the feet, *tarsi*, s. The *tibiæ* have usually two spurs, *calcaria*, t, at the end; the hind *tibiæ* often have two behind the middle, u; the fore *tibiæ* occasionally have an emargination on the inner side, the upper edge of which is often prolonged into a spur, v.

Fig. 19.

WINGS, *alæ*.   Figs. 1, 20—26.

There are two pairs of wings, the fore wings, *alæ anteriores*, fig. 20, and hind wings, *alæ posteriores*, fig. 21, indifferently called *primaries* and *secondaries*, or *superiors* and *inferiors*—sometimes rudimentary or imperfect in the females, very seldom entirely wanting. The primaries lie with their hind edge on the fore edge of the secondaries, and cover the latter entirely in most of the nocturnal moths when in a state of repose. The secondaries are often folded together when at rest, and in that case usually have on the upper edge near the root, a strong elastic, sometimes double hair or bristle, which draws itself through a hook on the under side of the primaries and serves to maintain or render more easy the expansion of the secondaries. This is called the *frænum*, fig. 21, fr. This instrument is wanting in nearly all butterflies, which do not fold the secondaries when at rest.

The wings have three edges or margins, the anterior margin, *margo anterior*, on the upper side, A, the interior margin, *margo interior*, opposite the anterior, B, and the posterior margin or *seam*, *margo posterior* or *limbus*, C, which is opposite the root of the wing, *basis*, and binds the two other margins The angle, made

Fig. 20.   Fig. 21.

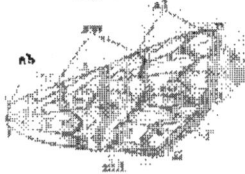

by the anterior margin and the posterior, is called the *anterior angle*, D, on the secondaries; on the primaries, this angle is called the *apex*; the angle between the posterior and interior margins E, is called the *posterior angle* on the primaries, and the *anal angle* on the secondaries. In many of the *Tineidae*, the interior margin and posterior angle are wanting, because the wings are very narrow and lanceolate, the edge proceeding in a regular curve from the apex to the base, figs. 27, 28.

The external limit or boundary of the wing is the *linea limbalis*, the scales extending beyond that are called the *fringe*, *ciliae*, fig. 20, F. In some micro-lepidoptera, especially in those with narrow wings, these *ciliae* are hair form and very long, and often longer on the secondaries than the breadth of the wing. A line of darker shade, parallel with the margin, often runs through the fringe. The margin is *straight*, *rectus*, when it proceeds in a straight direction; *curved*, when it forms a concave curve towards the base, fig. 20; *sinuate*, when it makes a convex curve towards the base, fig. 21; *entire*, when it forms an even, straight, curved or sinuate line, fig. 24; *undulate*, when it makes small rounded indentations, fig. 20; *dentate*, when there are sharp, angular, closely connected, tooth-like projections, fig. 21; *cucullate* (hood shaped) when small, rounded emarginations run into sharp angles toward the base, and *lobate*, when these emarginations are larger, fig. 23.

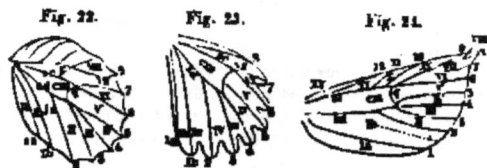

Fig. 22.   Fig. 23.   Fig. 24.

The wings themselves consist of a skin-like membrane which are held in a state of expansion by the ribs or nerves, *costae*, running across or through them. The structure and arrangement of these *costae* are of great importance in the systematic division of butterflies, and hence a special description of this structure and the determination of each costa are necessary, figs. 22—28.[1]

[1] [This nervular system of classification is of comparatively recent date, and is not closely followed in the present work.—M.]

From the middle of the root of each wing two ribs **proceed, which** usually are united in or behind the middle of **the wing, by** an interrupted or curved short cross nerve q, thus **inclosing a field** between it **and** the root or base. These are called **the** *anterior median nerve*, also the *subcostal*, 2c, and the *posterior median*, or *mediastinal*, 3d. From them and the cross nerve, a number of others proceed which terminate on the anterior and posterior margins. These are counted on the posterior margin from the posterior angle toward the anterior angle and are designated by the numbers 2, 3, 4, &c. &c., without any regard to the fact whether they **arise** separately from the median and cross nerves, or whether two or more unite towards the base and proceed from the common branch.

Besides these, there exist on the anterior margin of the wings from one to three nerves (on the primaries usually only one, seldom two), which arise from the base or root, and end on the posterior or interior margin; these are called *dorsal* **nerves.** These all bear the figure 1, and are distinguished by 1a, 1b, 1c. On the anterior margin of the primaries and for the most part on that of the secondaries, a nerve springs from the root, which **is** called the *costal* nerve, and which always bears the highest number, as No. 8, fig. 21. On the secondaries of many *Bombycidæ*, this **costal** nerve unites with the anterior median for a short **distance,** fig. 21, or it is entirely amalgamated with it at the base, so that it **seems** to proceed from the anterior median itself. The *frenulum* mentioned above is essentially also a nerve, which has remained **free from the membrane** of the wing. In most butterflies, which have no *frenulum*, there are in the **place of it,** on the anterior margin, one or more short curved nerves terminating on it, fig. 22. Nerve 6 of the secondaries is often wanting or is less distinct; this is also the case with nerve 6 of the primaries; their position is, however, easily determined by the larger space between 5 and 6, and they as well as other occasionally obsolete nerves are counted, so that each nerve, if possible, may always have the same numerical designation. That nerve at the apex of the primaries on the one terminating nearest to it, is called the *apical* nerve, fig. 21, 6.

The two median nerves with their ramifications, and the costal and dorsal nerves, are most prominent in the structure. Each of the medians runs off into three branches, the anterior of the secondaries into two, so that the individual branches, one after the other, proceed from the principal trunk. A more extensive result fication does not occur on the secondaries, and all the branches terminate in the outer margin; so also with the branches of the posterior median of the primaries. On the other hand, the two first branches on the primaries end on the anterior margin, nerves 11 and 10; the third proceeds as nerve 8 to the outer margin, but at or behind the cross nerve it furcates, and nerve 8, which here arises out of it, proceeds usually to the apex or near it, after it has again branched off, and nerve 7 is sent off to the outer margin and nerve 9 to the anterior, fig. 24. Nerve 10 also frequently furcates, in sending one branch towards the outer margin, impinging on nerve 8, usually at the place where nerve 7 originates, so that this is the continuation of that branch, which then cuts nerve 8. There are some deviations from this structure, especially in the microlepidoptera, of which the neuration of the primaries is more simple. It is not to be denied that the anterior margin and the apex of the primaries, on which the power of sustaining flight chiefly depends, acquire a greater strength from the complicated nerve structure, whilst the secondaries do not require it, inasmuch as they are closely united with the primaries; but on the other hand, on the interior margin they are furnished with more simple dorsal nerves, which are sufficient to sustain the wider superficies of the wings. The dorsal nerve of the primaries and the costal of the secondaries also appear to bear a mutual relation to each other, and this may also be true with regard to the corresponding margins. Both these nerves often have an inclination to furcate toward the root of the wings. In those cases, for instance, where the costa of the inferiors after its origin unites with the anterior median, it is essentially a furcation, in which case, however, the one branch constitutes part of the median, or coincides with it.

The spaces between the nerves are called *cells, cellulæ*, and are so distinguished by numbers, that the cell always contains the number of the nerve which it follows, counted from the interior margin. Thus the cell between the nerves 2 and 3 is called cell 2; the one between the nerves 3 and 4 is called cell 3, &c. &c. In fig. 25, they are distinguished by Roman letters. The cells, on the contrary, between the interior margin and nerve 2 are distinguished as cell 1a, 1b, 1c, 1d, fig. 25. The cell between the cross nerve and the two medians is called the median cell, *cellula media*, &c. Occasionally it is divided by one or two longitudinal nerves, in which case the distinct parts are called the *anterior median cell*

and the *inferior median cell*, fig. 25, sm and cm. In some genera,
the cross nerve between nerves 4 and 5 is obsolete, so that the
median cell is here open and passes into cell 4. There are also

sometimes small inclosed cells at the median, called *accessory* cells,
which are either situated at the root of the secondaries, fig. 22, r,
or *intrusive cells*, as fig. 25, s, or *appendicular* cells, as fig. 25, x.

In the family of *Tineidæ* with lanceolate secondaries, the nerve
structure declines. The median cell is indistinct or entirely obsolete, for all the nerves arise either from the root or other nerves,
or lose themselves in the membrane in the vicinity of the cross

nerve. The number of nerves, especially in the secondaries, also
diminishes.

In order to distinguish the wings lengthwise, they are divided
into three fields or areas, the *basal area*, figs. 1 and 20, ba, the
middle area, ma, and the *limbal area*, la. In many genera, these
areas or fields on the primaries are marked or distinguished by
simple, double or triple cross lines or narrow bands, which are
called, fig. 20, aa, *transverse anterior* (extra basillaire) or *posterior*,
ap (ligné coadée). These transverse bands or streaks are most
distinct and common in the *Noctuidæ*, fig. 20. In these, there is
in addition a cross line between the base and the anterior line,
which does not extend down to the interior margin, and which is
called the *basal half line*, sd (demi-ligne of the French); and another conspicuous cross line between the posterior line and the limb,
called the *undulate line*, rr (ligne-subterminal). In the field or
area, between these two, there are often arrow-shaped spots, which

are called *sagittate* spots. Besides these, the *Noctuida or moths*, have three distinguishing marks in the middle area; one in the cell, 1b, called the dentiform spot; a small, usually round one in the median cell, called the *orbicular*, mo, and behind it, a larger, kidney-shaped spot, called the *reniform*, mr. The two latter are often surrounded by a double edge, lighter than the ground color. Between both, there is usually drawn across the whole wing, a darker band, which is called the *transverse median shade*, am. Some species have a dark square spot between the two spots in the median cell, which often extends itself in a pyramidal form over the *orbicular* towards the root, so that both spots form a sort of recumbent pyramid, and is called the *pyramidal* spot. The posterior transverse streak alone is for the most part continued over the secondaries, which is then called, on both sides of the wing, the *arcuated line*.

The *reniform* mark appears on the under side as the *median lunula*, and all the dark spots on the cross nerve of both sides of the secondaries bear the same name, fig. 21.

In general, the structure of the several parts of the butterfly, as far as this is necessary to the determination of the species, genus, etc., can easily be recognized, without dissection. Difficulties sometimes occur in the frequently indistinct simple eyes, *palpuli* and *frenulum*. The last is usually present in species which fold their wings, when in a state of rest. A careful examination with a magnifying glass will readily detect the presence of this member. Much more difficult is a discrimination of the nerve structure, inasmuch as the nerves are frequently so covered with scales, that without removing them, the nerves cannot be seen. In this case, the under side of the wings should be particularly examined, inasmuch as the nerves on this side are more distinct than on the other. But if this will not suffice to determine all the points desirable to be known, the scales must be removed. In order to accomplish this, either take a sharp, fine penknife and move the blade or back gently over the nerves on the under side of the wings, until the nerves become distinct, or rub the whole wing with a soft, blunt hair pencil until all the scales are removed, but on the upper side only, when you wish to observe the furcation of the dorsal nerves of the primaries. This operation can be most satisfactorily performed when the specimens are fresh.

SYNOPSIS OF THE GENERA.*

. Section I. RHOPALOCERA.

Antennæ filiform, terminating in a knob or club. Wings, at least the primaries, elevated in repose; no bristle or *frenulum*; no *stemmata* or simple eyes—flight diurnal.

Fam. I. Papilionidae.

Larva with two retractile tentacles on first segment. Eyes prominent; palpi short; six feet adapted for walking; wings wide, nerves distinct, abdominal edge of the secondaries concave, discoidal cell in both wings closed, hooks of the tarsi simple, abdomen free.

A. Club of antennæ arcuate;
  Wings wide, secondaries with long tails or lobed.   Papilio.
B. Club straight;
  Primaries transparent at the summit, two black ocelli in the
  discoidal cellule, abdomen of the female with a corneous
  pouch. [No species east of the Rocky Mountains.]   Parnassius.

---

* [The present synopsis is believed to be approximately correct and generally agrees with the body of the book as far as the *Rhopalocera* are concerned, but in the *Heterocera* the conformity is not so rigid, owing to the indistinctness of some of our new American genera and an indisposition to create new families in which to place them. Further investigation will be required to determine their proper place in the system. The synopsis, however, gives a tolerably fair exhibit of our Lepidopteral Fauna, exclusive of the *Noctuidæ* proper, which may, however, hereafter be somewhat improved.

The Genus *Pinela*, p. 139, belongs to *Bombycidæ*, inadvertently placed where it now stands.—J. G. M.]

B

Fam. II. **Pieridae.**

Antennæ truncated at the extremity or clubbed. Secondaries with no concavity on abdominal edge, abdomen received into a groove, color whitish or orange to greenish-white on the upper side.

A. Antennæ abruptly terminating in an oval club;
    a. Wings narrow, elongate.
        * Secondaries wider than the primaries. [Mexican.] **Leptalis.**
    b. Wings of ordinary width.
        | Palpi with long fascicled hairs, last article shorter than
          the preceding.
           a. Antennæ rather long.   [Mexican.] **Euterpe.**
           b. Antennæ very short.   **Nathalis.**
        || Last article of the palpi at least as short as the pre-
          ceding.
           a. An auroral spot at the summit of the primaries,
             at least in the males.   **Anthocaris.**
           b. No auroral spot.   **Pieris.**
B. Antennæ truncated at the summit or terminating insensibly in
    an obconic club;
    a. Wings robust.
        * Primaries angulate.   **Rhodocera.**
        ** Primaries not angulate, secondaries entire.
          a. Antennæ rather long, terminating insensibly in a
           club.   **Callidryas.**
          b. Antennæ short, terminating in an obconic club.
                              Colias.
                                   Terias.
    b. Wings thin and delicate.

Fam. III. **Danaidae.**

Palpi remote, not extending much beyond the head, club of antennæ formed insensibly; wings wide, with the edges somewhat
sinuous, discoidal cell of the secondaries closed, thorax robust,
pectus with white dots, four walking feet.

Secondaries of the males with a black spot in relief.   **Danais.**

Fam. IV. **Heliconidae.**

Abdomen slender, elongate; wings narrow, oblong, abdominal
edge scarcely embracing the lower part of the abdomen, discoidal
cell closed.

Antennæ longer than the head and abdomen, nearly filiform, insensibly thickening towards the extremity, four walking feet.
    [Only one species; southern.]   **Heliconia.**

Fam. V. Nymphalidae.

Palpi nearly connivent, porrect, scaly, their anterior face as wide as the sides, discoidal cell nearly always open, nails of tarsi strongly bifid.

A. Antennae with a flattened club, primaries sinuous.   **Agraulis.**
           primaries not sinuous.   **Argynnis.**
  Under side of wings without nacred spots.   **Melitaea.**

B. Club of antennae not flattened;
  a. Primaries excised, angular, secondaries with a pale, silvery
    or golden mark like the letter L or C.   **Grapta.**
  b. Primaries subtriangular, less excised, apex truncate, palpi
    very hairy.   **Vanessa.**
  c. Primaries less angular, palpi less hairy.   **Pyrameis.**
  d.   Eyes naked, anterior legs less hairy.   **Junonia.**
  e. Primaries rounded at the summit, proboscis very long.   **Anartia.**
  f. Primaries dentate, sometimes prolonged to a tail.   **Nymphalis.**
  g. Primaries, fore margin arcuate, angle acute, tail prominent,
    color coppery.   **Paphia.**
  h. Primaries slightly dentate, secondaries with ocelli.   **Apatura.**
  i. Primaries not dentate, subfalciform—no ocelli.   **Aganisthos.**

Fam. VI. Libytheidae.

Larva without spines; palpi very long, contiguous, in the form of a beak, parallel to the axis of the body; wings angular, rather robust; discoidal cellule of secondaries open.   **Libythea.**

Fam. VII. Satyridae.

Wings robust, abdominal edge of the secondaries forming a groove; discoidal cellule closed; nervures of the primaries often dilated at their origin.

Costal nervure feebly inflated at base; color pale, dull, livid.
  [Extreme north.]   **Chionobas.**
Veins delicate, color uniform.   **Neonympha.**
Costal nervure much inflated, color dark brown; wings ocellate or
  with black spots.   **Erebia.**
One or two veins of primaries inflated; limb of secondaries dentate;
  secondaries marbled beneath; primaries ocellate.   **Satyrus.**
Eyes hairy; base of costal and median nerves of primaries dilated;
  secondaries lobed.   **Calisto.**
Costal nervure inflated; secondaries emarginate, slightly caudate.
    Debis.
The three principal nerves inflated, no ocelli.   **Coenympha.**

Fam. VIII. **Lycaenidae.**

Larva onisciform; discoidal cellule closed apparently by a small nervi form prominence.

Small; under side with small spots or ocellated points; often a
  marginal band of yellow spots; color of males usually blue.   **Argus.**
Under side ocellate; color fulvous.   **Polyommatus.**
Secondaries with filiform tails; sometimes simply dentate.   **Thecla.**

Fam. IX. **Erycinidae.**

Small; six walking feet in the males, four in the females.

Antennae long, annulated with whitish; abdomen shorter than the
  secondaries.   **Nymphidia.**
Antennae shorter, not annulate.   **Lemonias.**

Fam. X. **Hesperidae.**

Head wide, transverse; antennae often terminated by a hook.

Primaries triangular, often with pellucid spots; anal angle with no
  lobe, no silvery spots beneath.   **Hesperia.**
Anal angle with a short tail turned outwards, or an obtuse point,
  silvery spots beneath.   **Goniloba.**
Anal angle rounded.   **Nisoniades.**
Wings with orange-colored spots; color dark brown.   **Cyclopaedes.**
Primaries only erect in repose; disk in many species with an ob-
  lique velvety patch.   **Pamphila.**
Color brownish, with numerous translucent, angular and square
  whitish spots.   **Syrichthus.**

Section II. **HETEROCERA.**

Antennae variable, prismatic, pectinate, serrate, moniliform or
filiform; wings deflected in repose, secondaries mostly frenate;
stemmata or false eyes in many genera. Flight diurnal, crepuscular, most frequently nocturnal.

Fam. I. Epialidae.

Proboscis short or obsolete; palpi nearly obsolete; antennæ moniliform, shorter than the thorax; wings deflected, long, narrow, secondaries semi-hyaline. No stemmata.

Thorax not crested; body pilose; last abdominal segment of the female forming an elongated oviduct. **Epialus.**

Fam. II. Cossidae.

Body stout, pilose, head small, antennæ shorter than half the length of the wings, palpi small, eyes naked, proboscis short or obsolete, wings strongly veined, deflected; flight nocturnal; stemmata none.

Abdomen long, extending beyond the anal angle; hind tibia with two pair of spurs; palpi shorter than the head. **Cossus.**

Hind tibia with only terminal spurs. **Zeuzera.**

Fam. III. Conchilopodidae.

Body rather stout; proboscis not visible; antennæ of ♂ simple, rather serrated, pilose at the apex, which is acute; legs stout, pilose; hind tibiæ with four spurs; wings moderately broad, deflexed; abdomen a little tufted at the extremity. Larva oniaciform, or flat.

Fore wings, subcostal veins exterior to the disk, bifid, with two nervules from the disk. **Limacodes.**

With one nervule from the disk. **Adoneta.**

Fore wings, subcostal trifid, exterior to the disk. **Empretia.**

Fore wings, subcostal quadrifid, exterior to the disk. **Nochelia.**

Fam. IV. Zygaenidae.

Antennæ fusiform cylindric, often pectinate; proboscis long, convolute; wings longer than the body, primaries more narrow, secondaries rounded; stemmata present.

Costal vein bifid at base; antennæ fusiform. **Zygaena.**

Without costal vein. **Procris?** *Clemens.*

Antennæ not pectinate, thicker in the middle than at the apex. **Alypia.**

Fam. V. Glaucopididae.

Wings narrow, often limpid or with limpid spots; hind wings short; antennæ pectinated; flight diurnal.

b*

Hind wings without a discal nervule; median vein of hind wings
bifid; wings usually hyaline.   **Glaucopis.**
Median vein of hind wings trifid; subcostal vein with a marginal
branch; discal vein vertical,   **Ormetica.**
Hind wings with a discal nervule; median vein of hind wings bifid.
     Euchromia.
Median vein 3-branched.   **Cyanopepla.**

Fam. VI. Ægeriidae.

Primaries narrow, usually vitreous to the margin; secondaries
shorter, altogether vitreous; abdomen often with a caudal tuft.

Antennæ gradually thickened nearly to the end, curved; proboscis
nearly obsolete; male, with a caudal tuft.   **Trochilium.**

Fam. VII. Thyridae.

Antennæ feebly thickened in the middle, first article inflated; no
stemmata; wings broad, subtriangular, more or less angulate and
indented, opaque with semitransparent spots.

Body short and thick, abdomen conical, tufted at the end.   **Thyris.**

Fam. VIII. Psychidae.

Proboscis obsolete, palpi hirsute, antennæ pectinate or ciliate,
wings more or less rounded. Female mostly apterous.

Antennæ of the male pectinated more than half the length; abdomen of the male very long. Female wingless.   **Oiketicus.**
Antennæ of the male pectinated almost to the apex; abdomen extending beyond the wings. Female wingless.   **Thyridopteryx.**
Primaries acuminate at the apex. Female winged.   **Perophora.**

Fam. IX. Sphingidae.

Fore wings entire.

A. Terminal margin obliquely convex;
    Antennæ clavato prismatic, with hook and seta;
    Tongue twice or nearly twice as long as the body.   **Macrosila.**
    Tongue as long as the body, or somewhat longer.   { **Sphinx.** / **Dolba.** }

    Tongue two-thirds as long as the body.   { **Pachylia.** / **Darapsa** *pars.* / **Lapara.** }

    Tongue about one-third as long as the body.   { **Ceratomia.** / **Daremma.** }

    Tongue as long as palpi.   **Ellema.**

Antennæ slender, minutely serrate-setose;
Abdomen more or less tufted ;
Tongue moderate.   Oenosandra.
Tongue rather short.   Perigonia.
Tongue one-half as long as body.   Macroglossa.
Antennæ subclavate or fusiform ;
Abdomen not tufted at the tip.   { Arctonotus,
                                       { Deilephila.

Abdomen tufted at the tip.   { Smia.
                                       { Macroglossa.

B. Terminal margin wavy.   Anceryx.[*]
C. Terminal margin nearly straight or slightly sinuate ;[†]
   Antennæ with a long hook ;
   Tongue two-thirds as long as the body.   Pachylia.
   Tongue as long as the body.   Philampelus.
   Antennæ somewhat fusiform, rather short ;
   Tongue as long as the body.   Chærocampa.
D. Terminal margin excavated by the tip, convex from the middle;
   Abdomen without apical tuft ;
                                  { Ambulyx.
   Tongue not quite as long as body or as long.   { Pergesa.
                                  { Chærocampa *pars.*
   Tongue nearly obsolete.   S. Juglandis ♂ .
   Tongue about half as long as the body.   Darapsa.
   Abdomen with apical tuft ;
   Fore wings with silvery streaks.   Calliomma.

FORE WINGS NOT ENTIRE.

Fore wings indented above interior angle ;
   Abdomen with apical tuft.   Proserpinus.
   Abdomen without apical tuft.   Unzela.
   Fore wings excavated near tip and anterior angle.   Thyreus *pars.*
   Fore wings truncate at the tips ;
      Angulated and denticulated.
   Tongue nearly as long as the body.   Thyreus *pars.*
      Angulated in the middle.
   Abdomen with apical tuft.   { Enyo.
                               { Perigonia.

   Abdomen without tuft or scarcely tufted :
   Tongue about as long as palpi.   Smerinthus *pars.*
   Tongue two-thirds as long as the body.   Deidamia.
   Not angulated in the middle.   Perigonia *pars.*

---

* M. cnerus and the ♀ of S. juglandis.   † A. cnicus.

Fore wings denticulated;
With silvery streaks and angulated.   Calliomma *pers.*
Without silvery streaks, not angulated.   Smerinthus.

Fam. X. Drepanulidae.

Body slender; proboscis inconspicuous, palpi very short, antennæ longer than the thorax, feet slender, naked; wings wide, primaries falcate; antennæ of the males moderately pectinated—of the female scarcely longer.   Drepana.

Fam. XI. Saturniidae.

Antennæ setiform, bipectinate in the male; no stemmata; secondaries wide, fringe short, without a frænulum; body thick, densely pilose.

Antennæ of males bipectinate, females unidentate.   Saturnia.
Antennæ of both sexes strongly pectinate; wings with vitreous, diaphanous spots.   Attacus.
Antennæ of the male deeply pectinated to much beyond half the length, minutely serrated from thence to the tips—of the female, simple.   Dryocampa.
Antennæ of the male merely serrated for more than one-third; of the female, simple.   Ceratocampa.

Fam. XII. Bombycidae.

Antennæ in both sexes pectinated, strongly in the males; body robust, pilose; wings strong; cocoons of the larvæ silky, hence called spinners.

A. Limb of the wings denticulate;
    a. Antennæ very short.
        a. Body thick.   Gastropacha.
B. Limb of the wings not denticulate;
    a. Antennæ of the male equally pectinate.
        | Primaries with veins not punctate.
        O Primaries with no pale discal spot; subacuminate at
            the apex.   Clisiocampa.
        — Primaries rounded at the apex.   Pinsala.
        || Primaries, veins punctate.   Artace.

Fam. XIII. Notodontidae.

Body usually robust, pilose, extending beyond the wings; antennæ of the male usually pectinate, rarely simple—of the female, simple, rarely pectinate; wings entire, often long.

Antennæ of the female pectinate. Cossus.
Antennæ of the female serrate. Notodonta.
Antennæ of both sexes pectinate. Ichthyura.
Antennæ of the male pectinate, naked at the apex. Heterocampa.
Antennæ of the male not pectinate to the apex. Edema.
Antennæ setaceous, minutely ciliated. Eudryas.
Antennæ of male minutely pectinated; of female minutely serrated.
Datana.
Antennæ moderately pectinated. Nadata.

Fam. XIV. Arctiidae.

Stature robust; stemmata conspicuous; maxillæ short; antennæ moderate, those of the female, when not nearly obsolete, bipectinate or ciliate, sometimes serrate or simple; abdomen thick, often muscular; frenulum conspicuous; flight often heavy, nocturnal.

Thorax not fasciculate, wings rounded. Arctia.
Primaries not dilated; body maculate. Spilosoma.
Wings rather long, third article of palpi very short. Lophocampa.
Body slender, third article of palpi globose. Nemeophyla.
Antennæ simple, ciliate; abdomen not extending beyond the wings; scale of prothorax straight. Phragmatobia.
Primaries long. Bombatheria.
Antennæ in both sexes simply ciliate, with two strong ones at each joint. Callimorpha.
Body fusiform; antennæ minutely pectinate. Apantesis.
Antennæ deeply pectinate; tibiæ with only terminal spurs. Orgyia.
Antennæ simple in both sexes—those of the male sub-plumose below. Deiopeia.
Antennæ of male deeply pectinate—of female moderately so. Dasychira.

Fam. XV. Lithosiidae.

Body slender, elongate; no stemmata. Antennæ usually ciliate or simple. Thorax not crested. Abdomen not extending beyond the wings, or very little. Wings often subelliptical, primaries narrow, secondaries often twice as wide as the primaries. Frenulum conspicuous. In repose, the primaries placid.

Antennæ setaceous, simple; wings not long. Euprepia.
Antennæ setaceous, simple, shorter than the body; wings narrow. Eubaphe.
Antennæ setaceous, simple, minutely pubescent; wings long, narrow. Mirina.

Antennæ of the male setaceous.   **Gnophria.**
Antennæ deeply pectinated.   **Lagoa.**
Antennæ setiform, scarcely ciliated in the males; wings rather
  broad, semi-diaphanous, rounded.   **Nudaria ?**
Antennæ rather deeply pectinated; wings narrow, rather long.   **Lexica.**
Antennæ moderately pectinated; wings moderately long and broad.
                                                                  Apistosia.
Antennæ moderately pectinated; wings rather long and narrow.   **Ardonea.**
Wings moderately broad, not long.   **Hypoprepia.**
Wings very narrow, somewhat pointed.   **Lymire.**
Wings narrow, not long.   **Fercota.**
Hind wings much broader than the fore wings.   **Lithosia.**

Fam. XVI. Ctenuchidae.

Hind wings without costal vein; subcostal bifid from the origin
of the discal; discal vein simple, angulated usually beneath the
middle of the disk; median vein 4-branched.

Wings very narrow; hind wings broader than the fore wings: antennæ moderately pectinated in the male.   **Acoloithus.**
Hind wings narrower than the fore wings; rather deeply pectinated
  in the male.   **Aglaope.**
Wings broad or narrow, elongate-trigonate; antennæ deeply pectinated in the male.   **Ctenucha.**
Fore wings rather broad, obovate; antennæ rather thick, tapering
  at the tips, pectinated.   **Malthaca.**

Fam. XVII. Lycomorphidae.

Hind wings without costal vein; subcostal bifid; median 3-
branched.

Wings narrow; fore wings nearly fusiform; antennæ biserrated or
  very minutely pectinated.   **Lycomorpha.**

Fam. XVIII. Melameridae.

This family has much affinity to the *Glaucopidida*, and also to
the *Pyralites*. Wings generally more or less black, occasionally with
a metallic hue, frequently adorned with bright colors or partly limpid. All the species are Mexican or West Indian.

Body nearly linear and cylindrical; wings black, generally narrow,
  with yellow, lateous or white stripes, bands or spots.   **Josia.**
Wings mostly limpid; generally long and narrow.   **Dioptis.**
Wings rather broad; fore wings not angular.   **Uraga.**

Fam. XIX. Pericopidae.

Species large, often with pale dots on the head and thorax; wings ample, more or less vitreous. Mexican and West Indian.

Wings long, rather broad, more or less semi-hyaline.	Pericopus.
Wings long, rather narrow, with semi-hyaline spots.	Composia.
Wings ample; fore wings with a semi-hyaline band.	Eucyane.

Fam. XX. Nyctemeridae.

Some of the genera, like a few of the *Pericopidae*, have much resemblance to the *Rhopalocera*. The body is slender and the wings ample, and they have likewise a general resemblance to some of the *Geometrites*. They are nearly all Mexican and West Indian.

Wings moderately broad; fore wings straight in front, rounded at the tips, oblique along exterior border; antennae moderately pectinated.	Carallea.
Wings long and narrow; antennae of ♂ minutely pectinated.	Dubale.
Wings short, somewhat triangular; antennae of ♂ pectinated on both sides.	Psycomorpha.
Wings broad, not long, generally black with semi-hyaline white spots.	Melanchroia.

LEPIDOPTERA

OF

NORTH AMERICA.

.

_____

SEC. I. RHOPALOCERA.

Antennæ filiform, terminating in a knob or club. Wings, at least the primaries, elevated in repose; no bristle or *frenulum* at the anterior edge of the secondaries. No *stemmata* or simple eyes on the vertex. Flight diurnal.

FAM. I. PAPILIONIDAE.

Larva elongated, with two retractile tentacles on the first ring. *Perfect insect* with the abdominal edge of the secondaries concave. Discoidal cellule closed. Hooks of the tarsi simple. Six feet adapted to walking in both sexes.

PAPILIO LINN.

Head large; eyes prominent; palpi very short, joints scarcely distinct; antennæ elongate, club pyriform; body, more or less hairy, free from the wings; wings robust, borders more or less dentated, often terminated by a tail; central cell closed; nerves prominent.

Larva smooth, or bearing fleshy tubercles; provided with two retractile tentacles protruding from the first segment; emitting a strong odor when alarmed.

Chrysalis without metallic spots, moderately angular, occasionally a horn on the back; head square, bifid, or truncate; fastened by the tail and suspended by a thread across the back.

1

1. **Papilio turnus** Linn. Boisd. et Lec. pl. 6, 7. Say's Amer. Ent. pl. 1. Pal. de Beauv. VII, pl. 2. Lucas, Hist. Nat. des l'ap. Exot. pl. 118. Cram. Pap. Exot. pl. 38. *P. alcidamas* Cr.

Wings pale yellow, border black—that of the primaries divided by eight or nine yellow spots; wings traversed by four unequal black bands.

Secondaries with a marginal range of six lunules, two rufous, four yellow; anal emarginations bordered with yellow. These lunules are surmounted with groups of bluish atoms. Emarginations large, obtuse; tail black, bordered with yellow within.

Under side of primaries similar to the upper, the marginal points forming nearly a continuous ray, preceded by a range of grayish atoms.

Under side of secondaries has the border sprinkled with grayish yellow, with all the marginal lunules rufous in the middle; a range of bluish lunules above the border, three or four of which are surmounted with a little rufous.

Body blackish above; two yellow rays on the thorax, yellowish ray below.

Larva green above, whitish below; sides with seven oblique greenish stripes; between the fourth and fifth segments, a transverse band, yellow before, black behind; on the third segment a lateral, ocellated spot, with two blue pupils; head flesh-color, neck yellow; feeds on various species of *Prunus.*

The chrysalis is brown, more or less deep, with a conical point on the breast.

The perfect insect measures from three to four inches across the wings, and is found in the United States generally.

Boisd.

2. P. **glaucus** Linn. (Most probably a *Southern female variety of P. turnus.*) Boisd. et Lec. pl. 8, 9. Cram. Pap. Exot. pl. 139. Pal. de Beauv. VI, Liv. pl. 1.

Size and habits, and when held towards the light, showing the markings of *P. turnus;* varies from pale brown to deep black.

Wings blackish brown; primaries, with a marginal series of eight oblong, yellowish spots, preceded by arcuated groups of bluish atoms. Secondaries sprinkled with blue, except at the base; outer limb divided by a range of seven lunules, some yellow, others rufous, surmounted by cuneiform spots of pulverulent blue, forming one wide arcuated band; outer border dentated; tail spatulate, bordered with yellow inside, as well as all the emarginations of all the wings.

Beneath primaries paler brown, with three blackish bands, proceeding from the anterior margin, the two outer abbreviated, the basal continuous. Secondaries brown; a transverse line gradually narrowing towards its end. Marginal lunules, rufous, slightly bordered with yellow; the band of bluish atoms (in the fresh subject) surmounted by four or five triangular rusaety spots.

Body black, with two yellow spots on the sides.

Larva similar to that of *P. turnus*.

Inhabits the Southern States.

BOISD.

3. **P. rutulus** *Boisd.* The figure, size, and *facies* of *P. turnus*, of which it is perhaps only a modification. Ann. Soc. ent. de France, X, 2me sér. 279.

Upper side ochry yellow, with the extremity of all the wings rather widely bordered with black; primaries cut by the nerves, and marked with five unequal transverse black bands, the first continuing from the base the whole length of the abdominal edge of the secondaries; the second descending to the anal angle of the latter, and abruptly bending to unite with the first; the third a little divided, and ending on the first branch of the median; the fourth at the extremity of the discoidal cellule and not passing the median; the fifth somewhat shorter; the border of the primaries is divided by a ray of ochry yellow oblong points; secondaries with a streak or blackish arc on the extremity of the discoidal cellule; a marginal row of six crescents, of which the anal is fulvous and the other five yellow; anal emargination bordered with fulvous, surmounted as well as the internal crescent with a group of blue atoms; the exterior edge with wide obtuse teeth, and a spatulate black tail, edged with yellow within, as well as all the emarginations.

Under side similar to the upper, the marginal points forming a continuous ray, preceded by a ray of grayish atoms; that of the secondaries has the border powdered with yellowish gray, the marginal crescents being ochry as above. A row of bluish crescents on the anterior edge of the border. *Body* blackish above, yellowish below, with two black central rays.

It differs from *P. turnus* in that the upper side of the secondaries have not the fulvous crescent on the internal angle, and the under side has not the fulvous crescent in the border, nor the sagittate spots between the border and discoidal cellule of *P. turnus*.

California.—In the spring and summer.

BOISD.

4. P. eurymedon *Boisd.* Ann. Soc. ent. 2me sér. 280.

The general appearance of *turnus*, but the black predominates more, and the bands are nearly white. Ground color very black; primaries with four bands, white a little yellowish; the first at the base; the second before the discoidal cellule; the third, very short, represented by a simple streak at the end of the cellule; the fourth bifid at its summit and united below to the second; a row of marginal oblong points diminishing before the internal angle. Secondaries with two wide whitish bands, or rather with a whitish disk, cut by a black ray as in *P. turnus*; the border divided by a row of five crescents, and two fulvous anal ones; anal emargination fulvous, surmounted, as well as the internal crescent, with a group of blue atoms; tail black, spatulate, edged with whitish as well as the emarginations. Under side of primaries, nearly like the upper. That of the secondaries similar to *turnus* but much more black; the border sometimes divided by fulvous crescents, and sometimes of the ground color, except the two anal and the anal emargination which are always fulvous; all the crescents are surmounted by a row of blue spots. *Body* black above, with two white rays on the thorax; whitish below, with two black ventral rays.

California.

Gray regards *P. eurymedon* as a mere variety of *P. rutulus*. Catalogue of Lep. Ins., in collection of Brit. Mus., pt. 1, p. 24.

BOISD.

5. P. rutulus *Boisd.* Ann. Soc. ent. 2me sér. 280.

Primaries black, traversed by an oblique, yellow band, divided into eight spots by the black nerves; this band is preceded by two streaks and a spot of the same color; the border divided by eight yellow points. Secondaries with a black arc at the end of the discoidal cellule; abdominal edge black, powdered with yellow, tail linear, black, obtuse, bordered with yellow on one side.

The anal eye bright fulvous, circled with yellow fulvous, body black, with a lateral yellow band.

California.

BOISD.

6. **P. troilus** *Linn.* Bois.L et Lec. pl. 10. Sm. Abb. vol. 1, pl. 2. Cram. Pap. Exot. pl. 207. Herbst, pl. 17 (mas.) pl. 29 (foem.). Drury, 1, pl. 2. Lucas Hist. Nat. des Pap. Exot., pl. 19. *P. ilioneus,* Sm. Abb.

Wings blackish, dentate, emarginations yellowish white. *Primaries,* with a range of seven or eight spots of pale yellow on the outer margin, gradually decreasing in size upwards. *Secondaries,* with a marginal range of seven greenish lunules, the upper one, orange yellow. Above these, a wide bluish gray band divided by the nervures. The lunule of the anal angle, is orange yellow inside greenish gray outside, tail black.

Under side of primaries, deep brown, two marginal series of yellow spots, besides one or two towards the upper edge.

Under side of secondaries, has two series of rufous lunules, separated by a band of bluish atoms; anal spot rufous.

Body black, with yellow spots on the thorax and a line of yellow points on each side. Expands three inches.

Larva green, with a yellow marginal band; two series of blue points on the sides and in the fourth segment two carneous spots, on the third, a carneous ocellated spot, pupilled with deep blue, on the first, a black band; the under side ferruginous, at the base of the membranaceous feet, a series of seven blue points. Feeds on *Laurus sassafras* and other species of *Laurus.*

Chrysalis a little gibbous, pale ferruginous striated with a deeper tint.

Bois.

7. **P. asterias** *Fab.* Sm. Abb. 1, pl. 1. Cram. Pap. pl. 385. Bois.d. et Lec., pl. 4. Lucas Hist. Nat. des Pap. Exot. pl. 20. Haldeman, in Stansbury's Expl. p. 366. *P. troilus,* Sm. Abb.

Wings deep blackish brown, with two macular pale yellow bands; the first, composed of eight spots, nearly triangular, traversing the middle of the secondaries; the second is marginal, and the spots are smaller, eight or nine of which are on the primaries and six on the secondaries, mostly lunular. Besides these, the primaries have one or two spots toward the upper margin, and the secondaries, six or seven blue lunules between the spots. At the anal angle, a rufous spot, with a black point—emargination yellowish—tail black.

Under side of primaries, paler; the first band is pale rufous, except the first two or three triangular spots, which are yellow.

Under side of secondaries, orange, except the two last of the marginal band, which are yellow. In the female the spots of the first band are smaller, sometimes obsolete on the secondaries.

Body black, rufous points on the thorax, and three series of yellow spots on the sides. Expands four inches. United States.

Larva apple green, with a transverse band on each segment formed of alternate bands of black and yellow, excepting on the first three, where the black band is interrupted by the yellow points only towards the spiracles; whilst on the back, the yellow are placed before the black band; three black points on the anterior part of the first segment and two black lines on the head. The feet have black points at their base.

Feeds on *Daucus carota, Anethum faeniculum* and other umbelliferous plants.

Chrysalis grayish, with ferruginous wavy streaks.

Boisd.

8. P. philenor *Fab.* Boisd. et Lec. pl. 11. Sm. Abb. 1, pl. 3. Say's Amer. Ent. pl. 3. Cram. Pap. pl. 205. Drury 1, pl. 2. Herbst, pl. 19. Lucas Hist. Nat. des Pap. Exot. pl. 8. *P. astinous,* Cram.

Primaries black, with a greenish reflection towards the outer border—emarginations, whitish; in some specimens, a series of whitish spots along the outer border, obsolete in others.

Secondaries blackish, with a greenish hue except towards the base, a range of six whitish lunules—tail black, whitish at the base.

Under side of primaries, dull black; a marginal range of five or six whitish spots.

Under side of secondaries has a brilliant greenish reflection, except at the base, where there is a whitish spot. Seven lunules of bright rufous, surrounded with black. Four or six of those above bordered with white on one side; expands three and a half inches. North America.

Larva brown, with two lateral series of smaller reddish tubercles. The first segment has two long processes—nine of moderate length below and others in the three last segments.—Feeds on *Aristolochia serpentaria.*

Chrysalis grayish violet, back yellowish; head truncate.

Boisd.

9. P. chalcas *Fab.* Boisd. et Lec. pl. 6. Herbst, pl. 62; Drur. I, pl. 19. Cram. Pap. Exot. pl. 93. *P. palamedes* Drur. Cr.

Wings olive black, traversed by an interrupted, pale yellow band, continued over the secondaries, formed of triangular spots in the primaries—a yellow spot near the upper edge and nearer the base, a short, yellow, narrow line. Towards the outer edge, a marginal range of roundish, yellow lunules; anal angle, with a bluish crescent; a little dusty yellow between the base and the marginal points. Emarginations, yellow. *Tail* black, with a yellowish ray in the middle.

Under side of primaries, paler; near the base, a transverse line of grayish atoms.

Under side of secondaries is traversed by a rufous line. The transverse band, macular, whitish within, rufous without. The marginal lunules are whitish—the middle rufous, and the interval sprinkled with yellowish dust; a band, also, of blue crescents.

Body black; a yellow line on each side of the thorax and abdomen.

Southern States.—Expands four and a half inches.

Larva green, punctured with pale blue; under size and feet, carneous; head, yellow, ferruginous with a black arc; the third segment has a lateral, carneous eyelet with a blue pupil, surmounted with a blue point. The fourth has a lateral, carneous spot. The green is separated from the reddish, by a marginal, yellow line. Feeds on *Laurus*.

Chrysalis, uneven, or humpbacked; ferruginous on the back, roseous beneath and four ranges of small bluish points.

Nolan.

10. P. thoas *Linn.* Boisd. et Lec. pl. 12. Cram. Pap. Exot. pl. 167. Drur. pl. 22. Herbst, pl. 39. Lucas, Hist. Nat. des Pap. Exot pl. 15. *P. cresphontes* Cram. *P. aristus* Hbnr.

Wings deep black above, traversed by a yellow macular band, extending across the base of the secondaries. The third spot is oblong, surmounted by two or three others. The primaries have besides, four yellow lunules near the inner angle.

The secondaries have a curved series of six or seven yellow lunules; the anal angle has a rufous crescent with a group of blue atoms above it; dentate and the emarginations of both, yellow.

Tail black, with an oval yellow spot.

Under side of primaries much paler ; on the base, a large, radiated yellow spot, which fills the discoidal cellule and eight marginal spots.

Under side of secondaries, yellow, divided by six or seven blue lunules, three or four of which are associated with as many ferruginous spots. The anal spot corresponds with that of the opposite side. Expands five inches.

Body yellow; back black; thorax, black above, with two yellow lines. Southern States.

Larva brownish below, back covered with large, whitish blotches, irregular, spotted with brown.

Chrysalis brown, marked with blackish points. Feeds on the orange tree.

BOISD.

11. P. ajax *Sm. Abb.* Boisd. et Lec. pl. 1. Sm. Abb. I, pl. 4. Pal. de Beauv. IV, pl. 2.

Upper side of the wings, blackish brown, with bands, whitish yellow ; the first, which is at the base of the primaries, is very small ; the second is wide and descends beyond the middle of the secondaries ; the third is only a whitish line ; the fourth is wide, bifid above, and descends on the disk of the secondaries ; the fifth and sixth are short and of unequal length ; the seventh is marginal and interrupted.

The secondaries have fewer whitish lunules, two other bluish lunules, and at the anal angle a bilobed red spot, resting on a black crescent, which is cut transversely by a blue line and surmounted by a group of grayish atoms. Emarginations whitish.

Tail black, linear, white at the extremity and on the sides.

Under side paler, a narrow grayish band on the internal side of the marginal band of the primaries.

Under side of secondaries differ considerably from the upper.

The white marginal lunules are preceded by a black streak and the blue lunules by an equal number of grayish crescents. A slightly flexuous scarlet line, bordered with white, separates the two whitish bands. The bilobed spot is surmounted with white. Expands three inches. Southern States.

Body blackish, with two whitish lines on the sides; antennæ brown, with the lower side of the club blackish. Its flight is low, rapid, not sailing.

Larva green, with the stigmata yellow and a tricolored transverse band in the fourth segment, black in the middle, and yellow behind. Feeds on *Porcelia pygmara* and *Anona palustris*.

Chrysalis ferruginous, with clearer lines and darker striæ.

Bomo.

12. **P. marcellus** *Cram.* Boisd. et Lec. pl. 11. Cram. Pap. Exot. pl. 98. Esper, Pap. Eur. Part 1, pl. 51. *P. ajax* Illbr.

Resembling *ajax* but somewhat larger. *Wings* deeper black, transverse bands more narrow; secondaries more elongate; tail longer, the posterior half of which is whitish. The red anal spot is not bordered with white in front as in *ajax*. It sometimes forms a large round spot, sometimes a transverse ray, and again bilobed, or divided into two spots; no blue crescent between this red spot and the anal emargination; all the whitish bands, more narrow on both sides, excepting that along the abdominal border, which is wider. All the other characters as in *P. ajax*. Southern States. Flight more graceful than that of *P. ajax*.

The *larva* differs much from that of *P. ajax*. It has a whitish ground, striated transversely with violet, with a yellow semi-circular band on the middle of each ring; the band of the fourth ring is bordered before with black. Chrysalis ferruginous. Feeds on *Porcelia pygmæa*.

Bomo.

Gray in Cat. Lep. Ins. Brit. Mus. considers *P. ajax* and *P. marcellus* to be varieties of the same insect. This is now the opinion of all the collectors in this country. One of them declares that *P. ajax* is the spring, and *P. marcellus* the fall brood of the same species.

J. O. M.

13. **P. sinon** *Fab.* Boisd. et Lec. pl. 3. Cram. pl. 318. Herbst, pl. 45. Drur., 1, pl. 22. (Drury's fig. is not exact; Cramer's, too green.) *P.* protesilaus Drur. *P. celadon* Lucas.

Size of *P. ajax*, and analogous. *Wings* deep black, with the bands yellowish white, ordinarily a little greenish. The first, at the base, is linear and descends on the secondaries, even to the red spot; the second, of the same width, a little bent, widening on the secondaries; after this, there is a small, very narrow line, sometimes obsolete; then, a band wide in the middle, bifid above, and terminating in a point on the disk of the secondaries; then, a small, short band, a whitish or greenish point, and finally, a marginal,

macular band composed of eight lunules. The secondaries have
six whitish crescents, marginal, and a large, red, bilobed anal spot,
placed a little obliquely and wider internally.

Tail black, linear, whitish at the end.

Under side of primaries, brownish, on which all the characters
of the upper side are visible.

Under side of the secondaries also presents the same bands as
the opposite surface, but there is, besides, a red line placed on the
black band between the two principal white bands; near the anal
angle, this line is bent, as in *P. ajax*, but instead of widening, as in
the latter to form two red lunules, it continues in the same width
on the disk; this line is bordered with white, but only in the place
where it corresponds to the red spot above. Some grayish atoms
above the two last white crescents.

Body blackish, with two whitish rays on the thorax; abdomen
blackish, *annulated* with white above, grayish below. Antennæ
blackish. Southern States.

Larva unknown.

P. sinon is easily distinguished from the neighboring species by
its greenish bands, the macular posterior band; the red line on the
under side not forming a crescent and the body annulated with
white.

Boisd.

14. P. celadon *Lucas*. Guér. Rev. Zool. 1852, 130.

A little smaller than *P. sinon*, with which it has been confounded by Cramer. Upper side of wings, black, with bands of a
clear green thus disposed; the first, linear, common, running along
the abdominal edge of the secondaries, nearly to the red spot of
the anal angle; the second, also common, descends a little lower
on the secondaries; the third, very wide, principally in the secondaries, common, and sending out on them two prolongations, which
reach the costal edge; on the secondaries it does not extend beyond
the intermediary band; the fourth, narrow, not passing the median nervure of the secondaries; the fifth, smaller than the fourth,
is placed beyond the summit of the discoidal cellule, and is divided
into three spots by the nervures, which are of a russety brown; the
sixth, macular, forming, on the second, a range of spots, more or
less rounded, nearly marginal, but sinuous and not touching the
posterior edge of the primaries, as in *P. sinon*. Under side, like

the upper, with the black inclining towards russety. The secondaries, besides the characters already mentioned, present a marginal range of lunules of a clear green and an anal spot of red vermilion, but much smaller than in *P. sinon*. The external edge is dentated as in *sinon* by a tail less long and entirely black; emarginations less bordered with whitish than in *sinon*. Under side russety white, with the red spot more narrow than above. There is also a reddish, feeble line, which goes from the middle of the edge, without passing the superior nervure of the discoidal cellule; antennæ black; palpi clothed with white hairs; head black, with a yellowish ray on each side, which continues on the sides of the thorax, thorax black: abdomen black, annulated with yellowish white on the sides; below, of this color, with a longitudinal narrow black ray.

Expands 58 mill.   California—Oregon?

Lucas.

11. *P. arcesilaus Lucas.* Guér. Rev. Zool. 1852, 131.

Male, a little smaller than *P. ajax*. Upper side brown black, with bands of a pale yellowish white thus disposed; first, linear, common, touching the abdominal edge of the secondaries so as nearly to join the red spot of the anal angle, from which it is separated only by a small line of black; the second is a little wider; the third, more narrow, not passing the discoidal cellule; the fourth, very wide, bifid in parting from the median nervure: the fifth, very short, wider and less elongated than the third; the sixth, nearly marginal, feeble, interrupted by the nervure; under side of a black more clear, with the same designs as above; upper side of secondaries deeper black, with the spot of yellowish white very large, occupying all the centre and losing itself posteriorly in a space powdered with yellowish; anteriorly, it is interrupted by a black band very short, which proceeds from the middle of the edge; the red spot is large, transverse, oblique and supported behind on two yellowish spots; the exterior edge presents a marginal space of yellow lunules, dentated; tail black, yellow at the extremity. Under side resembles the upper, and has besides in the middle, a red sinuous ray, bordered with black on the internal side at its anterior part, and slightly edged with this color on the external side; the red transverse band is more narrow than on the upper side, edged with white behind, with the lunules of the anal angle pow-

dered with whitish atoms; tail much more edged with yellow on
the internal side than above; palpi yellowish white; this color continues on the sides of the thorax, which is black. Abdomen black
above, yellow in the sides or below—a ray in each side.

California—Oregon? Expands 62 mill.'

LUCAS.

16. P. machaon *Linn.*   Figured by most European authors.

Upper side yellow, with a rather wide black border, sinuate
within, divided on the primaries by a row of eight yellow marginal
points and in the secondaries by a marginal row of six lunules of
the same color, of which four or five of the intermediary are largest;
all these lunules are preceded by an orbicular spot formed of blue
atoms; the anal angle is marked by a reddish yellow ocular spot,
surmounted by a whitish violet crescent. Primaries with four
black spots along the upper edge, of which the outer one is the
smallest and nearly round; the two following are transverse, not
passing the median nervure; the fourth is very large, occupying
all the base, and powdered with yellowish gray, as well as that part
of the border comprised between the marginal points and the
ground color; the branches of the median nerve black and dilated.
Secondaries have a black arc at the extremity of the discoidal cellule; the abdominal edge black, powdered with yellowish; the contour with short teeth and a black linear tail of moderate length,
obtuse at the extremity, bordered with yellow in the internal side;
emarginations bordered with yellow as well as the sinus of the primaries.

Under side nearly similar to the upper with all the nervures
black and the yellow more mingled with the black and occupying
more space. The blue spots of the secondaries are more narrow,
somewhat lunulate; the second, third, and sometimes the sixth are
each surmounted with a russety spot. Body yellow, with a dorsal
band; antennæ black.

California—Europe—Asia.

BOISD.

17. P. villiersii *Boisd.*   Boisd. at Lec. pl. 14.   *P. devilliersi* Godt.

Nearly same size as *P. troilus*. *Wings* greenish blue, shining,
dentated, emarginations white, a marginal range of bluish lunules,
much smaller on the primaries than on the secondaries.

Tail moderate, spatulate.

Under side of primaries, shining, blackish bronze to the middle, with an arc of white spots at the end of the discoidal cellule, and a marginal range of silver white triangular spots.

Under side of secondaries, brown, with the origin of the base and outer border, yellowish white; in the middle, three large, silver spots. Towards the edge, a range of five to seven silver spots, separated from the external border by a black zigzag line, surmounted by ferruginous crescents, reposing on a deep bronze ground.

Body black bronze, with white points on the prothorax, breast and sides of the abdomen. Southern States.

BOISD.

18. **P. polydamas** *Linn.* Boisd. et Lec. pl. 15. Cram. Pap. pl. 211. Drury I, pl.17. Herbst, pl. 10. Seba Mus. p. 39. Merian, Surin. pl. 31. Lucas Hist. Nat. des Pap. Exot. pl. 17.

Size of *P. asterias.* *Wings* greenish black, traversed towards the extremity by a band of yellow more or less pale, of moderate width, somewhat macular; formed, on the primaries, of enneiform, pointed spots, and on the secondaries, of cuneiform, truncated spots. The primaries sinuate, slightly dentate; the secondaries dentate. Emarginations yellow.

Under side brown; that of the primaries more clear towards the base, with the same markings as above; that of the secondaries is more obscure towards the extremity, with a marginal range of seven reddish brown spots, linear, transverse, a little flexuous, of which the three outer are usually bordered with silver white. At the base, there is also a reddish spot.

Body black, the prothorax, the sides of the breast, and of the abdomen, with rufous spots or streaks.

Georgia.

Larva which lives on *Aristolochia*, is brown, with fleshy spines of the same color; the body radiated with red and each segment having, besides, four ocellated spots, half yellow, half red.

BOISD.

PARNASSIUS Latr.

Head rather small; eyes not prominent: palpi longer than the head, elevated beyond the front, furnished with long and fine hairs, and composed of three distinct, equal articles; the first arcuate, the second straight, the third linear; antennæ short, terminating in a straight, ovoid, elongated club.

Body thick, hairy; abdomen of the female provided with a pouch or horny valve. Wings, parchment like, nerves prominent, not dentated, and nearly destitute of scales on the under side and towards the summit on the upper side. Secondaries have the abdominal edge sloped, leaving the abdomen entirely free.

Larva smooth, cylindroid, thick, with small tubercles, a little hairy. The first ring provided with a furcate tentacle of the shape of a **Y**. Head small, round. ·

Chrysalis cylindrico-conical, powdered with a bluish efflorescence, enveloped between leaves in a light tissue of silk and sustained by transverse threads.

1. P. clarina *Everm.* Bullet. de Moscou, XVI, 839, fig. 1.

Primaries white, with two black streaks in the discoidal cellule; the extremity semitransparent, gray, divided by a row of white spots; internal angle sometimes without spots and sometimes marked with a small blackish spot.

Secondaries white, with two small red ocelli; anal angle with a black arc, often obsolete in the males.

Under side of the secondaries with two ocelli as above; the base usually with the impression of red obsolete spots; the arc of the anal angle black or red. Body blackish, with whitish hairs, very short on the thorax; palpi covered with yellow hairs. The *female* has the anal arc distinct, reddish on the under side; wings divided above by a blackish marginal festooned line; the horny pouch of the under side of the abdomen, large, entirely white and bordered with yellow hairs.

Northern California.

Everman.

2 P. nomion *Fisch.* Fisch. Entomograph. de la Russie, II, pl. 6. Boisd. Icon. pl. 4, fig. 3. Godt. Dup. Suppl. pl. 43. Boisd. Spec. Gen. pl. 2. Gray. Cat. Lep. Ins. Brit. Mus. fig. 316, 409, 410.

Base of the wings black; transverse sinuous ray of the extremity well defined on all the wings; two spots between the discoidal cellule and this ray, on the primaries, marked with reddish; the spot on the middle of the internal edge has the middle of it reddish;

secondaries with a reddish spot at the base; abdominal edge
covered with a space more deeply blackish, ascending in the form of
an anchor or hook, to the extremity of the discoidal cellule; fringe
intersected with black; antennæ strongly annulate with black.
Female a little larger than the male, wings powdered with blackish;
pouch of the under side of the abdomen small, brownish, not
prominent, formed of two wrinkled valves, separated by a longitudinal groove.

Rocky Mountains.

Boisd.

2. P. clodius *Menetries*. Voyage de M. Wosnesensky. *P. clarius*, Boisd.

Very near to P. *clarius* Everam. but larger; wings of a dead
white, a little yellowish (the transparent part and the row of spots
on the external edge as in *clarius*.)

On the *under side*, the primaries have the same black spots as in
clarius, but the two discoidal spots of the anterior edge are very
narrow; the base is widely powdered with black; near the internal
edge there is a well defined small black spot.

The secondaries have the base powdered with black, the two
ocelli are small and irregularly round, pale reddish, with a deep
black edge; no anal spot.

Under side paler white and glossy; with the same markings as
above but less distinct.

The four spots at the base of the secondaries are pale red, each
one limited outwardly by a black trait. (These spots do not occur
in *P. clarius*.) Towards the anal angle, there is a caneiform spot
of a similar red, with a black line above and below it, and near it
and more outwardly, there is a black point.

The whole body is covered with long, yellowish hairs, which on
the front, the anterior of the thorax and under the abdomen are
shorter, closer and rusty. Expands three inches and a half.

California.

Menetries.

Fam. II. PIERIDAE.

Larva slightly pubescent, somewhat attenuated at the
extremity. *Perfect insect* with the abdominal edge of the
secondaries without a concavity. Discoidal cellule closed.
Hooks of the tarsi unidentate.

PIERIS Schr.

Head rather small, short; eyes naked, moderate; palpi rather long, somewhat compressed, a little cylindrical, clothed with rigid hairs, slightly fasciculate; the last article slender, *nearly as long as the preceding*, forming a small acicular point; antennae moderate, the joints distinct, the club *ovoid* compressed. Abdomen not robust, a little shorter than the secondary wings. Wings moderately strong, the discoidal cellule closed; the internal edge of the secondaries convex, embracing more or less the lower part of the abdomen.

Larva cylindrical, elongate, pubescent, marked with longitudinal rays and small granules more or less visible.

Chrysalis angular, terminated before by a point more or less long, sometimes nearly smooth, and sometimes furnished with tubercles more or less sharp, attached by the tail and a transverse line.

Pieris may easily be distinguished from the neighboring genera by the antennae not being truncated, the palpi less compressed, of which the last article is always nearly as long as the preceding; by the less robust body and the wings more thin. *They never have those central silver or ferruginous spots which are always present on the discoidal cell of the under side of the wings of the true Colias.* The prevailing color is white, more or less spotted with black.

1. P. monuste *Hübn.* Samml. Exot. Boisd. et Lec. pl. 16. Hübn. Pap. Exot. Cram. 151. *P. eratis* Godt. *P. cleomes* Boisd.

Male. Upper surface of primaries, white with a black border, wider at the summit, serrated within. Upper surface of secondaries, entirely white in the males. Under surface of primaries white, with the border pale brown, or yellow ochre.

Under surface of secondaries, yellow ochry, more or less pale, with the border pale brown, and a saffron spot at the base.

The female has an arcuated black line on the middle of the primaries, and a marginal series of black triangular spots in the secondaries.

Body white; thorax obscure; shoulders grayish; neck ferruginous. Antennæ black, annulated with white; tip of the club greenish. Expands two to three inches.

Larva violet, with longitudinal bands of citron; head, feet, and lower part of the body yellow—a little greenish.

Chrysalis pale, yellowish, shaded with blackish, with a raised point on the back.

Feeds on *Cleome pentaphylla*.

Georgia to Brazil.

Boisd.

2. P. protodice *Boisd.* Boisd. et Lec. 45, pl. 17.

Male. Primaries white, with a large black trapezoidal spot near the upper edge, and an oblique, macular, black band; the summit, near the border, has four or five black triangular spots on the nervures.

The *upper side* of the secondaries entirely white, sometimes with a small group of blackish atoms near the internal angle.

The *under side* of the primaries resembles the upper, but the black markings are paler—a little greenish at the summit.

The *under side* of the secondaries white, slightly tinted with yellow or greenish, with the nervures more pale or ochry; a slight blackish spot on the border of the discoidal cellule, besides a marginal impression of dark atoms scarcely distinct from the ground color.

The *female* has the black of the primaries more intense; the secondaries are white, tinted with grayish; exterior edge dark, with five or six white trapezoidal spots.

Under side washed with greenish brown in the nervures, and a submarginal band of the same color.

Expands two and a half inches.

United States.

Boisd.

P. sisymbrii *Boisd.* Ann. Soc. ent. 2me sér. X, 284.

Upper side white; primaries with a subcostal spot; a transverse, interrupted ray, and some longitudinal streaks at the end of the nerves, blackish brown; secondaries without spots.

Under side of primaries similar to the upper, except the streaks, which are powdered with greenish brown.

2

Under side of secondaries white, with the nerves widely edged with greenish brown, dilated towards the marginal edge, and nearly united between this edge and the cellule by a transverse ray; obsolete, more or less interrupted.

California—rare.

Bois.

P. laucodice *Erwm.* Figured in Bulletin, Moscow, XVI, pl. 7, f. 2.

Wings on both sides white; nerves black; primaries on both sides, with the usual median spot, occupying the transverse nervure and external fascia, black; secondaries below, with the external fascia, blackish.

Northwestern America.

EVERSMANN.

P. autodice *Hübn.* Samml. Exot. Boisd. Spec. Gén. 639.

Upper side of the male white; primaries, with some marginal triangular blackish marks at the summit, preceded by a macular transverse ray of the same color; a black oblong spot in the form of a transverse ray on the extremity of the discoidal cellule.

Upper side of female white, a little yellowish, with a marginal row of black triangular marks on the four wings, nearly touching, preceded by a sinuous row of sagittate spots, of which the concavity is turned inwards; the black spot of the discoidal cellule of the primaries is large, quadrangular, and a little prolonged on the upper edge.

Under side of the primaries differs from the upper in having the discoidal spot cut by a white vein; in having the summit of a pale yellow, with the marginal marks less distinct, paler, and each one divided by a whitish gray nervure.

Under side of secondaries pale yellow in both sexes, with the nervures whitish gray, slightly edged with blackish, a little dilated on the posterior edge; a transverse ray of six sagittate spots, blackish, corresponding to those on the upper side of the female; the upper edge, and two points at the base, saffron yellow; a vein of the same color, but paler in the discoidal cellule, and another not far from the abdominal edge, a little mingled; a small white space on the extremity of the discoidal cellule, and a small blackish, oblong spot, pupilled with whitish, situated between the costal and subcostal nervure.

Body whitish; head saffron yellow; antennæ black, annulated
with white, with the club greenish white.

California—Chili.

3. P. oleracea *Harr.* Ins. Mass. (1842), 314.

All the wings white; base of the primaries dusky.

Under side of primaries yellowish at apex; cervures darkish.

Under side of secondaries straw color, with broad dusky nervures; base, deep yellow.

Body black; antennæ blackish, annulated with white; ochry at
the end of the club.

Northern States.—Expands two inches.

HARRIS.

P. casta *Kirby.*—*P. cruciferarum* Boisd. Spec. Gén. 519. Figured in
Kirby Faun. Bor. Amer., IV, pl. 3.

Antennæ black, annulated with white; wings white; primaries,
at the anterior margin, sprinkled with blackish; secondaries, underneath, with a few scattered black scales accompanying the nervures;
wings rounded and very entire.

KIRBY.

P. menapia *Felder.* Wiener Entom. Monatschrift, III, No. 9, 271.

Wings tender, white; veins black at the base; elongate; con-
colored; costal streak and apical edge black; this edge profoundly
sinuate within, and divided on the under side with six (in the male
five) large white spots.

Secondaries of the male with a submarginal streak, flexuous;
blackish above, with black points situated at the extreme of the
veins; below more distinct.

Secondaries of the female with the same streak, but much more
distinct and obscure; below, the veins widely margined with fuscous; the costa, the basal and other spots a little livid; abdomen
above blackish, below whitish.

Utah.

FELDER.

ANTHOCARIS Bom.

Head rather small, short; eyes moderate, a little prominent; palpi rather long, somewhat divergent, bristled with stiff hairs, somewhat fasciculate; last article thin, very distinct, acicular, scarcely as long as the preceding; antennæ rather short, joints distinct, terminated more or less abruptly by an ovoid, compressed club. Abdomen not robust, a little shorter than the secondaries. Wings delicate, discoidal cellule closed; the secondaries lightly embracing the under part of the abdomen.

Larva slender, pubescent, attenuated at both extremities.

Chrysalis naked, navicular; rings immovable, carinated, more or less arcuated, destitute of lateral points; attached by the tail and a transverse line.

Anthocaris differs from *Pieris* in the form of the chrysalis, which is navicular, equally attenuated at both ends, and in the antennæ of the perfect insect. It can easily be distinguished from the allied genera by the delicate texture of the wings and the auroral or reddish spot which covers more or less of the summit of the primaries, at least of the males in two of our species.

1. A. genutia *Fab.* Ent. Syst. III, 1, 193. *Ihermisirri* (fem.) Godt. A. *Midea?* Hübn.

Wings white; primaries, with external border concave, and the summit pale orange; upper edge near the base, sprinkled with grayish, a small black point near the middle.

The fringe of the secondaries bordered with a range of small black spots.

Under side of primaries white, with the summit greenish, small black point in the middle.

Under side of secondaries marbled with green.

Expands an inch and an eighth.

The female is destitute of the orange summit, but has blackish spots along that edge. The black spot on the middle of the primaries is larger than in the male.

Southern States.

Bom.

2. A. lanceolata *Boisd.* Ann. Soc. ent. 2me sér. X, 254.

A little larger than *A. genutia*, but destitute of the auroral spot in the male as well as in the female.

Upper side white; primaries with a black spot at one end of the discoidal cellule, and at the other, some brownish black streaks.

Under side of primaries with the costal spot as above, and the summit reticulated with greenish gray.

Under side of secondaries entirely marbled and finely reticulated with greenish gray, with the edge marked with some small white spots, of which one is largest.

California—rare.

Bomb.

3. A. eara *Boisd.* Ann. Soc. ent. 2me sér. X, 245.

Upper side white, or white slightly tinted with yellow; that of the primaries marked at the summit with a large triangular orange red spot, bordered with black; the black spot of the discoidal cellule is connected with the black border.

Upper side of the secondaries transparently showing the markings of the opposite side, and with some blackish, marginal spots, more or less distinct.

Under side of primaries a little more pale than above.

Under side of secondaries finely pointed, and marbled with white and greenish, like *A. genutia*.

The females with a paler spot, not edged with black, and divided at the extremity by a series of sulphury white marginal points.

California

Bomb.

NATHALIS Bomb.

Head rather large, bristled; palpi long, separate, extending beyond the eyes, covered with stiff hairs; second article long, the last much shorter than the preceding; antennæ very short, joints distinct, terminated abruptly by an oval, flattened club, a little truncated at the summit; body moderate. Abdomen as long as the secondaries. Wings not robust, discoidal cellule closed; the secondaries embrace a portion of the under side of the abdomen; the anterior border, in the male, with a small, oval, glandular, naked impression.

It differs from *Terias* by its long, separate, and bristly palpi; from *Anthocaris* and *Pieris*, by the shortness of the antennæ, and especially by the small glandular space mentioned above.

1. N. iole *Boisd.*   Spec. Gén. 1, 589.

Wings saffron yellow; the primaries have at the summit a black, rather large, triangular space, marked on the side with two small yellow streaks. Below this space, not far from the internal angle, a spot of the same color, surmounted by a small black point. Secondaries without spots, or with the border, with small, blackish, separate lines, nearly obsolete; the costal border blackish, marked with a lenticular space of dull gray, partly denuded.

The *under side* of the primaries differs from the upper, the ground color being paler, except along the side, where it is orange yellow; there is a small, discoidal, black point, and below the apical blackish space there are three blackish spots.

The *under side* of the secondaries is greenish yellow, strongly powdered with obscure atoms, especially towards the base, with two transverse obsolete lines, formed by the condensed atoms.

Body blackish, powdered with yellowish atoms; antennæ short, blackish, annulated with whitish, with the club much compressed, and of a russety tint. Expands one inch.

Texas.

Boisd.

2. N. irene *Fitch.*

" Differs from *N. iole* in having the under side of the primaries destitute of a blackish central dot, and of the three blackish spots towards their inner angle, the hindmost one is here prolonged into a broad stripe extending to the base of the wing, and slightly separated from its inner edge; and the base of the wing instead of its outer edge is orange yellow."

Mississippi Valley.

Fitch.

RHODOCERA *Boisd.*

Head small, retracted; eyes naked, not prominent; palpi much compressed, contiguous, furnished with short hairs, scaly; last article very short; antennæ rather short, *truncated, more or less* arcuated, *enlarging from the middle to the extremity;* thorax rather robust, covered with fine silky hairs. Wings rather robust, discoidal cellule closed. The primaries always have the summit more or less sharp and angular; the secondaries sometimes furnished with a prominent angle, forming a groove, which embraces the lower part of the body; body shorter than the secondaries.

Larva feebly pubescent, attenuated at both extremities, green, with a paler lateral ray.

Chrysalis much arcuated, spindle-shaped at both ends; always attached by the tail, and a transverse line over the body.

Rhodocera strongly resembles the next genus, *Callidryas;* but it differs from that in the arcuated antennæ and angular wings. The ground color is yellow, more or less pale. Ordinarily, there is a ferruginous spot at the extremity of the cellule of each wing. The median nervure of the secondaries is more prominent than in the other genera. The males differ from the females in the more lively yellow of the wings. In the American species, the costal border of the primaries of the males is hispid, and rough to the touch.

1. R. maerula *Fab.* E. S. III, 1, 212. Figured in Cram. Pap. II, pl. 129. Illust. Pap. pl. 102. Donov. Gen. Illust. of Ent. pl. 2. Boisd. et Lec. 71, pl. 23. *R. eclipsis* Cram. Ebst.

Yellow citron above, with a black point on the middle of the primaries, and one of pale orange, slightly circled with black on the secondaries.

The *primaries* are somewhat falcate at the summit; along the outer border, a range of small orange points; secondaries, angular.

Under side paler than the upper; discoidal spot of each wing ferruginous, and marked with a white point.

Body of same color as the wings; antennæ reddish.

Female, more lively yellow than male. Expands three and a half inches.

Southern States.

Boisd.

2. R. lyside *Godt.* Encyc. Méthod. IX, 93.

Upper side whitish green; primaries, with the base, yellowish orange, and the summit washed with yellow russety. Secondaries, without spots.

Under side of primaries a little paler than the upper, with the summit somewhat broader russety.

Under side of inferiors yellowish, without spots, the median nervure very prominent; antennæ short, grayish rosy, with the end of the club ferruginous.

Female whiter, with the upper side of the secondaries ochry yellow, and the base of the primaries deprived almost entirely of the yellow spot.

Southern States.

Godart.

3. R. rhamni *Linn.* Figured in Boisd. Spec. Gén. pl. 2, B. fig. 7.

Upper side of the male citron yellow, that of the female greenish white, with an orange point on the extremity of the discoidal cellule of each wing, and some very small indistinct ferruginous points on the fringe.

Under side of the male paler than the upper; the discoidal orange spot is replaced in both sexes by a ferruginous point, a little whitish in its centre.

Body blackish above, yellowish below, with white silky hairs on the thorax and at the base of the abdomen. Expands over two inches.

California.

Bosd.

CALLIDRYAS Bosd.

Inferior palpi much compressed, with short hairs; last article conical, much shorter than the preceding; antennæ of moderate length, neatly truncated at the extremity, slightly arcuated, enlarging insensibly from the base to the extremity. Prothorax rather long. Body robust. Abdomen much shorter than the secondaries. Wings robust, discoidal cellule closed; secondaries forming a groove which embraces the under side of the body.

The *Callidryas* vary in color from orange yellow to pale saffron. Their wings, *always destitute of angles*, ordinarily have on the under side, at least in the females, one or two silvery or ferruginous points.   They are distinguished from *Colias* and *Rhodocera* by the absence of the rough costal edge of the primaries of the males, of the prominent angles, and by the form of the antennæ.   The sexual difference is very striking, and this has led some writers to describe the two sexes as different species.

1. C. eubule *Linn.*   Figured in Boisd. Spec. Gén. pl. 2, B. fig. 6.   Cram. 120.   A. B. 163.   A. B. C.   Boisd. et Lec. 74, pl. 24.   Sm. Abb. 1, pl. 5.   *C. marcellina* Cram.

Boisd. in Boisd. et Lec. p. 75, following the example of the old authors, confounded this species with *C. marcellina*, making the latter the male; but a subsequent comparison of the *larvæ* convinced him of his error.

Male.—*Upper side* yellow citron, with a thin indistinct border of yellow, more dull and dentated on the primaries; the fringe of all the wings is marked by distant ferruginous small points.

Under side more deeply yellow; primaries, with two ferruginous, geminate points at the end of the discoidal cellule, followed by a transverse, brownish, zigzag ray.

Under side of secondaries, with two discoidal, silvery points, circled with ferruginous, situated on a sinuous, brownish line, preceded by red ferruginous points, more or less distinct, and followed by a tortuous, brownish, indistinct line.

Female, or *C. eubule* of authors, of a more vivid yellow; secondaries rounded, fringe orange, interrupted by transverse brown lines or spots.   Primaries, with a large brown spot on the middle, cut by an orange arc; border narrow, brown, crenulate, preceded towards the summit by a tortuous, blackish, indistinct ray.

Under side more intensely yellow than the male, with the same markings more prominent and more ferruginous; the primaries have two discoidal, united silvery points; the secondaries have a part of the points of the base united in a tortuous line, so that they have three tortuous, transverse rays, of which the middle one is joined with that of the primaries.

Body yellowish, with greenish hairs on the thorax; antennæ, and under side of the last article of the palpi, rose brown.   Expands about two and three quarter inches.

Florida.

Boisd.

2. C. marcellina *Fab.* E. S. III, 1, 209. Figured in Donov. Nat. Repos. pl. 6. Sm. Abb. I, pl. 5. Boisd. et Lec. pl. 24. *C. eubule et marcellina* Godt.

It is almost impossible to distinguish this species from *C. eubule*. The most positive character is, that the secondaries are less rounded, and the anal angle more prominent.

The *upper side* of the male is similar to that of *C. eubule;* but the under side has the points and tortuous lines more obsolete; the geminate ferruginous points of the primaries are replaced by a red or ferruginous point, cut by a small yellow nervure; and the two discoidal, silvery points of the secondaries, are a little smaller.

The *upper side* of the female has the same designs as *Eubule,* only that the secondaries have the posterior border very indistinctly marked by small brown lines or spots.

Under side similar to *C. eubule*, only that it is ordinarily strewed with small ferruginous atoms.

Larva deep citron yellow, punctured with black, and a blue transverse ray on each segment; abdomen below and feet yellow, with a lateral range of small blue lines above the feet. Feeds on *Cassia.*

Southern States.

Bois.

COLIAS Fab.

Inferior palpi much compressed, covered with short silky hairs, rose red; *last article much shorter than the preceding;* antennæ straight, short, rose red, terminating in an obtuse cone, *which extends more than a fourth of their length.* Abdomen shorter than the secondaries; thorax robust; color more or less lively yellow; border black.

Colias differs from *Pieris* in the shorter antennæ, insensibly terminating in an obconical club; in the black border common to all the wings; in the primaries, usually having a black discoidal point, and the secondaries a central point, orange above and ordinarily silvery below, accompanied by another small point, in a small reddish or ferruginous spot on the insertion of the median nerve, at the base of secondaries below.

Larva smooth, slightly pubescent, a little attenuated at the extremities.

Chrysalis carinated above, not arcuate, destitute of lateral points, terminating anteriorly in a point; always attached by the tail, and a transversal line placed below the middle of the body.

1. C. cæsonia *Godt.* Encyc. Method. IX. 98. Figured in Boisd. et Lec. 67, pl. 22. Boisl. Suppl. Cram. pl. 41. Lucas, Hist. Nat. des Pap. Exot. pl. 39. *C. philippa?* Fab.

Wings beautiful yellow; primaries, with the summit, very sharp, sometimes a little falcate.

Primaries blackish at the base, a large black point in the middle; a wide black border, sinuate, or rather emarginate interiorly, making the yellow part bear a rude resemblance to a dog's head, of which the black point forms the eye. On the upper edge, near the summit, are three whitish oblong streaks. Fringe rosy.

Secondaries with a black border strongly dentated within; two large geminate discoidal orange spots, and some streaks of the same color near the border. Fringe yellow, washed with rosy.

Under side of the primaries dull yellow, except in the middle; a black eye with a silvery pupil.

Under side of secondaries deep yellow, with two silvery, discoidal, geminate points, circled with ferruginous; besides this, a transverse line of ferruginous points, as in most of the species.

Body blackish above; yellowish below; antennæ reddish.

The *female* is of yellow, less bright; the border of the primaries is of black, less deep, with some indistinct yellow streaks; the border of the secondaries is interrupted, and the surface here and there presents some traces of rosy. Expands two inches and a half.

Larva green, with a lateral white band, punctured with yellow; besides this band, there is on each segment a transverse black band, bordered with yellow. Feeds on different species of *Trifolium.*

Southern States.   Boisd.

2. C. edusa *Fab.* Ent. System. Godt. Encyc. IX, 101. Figured in most of the European works on this subject.

Wings yellow, inclining to fulvous, more or less mingled with greenish on the secondaries.

The primaries have a large black point at the extremity of the discoidal cellule, and a wide border of the same color, sinuated interiorly, a little dilated at the summit, and divided at this part by *fine yellow nervures;* the secondaries have on the disk an orange spot, and at the extremity a black border following that on the primaries, more or less sinuated within, and terminating in a point a little before the anal-angle.

Under side of the primaries differs from the upper in being a little more pale; all the part corresponding to the border is yellowish green, preceded by a transverse line of points, of which the three inferior are black, and the others ferruginous and smaller.

The *under side* of the secondaries is yellowish green, with two geminate, discoidal, silvery points, bordered with ferruginous corresponding to the orange spot, of which the outer is the smaller; besides this, there is a reddish line at the base, on the insertion of the median nerve; a small ferruginous spot on the costal edge, followed by a transverse line of ferruginous points in a line with those of the primaries.

The fringe of all the wings is yellow, interrupted with brown above and rosy below.

Body yellow greenish; back black; antennæ and feet rosy.

The *female* differs from the male in having the border divided by a yellow band, macular, interrupted on the primaries.

Larva, which feeds on *Trifolium,* is green, with a lateral ray mingled with white and yellow, marked with a fulvous point on each ring.

Chrysalis green, with a lateral yellow line and some ferruginous points.

Inhabits the four quarters of the globe.

Bosm.

3. C. chrysotheme *Hübn.* Pap. 426–8. Figured in Boisd. Spec. Gén. pl. 2, B. fig. 5. Boisd. Icones, pl. 9, fig. 3-4. Hübn. Europ. Schmett. pl. 85.

Resembles *C. edusa,* but paler; border browner, divided by fine yellow nervures. The primaries are broadly yellow on the edge; the discoidal point more narrow, transverse, surrounded with ferruginous. The discoidal spot on the under side of the primaries has a silvery pupil.

In the *female* the yellow orange occupies only the disk of the primaries, and the yellow spots which divide the border are larger, more distinct, and paler.

Inhabits North America and Europa.

Boisd.

4. C. philodice *Godt.* Encyc. Méth. IX, 100. Figured in Boisd. et Lec. 64, pl. 21. Swains. Zool. Illust. 1st series, pl. 60. Lucas, Hist. Nat. des Pap. Exot. pl. 39. *C. anthyale* Hübn.

Upper side canary yellow, with a black border, slightly sinuous within, and terminating on the secondaries, a little before the anal angle. *Primaries*, with a black point near the upper edge. *Secondaries*, with a pale orange point on the disk.

Under side of primaries canary yellow, with the edge and extremity a little russety ; the discoidal point usually pupilled with white.

The *under side* of the secondaries is yellow, a little russety, with two geminate, discoidal, silvery points, bordered with ferruginous, of which the outer one is the smaller; parallel to the outer edge of both wings there is a series of ferruginous points.

The fringe of the four wings is rosy below ; more dull above. *Body* and antennæ as in the other species.

The *female* has the border less black, a little wider, a little dilated at the summit, divided on the primaries by a macular band interrupted by the ground color; the discoidal point pupilled with whitish above.

A female variety is sometimes found with wings nearly white.

Inhabits the United States.

Boisd.

5. C. amphidusa *Boisd.* Ann. Soc. Ent. 2me sér. X, 286.

Wings with the border of the same form and width as *eduse* ; slightly powdered with yellowish atoms, and divided at the summit of the primaries by three or four fine yellow nerves. The upper edge slightly powdered with citron yellow.

Female, sulphury white.

California.

Boisd.

6. C. eurytheme *Boisd.* Ann. Soc. Ent. 2me sér. X.

Perhaps only a variety of *C. chrysotheme.*

Usually much larger, of a brighter orange fulvous, with the yellow nervures less numerous. The spots which divide the border of the secondaries in the females are less neat and less distinct than in *C. chrysotheme*.

California, Mexico, and some of the States.

                                Boisd.

7. C. pelidne *Boisd.* Boisd. et Lec. 66, pl. 21.   .

Upper side of all the wings yellow, inclining a little to greenish, with a black border, regularly sinuated on the internal side, and ending on the secondaries towards the middle of their outward seam.

Under side of the primaries is paler, with the edge powdered with darker atoms, and an oval, central, elongated point, pupilled with reddish.

Under side of the secondaries is greenish yellow, with a rounded, central, reddish point, surmounted by another much smaller point of the same color. The base also has a reddish point.

The fringe of all the wings is red; antennæ yellowish rosy, with the knob brownish above and yellowish below.

Labrador.

                                Boisd.

8. C. phicomone *Godt.* Encyc. Méthod. IX, 100.

Upper side greenish yellow in the male; greenish white in the female, covered in both sexes with a blackish powder, usually less abundant in the disk of the primaries, marked with a black discoidal point; a rather wide blackish border, and divided by a range of spots of the ground color. *Secondaries* have also a black border, divided by a band of the ground color; but the black often disappears, especially in the female, so that the border is formed by a yellow or whitish band; a discoidal yellow spot.

Under side of the primaries white, more or less greenish, with the summit russety yellow; a silver discoidal point, bordered with ferruginous, sometimes united to a smaller point; a small ferruginous spot on the insertion of the median nervure and the costal edge.

Labrador.

                                Boisd.

9. C. nastes *Boisd.* Spec. Gén. I, 648.

Smaller than *C. phicomone*, but very similar to it.

Under side yellow, a little greenish, powdered as in *phicomone*, with the fringe and the edge of the primaries a little more rosy;

primaries with a blackish border, insensibly mingling with the yellow, divided by small elliptical yellow spots, placed on the nervures; a black discoidal point, sometimes ocellated. Secondaries nearly like *phicomone*.

Under side of the primaries white, more or less greenish, with the summit yellowish, and a black discoidal point, pupilled with whitish.

Under side of the secondaries greenish yellow, covered with a fine blackish dust from the base to beyond the middle, and marked at the extremity of the discoidal cellule with a solitary small spot of a ferruginous reddish, pupilled with russety white. Antennæ red, with the under side of the club yellow.

Female whitish above, less powdered with blackish atoms than the female of *C. phicomone*, with the border of the primaries divided by regular elliptical spots.

Labrador.

Boisd.

10. **C. hyale** *Linn.* Figured in Fischer Entom. de la Russie, pl. 11. *C. palæno* Fisch.

Upper side saffron yellow, with a large black point at the end of the discoidal cellule of the primaries, and a pale orange spot, a little blotched, on the disk of the secondaries. Primaries with a black border at the extremity, widened at the summit; cut its whole length by a suite of spots of the ground color, of which the two intermediary are less distinct, and the following ones sometimes mingled with the general tint. Secondaries with a blackish border, narrow, often macular, and sometimes nearly obsolete, especially in the males.

Under side of the primaries has no border, summit yellow, a little russety, preceded by a transverse line of blackish points.

Under side of secondaries entirely russety yellow, with two geminate points, discoidal, silvery, bordered with ferruginous, corresponding to the orange spot of the upper side, of which the exterior is the smallest; besides this, a small reddish mark at the base, a small ferruginous spot on the costal edge, followed by a transverse line of ferruginous points, on a line with those of the primaries. Fringe reddish, as well as the upper edge.

Body yellow, with the head ferruginous; palpi, antennæ, and feet reddish.

Female pale saffron yellow, and nearly white above.
California—Europe—Africa—Siberia.

Bois.

11. *C. vosnesenski Ménétriés.* Figured in Cat. Petersburg Imper. Acad.
     Sci. 77.

Nearly the size of *C. caesonia;* but the primaries are much more
pointed at the summit, and the external edge more falcate.

The primaries have a beautiful, vivid, yellow spot on the disk;
a violet reflection over all the wing; base powdered with black, as
well as the whole length of the anterior edge; a black discoidal
point; the black border of the external edge is wider than in *C.
caesonia;* it is emarginated, square, somewhat, as in this species,
but it encroaches more on the yellow spot so as to nearly touch the
discoidal point, which completely destroys the likeness to a dog's
head, so distinctly marked in *C. caesonia.*

The fringe is rosy, with some yellow spots on each side of the
summit.

The secondaries are beautiful citron yellow, covered over with
orange yellow without any spot, only that the trace of the discoidal point of the under side is indicated by an orange point.

The *under side* of the four wings as in *C. caesonia,* only that the
discoidal point of the primaries is smaller, and the second silver
point of the secondaries is larger.   Head black; antennæ reddish;
thorax black, with some scattered yellow hairs.

Body black, a little yellowish below.
California.

Ménétriés.

THERIAS Swains.

Head short, inclined, somewhat concealed under the costal edge
of the primaries; eyes naked; palpi very short, covered with short
hairs, scaly; last article small, thin, naked, much shorter than the
preceding; antennæ slender, articulation distinct, terminating in
an *ovoid* or conic club, a little arcuate, slightly compressed laterally.

Body rather slender; prothorax very short. Abdomen compressed, extending the length of the secondaries. Wings thin,

delicate, rather wide, discoidal cellules closed; primaries having the coastal edge strongly arcuate towards the base; the secondaries embracing the abdomen below.

This genus has been sometimes confounded with *Pieris* and again with *Colias*. It differs from the first in having the palpi furnished with shorter and more closely set hairs, and the last article very short. It differs from the second in the delicate texture, the arcuate antennæ, the laterally compressed club, and the wings destitute of the discoidal silvery spots below.

The thin and delicate wings are usually yellow, with the summit of the primaries deep black, contrasting agreeably with the ground color.

1. **T. nicippe** *Fab.* Ent. Syst. III, 1, 209. Figured in Cram. Pap. pl. 210. Herbst. Pap. pl. 107. Boisd. et Lec. 53, pl. 20. Say's Am-r. Ent. pl. 30. Lucas' Hist. Nat. des Pap. Exot. pl. 33.

Upper side lively yellow orange, with a wide black common border, dentate within, wider at the summit of the primaries, where it is surmounted on the upper edge with three or four small yellow streaks. The primaries also have on the extremity of the discoidal cellule a small black crescent, and the upper edge towards the base is densely sprinkled with black.

Under side of primaries paler.

Under side of secondaries yellow, with brown atoms; a small discoidal black dot; a brownish spot on the middle of the costal edge; then a transverse band, undulate, more or less brownish.

Female differs from the male in being paler and often of a yellow color; *the black border of the primaries suddenly ceases a little before the internal angle,* and that on the secondaries is partly effaced towards the anal angle.

Larva, which feeds on *Cassia* and *Trifolium,* is pale green, with a dorsal ray more obscure, and a lateral white band, marked before with five yellow points.

Chrysalis green, a little arcuate, sprinkled with ferruginous spots.

United States.—Expands a little over two inches.

Boisd.

3

2. T. lisa *Boisd.* Boisd. Spec. Gén. 1, 661. Figured in Boisd. et Lec. 63, pl. 19. Boisd. Spec. Ova. pl. 2. *T. similæ* Godt.

Wings citron yellow above. *Primaries* have the base powdered with blackish; a small black discoidal point; a black border, beginning at the middle of the upper edge, dilated at the summit, and dentated within the whole length.

Secondaries have a narrow black border, dentated within, obsolete towards the anal angle.

Fringe of all the wings rosy above.

Under side of primaries yellow, with a small black discoidal point, and the upper edge embroidered with reddish.

Under side of secondaries yellow, sprinkled with obscure atoms, with three small blackish points, of which one is on the base, and two on the disk; a blackish, undulate, transverse, macular ray, followed on the external angle by a roundish, ferruginous spot.

The four wings are edged with red ferruginous, interrupted by small black points, and separated from the fringe by a thin line of silver white.

Female pale saffron yellow, with the base of the superiors more densely powdered with blackish.

Larva, which feeds on *Cassia* and *Glycine*, is green, with four longitudinal whitish rays.

Chrysalis green.

Southern States.—Expands nearly two inches.

          Boisd.

3. T. delia *Cram.* Figured in Cram. Pap. Exot. pl. 273. Herbst. pl. 17. Boisd. et Lec. pl. 18. *T. daira* Godt.

Primaries citron yellow, with a wide black border, dentated within, ending abruptly before reaching the internal angle. Upper edge sprinkled with blackish; a blackish *longitudinal* band, rather wide, *parallel to the internal edge*, bordered with marigold below, and not extending to the internal angle.

Secondaries yellow; a black, marginal, triangular spot on the outer angle, in a line with some small, indistinct, marginal points or streaks of the same color, situated on the extremity of the nervures.

Fringe of all the wings above rosy.

Under side of primaries yellow, with the edge and summit wine red, and two small black discoidal points.

Under side of secondaries wine red, two small blackish discoidal points, and a transverse, undulate, brownish, interrupted band.

The *female* is destitute, or nearly so, of the black longitudinal band, and of the marginal, marigold line. The base is sprinkled with blackish.

Larva, which feeds on *Trifolium*, *Cassia*, and *Glycine*, is green, with a longitudinal white line on each side above the feet.

Chrysalis green.

Southern States.—Expands an inch and a half.

Down.

4. **T. Jucunda** *Boisd.* Boisd. Spec. Gén. 1, 663. Figured in Boisd. et Lec. pl. 19.

Primaries like those of *T. delia*, except that the fringe is white, and the ground color of a less lively yellow.

Secondaries yellow saffron, with a blackish border, a little sinuated within, and nearly obsolete before reaching the anal angle.

Under side of primaries yellow in the middle; other parts whitish, sprinkled with grayish atoms.

Under side of secondaries white, finely aspersed with grayish.

Female paler; primaries densely powdered with blackish, destitute of the marigold line; border of secondaries a little wider, and sometimes interrupted by yellow streaks.

N. America.—Expands about an inch.

Boisd.

T. proterpia *Boisd.* Boird. Spec. Gén. 654. Figured in Lucas' Hist. Nat. des Pap. Exot. pl. 38.

Upper side orange red in the male, and russety yellow ochre in most of the females; nervures black towards the extremity. *Primaries*, with a black border along the upper edge, rather wide, continuing more or less on the outer edge. *Secondaries* without a border, or with a blackish border effaced; outer edge angular in the middle.

Under side of all the wings paler than on the upper; that of the primaries without border or spots, that of the secondaries more or less sprinkled on the disk with spots or atoms a little more obscure, sometimes nearly obsolete.

The nervures of the ground color, or only those of the primaries blackish at the extremity. *Secondaries* without any border, with the exterior angle much more prominent and prolonged, in the form of a tail.

Under side of secondaries more densely sprinkled or speckled with atoms and ferruginous spots.

Texas—Mexico.—Expands 18 to 22 French lines.

Boisd.

T. mexicana *Boisd.* Boisd. Spec. Gén. 679. Figured on pl. 3, C. fig. 1, of Boisd. Spec. Gén.

Wings brilliant citron yellow; primaries with a black border at the extremity, rather wide, ending squarely at the internal angle, showing near the middle a rather deep quadrangular sinus; the outer edge slightly sinuate, and whitish; secondaries, with the middle of the exterior edge prolonged to a prominent angle, in the form of a tail; a black border of moderate width, a little dentated on its internal side, not reaching the internal angle; costal edge washed with orange yellow, mingling with the ground color.

Under side of the primaries pale citron yellow, with a black central point, the edge intersected with brown points; the outer edge reddish near the fringe.

Under side of secondaries yellow, sprinkled with ferruginous atoms, with a blackish central point; edge intersected with ferruginous points, and marked near the external angle with a spot of the same color; the posterior half having four or five other spots of the same color, of which two or three are in a line, and tending to form a transverse band; the middle of the outer edge more or less washed with ferruginous.

Female differs from the male in the upper side being yellowish white, with a wider border, the quadrangular sinus more profound; the anterior edge of the secondaries widely orange yellow, and below, three ferruginous posterior spots form on the secondaries a narrow, transverse, ferruginous band.

Texas—Louisiana—Mexico.

Boisd.

Fam. III. DANAIDAE.

Larva smooth, cylindric, with five pairs of simple, fleshy, flexible processes. *Chrysalis* rather short, cylindric, with brilliant golden spots. *Perfect insect;* palpi separated; thorax and pectus with spots. Wings wide, discoidal cellule closed. Hooks of the tarsi simple.

DANAIS Boisd.

Head a little more narrow than the thorax; antennæ rather long, insensibly terminating in a club; palpi remote, with the last article short, acicular, and straight; white points on the head, prothorax, thorax, and breast. Abdomen rather thin, nearly as long as the secondaries. Wings wide, with the outer edge somewhat elongate. Secondaries of the males have usually, towards the anal angle, a very black spot or tubercle, divided by a grayish ray in relief, placed on the extremity of the nervure.

Our two species have two ranges of whitish points on the blackish border of the wings.

1. D. berenice Cram. Figured in Cram. Pap. pl. 205. Sm. Abb. vol. 1, pl. 7. Boisd. et Lec. pl. 39. D. erippus Godt. Fab. D. gilippus Sm. Abb. Godt.

Wings rufous brown, often more obscure at the base, with a black border extending from the upper edge of the primaries to the anal angle of the secondaries.

The *primaries* have on both sides a number of white spots on the upper edge and disk, forming usually two marginal ranges, of which the outer divides the border.

The *secondaries* have sometimes the black border without any points, and sometimes it is divided by one or even two ranges of white points.

The *under side* of the primaries differs very little from the upper; but the under side of the inferiors is divided by wide black veins, bordered with whitish. The disk has three or four white points, situated on the edge of the discoidal cellule. The black marginal border is divided by two rows of white points.

The nervures on the upper surface of the secondaries in the female are finely lined with grayish white.

The *larva*, which feeds on *Nerium*, *Asclepias*, &c., is whitish violet, with transverse stripes of a deeper color; a transverse band of reddish brown, on each ring, divided in its length by a narrow yellow band. Along the feet a longitudinal band of yellow citron. Long, fleshy processes, of brown purple, disposed in pairs on the second, fifth, and eleventh rings.

Chrysalis green, with golden points on the anterior side, and a semicircle of the same color on the dorsal side, a little beyond the middle, separated from a blue band by a row of small black dots.

Southern States.—Expands three and three quarter inches.

Boisd.

2. D. archippus Sm. Abb. Figured in Sm. Abb. vol. I, pl. 6. Cram. 2d. Hübn. Exot. Samml. Say's Amer. Ent. III, pl. 54. Boisd. et Lec. 137, pl. 40. *D. megalippe* Hübn.

The four wings somewhat sinuate, fulvous above, with a rather brilliant reflection; all the wings entirely margined with deep black, having, in fresh specimens, a bluish reflection; nervures same color. The summit of the primaries has three oblong, fulvous spots, preceded by eight or ten smaller, white or yellowish white extending to the middle of the upper edge. Two rows of white spots on the outer borders of all the wings; occasionally the inner row is ferruginous. The fourth nervure of the secondaries has a large black spot or tubercle.

The *under side* presents the same markings as the upper, but the points of the posterior edge are larger and all white. The ground color of the secondaries is nankin yellow, with the nervures slightly bordered with whitish. The emarginations of all the wings white.

Body black, with yellowish points on the thorax and breast.

The *female* has wider nervures, and is destitute of the black tuberculous spot on the secondaries.

Larva whitish, transversely fasciated with black and yellow. It has two pairs of fleshy processes, blackish, of which the anterior pair are situated on the second ring, which are much longer than the other pair, situated on the eleventh ring. Feeds on *Asclepias*.

Chrysalis pale green, with golden points before; a semicircle of gold behind, bordered below by a range of small black dots.

Middle and Southern States.—Expands four and a half inches.

Boisd.

FAM. IV. HELICONIDAE.

Larva cylindric, spinose the whole length. *Perfect insect;* palpi short, separate, not much elevated. Abdomen thin, elongate. Wings oblong, narrow, elongate. Abdominal edge of the secondaries scarcely embracing the under side of the abdomen. Discoidal cellule closed.

HELICONIA Fab.

Palpi extending a little beyond the clypeas; second article much longer than the first; antennæ filiform, gradually enlarging towards the extremity. Wings *oblong, narrow.* Abdomen elongate; four walking feet in both sexes.

1. **H. charitonia** *Linn.* Linn. Syst. Nat. II, 757. Figured in Cram. pl. 191. Boisd. et Lec. 140, pl. 41. Lucas' Hist. Nat. des Pap. Exot. pl. 50.

Wings black, with bands of citron yellow. The *primaries* have three, of which the two outer are transverse and oblique; the inner one proceeds directly from the base to the middle, where it makes an elbow to gain the posterior edge above the internal angle.

The *secondaries* have two transverse bands, of which the upper is the wider, straight and continuous; the lower is curved, and formed of spots of different sizes. The posterior edge, which is slightly sinuate, has, towards the anal angle, a range of six or seven small yellow points, and near the base there are one or two points of carmine.

The *under side* resembles the upper, except that the yellow bands are paler; the primaries have the upper edge reddish at the base; the secondaries have four blood red points, disposed two by two near the abdominal edge, and separated by the upper band; and, finally, the marginal points of these secondaries are whitish, and extend to the summit.

Body black, with yellow points on the head and thorax, and lines of the same color on the sides of the breast and abdomen.

Georgia and Florida.—Expands three inches and a half.

Boisd.

2. **H. diaphana** *Drury.* (Westwood's Ed.) Figured in Jardine's Nat. Libr. vol. IV, pl. 12, fig. 3. Drury, vol. II, pl. 7.

Upper side: antennæ black and very long; thorax and abdomen dark brown.

Wings transparent, vitreous. *Primaries* with the anterior edges bending inwards. A small narrow border of dark brown runs entirely round the edges of these wings, and on the anterior edges about a third from the tips, runs a dark brown streak towards the middle of the wings, close to which is a small white spot, joining to the anterior edge. *Secondaries* having also a very narrow border, running about two-thirds round them, and stopping at the abdominal edges. Some long yellowish hairs are placed on the anterior edges near the body.

Under side: palpi, sides, breast, ash colored. The dark brown borders surrounding the wings appear on this side orange brown; the rest as on the upper side; margins of the wings entire.

Texas.

FAM. V. NYMPHALIDAE.

Larva cylindric, spinose the whole length, or only on the head. *Chrysalis* variable. *Perfect insect;* palpi usually close, elevated, very scaly; the anterior face of their first two articles nearly as wide or wider than their sides. Abdominal edge of the secondaries forming a deep groove to receive the abdomen. Discoidal cellule nearly always open. Hooks of the tarsi bifid.

ACRAULIS Boisd.

Head large, at least as wide as the thorax; antennæ rather long, terminated by a flattened club, more elongate, and less rounded than in *Argynnis;* palpi ascending, a little divergent at the summit, covered with close-set hairs; the first article very short, obtuse. Abdomen shorter than the secondaries; discoidal cellule of the latter always open; primaries elongate, with the posterior edge sinuate; the secondaries denticulate.

1. **A. vanillae** *Linn.* Linn. Syst. Nat. II, 787. Figured in Cram. pl. 212. Stoll. Suppl. pl. 1. Salz. Genoh. pl. 18. Clerck, Icon. pl. 40. Bolsd. et Lec. 143, pl. 42. *A. passiflorae* Fab.

Male, bright fulvous; female, more dull; primaries elongate, posterior border a little concave, divided at the summit by the veins, and lower down by streaks, widest at the edge, black. Disk, with some black spots, of which two or three of those situated in the discoidal cellule are pupilled with white. In some specimens, these pupils are obsolete.

The *secondaries* are bordered by a black band, crenated on the outside, and divided by large spots of the ground color. Between the centre and outer edge there are three or four black spots.

The *under side* of the primaries differs from the upper in having the summit dull yellow (the color of dead leaves), with six or seven silver spots, and the costal spots papilled with silver.

The *under side* of the secondaries is dull yellow, with about seventy-two very brilliant silver spots, elongate, of which the marginal are smaller. The upper edge at the base is also silvery. Among the spots in the middle, one is strongly emarginate, or nearly separated in two.

Body fulvous above, yellowish below, with white dots on the head, and silvery lines on the breast.

Larva cylindric, pale, fulvous, with four blackish longitudinal bands, of which the two dorsal are sometimes obsolete; furnished with ranges of blackish ramose spines, of which two are placed on the summit of the head. Head with a whitish ray on each side, lined with black; feet black.

Chrysalis russety brown, with some paler shades. Feeds on *Passiflora.*

Southern States.—Expands four inches.

Boisd.

ARGYNNIS Fab.

Head large, at least as wide as the thorax; antennæ rather long, abruptly terminated by a flattened club, *grooved;* palpi pilose, somewhat remote; the first article slender, naked at its extremity, and pointed like a needle. Abdomen shorter than the secondaries. Wings sinuate or denticulate.

Ground color fulvous, usually with black points, forming sinuous, transverse lines, and sometimes with a blackish border, more or less wide; the under side usually has nacred spots, or violet or ferruginous nacred reflections.

1. A. idalia Fab. Fab. Ent. emend. III, 145. Figured in Cram. pl. 44. Drury I, pl. 13. Herbst. pl. 252. Boisd. et Lec. 147, pl. 43. Lucas' Hist. Nat. des Pap. Exot. pl. 66.

Upper side of primaries fulvous, with about fifteen black spots, of which the upper are linear, situated in the discoidal cellule; below these they form a zigzag, transverse line; the others are round, smaller, and disposed in a line parallel to the outer edge; this edge is covered by a wide black band, dentated within, and divided, in the male, by a range of yellowish crescents; and in the female, by a row of white spots.

The *female* has also some white spots on the summit, where the border dilates considerably.

The *upper side* of the secondaries is steel blue, with the base russety, traversed by two rows of large white points, of which the outer are yellow in the male.

The *under side* of the primaries resembles the upper, except that the terminal band is less deep, and the spots which divide it are nacre.

The *under side* of the secondaries is dull brown (dead leaves), with about twenty-eight nacred spots, of which the seven marginal are crescents; those of the disk are conic, divided or bordered by a black line; the edge at the base nacre. Emarginations of the wings whitish.

Body blackish, with yellow hairs on the thorax.

United States.—Expands nearly five inches.

Boisd.

2. A. diana *Cram.* Cram. II, 4. Figured in Cram. pl. 98. Herbst. pl. 253. Say's Amer. Ent. pl. 17.

Wings slightly dentate; black brown from the base to the middle, then fulvous to the edge. The fulvous forms a wide band, crenate within, having on the primaries two transverse rows of black points, and on the secondaries only one row.

The black points are obsolete on the *under side* of the primaries; the dark part is marked with two nacre spots, preceded within by three fulvous streaks, and outwardly by three small yellowish spots.

Under side of secondaries much paler than the upper, with nine nacre spots, of which three are triangular, situated between the base and the middle of the outer edge; the seven others are crescent, on a line with the posterior edge.

Southern States.

Say.

3. A. cybele *Godt.* Godt. Encyc. Méthod. IX, 263. Figured in Cram. pl. 57. Herbst. pl. 256. Boisd. et Lec. 151, pl. 45. *A. daphnis* Cram. *A. aphrodite* Fab.

Upper side obscure from the base to the middle; deeper in the female; then fulvous, with three transverse rows of black spots, of which the interior are in a zigzag line. Those intermediary are round; the exterior crescent. In the discoidal cellule there are some marks as in the analogous species. The outer edge is preceded by a black line crossed by nervures of the same color.

Under side of the primaries like the upper, except that the base is fulvous; and opposite the summit there are some silvery spots, of which four or five rest on the black crescents.

Under side of the secondaries brown ferruginous, with the base and about twenty-four spots, nacre; the spots at the base are small; those of the middle larger; those of the edge triangular, and separated from the preceding by a yellowish band, losing itself in the ferruginous.

Body brownish; antenna blackish; club black, tipped with fulvous.

This species is usually confounded with *A. aphrodite*, but is different, as will be seen from the description.

United States.—Expands nearly three inches.

Boisb.

4. **A. aphrodite** *Fab.* Fab. Syst. Ent. III, 1, 144. Similar to *A. cybele*, for which it is usually taken.

Primaries tawny orange brown at base, spotted, inscribed and reticulated with black; at the posterior margin, a deep orange band, edged with black; above this, a series of black crescents, succeeded by one of round spots; the costal margin is barred with black, the three anterior bars being angular, and the fourth shaped like the letter Γ; this is followed by three others less distinct; the reticulations of the disk terminate posteriorly in a zigzag black band; underneath, at the external angle, are five silver marginal series of crescents, above which the wing is spotted with black, with a few paler spots surmounted by a black crescent; underneath they are reddish brown, with a pale, tawny, marginal band. A marginal series, consisting of seven silver triangular spots, edged with black, next follows; and a second series, consisting of the same number, differing in shape, edged also with black, the intermediate one being the smallest; a third series of four spots succeeds, that next the costal margin is crescent-shaped; the second is subtriangular, divided by a black line; the third is oblong; the fourth minute. At the base are five spots, varying in form; on the shoulders is also a silver spot, and the inner margin is silvered, but less conspicuously. Fringe pale, barred with black.

Fabricius does not mention the two costal silver spots of the

prone surface of the primaries. In some specimens these appear
not silvered.

United States—Canada.—Expands 2¼ to 2½ inches.

KIRBY.

Doubleday, in *lit.*, says: " *A. aphrodite* is smaller and rather
brighter than *A. cybele*. It has the outer margin of the primaries
quite black, instead of the fulvous markings of *A. cybele*. The
margins of the secondaries have an additional black line ; flight also
different."

5. **A. columbina** *Godt.* Godt. Encyc. Method. IX. Figured in Cram.
     pl. 209 et 69. Boisd. et Lec. 153, pl. 41. *A. hegesia* Cram. *A. claudia*
     Cram.

Wings bright fulvous above, paler in the female, with a transverse, posterior row of black points ; outer edge black, divided by
a range of fulvous crescents ; the four wings are traversed by two
black zigzag lines.

The *primaries* have, besides, two annular black spots on the
discoidal cellule.

The *under side* of the primaries has the upper edge fulvous ; the
second zigzag line is obsolete, and at the summit there is a grayish
triangular space more or less distinct.

Under side of secondaries yellow russety, tainted with brownish ;
two whitish transverse bands, of which the anterior is discoidal,
extending somewhat on the nerves ; the second is marginal, narrow,
dentated within, separated from the first by a row of black spots
pupilled with grayish.

Body of same color as the wings.

This species varies much according to localities. There are
some on which the second zigzag ray is obsolete ; others, on which
the first is apparent only in the primaries ; others again, which
show scarcely any trace of the whitish transverse on the under side
of the secondaries.

Larva spiny, reddish yellow, with two lateral bands, and a series
of dorsal spots, white ; abdomen whitish, with the head and feet
black ; spines blackish, and the two on the first ring are much
larger, and directed towards the front like antennæ.

Chrysalis white, moderately angular, scattered with black dots
and streaks ; dorsal points yellow.

Southern States.—Expands three inches.

BOISD.

6. **A. myrina** Cram. Cram. Ency. Méthod. IX, 269. Figured in Cram. pl. 189. Herbst. pl. 255. Boisd. et Leo. 155, pl. 45. Say's Amer. Ent. pl. 46. *A. myrina* Godt.

Upper side fulvous with black spots, some irregular, disposed confusedly towards the base; the others are in the form of points or dots, in a line parallel with the outer edge, which has a black band, divided by a series of fulvous crescents.

Under side of primaries paler, except at the summit, where it is a little ferruginous, and marked with two or three nacre spots. The outer edge also has a range of triangular silver lunules.

The *under side* of the secondaries is red ferruginous, with two or three yellow spaces, and about twenty-four silver spots, some irregular and unequal towards the base, the others disposed in two transverse series, of which the one forms marginal crescents; these two rows are separated by a series of brownish black points. Towards the base of the wings there is a black silvery circle.

Body blackish above, grayish yellow below; antennæ black, and annulated with white, and the extremity of the club yellow.

Female with a taint a little less vivid than the male.

United States.—Expands one and three quarter inches.

Boisd.

7. **A. bellona** Godt. Godt. Ency. Méthod. IX, 271. Boisd. et Leo. 164, pl. 45.

Size and form of *A. myrina*, but the primaries are a little more sinuous.

Wings fulvous, with a large number of black spots, some placed confusedly towards the base, where the ground color is more obscure, the others forming two parallel rows on the outer edge, which is sometimes a little intersected with black.

Under side of primaries fulvous and spotted, as above, with the summit washed with brown and pale yellow, and marked with a small transverse line of whitish violet.

The anterior half of the *under side* of the secondaries is yellow russety, with ferruginous undulations and atoms, a bifid spot of whitish violet towards the base, inclosing in its angle an orbicular spot of reddish yellow. The other half is violet or coppery purple, with a transverse row of six or seven brown points pupilled with whitish, followed on the terminal edge with obscure lunules, more or less distinct, and forming nearly a continuous marginal ray.

Body and antennæ as in the analogous species.
Southern States.—Expands an inch and a half.

Boisd.

8. **A. freya** *Godt.* Gall. Encyc. Method. IX, 273. Figured in Herbst.
   pl. 272.

Stalk of the antennæ yellow, with a large compressed brown
knob, red underneath, at the base and tip.

Wings tawny, dark brown at the base, with a narrow black band
occupying the posterior margin, followed by a series of black
arrow-headed spots, next to which in the primaries is a zigzag,
angular, discoidal, black band, and at the anterior margin, five
transverse spots of the same color.

The *under side* of the primaries is tawny, variegated with black
and white spots and lines.

Under side of the secondaries is reddish, variegated with white
and yellow spots and band, with a discoidal, arrow-headed, white
spot in the centre. Fringe of the wings alternately white and
yellow.

Canada.

ERNST, FABR. BOS. 291.

9. **A. aglaia** *Linn.* Syst. Nat. II. Figured by many European authors.

Reddish yellow with black marks.

Under side of the secondaries greenish, yellow near the seam;
no reddish spots with silver pupils; the sacred spots usually small
and round, in number about twenty-one, not including those at
the origin of the upper edge and internal edge, which are also
silvery.

In the *female*, the marginal lunules of the upper side of the
primaries are yellow, not fulvous.

California and Europe.

GODART.

10. **A. callippe** *Boisd.* Boisd. Ann. Soc. Ent. 2me sér. X, 302.

Upper side fulvous, traversed by a black zigzag ray, preceded
from the side of the base by black sinuous streaks, and followed
by a row of black points; all the exterior contour blackish,
divided by a line of lunules more pale than the ground color.

Under side of primaries reddish fulvous, paler at the extremity,
with the same markings as above, and a series of silvery marginal
lunules, preceded by two or three apical spots of the same color.

Under side of secondaries brownish, with about twenty silver spots, the edge of the wings towards the abdomen silvery.

In the *female* the ground color is paler, with the other markings blacker ; on the under side the general tint is paler, and nearly yellowish.

California—rare.

Bois.

11. **A. ashtaroth** *Fisher.* Figured in Proceed. A. N. S., Phila., 1849, p. 160, pl. 8. In the place cited, this species is named *asturte*, but was afterwards changed to *ashtaroth* by Dr. Fisher.

Upper wings with both surfaces fulvous; above with a broad, black exterior margin, containing a range of seven small whitish spots, parallel with the margin ; four large oblong spots of black proceeding from the exterior margin, the two intermediate ones reaching beyond the middle of the wing, the others shorter, with each a small fulvous spot near the tip ; and four spots of black descending from the subcostal nervure, of which the one nearest the body is linear, the next square, the third roundish, with a fulvous spot in the centre, and the fourth connate with the fourth of the before-mentioned spots proceeding from the exterior margin.

The *lower wings* are above bluish black, changing to brownish fulvous near the base, with an indistinct whitish spot below the centre.

The *under side* of the upper wings has seven spots of pearly white parallel with the outer margin, of which the five exterior ones are linear, and the two others round ; from these two round spots proceed two oblong black spots to the middle of the wing, and the two next have each a round black spot above them. From the subcostal nervure proceed four black spots, of which the two nearest the body are linear, the next triangular, inclosing a fulvous spot, and the fourth is almost confounded with the black upper margin. ·

The *under side* of the lower wings is brown, with four white subinnate spots, bounded above and below by black, and parallel with the lower margin. There are, likewise, two long black spots outside of the outer one of these spots; the whole base of the wing is occupied by six large pearly spots, radiating from the axilla, one of which occupies the precostal portion ; between the second and third (which are very wide) is a smaller spot, and the third is

crossed near its base by a short black bar.   The emarginations of
the wings are margined with white.

Body black; thorax thickly covered with brownish fulvous hairs.

The above described butterfly so nearly resembles the *Argynnis
idalia*, that at first sight it may easily be taken for a mere
variety.   The want of a double row of white spots on the upper
surface of the lower wings, although a remarkable difference, would
not perhaps constitute a specific mark; yet, when we come to
examine the under surface, instead of the twenty-four or twenty-
five spots of white, which are observed over its whole surface, we
find but two near the margin, and six large ones occupying nearly
the whole of the base, and radiating from the axilla, we cannot
hesitate to pronounce it distinct and certainly new.

The *larva* is unknown.   The interesting fact of so large a species
of butterfly being found at this time in New Jersey, and having
heretofore escaped the researches of all entomologists, has led me
to offer this short communication for publication in the Proceedings.   It was found by me in July of this summer, on Succasunna
Plains, near Schooley's Mountain, in Morris County.

FREEL.

Most probably a variety of *A. idalia.* (Morris.)

12. A. **cualnnus** *Herbst.* Boisd. et Lec. p. 157. Figured in Boisd. Icon.
Illst. pl. 19. Herbst. pl. 270. *A. tricklaris* Hübn.

Small; *upper side* fulvous, inclining to yellowish.

Under side of the primaries deeper fulvous; summit washed with
ferruginous; the lunules of the extremity are scarcely indicated.

Under side of secondaries reddish; all the spots are nacred,
except the transverse ray, which precedes the ocellated ones; marginal lunules small, not very triangular, bordered by a brown arc.

The nacred spots of the under side of the female are more dull
and smaller than in the male, and the transverse black points of
the primaries are nearly all pupilled.

Labrador.

13. A. polaris *Boisd.* Boisd. et Lec. p. 159. Figured in Boisd. Icon. Illst.
pl. 20.

Size of *A. myrina.* *Primaries* have nearly the same design as
A. frigga, of Europe. The base is less obscure, and the points
which precede the terminal edge are smaller.

Under side of secondaries ferruginous brown. The base is

marked with four small white spots. Towards the middle, there is a transverse, irregular white band, slightly powdered with brown, and divided by the nervures, which are rossety. Beyond this band, there is another white band nearly macular, of which each spot is bordered by a clear yellowish space, and is marked by a black-brown point, corresponding to those of the opposite surface; the terminal edge is divided by small white lines or streaks, inflated at their anterior extremity. These wings are bordered with white. Fringe alternately white and black, and the white part forms below with the small white marginal lines, a kind of T.

The *female* differs from the male only in having the spots and white bands of the secondaries a little clearer.

Labrador.

Bonn.

14. **A. charlotea** *Godt.* Encyc. Méth. IX, 270. Figured in Herbst, pl. 272.

Nearly the size of *A. myrina*.

Upper side fulvous, traversed by black zigzag lines and by a row of black points, situated before the marginal lunules.

Under side of primaries fulvous, with the apical extremity yellowish, and a terminal row of small streaks of yellowish-white, which intersect the fringe and terminate in a small blackish arrow-shaped spot.

Under side of the secondaries purple-brown, deeper towards the base, which is marked with three small nacred spots; a little before the middle is another nacred band, sinuous, bordered with black-brown, and often powdered with ferruginous, especially in the males; between the spots of the base and this band, there is an isolated silver point, usually pupilled with brown. The posterior half of these wings is of a clearer tint, with some whitish reflections, especially near the transverse band—a row of purple-brown points, corresponding to the black points of the upper side, and at the extremity a terminal series of nacred triangular lunules, pointed with brown. Often in the males, all these lunules are strongly powdered with brown, and then are only indicated by a small white line, similar to those of the primaries.

Female a little larger than the male, sometimes a little more sombre above. On the under side, the nacred spots forming the

4

transverse band and the marginal lunules are more brilliant and more rarely powdered with ferruginous brown.

Labrador.

B012.

MELITAEA Fab.

In generic characters nearly similar to *Argynnis*. *Wings* usually blackish and fulvous, *subdenticulate*, spotted like a chess-board. *The nacre on the under side of the secondaries of Argynnis is here replaced by yellow or violet pearly reflections.* Discoidal cellule of the secondaries always open.

1. **M. phaeton** *Fab.* Syst. Ent. 481. Figured in Cram. pl. 193. Drury I, pl. 21. Herbst, pl. 3. Boisd. et Lec. pl. 47, p. 167.

Wings obscure black, with a marginal series of fulvous spots, more or less triangular, preceded by two transverse rows of yellow points. The *primaries* have, besides, two fulvous spots in the discoidal cellule, followed outwardly by some yellow dots.

On the *under side*, the base of each wing is marked with fulvous spots intermingled with yellow dots.

Body black; *palpi* and *feet* fulvous; *abdomen* spotted with yellow below, and pointed with yellow on the sides; *antennae* blackish; club a little ferruginous.

United States.—Expands two and three-eighths inches.

Bois.

2. **M. ismeria** *Boisd.* Boisd. et Lec. pl. 46, p. 168.

Upper side yellowish fulvous, with a large number of black spots; some placed confusedly towards the base, forming zigzag rays; others forming two transverse sinuous rays on the primaries and a single one on the secondaries, where it is followed by a row of points of the same color.

The outer edge of the four wings is black, divided on the primaries by fulvous spots and on the secondaries by a line of crescents, which are yellowish-white. Besides these, the summit of the primaries is marked by four or five white dots.

The *under side* of the primaries has a whitish macular band before the outer edge, preceded by three or four spots of the same color.

Under side of the secondaries fulvous, with white spots towards the base; then a median, transverse, irregular band, and finally marginal lunules of the same color. These last are separated from the transverse band by a series of blackish points corresponding to those of the upper side.

Fringe of all the wings blackish, intersected by white.

Body and *antennæ* as in the analogous species.

Larva yellow, with spines and three longitudinal rays, blackish.

Head black, as well as the scaly feet and abdomen on under side; other feet yellow.

Chrysalis ash-gray, with some clearer spaces; the small dorsal tubercles nearly white.

Southern States.—Expands one and three-eighths inch.

BOISD.

3. M. tharos Cram. *M. tharossa* Godt. Encyc. Method. IX, 289. Figured in Cram. pl. 169. Drury, I, pl. 21. Boisd. et Lec. pl. 47, p. 170.

Wings fulvous, with black wavy lines, more or less wide, often confluent or interlaced. A wide black border on the outer edge, a little sinuous within, marked on the primaries with a fulvous yellow spot, and divided on the secondaries by a regular sinuous line of grayish, preceded by a row of black ocular dots.

The upper edge of primaries black; from which, at the end of the discoidal cellule, there proceeds a black streak, which loses itself in the sinuous lines.

Under side of the primaries fulvous, with ferruginous wavy lines, very fine and indistinct. The border is more brown, mingled with the fulvous and marked with a yellow spot larger than that on the upper side.

The under side of the secondaries is ochre yellow, with a large number of wavy, brown ferruginous lines; a brown border, touching neither the anal nor external angle, marked by a yellow crescent. This border is preceded by a row of small brown dots, corresponding to those on the upper side.

Body black above, yellowish below.

United States.—Expands an inch and an eighth.

BOISD.

4. M. editha Boisd. Ann. Soc. Ent. 2me sér. X, 305.

Boisduval says, it is possible that this species is the same which Doubleday and Hewitson have figured in pl. 33 of their work as

M. onicia, but unfortunately they have not represented the under side, which in many species it is important to know. The upper side of the secondaries of their *M. onicia* has a marginal series of three fulvous bands, whilst in this species the intermediary range is pale yellow.

Upper side blackish-brown, with the fringe whitish, some spots of bright fulvous and some yellow spots disposed in transverse bands; the four bands of the secondaries alternately yellow and fulvous, interrupted; the one before the last yellow and that which precedes it fulvous, the spots slightly pupilled with yellow; the upper edge of the primaries reddish.

Under side fulvous, with bands ochry yellow, more or less edged with brown; that of the secondaries, with each spot of the antepenultimate band, pupilled with ochry yellow.

The *female* is nearly similar to the male, with the primaries a little more rounded at the summit.

California.

                                                                Boisd.

                              •

5. **M. palla** *Boisd.* Ann. Soc. Ent. 2me sér. X, 306. *M. nyctais* Doubleday.

Upper side bright fulvous.

Under side of primaries fulvous, with a terminal band of ochry yellow.

Under side of secondaries fulvous, with two bands of ochry yellow, edged with brown, and some basal spots of the same color, forming an irregular band; posterior band nearly terminal, formed by crescents more or less large; that which precedes it is cut longitudinally by two irregular blackish lines.

The *female* is very different from the male; the spots of the under side are usually of a pale ochry yellow, except the small marginal crescents and the antepenultimate band of the secondaries, which are fulvous. On the under side the ochry yellow bands cover nearly the whole surface, and the fulvous is reduced on the secondaries to marginal crescents, a row of five or six large points, and some basal spots.

California.

                                                                Boisd.

6. M. serene *Boisd.* Ann. Soc. Ent. 2me sér. X.

Upper side bright fulvous, as in *M. cybele*, with the black markings as in the species of the same group.

Under side of primaries fulvous, with the markings of the upper. The summit has spots of a yellowish-white, and the edge is divided by small crescents of the same color.

Under side of secondaries ferruginous gray, with spots of yellowish-white, as in the neighboring species, but not silvery; the spots of the middle and the marginal crescents are environed and surmounted with ferruginous, more obscure than the general tint.

Female a little larger than the male, with the under side ferruginous gray, paler, and sometimes the marginal crescents a little silvery.

California.

Boisd.

GRAPTA Kirby.

Nearly allied to *Vanessa*, from which it may be distinguished by its more excised and angular wings, and its less hairy palpi. All the known species have the upper surface more or less brightly fulvous, spotted with black; lower surface crowded and veined with different shades of brown; the secondaries have a more or less angular silvery or pale golden mark, resembling sometimes the letter L or C, whence the name *C-album*, &c. &c.

The *larvæ*, like those of the neighboring genera, have the second and third thoracic and also the abdominal segments armed with spines, which are set round with whorls of delicate bristles.

Pupa angular and tuberculated; head rather deeply notched, generally brown or grayish-brown, with silvery or golden blotches.

1. G. interrogationis *F.* B. 8. III, 1, 78. *G. aureum* Cram. Figured in Cram. pl. 19. Sm. Abb. I, pl. 2. Boisd. et Lec. pl. 51, p. 192.

Upper side of all the wings fulvous or ferruginous fulvous, with seven or eight unequal black spots, and the outer edge sometimes brown, obscure, and sometimes of a ferruginous tint, mingling insensibly with the ground color.

Upper side of secondaries deep brown, with a greenish blue reflection and the base red ferruginous.

Under side of all the wings grayish, marbled with brown; sometimes ferruginous or brownish, with the extremity a little more clear; often brown, slightly glossed with greenish white, especially on the secondaries. On the disk, a silvery spot, sometimes in the form of a C, sometimes in the form of an interrupted C or mark of interrogation. In most of the varieties, there is a row of black points on the terminal edge of each wing. The secondaries are furnished with prominent tails.

Larva deep brown, with the body pointed and striated with yellowish and whitish. Head and feet reddish, spines blackish. Along the feet a ray of citron yellow, and above the stigmata another ray of the same color, marked with a row of red spots.

Chrysalis angular, obscure, with golden spots. Feeds on *Ulmus* and *Tilia.*

United States.—Expands two and three-quarter inches.

BOISD.

2. G. comma *Harris.* Ins. Mass. 221 (1842).

Upper side tawny orange; fore wings bordered behind and spotted with black; hind wings shaded behind with dark brown, with two black spots on the middle and three more in a transverse line from the front edge, and a row of bright orange-colored spots before the hind margin; hind edges of the wings powdered with reddish-white.

Under side marbled with light and dark brown, the hinder wings with a silvery comma in the middle.

The *caterpillar* has a general resemblance to that of *G. interrogationis.*

Chrysalis brownish gray, or white variegated with pale brown, and ornamented with golden spots; there are two conical ear-like projections on the top of the head, and the prominence on the thorax is shorter and thicker than that of *G. interrogationis,* and more like a parrot's beak in shape.

Expands from two and a half to two and three-eighths inches.— *Harris, Insects of Mass.,* p. 221.

Harris thinks that his *G. comma* is different from the European *G. C-album,* which Boisd. et Lec., p. 190, describe as occurring here, and for the purpose of comparison, their description is inserted :—

3. G. C-album *Linn.*

Nearly the size of *G. progne.* ·

Upper side fulvous or ferruginous, with scattered black spots; outer edge more or less obscure.

Under side sometimes brownish-black, sometimes brownish-yellow, with green atoms on the outer half, which, with the exception of the costal margin, is always lighter.

Under side of secondaries has a G or C of pure white on the disk.

Body blackish, with greenish hairs on the thorax.

Antennæ black above, brown below, with white rings; extremity of the club reddish.

Environs of Philadelphia only.

Bois. et Lec.

VANESSA Fab.

Clothed with long hairs, eyes densely hairy; labial palpi porrect, projecting beyond the forehead, scaly and densely hairy all round; first joint much curved, second swollen beyond the middle, third nearly acicular. Antennæ about three-fourths the length of the body, with two distinct grooves below; club rather short, last joint minute, pointed. Thorax clothed with long hairs. Primaries subtriangular, apex truncate. Anterior margin but little curved, sometimes deeply emarginate; inner margin nearly straight, costal nervure rather stout, extending about to the middle of the anterior margin. Secondaries somewhat obovate. Inner margin the longest; outer margin more or less sinuate, dentate, prolonged into a tooth or short tail at the termination of the third median nervule. Abdomen about two-thirds the length of the inner margin of the posterior wing. Larva cylindric, head and first thoracic segment unarmed, the rest armed with long spines, set with setæ in whorls. Pupa very angular and tuberculate; head deeply bifid, often adorned with golden spots.

Vanessa differs from *Grapta* in the palpi, which are much less,

hairy, and in the wings in not having the inner margin of the
primaries emarginate. The larva of *Vanessa* differs in wanting
the spines on the head.

1. V. J-album *Boisd.*   Figured in Boisd. et Lec. pl. 50, p. 185.

Upper side dull yellow or fulvous, with the base of the primaries and a part of the secondaries more obscure. A little before
the outer edge, there is a brown ferruginous or blackish ray, which
on the primaries of the male often blends with the terminal edge,
which is nearly always powdered with blackish. The primaries
have four or five unequal spots on the middle and on the upper
edge, three short transverse bands of the same color, of which that
on the summit is separated by a white spot. The secondaries have
the upper edge black, divided by a white spot.

Under side of the wings brown, from the base to the middle,
with waves more pale and others more obscure; then, grayish-
white reticulated and a marginal interrupted ray of ashy blue. On
the middle of the inferiors, there is a small grayish mark in the
form of a J.

North and West.—Expands three inches.
                                            Boisd.

2. V. milberti *Godt.*   Encyc. Méthod. IX, 307.   *V. furcillata* Say.
Boisd. et Lec. pl. 50, p. 187. Say, Amer. Ent. II, pl. 27.

Upper side brownish-black, traversed between the middle and
the extremity by a wide fulvous band, a little sinuous within, where
it has a paler tint, followed on the secondaries by a marginal row
of violet-blue crescents.

The *primaries* have two fulvous spots in the discoidal cellule, a
black spot in the band on the costal edge, and a white spot besides.

Under side blackish, with waves more obscure, and a band of
paler tint corresponding to that of the upper side.

Body blackish-brown.

Northern States.—Expands an inch and a half.
                                            Boisd.

3. V. progne *Cram.*   Figured in Cram. pl. 65.   Boisd. et Lec. pl. 50, p. 186.

Upper side bright fulvous, a little paler at the extremity of the
primaries. These have five black spots, of which two are in the
discoidal cellule and three below the median nervure; two short

brown bands along the upper edge, one at the end of the discoidal cellule and the other near the summit, from which it is separated by three or four crescents paler than the ground color. Towards the internal angle, there is a brown spot slightly united to the border, which is deep brown.

The *secondaries* have the extremities blackish, insensibly mingling with the fulvous, which is marked with two small black spots. A little before the outer edge, there is a row of fulvous spots, sometimes indistinct. The angulated tails of the secondaries are tinted with grayish-violet, and the emarginations of all the wings are bordered with yellowish-gray.

Under side brown, striated with blackish, with a paler band towards the outer edge, angulated on the primaries; a white mark on the disk of the secondaries, which has a faint resemblance to the letter L.

Some *female* specimens have along the marginal edge on the *under side* some shining greenish crescents, more or less distinct, and nearly united in a continuous line. These have the *upper side* of a less brilliant fulvous.

United States.—Expands two inches.

Boisb.

4. V. antiopa *Linn.* Syst. Nat. II, 776. Figured in most of the European works.

Upper side velvety black chestnut, with a yellowish terminal band, the internal side of which is a little sinuous, preceded by a line of seven or eight dots of violet-blue.

The *primaries* have the upper edge finely interrupted with yellowish-white, and marked between the middle and the bluish points with two transverse and parallel spots of the same color as the border.

Under side obscure black, with wavy lines of deeper color, and a small central grayish point.

Body and *antennæ* black; club ferruginous.

United States and Europe.—Expands three inches.

Boisb.

5. V. lintneri *Fitch.* Third Report to N. Y. State Agr. Soc., p. 488 of Trans.

Wings of the same form and color of *V. antiopa*, but their pale border is twice as broad, occupying a third of the length of

the wings, and is wholly destitute of the row of blue spots which
occur in *V. antiopa* forward of the border. Ground color deep
rusty brown, much more tinged with liver reddish than in *V. antiopa*. The fore margin of the anterior wings is black, freckled
with small transverse white streaks and lines, but is destitute of
the two white spots of the other species. The broad outer band
is of a tarnished pale ochre yellow hue, speckled with black, and
becomes quite narrow at the inner angle of the hind pair. Wings
beneath similar to those of *V. antiopa*, but are darker and without
any sprinkling of ash-gray scales or any whitish crescent in the
middle of the hind pair, and the border is speckled with gray and
whitish in wavy transverse streaks, without forming the distinct
band which is seen in *V. antiopa*.

Fitch.

[Probably a variety of *V. antiopa.*—J. G. M.]

6. V. californica *Boisd.* Ann. Soc. Ent. 2me sér. X, 306.

Upper side bright fulvous; primaries with three black bands on
the upper edge, as in the allied species, and only three large points
on the disk; a white ante-apical streak; the edge of all the wings
blackish, but destitute of blue crescents.

Under side paler, with the transverse band very angular.
California.

Bosn.

PYRAMEIS Doubled. & Hewits.

Differs from *Vanessa* in having the wings less angular, palpi less
hairy, and in somewhat different form; the club of the antennæ is
rather more pointed; larvæ have all the segments except the head
and prothorax armed with long spines, set round with whorls of
stiff bristles. They differ also in habits; those of *Pyrameis* are
always solitary, drawing together the sides of a leaf with silken
threads, and thus forming a cylindric dwelling; the pupæ are
similar in shape and markings.

1. P. atalanta *Linn.* Syst. Nat. II, 779. Figured in most European
works on Lepidoptera.

Upper side black, with a red band. The band of the secondaries is marginal, with four black dots on it, terminated at the anal

angle by a double bluish spot. The band of the primaries is
arcuate, slightly interrupted in the middle. Summit slightly
bluish, with six white spots, of which the interior, in the form of a
transverse band, rests on the costal edge.

Under side of the primaries nearly similar to the upper, but the
summit is brown mixed with gray. The red band is paler at each
extremity, and separated from the white spots by a bluish ring.
At the base there are several streaks of the same color.

Under side of secondaries brown, slightly marbled with gray;
a yellowish spot on the middle of the costal edge, and some bluish
atoms on the lower edge, which is more or less grayish. Emarginations white.

Body of same color as the wings. *Antennæ* annulated with
white and black; club yellowish.

Larva differs in its tints—sometimes of a yellowish-green, sometimes violet powdered with gray; spines moderate, and a sinuous,
lateral band of citron yellow. Feeds on *Urtica*, and is almost
constantly enveloped between several leaves, drawn together by
silk threads.

Chrysalis blackish, moderately angular, covered with a grayish
efflorescence, and ornamented with golden spots.

United States and Europe.—Expands two inches and a half.
Boisd.

2. P. cardui *Linn.* Syst. Nat. II, 776. Figured in most European works.

Upper side of primaries at the base and lateral edge russety
brown; the middle fulvous, nearly cherry-red; border black,
transverse and angulate. Summit widely black, with five white
spots, of which the interior is largest, and rests transversely on the
edge; the four others are in the form of unequal dots, and ranged
in an arc. Posterior edge entirely black, with white emarginations.

Upper side of secondaries fulvous, more or less reddish, with
the base, the internal edge and disk russety brown, and three posterior and parallel rows of black points, of which the intermediary
are oblong and smallest; the exterior are marginal, the interior
only four in number, and sometimes slightly ocellate.

The *under side* of the primaries has the same markings as the
upper, but the fulvous of the middle still more approaches red.
The black band which divides it is marked with white near the
costal edge, and the summit is greenish-brown.

Under side of secondaries marked with brown, white and yellowish, with a row of four ocular spots, separated from the edge by a grayish line, along which there is a series of small bluish crescents formed by atoms.

Body russety brown above, whitish below, with black rings on the abdomen.

Larva spinous, brownish or gray, with lateral and interrupted yellow lines. Feeds on various species of *Carduus*, *Serratula*, and *Cirsium*.

Chrysalis grayish, moderately angular, scattered with golden spots, which sometimes cover nearly the whole surface.

Inhabits the four quarters of the globe.—Expands two and a half inches.

8. P. huntera *Sm. Abb.* *P. virginiensis* Drury. *P. iole* Cram. Figured in Sm. Abb. pl. 9. Cram. 12. Drury I, pl. 5. Boisd. et Lec. pl. 46, p. 1:0.

Size of *P. cardui*, and in many respects similar, but the outer edge of the primaries is usually more emarginate; the summit has a slight blue reflection, and it is browner on the under side. The interior white spot is more narrow and bent outwards. There is a white point between the extremity of this band and the internal angle.

Upper side of secondaries also very similar to *P. cardui*.

The *under side* is brown, slightly obscure, with nervures of a yellowish-white, crossed near the base by two lines of this color. In the middle, there is a transverse band of white, a little grayish, or of a rosy white, followed exteriorly by *two ocellated spots*. Near the posterior edge, there is a marginal band of nearly the same tint, divided in its length by a violet undulated line.

In the *females*, the tint of the upper side is sometimes carmine or brick color.

Larva blackish-gray striated with yellow, with the segments more clear, and the first rings more obscure. Along the feet, and below the stigmata, a yellow lateral ray, and above these another yellow ray, marked with a small orange spot above each stigma. The spines are yellow. Feeds on *Gnaphalium obtusifolium*.

Chrysalis yellowish, of the same form as that of *P. cardui*, scattered with a large number of golden spots.

United States.

Boisd.

JUNONIA Doubld. & Hew.

This may be distinguished from the allied genera by the naked
eyes and less hairy anterior legs. In the other genera, these legs
are densely clothed with long hairs, and this is also the case with
the females of *Vanessa* and *Pyrameis*, but in *Junonia*, though the
legs of the males are thickly set with fine hairs, they are short, and
do not so entirely cover the legs as to make it difficult to detect
their form and even their articulations. The cells of both pairs
of wings are always open, except in a few aberrant species.
Larvæ, with the head and all the segments armed with spines,
which make them resemble the larvæ of *Argynnis* rather than,
those of *Vanessa*. Pupa tuberculated, scarcely angular.

1. J. cœnia *Hubn*. J. orythia *Sm. Ab*. J. lavinia, var. Godt. J. junonia
    Hubn. Figured in Hubn. Exot. Samml. Sm. Abb. I, pl. 6. Boisd.
    et Lec. pl. 49, p. 182.

Upper side obscure brown, with two black ocellated spots; iris
grayish-yellow; pupil blue—the lower one much the larger. They
are preceded by a fulvous ray, followed by a double grayish marginal ray, almost obsolete in the primaries. These have towards
the base two fulvous streaks bordered with black, and between the
two ocellate spots a white band or yellowish-white, going from
the summit to the terminal edge. There is also a small white spot
above the upper ocellus.

The two ocelli of the secondaries are also of unequal size. The
upper one is in part encircled by fulvous, in part by black. It is
nearly covered with violet-blue atoms. The inferior one is similar,
but much smaller.

The *under side* of the primaries is fulvous towards the base,
with some grayish lines bordered with black; paler towards the
end, with the two ocelli and the separating band as on the upper
side, and ordinarily a second small eye above that of the summit.

The *under side* of the secondaries is ferruginous gray, with more
obscure wavy lines and a transverse ferruginous brown band,
marked with two or three small eyes and two blackish points.

Body of same color as the wings. *Antennæ* whitish, with the
club blackish. Expands two inches and a half.

Larva blackish, pointed with white; lower side of abdomen and feet fulvous. It has two lateral white lines, of which the upper is marked with a row of fulvous spots. Spines blackish.

Chrysalis like those of *P. cardui* and *P. huntera*, but blackish, varied with whitish, without any metallic spots.

Southern United States.

Boisd.

ANARTIA Doubleday.

Head rather small, scaly; eyes round, a little prominent; proboscis twice the length of the body; labial palpi scaly; antennæ nearly as long as the body; club short, compressed, pointed; thorax oval, rather robust; primaries subtriangular, rounded at the summit; external edge a little emarginated towards the middle; internal edge slightly emarginate, external edge of secondaries sinuous, dentate, and forming a tooth at the end of the third median nervure; internal edge emarginate before the anal angle; feet of the first pair of the male scaly, femora scarcely more robust than the tibiæ; tarsi subcylindrical, thin; those of the female scaly, more robust, femora nearly cylindrical; tarsi of five joints nearly as long as the tibiæ; feet of the second and third pairs rather elongate; abdomen thin, rather short.

1. A. jatrophæ Linn. Syst. Nat. II, 779. Figured in Cram. pap. pl. 202. Herbst, tab. 172.

Upper side with a more or less livid tint, with brownish, transverse, undulated lines, and three black, ocellate spots, of which one is on the primaries towards the internal angle, and the other two on the secondaries. Some specimens have the extremity of the wings rossety, and the line which divides it forms parallel to the edge, a double row of lunules of this color.

Under side paler, and the ocellate spots have a small whitish pupil. *Antennæ* black, with the club ferruginous. *Body* dark above, whitish below.

Texas—Brazil.

Govt.

Fam. VI. LIBYTHEIDAE.

Larva without spines, slightly pubescent, finely shagreened. *Chrysalis* short, a little angular. *Perfect insect;* palpi very long, contiguous, in the form of a beak, parallel to the axis of the body. Wings angular, rather robust; discoidal cellule of the secondaries open.

LIBYTHEA Fab.

Inferior palpi in the form of a rostrum or beak. Primaries angular. Antennæ short, stiff, fusiform.

1. L. motya *Boisd.* Figured in Boisd. et Lec. pl. 64.

Wings brown; middle of primaries fulvous, beginning at the base; towards the upper angle three white spots, one near the costal edge, oval, the other two smaller and square.

Secondaries with a large pale yellow space in the centre, commencing at the base, and a whitish one on the side.

Under side of primaries similar to the upper, excepting that the fulvous part and the spots are intersected by the nerves, black.

Under side cinereous, with a darker band extending over half the wing, and a crescent streak near the outer edge.

United States.—Expands nearly two inches.

                                                        Boisd.

2. L. bachmani *Kirtland.* Var? of *L. motya.* Figured in Silliman's Journ., XIII, New Series, 356.

Body, dark brown; upper surface of primaries brownish, with three white spots placed in a triangle near the tip, the superior and interior spots oblong and irregular, the exterior smallest and oval, the inferior quadrangular. An ochry yellow band is situated on the humerus, and a second on the posterior margin, but does not reach the tip of the wing. A similar band extends across the lower half of the secondaries.

Under side of primaries similar to the upper; that of the secondaries reticulated with brown.

Expands one and five-eighths of an inch, while *L. motya* expands more than two inches.

The form and size of the white spots in the primaries differ;
the absence of a large white quadrangular spot and a different
arrangement of the yellow bars mark this as a new species.

Ohio.

KIRTLAND.

NYMPHALIS Latr.

Head a little more narrow than the thorax; eyes large, prominent; palpi moderate, a little longer than the head; last article
much shorter than the preceding, obtuse; *antennæ* nearly the
length of the body, insensibly enlarging in an elongate club;
wings wide, rather robust, dentate, *always destitute of oculli and
prolongations in the form of a tail.*

1. **N. ursula** *Fab.* Ent. Syst. III, 1, 82. *N. ephestion* Godt. *N. astyanax*
   Fab. Figured in Stoll, suppl. à Cram. pl. 25. Sm. Abb. I, pl. 10.
   Bsisd. et Lec. pl. 63, p. 199.

Wings slightly dentate; blackish-brown above, glossed with a
bluish tint, much more deep towards the extremity of the secondaries. These have parallel to their terminal edge a double festooned black line, preceded by a bent transverse ray of the same
color; three rows of bluish crescents, of which the interior are
much the largest. In the female, the blue occupies less space, and
the crescents which form the first row are truncate, less marked,
smaller, and each one supported behind by a fulvous point.

The *primaries* have the summit more brown than the rest of the
surface, and marked by one or two small white spots. The posterior edge has two rows of blue or slate-colored crescents, preceded
within by a row of fulvous points often indistinct, and existing
sometimes only on the half of the wing nearest the upper edge.

Under side is brown, a little reddish, glossed, in the male by a
violet-blue tint, except at the summit of the primaries. The base
of these is marked in the cellule by two fulvous spots, surrounded
with black and environed with blue; the base of the secondaries
has three nearly similar spots; the origin of the upper edge of all
the wings is fulvous; the terminal edge of all has two rows of blue
crescents, preceded within by a row of fulvous spots bordered with
black behind.

Body blackish, with the under side of abdomen whitish.

Larva whitish or russety white with green shades, which cover a part of the back; the second ring is armed with two long ferruginous horns, a little arcuate; the fifth bears two roundish tubercles, of the same color. The other tubercles are greenish and not prominent.

Chrysalis russety, with the under side of the abdomen whitish, and a prominent projection on the back. Feeds on *Salix, Vaccinium*, and *Cerasus.*

United States.—Expands three and a half inches.
                                                                              BOIS.

2. N. arthemis *Drury. N. lamina* Fab. Godt. Figured in Drury, II, pl. 10. Boisd. et Lec. pl. 54, p. 202. Say Amer. Ent. II, pl. 23.

Upper side brownish-black, with a common white band a little beyond the middle, and a double series of blue marginal crescents on the secondaries, and only one on the primaries. These have at the summit two or three small white spots, and the secondaries, in the males, a bent row of seven roundish spots, or large fulvous dots, situated between the band and the blue crescents.

The *lower side* differs from the upper in having the ground color more pale, excepting on the outer edge where it remains blackish; at the base of each wing there are some bluish spots, accompanied by large reddish points; the primaries have a series of reddish points before the double line of blue lunules of the extremity.

Emarginations of all the wings white. *Body* black, with three white lines along the abdomen. *Antennæ* black.

The *female* is larger than the male; the bent row of large fulvous points is replaced above by lunules formed of bluish atoms; below, it has the same markings as the male.

Northern States.—Expands three and a half inches.
                                                                              BOISD.

3. N. disippus *Godt.* Encyc. Méthod. IX, 392. *N. misippus* Fab. *N. archippus* Cram. Figured in Cram. pl. 16. Boisd. et Lec. pl. 55, p. 204.

Upper side fulvous, with nerves and edges black; the terminal edge has two rows of white points, the exterior are the smaller, and placed in the emarginations; near the summit of the primaries, where the black dilates sensibly, are three white points, followed by a macular and transverse band of four fulvous spots.

The *secondaries* are traversed beyond the middle, reaching from the external edge to the anal angle, by a bent, black ray.

Under side has the ground color and fulvous spots of the summit more pale ; the interior points of the terminal edge are replaced by a double series of white baules ; there are two white spots on the costal edge towards the base, and sometimes a point near the base of the cell.

Antennæ black as well as the body ; the latter is pointed with white on the head and breast.

The *female* is somewhat larger than the male, and the second row of crescents on the under side of the wings is a little bluish.

Larva green, varied with white ; the first rings are russety. The second ring bears two spiny horns, a little arcuate in front ; the third, fifth, sixth, seventh and tenth has each a small spiny process, and the eleventh two short spines. Feeds on *Salix* and *Prunus.*

Chrysalis russety, with the sides of the abdomen varied with white, and a prominent projection on the back.

United States.—Expands from two inches and a half to four inches.

Bodd.

4. *L.* lorquini *Boisd.* Ann. Soc. Ent. 2me sér. X, 301. *L. eulalia* Doubled.

Upper side brown-black, traversed toward the middle by a white macular band, preceded on the primaries in the discoidal cellule by a spot of the same color ; primaries, with the summit very widely ferruginous red, separated from the brown part by three or four white spots. Secondaries with two large fulvous points towards the anal angle.

Under side brown, with the same band and the same white spots as above ; the common band followed by a ferruginous space, divided by a series of whitish sagittate crescents, bordered with black at the summit ; that of the primaries with two ferruginous streaks in the cellule ; that of the secondaries with the edge whitish, and the base intersected by whitish-gray spots.

California.

Bodd.

PAPHIA Doubleday.

Wings with a metallic gloss, under side indistinctly reticulated ; female with the upper side more variegated with brown or pale-colored spots than the male. Head not tufted in front ; eyes large, prominent. Labial palpi thickly squamose, broad in front. Antennæ short, slender; club slender, obliquely rounded off at tip. Primaries large, fore margin strongly arched, somewhat elbowed near the base, apical angle more or less acute; apical margin sometimes deeply emarginate near the tip. Secondaries subovate, costal margin rounded, outer margin sometimes scolloped; the extremity of the third branch of the median vein being extended into a tail. Abdomen rather small and subovate.

1. P. glycerium *Doubleday.* Figured in Doubleday and Hewitson's Genera, pl. 50.

Upper side copper red; margin of all the wings brownish interiorly, powdered with the same color; primaries with two short brownish bands commencing on the costal, the one nearest the apex undulate; the brownish margin extends about one-third on the anterior edge, with a deep emargination near the summit.

Under side paler, of the color of dead leaves; the bands on the primaries longer than above, and a transverse band on the secondaries separating the deeper shade of the base from the other part; an indistinct white spot near the upper edge.

Female larger, paler, markings in the primaries more distinct and wide; similar below.

Texas—Illinois.

APATURA Fab.

Eyes large, prominent; *antennæ* rather long, terminated by an elongated cylindrical club, the end of which is yellow; *palpi* contiguous; *thorax* long and robust; *abdomen* proportionately small; *wings* slightly dentate, often with a bluish reflection, the secondaries with the cellule open and having at least one ocellus on the under side; the primaries always have the outer edge more or less concave, and in the discoidal cellule on the under side two or three black transverse streaks. The secondaries are also somewhat concave above the anal angle.

The *Apaturæ* resemble *Satyri* in the form of the *larva* and in the *ocelli* on the under side of the wings, but differ in habits; the former live on trees, the latter on low grounds and grasses.

1. **A. clyton** *Boisd.* Boisd. et Lec., 209, pl. 66, p. 208.

Primaries reddish-yellow or fulvous, with the extremity brownish, marked with two rows of small spots and a marginal interrupted ray, ochry yellow. The fulvous portion has two black streaks on the discoidal cellule, and is separated from the brownish by a sinuous blackish ray.

The *secondaries* are obscure rufous, gradually becoming brownish towards the extremity. This part is divided by a row of five black points ocellated with rufous, preceded by a series of quadrangular spots a little more clear than the ground color and followed by a yellowish marginal ray, as a continuation of that on the primaries. Besides these, there is near the middle a blackish, sinuous, transverse ray, very distinct at its origin on the upper edge.

Under side of all the wings is russety gray, with a violet reflection; an obscure marginal ray, and a median, black, transverse, flexuous ray, corresponding to that on the upper side, more distinct on the primaries, where it is preceded by two black streaks and followed by the same spots as above, but paler. This same ray is preceded, in the discoidal cellule of the secondaries, by two black streaks. The ocellated points have the pupil bluish-white. The emarginations of all the wings are feebly white.

Larva, which feeds on *Prunus* and other drupaceous plants, is green, with four rays of greenish yellow. Head yellowish-green, marked with two black spots and surmounted by two short ramose yellowish spines; the two small anal points are a little elevated.

Chrysalis green, with the envelopment of the wings and some indistinct dorsal rays greenish-yellow.

Southern States.—Expands nearly two inches and a half.

             Boisd.

2. **A. celtis** *Boisd.* Boisd. et Lec., p. 210, pl. 67.

Same size and form of *A. clyton*.

Upper side pale russety gray. Outer half of the primaries brownish, marked with about a dozen small white spots disposed in two lines a little sinuous, of which one or two near the summit are ocellated with black and very small. The exterior edge has a russety line, preceded near the external angle by a black eye ocellated by yellowish-red, on a line with the white spots of the second row. There are two black transversal streaks in the discoidal cellule.

The *secondaries* are traversed, towards the middle, by two indistinct carved lines of blackish-gray, and near the marginal edge by two parallel undulated lines of the same color, very distinct. These lines are preceded by a curved row of six black eyes, of which the second, counting from above, is the largest; the others sensibly diminish in size. The anal is very small and often wanting.

The *under side* is whitish, and has nearly the same markings as the upper. On the secondaries, the two carved lines of the middle are preceded, towards the base, by two or three small angular brownish spots. The ocelli are pupilled with white, and surrounded by a small yellow iris.

Upper side of the body brownish-gray. *Under side* whitish-gray. *Antennæ* brownish, with the club yellowish.

. *Larva*, which feeds on *Celtis occidentalis*, is yellowish, with the sides more pale and nearly whitish. The back has a ray yellowish-green, bordered on each side by an obscure green line. The whitish part is also divided longitudinally by a green obscure ray. Head green, surmounted by two small blað spines. The small anal points are a little raised.

Chrysalis yellowish-green, a little blað.

Southern States.

Bois.

AGANISTHOS Bois.

Head nearly as wide as the thorax; *eyes* large, prominent; *antennæ* long, terminated by an elongated cylindrical club; *palpi* near together, converging at the extremity; *thorax* long, thick, very robust; *abdomen* proportionately small; *wings* not dentale, very strong and robust; the primaries have the outer edge very emarginate and the summit prolonged, which gives them a falcate form; the secondaries are rounded, without tails, the anal angle a little prominent; *both sides destitute of ocelli*.

1. **A. orion** Fab. Syst. Ent. 457. *A. odius* Sulz. *A. demes* Cram. Figured in Cram. pl. 54. Sulz. Gesch. pl. 13. Boisd. et Lec. pl. 52, p. 195.

Expands about five inches. *Upper side* of primaries brownish-black, with a fulvous, longitudinal band, which covers the anterior surface, terminating a little distance from the outer edge. On the upper edge there is an oblong white spot of moderate size.

The *upper side* of the secondaries is brownish-black, with the base obscure fulvous.

The *under side* of all the wings is brown shaded with gray, with two transverse bands more deep near the base; then two black lines equally transverse, which unite towards the internal edge of the secondaries. A white spot on the primaries, corresponding with that on the upper side; the terminal edge of all the wings is grayish-white on each side.

Upper side of the body fulvous, with the extremity brownish; *under side*, color of the wings. *Antennae* ferruginous.

Florida. [Most probably not found in the United States.— Major Leconte *teste*, M.]

                                                          Boisd.

FAM. VII. SATYRIDAE.

Larva attenuate at the extremities and nearly pisciform, terminated by two anal points more or less prominent; head sometimes rounded, sometimes emarginate or bifid, or surmounted by two spines. *Chrysalis* cylindroid, not much angular. *Perfect insect*; palpi close, elevated, very hairy; body moderate; wings rather robust, abdominal edge of the secondaries forming a groove; discoidal cellule always closed; nervures of the primaries often much dilated at their origin.

CHIONOBAS Boisd.

Head not quite so wide as the thorax, closely connected with it; *antennae* terminating in an elongated club, forming insensibly and occupying nearly the half; *palpi* remote, covered with fine hairs; last article very short; *wings* rounded; *primaries*, with the costal nervure feebly inflated.

The species of this genus differ from the other *Satyridae* in their pale, dull, livid, and, as it were, *diseased* color, indicating their far northern habitat.

1. **O. also** *Boisd. et Lec.*, p. 222. Figured in Boisd. Icones, pl. 40.

Wings of a dirty grayish tint, mixed with yellow, slightly transparent with some small brownish atoms, a little more dense near the fringe. The primaries have a little more uniform color, deeper at the base, with an oblique shadow on the median nerve. The secondaries are sufficiently transparent to observe the markings on the opposite side.

The *under side* of the primaries is more deeply powdered with brownish than the upper, with the upper edge and summit variegated with grayish and blackish.

The *under side* of the secondaries is brownish to the middle, with some grayish atoms, and marbled with the same color near the external edge. The posterior portion is grayish violet, with blackish atoms and small undulations.

The *fringe* is grayish-white, interrupted with blackish.

Rocky Mountains of New Hampshire.

Boisd.

[Most probably *Sat. semidea* Say.—M]

2. **O. balder** *Boisd. et Lec.*, p. 216. Figured in Boisd. Icones, pl. 39. Boisd. Iconograph. du Regne Animal, pl. 50.

Upper side livid yellowish-brown, with the border a little more obscure. Primaries at the extremity have three pale yellow spots, of which two have a central black point. Secondaries, near the extremity, have a row of four or five pale yellow spots, cuneiform; the one nearest the anal angle usually has a black point.

Under side of primaries is more yellow than the upper, with the costal edge, apical point, and a part of the extremity, pale ash, sprinkled with brown.

Under side of the secondaries brownish, varied with ash-gray; a little bluish. It is traversed in the middle by a broad band, dentated, and forming a suite of nearly equal angles. The edge of this band and the extremity of the wing are more gray than the rest. Fringe white and black. Body brown; antennæ grayish at the base, pale testaceous to the end.

North Cape—Greenland—Labrador.

Boisd.

3. C. booten *Boisd. et Lec.*, p. 218. Figured in Boisd. Icon. pl. 37.

Upper side yellowish-brown, mixed with gray; primaries towards the extremity with a blackish marginal ray, interrupted or indistinct. The arc which closes the discoidal cell is blackish, followed by a brownish angular impression.

Upper side of secondaries yellowish, with an obscure impression on the middle and towards the base. The border is of the same color as that of the primaries, and separated from the yellowish by a blackish macular ray. Fringe grayish-white divided by black.

Under side of primaries yellowish, with the summit and costal margin whitish, with brown points. The cellule is traversed by a blackish ray; beyond this, there is another blackish ray, more distinct, and bent into an acute angle on the median nerve.

Under side of the secondaries is whitish, the base varied with black—a wide, sinuous band traversing the middle. Extremity russety, pointed with brown; a macular, blackish ray; nerves white. Body brown; antennæ fulvous; base gray.

North Cape—Labrador—Greenland.

Boisd.

4. C. osno *Boisd.* Figured in Boisd. Icones, pl. 39.

Wings thin and delicate; color livid brown, mixed with yellowish. Primaries nearly transparent at the extremity, which is more yellowish; apex and edge with some blackish atoms. Secondaries transparent, with some black atoms towards the edge.

Under side of the primaries more yellowish, with the summit and costal edge pointed with brownish.

Under side of the secondaries is marked with white and black, traversed by a blackish band, crenate. The extremity, with blackish atoms, forming a macular ray. Fringe white and black. Body brown. Antennæ as in the preceding species.

Lapland—Siberia—Labrador.

Boisd.

NEONYMPHA Hubner.

Body small, hairy; wings large, not diaphanous, uniformly colored above, more or less ocellated and strigose, especially beneath. Head small and slightly hairy. Antennæ very short, annulated with white, joints short, club robust, elongate; labial palpi densely clothed in front with long, straight, bristly hairs. Thorax oval, very finely hairy. Primaries large, entire, fringed with fine hairs; costal margin slightly arched, veins delicate. Secondaries sub-triangular, costal margin arched, outer angle rounded, anal angle rather obtuse, outer margin entirely fringed with long hairs. Fore legs of the males small and feathery; fore legs of the females very small, slightly feathery. Four hind legs short, scaly. Femora slightly clothed with hairs, tibial spurs distinct, claws much curved, entire, slender.

Larva elongate, thickest in the middle, longitudinally strigose, tail bifid. *Chrysalis* short and thick, with the head case rather incurved and obtuse.

1. **N. eurythris** *Fab.* Ent. Syst. III, 1, 137. *N. eymela* Cram. Figured in Herbst, pl. 198. Cram. pl. 132. Boisd. et Lec. pl. 61.

Wings entire, slightly brown on the upper side; primaries, at the extremity, with two black ocelli; iris yellow; double silvery pupil. These spots are separated from the outer edge by a triple blackish line.

Upper side of secondaries with three ocelli; the upper one small and widely separated from the two below; the middle one the largest, and it alone having the double silvery pupil.

The *female* has but two spots on the upper side of the secondaries.

Under side paler, with two brown wavy lines traversing the middle. Between the two ocelli, corresponding to those on the upper side, there are two double silver points.

Under side of secondaries has four spots, the upper and lower of which are the smallest. There are also two intermediary silver points, sometimes with an iris. Behind these spots are three blackish lines. Body brownish; antennæ annulated with white and black; club ferruginous.

United States.—Expands an inch and a half.

Boisd.

2. **N. gemma** *Hübner.* Figured in Boisd. et Lec. pl. 62.

Wings entire; upper side uniform pale brown, except on the lower edge of the secondaries, where there are three or four crescent-shaped black spots.

Under side paler. From the base of all the wings to the middle, there are short brown streaks. The primaries with two transverse brown lines, the outer one wavy, and the edge with a black ray. The secondaries are traversed by two wavy lines; towards the outer border, an irregular violet spot surrounded with black, enclosing two small silver points, one at each end. Between this and the edge is a series of silver points, confluent towards the anal angle.

United States.—Expands an inch and a half.

Bosc.

3. **N. sosybius** *Fab.* Ent. Syst. III, 219. *N. cememus* Cram. Herbst. Figured in Cram. pl. 293. Herbst, pl. 195. Bosc. et Leo. pl. 63.

Wings entire, brownish; upper side without spots; round the outer edge of all are three darker lines.

Under side, which is lighter, has three transverse, obscure, undulated lines. Discoidal cellule with a curved streak, and on the secondaries a similar streak extending obliquely from one line to the other, besides three fine lines round the edge.

The *primaries* have four or five ocelli, and the secondaries six.

The latter are black, with a simple white pupil and yellow iris; some of them are less distinct than others, and sometimes almost obsolete.

United States.—Expands an inch and a quarter.

Bosc.

4. **N. areolatus** *Godt.* Encyc. Méthod. IX, 494. Figured in Sm. Abb. I, pl. 13. Bosc. et Lec. pl. 63.

Wings entire, brownish; upper side without spots.

Under side paler, with two ferruginous transverse lines. Between these lines there is an elongated, ferruginous circle, in which the primaries have three or four ocelli, with a bluish pupil and yellow iris; the secondaries inclose in this circle six ocelli, of which the third, fourth and fifth are oblong, with the pupil oval.

Southern States.—Expands an inch and a half.

Bosc.

5. **N. canthus** *Linn.* Syst. Nat. 768. *N. boisduvalii* Harris. Figured in Bosc. et Leo. pl. 60.

Wings entire; bright brown above, darker towards the extremity, with four ocelli, two of which are not always distinct.

The *secondaries* have six ocelli; the anal one is of the ground color, with a black pupil, indistinct.

Under side paler, crossed with irregular wavy lines. The primaries have four ocelli, with the pupil white. The secondaries have six ocelli, five of which are contiguous.

United States.—Expands nearly two inches.

Boisd.

[Fabricius has united the following with the preceding, but Godart maintains that it is a distinct species.—J. G. M.]

6. N. canthous *Fab.* Ent. Syst. 486.

Nearly the same size as *N. canthus. Upper side* blackish-brown, without spots. *Under side* lighter, with two ferruginous, oblique, common lines. The *primaries* have three small indistinct eyes. The *secondaries* have six, of which the fifth is large; the sixth, which is at the anal angle, small.

North America.

Godart.

EREBIA Dalman.

Club of the antennæ gradual. Eyes naked. Tibia shorter than the tarsus. Only the costal of the primaries inflated. Species rather small in size; color dark brown; usually a ferruginous band or spots with small black eyes, pupils white. Sometimes the eyes are obsolete and in their stead only black spots. Under side paler; a dark band marbled. Outer edge rounded. Palpi with long hairs at the last joint; antennæ not annulated.

1. E. discoidalis *Kirby.* Faun. Bor. Am. IV, 298, pl. 3.

Body brown; antennæ annulated with white; wings entire, brown; costa spotted with gray; a triangular obscure reddish tawny discoidal stripe extends from the base to the posterior margin of the primaries, and is discoverable also on the under side, where the wing is faintly clouded with gray at the tip; the secondaries underneath are indistinctly marbled and clouded with gray or whitish; fringe whitish and brown alternately.

Canada.—Expands an inch.

Kirby.

2. E. nephele *Kirby.* Faun. Bor. IV, 299.

Color brown above and beneath, but paler beneath. Antennæ annulated with white ; knob slender.

Upper side is marked with an obsolete but broad submarginal band, in which there are two. eyelets with a clouded white or bluish-white pupil, and a small black iris with a very indistinct brown ring. The posterior wings are crenate, and marked with a minute or obsolete black spot.

Under side, the belt of the anterior wings is much more distinct, eyelets bright, and the outer ring of brown plain ; margin of the wing traversed with two or three lines parallel to the edge. Outer half of the hind wing paler and marked with six small eyelets, which form three rows, the largest eyelet being in the middle ; the anal angles divaricate, leaving a wide triangular space.

Canada.

KIRBY.

SATYRUS Fab.

Eyes naked. Tibia long, with a spur at the end. One or two veins on the primaries inflated. Wings wide, limb of the primaries seldom rounded, that of the secondaries dentate. Upper side brown or black, usually with a broad whitish or yellowish band before the limb, and with ocelli in the primaries. Under side of secondaries marbled.

[Westwood, in second volume of Doubleday's, Hewitson's, and Westwood's Genera, proposes to limit the genus *Satyrus* to those species generally of large size, which are distinguished by having the costal and median veins of the primaries dilated at the base, the sub-median being simple, and by having the eyes naked.— J. G. M.]

1. S. alope *Fab.* B. & III, 229. Figured in Boisd. et Lec. pl. 59.

Upper side blackish-brown ; under side paler and finely undulated with black. Primaries on both sides, with a wide, yellow ochry band, concave behind, sinuous before, touching neither the upper nor lower edge. This band bears two ocelli, with blue pupils, the lower one sometimes indistinct or obsolete.

The *upper side* of the secondaries, usually towards the anal angle, has a similar ocellated spot.

The *under side* has a row of six; iris yellow, pupil blue, of which the two extreme and the intermediary are smallest.

Body of the color of the wings; antennæ annulated with white and black.

The *S. pegala* of Fab. is most probably only a variety which has but one eye on the primaries.

United States.—Expands two and a half inches.

Boisd.

2. S. ariane *Boisd.*

Upper side blackish-brown; primaries with two black ocelli pupilled with white, the iris a little paler; secondaries with a smaller eye often preceded by another small one without a pupil.

Under side brown, with the markings more obscure; the eyes of the primaries with a fulvous iris, preceded by a transverse brown line, and followed near the fringe by three very fine parallel lines; that of the secondaries is traversed in the middle by two sinuous brown lines, followed by an irregular row of six small black ocelli and more or less marked with blue.

The *female* is much larger than the male; the ocelli of the primaries are larger, circled with fulvous yellow; the small ocelli of the under side of the inferiors much less distinct than in the male.

California.

Boisd.

3. S. sthenele *Boisd.* Ann. Soc. Ent. 2me sér. X, 308.

Upper side brown, with the fringe ash-gray, intersected with black; that of the primaries with two small black ocelli with white pupil; that of the secondaries without spots.

Under side ash-gray, deeper at the base; that of the primaries with two larger ocelli circled with fulvous yellow, that of the secondaries traversed by a wide brown angular band and marked towards the anal angle by two small black ocelli with white pupil.

California.

Bonn.

4. S. pegala *Fab.* Ent. Syst. III, 404.

Body brown; primaries obscure brown, with a wide russety band which does not reach the edge. On both sides an eye with a white pupil.

Upper side of the secondaries obscure brown, with a black eye, white pupil and yellow iris.

Under side of various colors, with six eyes, of which three are naked, the fifth very large. These eyes, which vary in number and form, are black, pupil whitish, and iris ferruginous.

North America.

GODT.

DIIRIS Boisp.

Body rather small, wings large; secondaries generally angulated in the middle with a row of large ocelli; eyes prominent, hairy; labial palpi rather elongated, clothed in front with moderately short fine hair. Antennæ slender, club slender, with short joints. Thorax short, thick, hairy. Primaries triangular, ovate; fore margin strongly curved, apical angle rounded, apical margin but little if at all emarginate, costal vein dilated at the base. Secondaries subovate, more or less scolloped along the outer margin, which is generally deeply angulated or rather shortly tailed at the extremity. Fore legs very minute and thickly clothed with long silky hairs; tarsus slender, as long as the tibia, and destitute of joints or claws. Fore legs of the females rather larger than those of the males, slender, scaly, destitute of hairs; tarsal articulations concealed by scales, obliquely truncate at tip, where there are a few short spines. Tibial spurs of the hind legs rather long.

1. D. andromacha *Hübn.* Figured in Say, Amer. Ent. II, pl. 36.

Body above and the superior surface of the wings brown; primaries beyond the middle, with a broad paler band, bifid before, and including a series of four fuscous oval spots or epupillate ocelli, of which the second and sometimes the third are small and the posterior one largest; between the band and the exterior edge is a single narrow pale line, sometimes obsolete; exterior edge alternately white and black; secondaries with a narrow fuscous, angulated line across the middle, and a broad pale band beyond the middle, in which is a series of five fuscous epupillate ocelli with a yellow iris, the third smallest, then the fifth, the first being largest, exterior margin slightly tinged with rufous and with one or two fuscous lines.

Under side pearlaceous, with a brown narrow band before the middle; beyond which is a broad lighter perlaceous band, in which on the primaries are four epupillate ocelli, two or three anterior ones small, and on the secondaries are six ocellate spots, consisting of a fuscous spot surrounded by a yellow line and having a white pupil; first spot distant, third small, fifth double; exterior margin with a yellow line.

Larva long, subcylindric, striate; head with two erect horns; body terminating in two porrected points.

Chrysalis short, thick, constricted across the abdomen.

North and West.

BAY.

2. D. portlandia *Fab.* Ent. Syst. III, 108. Figured in Bolsd. et Lec. pl. 58.

Upper side pale livid brown, inclining to russety, with three large black eyes on the primaries and five on the secondaries. These eyes have no pupils and are surrounded with a yellow iris. Sometimes the primaries have a small intermediate eye between the first and second, and the secondaries have a sixth small anal eye.

The *under side* is paler than the upper, with a violet reflection, traversed by two brown sinuous rays, between which there is a discoidal arc of the same color. The eyes are neater and blacker than above, with the iris yellow; those of the primaries are inclosed in an oblong white ring, and the first is often pupilled with white; those of the secondaries are nearly all pupilled with white, the anal is double and the pupils oblong. Besides this, the eyes are preceded on all the wings by a white sinuous band, and followed by a line of the same color, which is double in the secondaries. The marginal edge is fulvous yellow. Antennæ yellowish; body of the color of the wings.

Larva feeds on grasses; green, with two white dorsal lines and a lateral band of the same color. The anal points are prominent, rosy white; head surmounted by two points of the same color, which are elevated in the form of ears; the under side of the abdomen and the feet are whitish-green.

Georgia.

BOISD.

COENONYMPHA Westwood.

Body small, wings entire, rounded, sometimes entirely destitute of ocellated spots; the three principal nerves of the primaries inflated at the base; fringe long, costal edge moderately arcuated; secondaries oval and triangular, fringe long, external edge convex and entire, internal edge usually emarginate towards the end; antennæ thin, not annulated with black, club ovoid, elongate; labial palpi much compressed, straight, hairy in front; head small, hairy, without a frontal tuft; eyes prominent, naked; abdomen moderately long, thin.

1. C. semidea *Say.* Amer. Ent. III, pl. 50.

Body black, immaculate; antennæ fuscous, beneath bright rufous toward the tip, the club very gradually formed; primaries brown, the costal margin with alternate black and white spots; beneath dull ochreous, with obsolete, transverse, abbreviated, blackish lines; costal and broad tip margin alternated with vivid black and white lines; secondaries dark brown; towards the posterior margin obscure ochreous, with obsolete abbreviated, blackish, transverse lines; posterior margin with a slender black line and dirty white edging; beneath marbled with black and white, the black prevailing across the middle and base of the wing.

White Mountains of New Hampshire.

Say.

2. C. galactina *Boisd.* Ann. Soc. Ent. 2me sér. X, 309.

Upper side white, a little yellowish; without any other spot than by the transparency of the other side.

Under side of the primaries with a small black eye at the summit, most frequently without a pupil, preceded from the side of the base by a ferruginous transverse line a little bent; that of the secondaries washed with gray, and this part more obscure is separated from the other by a sinuous ray, followed by one, two, three or four small black eyes, often without pupils.

California.

Boisd.

CALISTO Hüb.

The hairy eyes, the dilatation of the base of the costal and median veins of the primaries, the insertion of all the branches of the post-costal veins beyond the extremity of the discoidal veins, the strongly angulated middle disco-cellular vein and the *lobed secondaries*, distinguish this genus.

1. *C. zangis Fab.* E. S. III, 216. *C. agnes* Cram. Figured in Cram. pl. 315. Herbst, pl. 203.

Upper side brownish-black velvety, a little paler towards the tip; a small black eye with a yellow iris at the lobe of the secondaries.

Under side ferruginous, with four black transverse and undulated lines, of which two are between the base and the middle, the other two near the terminal edge.

Primaries, opposite the summit, have a large black eye, with a rusty iris and a double white pupil.

Secondaries have two eyes, of which the anal one is like that on the upper side, the other similar to that of the primaries, but a little oblong and surmounted with three white points.

Body of the color of the wings.

Carolina.—Expands an inch and a half.

Brvc. Méth.

Fam. VIII. LYCAENIDAE.

Larva in the form of *Oniscus* (wood-louse.) *Chrysalis* short, obtuse at both ends. *Perfect insect;* abdominal edge embracing a little portion of the abdomen. Discoidal cellule closed apparently by a small norviform prominence. Hooks of the tarsi very small.

ARGUS Latr.

Head smaller than the thorax; *palpi* bent; second article covered with short and thick-set hairs; the last article naked, thin and filiform; *antennae* moniliform, terminated by fusiform club, compressed laterally at its extremity. The color of *Argus* is usually blue. The under side presents a number of small spots

6

or ocellated points, and often a marginal band of yellow spots. The females differ from the males in being often brown or blackish. *Wings* rounded, and ordinarily without tails. Some species have a small filiform process.

1. **A. Siennus** Porg. Cent. *A. Hanno?* Hübn. *A. obshtus* Godt. *A. pseudophiletes* Boisd. Figured in Hübn. Exot. Samml. Cram. 390. L. M. Boisd. et Lec. pl. 35, p. 114.

Upper side of the male blue, with a slight black border; fringe whitish. In both sexes there is a small black round spot near the marginal edge of the secondaries.

Under side ash-gray, usually more pale in the male than in the female, with a discoidal crescent on the middle of each, and three sinuous, common bands, formed of small black spots circled with white, of which the posterior are a little less distinct and somewhat sagittate. The space which separates the internal band of the median is usually whiter than the rest, and forms a band of small white quadrangular spots. The base of the secondaries has a transverse row of three very black points, circled with white; of which the external is largest. The secondaries have on the marginal edge and near the anal angle, a black eye, more or less circled with yellow, sprinkled behind with golden-green atoms.

Southern States.—Expands three-fourths of an inch.

Boisn.

2. **A. pseudargiolus** Boisd. et Lec. Figured in Boisd. et Lec. pl. 36, p. 118.

Upper side of the male tender violet blue, with a slight black edge, often widened on the primaries. Fringe whitish and black.

Upper side of the female paler blue and less violet, a wide black border on the primaries, and a marginal row of black points; a small black arc at the extremity of the discoidal cellula.

Under side obscure gray, with a brown discoidal streak, a transverse sinuous line of black points a little circled with white, and a marginal row of brownish triangular crescents, each one supported by a point more obscure. At the base of the primaries, a transverse row of three distinct black points.

Larva green, pubescent; back yellowish; a median interrupted ray, cut transversely by a wide arc; oblique streaks on the sides; near the feet a marginal ray, dark green; head black.

Chrysalis reddish ; wing envelopes greenish ; back with four rows of obscure spots.

United States.—Expands an inch.

Boisd.

POLYOMMATUS Latr.

Palpi very straight ; last article naked, rather long and subulate ; *head* more narrow than the thorax ; *antennæ* long, terminated by a fusiform elongated club ; anal angle of the secondaries in most males a little prolonged ; posterior edge usually somewhat emarginate before this angle, in the females.

Ground color of the wings more or less lively fulvous, at least in one of the sexes. The females always have some black points on the upper side.

1. P. comyntas *Godt.* Encyc. Méthod. IX, 660. Figured in Boisd. et Lea. pl. 36, p. 120.

Upper side of the male violet blue, posterior edge blackish.

Upper side of the female blackish-brown, sometimes uniform, sometimes with the base covered with bluish dust. Fringe white in both sexes ; secondaries, with a marginal row of small round spots, of which one or two, near the filiform tail, are surmounted with a reddish arc.

Under side gray, with a central arc, then a flexuous line of small ocellate points, circled with white, and two marginal lines of small brownish spots. *Secondaries*, with a row of two or three basal black points, and two anal triangular crescents, reddish-yellow, with black ends, each supported on a very black point, but separated from it by a small arc of shining gold-green atoms.

Larva dirty greenish-white ; an interrupted dorsal ray, and oblique lateral rosacy streaks ; near the head, a transverse streak blackish, and near the tail, two greenish triangular spots. Head black.

Chrysalis yellowish ; wing envelopes paler, and four dorsal rows of obscure points.

United States.—Expands a little over an inch.

Boisd.

2. P. phlaeas *Linn.* Syst. Nat. 793. Figured in most European authors.

Upper side of the primaries in both sexes shining fulvous, with the upper and side edge blackish-brown, and eight large black points.

Secondaries blackish-brown, with a central arc and some deeper points; then a fulvous crenated band, sometimes surmounted by a row of four or five blue points.

Under side of the primaries grayish-ash, with fifteen small scattered points, and a flexuous line.

Larva, which feeds on *Rumex*, is green, pubescent, with a rosy dorsal and marginal line, or sometimes pale green.

Chrysalis grayish, with obscure points on the back.

United States, Europe, Africa, &c.—Expands over an inch.
                                                                Boisd.

3. P. hypophlaeas *Boisd.* Ann. Soc. Ent. 2me sér. X, 293.

Closely resembles *P. phlæas*, but is smaller, with the points more distinct, the wings more rounded; *under side* of the secondaries white-ashy, with the yellow marginal band strongly marked.

North of California and Northern United States.
                                                                Boisd.

4. P. thoe *Boisd. et Lec.* Figured in Guér. Rég. Anim. pl. 81. Boisd. et Lec. pl. 38, p. 125.

Upper side of the male brownish, with a violet reflection and a light blackish border; three black points, of which two are in the discoidal cellule.

Secondaries have on the terminal edge an orange fulvous band, crenated behind, and a blackish arc on the end of the discoidal cellule.

Upper side of the primaries of the female fulvous, with a blackish border, and some black discoidal points, of which two or three are in the cellule, and the others disposed in a transverse line. That of the secondaries brownish, with some scattered brownish points disposed nearly as on the primaries, and a fulvous marginal band as in the male, but paler.

Under side in both sexes the same. *Primaries* fulvous, with the posterior edge ashy, two or three sinuous rows of black points, and four similar points between the base of the wing and the internal row.

Under side of secondaries pale ashy, with a fulvous band as above; some black points circled with white, without order, towards the base, but regular towards the extremity. Fringe of secondaries white and black.

United States.—Expands over an inch.

BOISD.

5. P. epixanthe *Boisd. et Lec.* Figured in Boisd. et Lec. pl. 38, p. 127.

Upper side brownish-black, with scattered black points. Primaries with the costal edge a little reddish; secondaries with a narrow marginal fulvous band, crenated behind. Fringe grayish.

Under side yellowish; primaries, with about fifteen black points disposed as in the analogous species; secondaries, with black points, but small; a crenated band of a more lively tint than that on the upper side.

Western States.—Expands about an inch.

BOISD.

6. P. crataegi *Boisd. et Lec.* P. terguinius Fab. Figured in Boisd. et Lec. pl. 37. p. 128.

Wings, blackish-brown; primaries, with a longitudinal sinuous yellow band, irregular at its extremity, and marked towards the base by a blackish interrupted line.

Secondaries, with the lower limb bright yellow, and a marginal series of black points.

Primaries of the female yellowish, with a crenate black border and two longitudinal interrupted black bands, the anterior the longer, and divided into three parts. *Secondaries* with the extremity yellowish, and four to six black points disposed in two rows.

The *under side* is reddish-yellow, glossed with whitish, with deeper spots slightly circled with white on the secondaries; primaries, with all the disk, of a yellowish tint.

Larva, which feeds on *Crataegus*, is green, with three dorsal white rays, and one at the base of the feet.

Chrysalis grayish; back darker, marked with prominent tubercles. Hind extremity pointed and a little arcuate.

United States.—Expands an inch and a half.

BOISD.

7. P. helloides *Boisd.* Ann. Soc. Ent. 2me sér. X, 292.

Upper side smoky yellow, with a beautiful violet reflection in the male. Markings nearly as in *P. phlæas*, except that the latter has only one black point towards the base of the primaries, whilst this species has two.

Under side of primaries nearly similar to *P. phlæas*; that of the secondaries reddish-gray, with a row of marginal lunules bright ferruginous.

San Francisco.

Boisd.

8. P. gorgon *Boisd.* Ann. Soc. Ent. 2me sér. X, 292.

Upper side with a bright violet reflection, a small black border, and the fringe intersected with white; primaries with a small subcostal black point; secondaries with a fulvous anal streak.

Upper side of the female dull brown, spotted with fulvous, as in the allied species, but of a paler tint.

Under side of both sexes ramsey on the primaries, pale grayish on the secondaries, with a great number of ocellate black points on each wing, and a row of fulvous marginal spots on the secondaries.

Mountains of California.

Boisd.

9. P. xanthoides *Boisd.* Ann. Soc. Ent. 2me sér. X, 292.

Size and general appearance of *P. gorgon*.

Under side of the male pale ashy-brown, rather glossy, with a black edge and white fringe slightly cut by the black of the nerves. Primaries with a small subcostal black streak, preceded by a small point of the same color; secondaries with a fulvous marginal streak towards the anal angle, and marked with two or three marginal black points in a line, and united with the border.

Under side ramsey gray, with a great number of black points; that of the secondaries with two or three fulvous lunules towards the anal angle, preceded by a ray paler than the general tint.

Mountains of California.   Rare.

Boisd.

10. P. arota *Boisd.* Ann. Soc. Ent. 2me sér. X, 293.

Upper side of the male brown, with a glossy red reflection, and some small points which are transparent from the opposite surface;

anal angle of secondaries with two small black marginal points, one on each side of the tail.

Upper side of the female brown, with the disk of the primaries and the greater part of the secondaries fulvous, spotted with black.

Under side of the primaries fulvous, the extremity ashy, with a great number of ocellate black points.

Under side of secondaries ashy, with smaller points and less distinct, a whitish band, terminal, sinuous within, deeper towards the fringe, and marked on each side of the tail with a black point. Distinguished from the allied species by the small tail.

California.   Boisd.

11. **P. amyntula** *Boisd.* Ann. Soc. Ent. 2me sér. X, 294.

Very similar to *P. comyntas*, of which it may be only a variety. It differs from it in the male not having fulvous lunules on the upper side, and in the under side of both sexes being more white, with smaller points; and finally, in having only the anal lunule powdered with golden atoms.

California.   Boisd.

12. **P. exilis** *Boisd.* Ann. Soc. Ent. 2me sér. X, 295.

The smallest species known.

Upper side clear brown; secondaries paler, with a blackish border.

Under side of primaries very clear brown, with white interrupted transverse striæ, more or less distinct.

Under side of secondaries white, with brown striæ and a marginal row of seven black ocelli powdered with golden atoms.

California.   Boisd.

13. **P. antaegon** *Boisd.* Ann. Soc. Ent. 2me sér. X, 295. *P. acmon?* Westw. and Hewits. Gen. Diurn. Lep. pl. 76, fig. 1.

Upper side beautiful violet blue, with a small blackish border and white fringe; inferiors with ante-marginal border fulvous, resting on a series of black points.

Under side ash-gray, with a great number of distinct and neat black points. · That of the secondaries has before the border a fulvous interrupted band, resting on a row of black ocelli, pow-

dered with very brilliant golden atoms; a black point between
the base and the discoidal spot of the primaries. The female is
sometimes all blue, sometimes only at the base, and sometimes
nearly black. In every case the band of the upper-side of the
secondaries is always more distinct than in the male.

California.

Bose.

14. P. xerces *Boisd.* Ann. Soc. Ent. 2me sér. X, 296.

Upper side of the male, blue; that of the female brown, with
some blue atoms at the base, without any other spot.

Under side of both sexes dark gray, with a central spot and a
sinuous interrupted band, formed of large white points; no marginal lunules.

California.

15. P. aneptoluus *Boisd.* Ann. Soc. Ent. 2me sér. X, 297.

Upper side blue, with a black border, wide on the primaries,
more narrow on the secondaries, the primaries having besides a
black costal point. Female entirely black, or powdered with blue
at the base.

Under side ash-gray in the male, dark gray in the female, with
a great number of black points as in the analogous species; that
of the secondaries with three or four fulvous marginal lunules,
more distinct in the female.

Mountains of California.

16. P. icarioides *Boisd.* Ann. Soc. Ent. 2me sér. X, 297.

Upper side violet blue, with a small black border and white
fringe. That of the secondaries with the border interrupted,
forming a series of marginal black points.

Under side clear and white; that of the primaries with a discoidal lunule and a transverse sinuous line formed of black ocellate spots; that of the secondaries with a central lunule and two
sinuous rows of white points scarcely pupilled with black. Female
brown, with the under side rather dark brownish-gray, marked
with a central lunule and two rows of distinct ocellate black points.

Mountains of California.

17. P. pheres *Boisd.* Ann. Soc. Ent. 2me sér. X, 297.

Upper side violet blue. *Under side* ashy-white; that of the primaries with a small discoidal cellule and a sinuous line of ocellate black points; that of the secondaries with white spots not ocellate. Female brown, with the base more or less bluish.

San Francisco.

18. P. heteronea *Boisd.* Ann. Soc. Ent. 2me sér. X, 297.

Upper side violet blue, with a small blackish edge, white fringe, and very prominent nerves.

Under side ashy-white; that of the primaries with a point and central lunule black, followed by two parallel sinuous lines of black points.

Under side of secondaries with two parallel rows of small obsolete spots, whitish-gray, little distinct from the ground color.

Upper side of the female brown, with the disk more or less fulvous, pointed with black, and traversed by a sinuous line of large black points. *Under side* like that of the male.

Mountains of Northern California.

19. P. enoptes *Boisd.* Ann. Soc. Ent. 2me sér. X, 298.

Upper side violet blue, with a rather wide black border; the fringe intersected with white and black on the primaries only, entirely whitish on the secondaries.

Under side ashy-white, with a great number of black ocellate points; the two stria of posterior points are separated on the secondaries by a series of five yellow lunules.

California.

Boisd.

20. P. piasus *Boisd.* Ann. Soc. Ent. 2me sér, X, 299.

Upper side blue, fringe whitish; that of the female with a blackish border on all the wings.

Under side of both sexes ashy-white, with a multitude of black ocellate points disposed as in the analogous species. Those of the posterior row are followed by one of clear white, which forms a transverse band, and occupies the whole space between it and the crescents of the extremity, which are nearly effaced, and resting behind on a grayish marginal band, crenate, more obscure than the ground color.

California.

Bonn.

21. P. antiacis *Boisd.* Ann. Soc. Ent. 2me sér. X, 300.

Upper side violet blue, with a slender black margin and whitish fringe.

Under side ash-gray, with the base greenish-blue; a transverse line of black points strongly ocellate with white, near the extremity, preceded on the primaries by a central lunule and on the secondaries by a central lunule and two ocellate points. Female blackish above, with the base more or less bluish.

San Francisco.

Bonn.

22. P. doroas *Kirby.* Faun. Bor. IV, 299. Figured in Kirby Faun. Bor. Amer. IV, pl. 4, fig. 1.

Body black above, white below. Antennæ black, with white rings. Knob tipped with orange; wings brown, with a reddish tint, underneath tawny; primaries with an angular band, formed by faint black spots; behind these nearer the costa is a black bar, above which are two more spots; between the band and the posterior margin are three more black spots, arranged transversely, and above the base are three more black spots forming a triangle; the secondaries have a slight sinus near the anal angle, the fringe of which projects so as to assume the appearance of a short tail; across the disk runs an angular band formed of faint black spots, above which is a crescent of the same color; at the anal angle is an orange-colored angular bar, or abbreviated band; underneath, these wings have several indistinct black dots, the three external ones of which form an obtuse angle with the four internal ones.

"This species seems to be the American representation of *P. phlœas,* but its color is much less vivid."

Canada.

Kirby.

23. P. lucia *Kirby.* Faun. Bor. IV, 299. Figured in Kirby Faun. Amer. Bor. IV, pl. 3, fig. 8, 9.

Wings above silvery blue, terminating, especially at the posterior margin, in a very slender black line; fringe white, barred with black; primaries underneath ash-colored, mottled with white; in the disk is a black crescent and a curved macular band, consisting of mostly oblique black crescents edged with white, especially on their under side. The wing terminates posteriorly in a broadish brown band, formed chiefly by obsolete eyelets; secondaries brown, underneath spotted and striped with black and white; towards the posterior margin the white spots are arranged in a transverse band parallel with it, and as in the primaries; the wing terminates in several obsolete eyelets.

Canada.—Expands one inch.

KIRBY.

24. P. americana *Harris MS.*

The fore wings on the *upper side* are coppery-red, with about eight small square black spots, and the hind margin broadly bordered with dusky-brown; the hind wings are dusky-brown, with a few small black spots on the middle, and a broad coppery-red band on the hind margin. The wings expand from $1\frac{1}{4}$ to $1\frac{1}{2}$ inch. The caterpillar is long oval, and slightly convex above, and of a greenish color; it probably lives like the *P. phleas*, on the leaves of dock and sorrel. The *chrysalis*, which is usually suspended under a stone, is light yellowish-brown and spotted with black dots.

Massachusetts.

HARRIS.

THECLA Fab.

Palpi nearly straight, sometimes longer than the head; last article naked, rather long, subulate or a little acicular; *head* more narrow than the thorax; *eyes* rather prominent; *antennæ* of moderate length, terminated by a club usually elongate and sometimes nearly fusiform; *secondaries prolonged in one or more thin tails,* sometimes but rarely simply dentate.

1. **T. halesus** *Fab.* Syst. emend. III, 278. *T. delichus* Hübn. Figured in Cram. 98.* Herbst, pl. 295. Hübn. Zutr. 219. Boisd. et Lec. pl. 23, p. 88.

Upper side of the males, beautiful glossy blue. *Primaries* have at the extremity a black border of moderate width. *Secondaries*

terminated by two black tails, of which the external one is much
shorter. At the external angle, near the summit, there is a wide
black border, which does not reach the anal angle. The latter is
extended somewhat in the form of a spatule, powdered on both
sides with golden atoms, which extend to the base of the tails.

The *upper side* of the females is pale greenish-blue, and this
color extends scarcely beyond the middle of the wings; spatule
and base of the tails, as in the males. ·

Under side of all the wings in both sexes is brownish-black, with
three red spots, of which one is at the base of the primaries, and
the two others at the base of the secondaries. The latter have
besides, towards the anal angle, a macular ray of golden green,
followed by several white spots, powdered with some golden atoms.
The males often have along the edge of the superiors, a blue ray,
more or less distinct.

Body and *thorax* above of the color of the wings.

Abdomen red below and on the sides, and in some specimens
this color extends to the back.

Under side of the breast black, with some white points which
extend to the base of the primaries.

Head pointed with white; *antennæ* black, with the club more
fusiform than in most of the species of this genus.

Larva, which feeds on *Quercus*, green, slightly pubescent.
Head and scaly feet testaceous. On the back, there is a small
ray, and on the sides nine oblique bands of obscure green. At
the base of the feet, a marginal ray of greenish-yellow. ·

Chrysalis russety, pointed with brown.

Southern States.—Expands an inch and a half.

Bois.

2. T. M-album *Boisd. et Lec.* Figured in Boisd. et Lec. pl. 26, p. 88.

A size smaller than *T. halesus*. *Upper side* of the male blue, a
little violet, with a wide black border commencing at the base of
the primaries and extending nearly all round.

The *upper side* of the female is a little more pale, and the black
border is usually wider.

In both sexes, the secondaries are furnished with two small
black tails, of which the external one is shorter.

The *under side* of the wings is cinereous; that of the primaries
is traversed towards the middle by a small white ray which begins

on the upper edge and ends on the median nervure. The secondaries have beyond the middle a whitish line, straight in its first half, angular towards the anal angle, where it describes a kind of M, and then continuing to the side. Between this line and the outer edge there is another line, less distinct, shaded outwardly with blackish, interrupted by a red spot, situated in the space between the two tails. The anal angle has a black spatula, separated from the internal tail by a square pale blue spot. At the base of the tails there is a small white or grayish line which separates the fringe, which is also white in this part of the wings. The base of the upper edge of the primaries is reddish, and the middle of the secondaries, near the upper edge, is marked with a whitish point.

Body, bluish above; ashy gray below.

Antennæ blackish, annulate with white; club blackish, tipped with fulvous.

In some specimens there is a small red spot on the spatula of the anal angle.

Larva slightly pubescent, pale green, a little yellowish, with a dorsal ray and seven oblique streaks, green.

Head black; marginal ray yellow, slightly shaded with obscure green on its upper side. Feeds on *Quercus.*

Chrysalis brownish-gray, with the anterior part and envelope of the wings pale gray, a little greenish.

Southern States.

BOISD.

3. T. payaha *Boisd. et Lec.* p. 88. Figured in Boisd. et Lec. pl. 27.

Same size as *T. M-album,* and most probably a mere variety. The four wings glossy blue, a little violet, with a wide black border as in *T. M-album.* The primaries sometimes have the costal margin a little reddish at the origin.

Secondaries with two tails; generally a small red spot at the anal angle; sometimes a small white spot on the disk of the primaries, in the male.

Under side dark, cinereous. Primaries traversed in the upper half by two whitish rays, meeting at their lower extremity. Secondaries traversed to the middle by a white ray describing a sort of M. Between this ray and the external edge there is another, which is interrupted between the two tails by a red spot. Near the larger tail there is a bluish space, bordered interiorly with black.

Southern States.

4. T. hyperici *Boisd. et Lec.* p. 90.　*T. favonius ?* Boisd.　Figured in Boisd. et Lec. pl. 28.

Probably a variety of *T. favonius.　Upper side* blackish-brown, uniform in the female, a more obscure tint in the disk of the male, forming a sort of indistinct spot.

The *secondaries* have two tails, of which the lateral is the longer. They are preceded by one or two fulvous crescents, supported by a black spot, separated from the fringe by a pale bluish-gray ray. The edge of the anal spatule is also a little bordered with fulvous.

The *under side* of the wings is ash-gray. The *primaries* are traversed in their posterior half by two rather wavy rays, of which the anterior one is white, bordered with reddish-brown, and the other brown, feebly lined with whitish.

The *secondaries* are traversed by two white rays, shaded with brown before. The anterior one is angular towards the anal angle, and the other is interrupted between the two tails by a fulvous spot, marked with black behind. The anal spatule is more widely fulvous than above, and between this and the other fulvous spot there is a space of pale blue. Besides these, the four wings have at the origin of the fringe a small brownish line more or less apparent, and the costal edge is a little marked with fulvous at its origin.

Body like the wings; lower side of the head and the extremity of the abdomen of the female a little fulvous. *Antennæ* blackish, with white rings; club tipped with reddish. Breast and under side of abdomen white.

Larva above reddish, with three brown rays, of which one is on the back. Lower side of abdomen, head and feet, green. Feeds on *Hypericum*.

Chrysalis yellowish, with the rings of the abdomen a little violet, marked with four rows of black points.

Southern States.—Expands a little over an inch.

8. **T. falacer** *Godt.* Encyc. Méthod. IX, 633. *T. calanus* Hubn. Figured
in Boisd. et Lec. pl. 29, p. 92.

Upper side uniform brownish-black. Primaries with a small,
oval, grayish shining spot on the disk of the males. Secondaries
terminated by two small tails, a little whitish at the extremity, of
which the internal one is much the longer. At the base of these
tails, near the fringe, there is a small grayish-white line, sometimes
preceded by an indistinct fulvous spot.

Under side ashy brown, with a short, geminate, bluish ray on
the disk of each wing. The primaries are traversed by two small
rays of bluish-white, shaded with brown on one of their sides, of
which the exterior is indistinct. The secondaries are traversed by
two similar rays which form an angle towards the abdominal edge.
Between the tails there is a fulvous spot, bordered with black on
the outer side, followed by one or two small spots of the same
color—an ashy blue space, bordered with a black spatula. The
anal emargination is also bordered with fulvous; a small white
marginal line at the fringe.

Body, like the wings; breast, with some bluish hairs; abdomen
whitish. *Antennæ* blackish, with white rings; club blackish.

Larva, which feeds on *Crataegus*, pale russety; a little greenish
on the sides, which are marked with oblique brown streaks; a
wide brown band on the back, which disappears on the middle
rings, where it is replaced by two parallel brown lines; the brown
band reappears on the posterior rings.

Chrysalis yellowish-brown, powdered with brown atoms.

Southern States.—Expands a little over an inch.

Bosd.

9. **T. favonius?** *Godt.* Encyc. Méthod. IX, 635. *T. melinus?* Hubn.
T. humuli Haw. Figured in Sm. Abb. pl. 14. Boisd. et Lec. pl. 30.

Form and size of *T. falacer*. "*Upper side* dusky brown, with
a tint of blue gray; and in the males there is an oval darker spot
near the front edge; the secondaries have two short thread-like
tails, the inner one the longer and tipped with white; along the
hind margin of these same wings is a row of little pale blue spots,
interrupted by a large orange-red crescent, inclosing a small black
spot; *under side* slate gray, with two wavy streaks of brown,
edged on one side with white; and on the secondaries an orange-

colored spot near the hind angle, and a larger spot of the same
color inclosing a black dot just before the tails.   It expands one
inch and one-tenth." *Larva* feeds on *Humulus* (Hop).

. HARRIS, INS. MASS., p. 217, ed. 1842.[1]

7. T. liparops *Boisd. et Lec.* p. 99. · *T. favonius* Sm. Abb. Figured in
Boisd. et Leo. pl. 31.

Form and size of *T. falacer.*   *Upper side* clear brown; on the
disk of the primaries a fulvous, oblong spot, transversely disposed
and mingling more or less with the ground color.   In the female?
this fulvous space is preceded by a small black spot.

Secondaries terminated by two tails, of which the internal is the
longer.   Between these tails, usually a fulvous spot in the female.
In both sexes, there is a small black spot at the base of each tail,
separated from the fringe by a whitish or bluish ray.   The anal
spatule is also marked by a blackish spot surmounted with a little
white.

Under side pale ash-gray; primaries traversed by four white
lines, more or less distinct, after uniting towards the lower edge.
Between these lines and the outer edge there is another sinuous
white line.   Secondaries traversed by two double rays, of which
the anterior form a sharp angle below.   Behind these rays, there
is a fulvous macular band, formed of from three to six spots, bordered slightly with black.   Anal spatule is marked with a little
black, and between it and the long tail there is a bluish space.

Under side of the body like the wings.   Breast, abdomen below,
and feet grayish-white.   Antennae black, with white rings; club
tipped with fulvous.

Larva yellowish-green, with a dorsal line and eight oblique
streaks of dark green.   Marginal ray green, yellow below.

[1] There is an almost inextricable confusion in the determination of these
species.   T. humulus Harr. has been mistaken for T. favonius Sm. Abb.,
but is different.   Boisd. has figured this species as F. favonius in Boisd. et
Lec. pl. 30, but he is doubtful himself of its correctness.   He says, "I am
by no means certain that Abbot's *Favonius* is the same as the one I give.
. . . . . After having carefully examined my specimens and attentively
compared them with the original drawings and notes of Abbot, I have
come to the conclusion that my *Hyprrici* is the same as my *Favonius* . . . .
and that T. liparops is the true *Favonius.*"

Chrysalis ash-gray, with two rows of blackish points on each side of the abdominal rings.

Southern States.

Boisd.

8. T. iris *Godt.* Encyc. Méthod. IX, 574. Figured in Boisd. et Lec. pl. 31, p. 101.

Upper side of the male blackish-brown, with a small grayish ovoid spot near the costal edge; the female is deeper brown, with the extremity more or less russety.

Wings denticulate; fringe whitish.

Under side brown, with a white transverse line, sinuous. Extremity of the wings a little russety, divided by an indistinct ray, divided by the nervures. The extremity of the secondaries are powdered with ash-gray, and divided by a transverse interrupted line of brown purple, often marked by one or two small brown spots. The base is slightly powdered with gray, and separated from the tint of the middle by a wavy transverse line.

Larva, which feeds on *Vaccinium*, is yellowish-green, with two dorsal interrupted rays; one lateral ray and eight oblique streaks pale green.

Chrysalis ferruginous, pubescent; two longitudinal obscure rays.

Georgia.—Expands an inch and an eighth.

Godart.

9. T. arsace *Boisd. et Lec.* Figured in Boisd. et Lec. pl. 32, p. 103.

Same size as *T. iris*, and in some respects similar.

Upper side of the male brownish-black, with a small ovoid spot near the costal edge; the female is deeper brown, with the extremity reddish-yellow, forming on the primaries a large spot mingling with the ground color, and on the secondaries a smaller spot situated near the anal angle. *Wings* denticulate as in *T. iris*.

Under side brown, traversed in the middle by a sinuous brown line; extremity of the primaries paler, divided by two transverse rays more obscure and indistinct; extremity of the secondaries is powdered with gray as in *T. iris*, divided by a row of indistinct brownish spots, and forming nearly a curved ray.

Larva reddish; back white from the second to the ninth ring, and divided by two parallel interrupted lines of obscure green. Near the base of the feet, there is a marginal ray of the same color,

7

bordered with white below, and between that and the dorsal rays a row of seven or eight oblique streaks.

Chrysalis reddish before, and the wing envelopes greenish.

Southern States.

BOISD.

10. **T. niphon** *Hubn.* Figured in Hubn. Zutr. fig. 203. Boisd. et Lec. pl. 33, p. 105.

Size, color, and *upper side* markings of *T. iris* and *T. urnea.*

Under side rather clear russety brown; the discoidal cellule of the primaries has two black transverse streaks, and beyond the middle a black sinuous ray edged with white, followed by a row of black sagittate spots, uniting in a curved wavy line, separated from the fringe by small grayish spaces. The secondaries are traversed by two tortuous black rays, of which the one towards the base is edged with white within and the other with white without, and connecting with the ray of the primaries. Between these two rays there is a black streak, and the outer one is followed by an angular black ray, of which the posterior concavity is filled by a pale tint, which separates it from a marginal purple line, more or less mingling near the fringe, with an ashy tint.

Larva green, pubescent, with three longitudinal rays on the back, the middle one pale yellow, the other two white. Near the feet, usually a small marginal white line. Head brown. Feeds on *Pinus.*

Chrysalis grayish, with four rows of small spots, of which the two middle ones are blackish and indistinct, and the others ferruginous.

Georgia and Florida.

BOISD.

11. **T. smilacis** *Boisd.* Figured in Boisd. et Lec. pl. 33, p. 107.

Upper side blackish-brown, with a pale whitish spot near the middle of the costal edge; the secondaries have two thin tails, as in the analogous species.

Under side greenish, often washed with a little reddish, with a transverse whitish ray sinuous on the primaries, tortuous on the secondaries, bordered in front by a ferruginous tint. Between this ray and the base, the secondaries have another short transverse sinuous ray of the same color. The extremity is marked by two or three ashy crescents, of which the intermediary is black in front, and the third in a line with two or three small ferruginous spots, more or less distinct. The anal palette is black, and near the fringe there is a small white marginal line.

Larva, which feeds on *Smilax*, is green, with the head and feet blackish. It has four rows of red spots, of which the two dorsal are formed of smaller spots, and one on each side composed of spots somewhat larger.

Chrysalis grayish-brown, with the abdomen more clear and reddish.

Bosd.

12. T. sylvinus *Boisd.* Ann. Soc. Ent. 2me sér. X, 287.

Upper side brownish-black in both sexes, with a stigma on the primaries of the male, and one or two fulvous spots near the anal angle of the secondaries of the female.

Under side pale ashy, with a small discoidal spot on each wing, and two sinuous striæ of points of the same color towards the extremity; the anal angle of the secondaries with a space of bluish ashy, preceded before the tail by a yellow lunule supported by a black point.

California.

Bosd.

13. T. saretorum *Boisd.* Ann. Soc. Ent. 2me sér. X, 287.

Upper side blackish-brown, with a stigma on the primaries and two obsolete fulvous spots towards the anal angle of the secondaries. *Under side* brown, with two wavy rays on the secondaries, blackish, indistinct, of which the posterior is nearly marginal and supported in two small fulvous crescents; edge of the anal angle black.

California.

Bosd.

14. T. saepium *Boisd.* Ann. Soc. Ent. 2me sér. X, 287.

Upper side reddish-brown, without spots, in both sexes; the male with a stigma on the primaries. *Under side* brown, a little more pale towards the extremity, traversed a little beyond the middle by a small white line, wavy, and near the extremity by a line more obscure, obsolete, equally sinuous, blending towards the anal angle of the secondaries into a grayish-blue space preceded by a small black crescent.

California.

Bosd.

15. **T. grunoa** *Boisd.* Ann. Soc. Ent. 2me sér. X, 289.

Female ; *upper side* brown, with the disk obscure fulvous, especially on the secondaries. *Under side* pale yellowish, traversed a little beyond the middle by an indistinct ferruginous line. On the right and left of the tail there is a small fulvous crescent, surmounted by a blackish arc.

California.

Boisd.

16. **T. iroides** *Boisd.* Ann. Soc. Ent. 2me. sér. X, 289.

Upper side brown, without spots in the male, the disk a little ferruginous in the female, and angle of the secondaries deeply emarginate. *Under side* brown. *Under side* of secondaries ferruginous brown, sometimes a little vinous, with the base widely obscure, and the extremity with a row of blackish points, more or less distinct.

California.

Boisd.

17. **T. eriphon** *Boisd.* Ann. Soc. Ent. 2me sér. X, 289.

Upper side brown, with the disk more or less marked with ferruginous. *Under side* paler brown ; that of the primaries with a small central point, an undulated ray, edged with white and marginal sagittate spots, blackish ; that of the secondaries washed with vinous red, and traversed by three black rays profoundly sinuous, edged with white, of which the posterior is serrate, forming sagittate spots.

California.   Rare.

Boisd.

18. **T. dumetorum** *Boisd.* Ann. Soc. Ent. 2me sér. X, 291.

Wings olive brown, without spots ; anal palette of the secondaries nearly obsolete. *Under side* of primaries russety, a little greenish ; that of the inferiors greenish, with a transverse row of small white points.

California.

Boisd.

19. **T. damaetas** *Godt.* Encyc. Méthod. IX, 646.   *T. damon* Cram. Figured in Cram. pl. 390, fig. C. D.

Upper side blackish-brown, with the disk fulvous.

Under side green, with two black bent lines, and bordered with white to the extremities of the primaries ; with three similar lines, but flexuous, on the surface of the secondaries. The anal angle of secondaries has a suite of three small ocelli with a white iris.

Virginia.—Expands scarcely half an inch.

GODART.

20. T. acis *Drury. T. mars* Fabr. *T. irion* Fabr. Figured in Drury, I, pl. 1, fig. 2.

Upper side. Primaries entirely dark brown, without any marks or spots. Secondaries the same, with four tails, the inner ones much longer than the others ; close above which latter are two red spots, edged at the bottom with black, and two more placed at the anal angle. The cilia white.

Under side. All the wings of a dark lead color. A very narrow black and white line crosses the primaries, parallel to the external edges ; another indented irregular line crosses the secondaries, beginning near the middle of the anterior edge, and meeting just below the extremity of the body. Four long reddish spots are very visible on this side, below which are four black ones.

Jamaica.—Drury gives New York as its habitat. Doubtful.

21. T. strigosa *Harr. MS.*

" The streaked *Thecla* has a long and a short tail on each of the hind wings, and is of a dark brown color, without spots on the *upper side ;* the wings beneath are ornamented with wavy transverse white streaks, and near the hind margin of the posterior wings is a row of deep orange-colored crescents, with a large blue spot near the hindmost angle. It measures 1 $\frac{1}{10}$ inches across the wings. In the markings of the *under side* of the wings it nearly resembles *T. liparops.*"

Massachusetts.

HARRIS MS.

22. T. auburniana *Harris MS.*

The outermost of the tails is very short, and often nothing remains of it but a little tooth on the edge of the wing. It varies considerably in color; the females are generally deep brown above, but sometimes the wings are rust-colored or tawny in the middle, as they always are in the males; the oval opaque spot which characterizes the latter sex is ochre yellow. Upon the *under side*, the wings in both sexes are green, the anterior pair tinged with brown from the middle to the inner edge; externally, next to the fringe, they are all margined by a narrow wary white line, bordered internally with brown; at some distance from the posterior margin is another broader white line, or series of contiguous spots, bordered internally with brown; this line, on the fore wings, does not reach the inner margin; on the hind wings it consists of six spots arranged in a zigzag manner, and the last spot, next to the inner margin, is remote from the rest; besides these, there are on the same wings three more white spots bordered with brown, between the zigzag band and the base; and between the same band and the margin three black spots, behind the middle one of which is a rust-red spot with a black centre. The wings expand from $1\frac{1}{3}$ to $1\frac{1}{2}$ inch. This pretty species is found on the mouse-ear (*Gnaphalium plantagineum*) in May, and on the flowers of the spearmint in August.

Massachusetts.

Harris MS.

23. T. mopsus *Hübn*. Figured in Hübn. Zutr. fig. 133. Boisd. et Lec. pl. 34, p. 109.

Upper side of the male blackish-brown, with the usual ovoid spot on the costal edge. The female is more dull, without the costal spot, but with one or two yellow lunulate spots towards the anal angle of each wing. The secondaries are without tails.

Under side of the male is grayish-brown, traversed by a row of black points circled with white, followed on the secondaries by a marginal band of reddish and somewhat macular, and on the primaries by a second row of black points lightly circled with white.

Under side of the female is a little more clear. The series of ocellated spots is preceded in the secondaries by a discoidal black streak circled with white; the red marginal band is more sensibly edged with white in front, and continues a little on the primaries, where it replaces the second row of black points on the male.

Larva, which feeds on *Eupatorium celestinum*, is greenish, with the back a little more whitish. The anterior and dorsal part has a brownish quadrangular space, bifid behind, and marked with four white spots. The three hind rings have a wide white border, edged with brown. Head and feet brownish.

Chrysalis resembles that of *Sentieris*, but differs in having on each side a row of yellow ferruginous points.

Southern States.—Expands an inch and a half.

Boisd.

24. T. poeas *Hübn.* *T.* bous Godt. Figured in Boisd. et Leo. pl. 35, p. 100.

Upper side blackish-brown, with the base of the primaries and the extremity, or even the whole of the secondaries, pale blue. Some specimens have the base of the primaries entirely blackish, and sometimes even all the wings, without any traces of the blue. The secondaries have tails, white at the summit. Some, which have the extremity blue, have a row of small marginal, unequal lunules, blackish-brown.

Under side is russety gray.

Southern States.

Boisd.

25. T. augustus *Kirby.* Faun. Bor. IV, 298. Figured in Kirby, Faun. Bor. Amer. IV, pl. 3.

Antennæ annulated with white; inch elongated; wings dusky black, with a dull ferruginous disk; fringe alternately white and black; secondaries underneath black at the base; at the apex dusky ash-colored, with a transverse series of about eight black spots, rudiments of which appear on the lower surface of the primaries.

Canada.—Expands one inch.

Kirby.

Fam. IX. ERYCINIDAE.

Larva very short, pubescent or hairy. *Chrysalis* short, contracted. *Perfect insect;* nearly constantly six feet in the females and four in the male. Abdominal edge of the secondaries not prominent. Discoidal cellule sometimes open, sometimes closed, and sometimes closed apparently by a false nervure. Hooks of the tarsi extremely small.

NYMPHIDIA *Fab.* *Erycina Latr.*

Head of the width of the thorax; *antennæ* long, annulate with whitish, terminated by a small elongated club; *palpi* short, straight, scarcely extending beyond the eyes; thorax slender, rather long; abdomen a little shorter than the secondaries; the four wings rounded; discoidal cellule of the secondaries open; six feet in the female, four in the male.

L. W. pumila Boisd. Figured in Boisd. et Lec. pl. 37, p. 181.

Upper side reddish ferruginous, with wavy, blackish, flexuous lines, nearly macular. Besides these black lines, the extremity has two others of a black lead color, separated by a row of black points, of which the internal one is strongly sinuous. *Under side* fulvous yellow, with the transverse lines more macular. Body above ferruginous, below yellowish.

Georgia—Florida.

Boisd.

LEMONIAS Ill.

Head hairy; eyes naked. Antennæ rather long, slender; club long, slender. Primaries more or less triangular; costal margin nearly straight; apical angle subacute, post-costal vein with only three branches. Secondaries subovate; post-costal curved at its base, forked at a moderate distance from the base. Fore legs of the males very small, densely clothed with soft silky hairs; fore legs of the females longer, slender, scaly; tarsus armed beneath with some short spines at the tips of the joints. Four hind legs long, slender, scaly. Tibiæ not armed beneath with spines. Nails and appendages minute.

L. L. mormo *Felder*. Wiener Entom. Monatschrift, III, No. 9, 271.

Wings subrepand; ciliæ widely intersected with white, above obscurely fuscous, beneath paler. *Primaries* on both sides ferruginous fulvous from the base to the disk, with two basal points, a third larger, internal, a discal spot, a macular band, sinuate and seven points, submarginal, surrounded with black and white, the disk paler and the submarginal points much larger, elongate, spotted with black, veins fulvous.

Secondaries a little fulvescent above the base, with two points, marked with white; two discal spots, one larger, the external band macular, much interrupted, repand, minute white spots surrounded with white, beneath much paler; costa white at the base, the spots and points of the upper surface, but much larger and nearly confluent. *Antennæ* annulated with white. *Thorax* and abdomen black above, below with the palpi and feet whitish.

Utah.

PILOSA.

FAM. X. HESPERIDAE.

Larva cylindric, without spines; first ring small, head prominent. *Chrysalis* cylindroid, elongate, hardly angular. *Perfect insect;* head wide, transverse. Antennæ often terminated by a hook. Palpi short, last article very small.

HESPERIA Linn.

Head broad; body robust. Labial palpi compressed in front and incurved, with the sides convex and angulated. Antennæ of moderate length or elongate, straight, slender, with a subterminal club, tip hooked. Primaries elongated triangular; apical margin, more or less convex; costal margin not reflexed, and the disk in the males not marked with the oblique silky patch; often marked with pellucid spots. Secondaries subtriangular, with the outer and anal angles rounded, or with the outer margin rounded and sometimes dentated. Anal angle not produced into a prominent lobe or short tail, and the disk beneath not marked with silvery spots.

1. **H. celius** *Boisd.* Figured in Boisd. et Lec. pl. 73.

Wings brown; primaries with a broad yellow band across the middle, the top of which is whitish; a whitish spot at the upper edge. Secondaries without spots on the disk. Fringe dull yellow or greenish; more distinct on the upper angle of the secondaries. *Under side* paler; markings of primaries the same, except that lower edge is yellow. Secondaries with two bands of deep brown.

United States.—Expands two inches.

BOISD.

2. H. lycidas *Godt.* Encyc. Méthod. IV, 751. Figured in Boisd. et Lec. pl. 71.

Wings deep brown, a little yellowish near the base; primaries with four or five yellow spots, forming a short irregular band; between this band and the summit are two or three points of the same color. Secondaries without spots.

Under side of primaries with a yellow band, narrow at the costal edge, widening downwards but not reaching to the lower edge; beyond this, is an interrupted line of yellow spots and a pale purple streak.

Under side of secondaries ash-gray, a large silvery spot on the outer edge, surmounted by two points of the same color: fringe white and brown.

United States.—Expands two inches.

Boisd.

3. H. proteus *Godt.* Encyc. Méthod. IX, 730. Figured in Boisd. et Lec. pl. 69. Sm. Abb. 1, pl. 39. Cram. pap. pl. 260. Clerck, icon. Ins. pl. 42.

Wings brown; light green at the base of the primaries, and covering half of the secondaries. Primaries, with four or five white spots oblong or square, and an arcuated line of white points intersected by the nerves. Secondaries extending to long tails. Body greenish above.

Under side purplish brown; markings similar to the upper except the black border of the spots and arc on the primaries, and two interrupted narrow bands on the secondaries.

United States.—Expands over two inches.

Boisd.

4. H. bathyllus *Sm. Abb.* Figured in Sm. Abb. pl. 22. Boisd. et Lec. pl. 74.

Wings deep brown, with a narrow, interrupted transverse band of white on the primaries, and three small dots intersected by the nerves, near the summit. Secondaries without spots.

Under side paler, with dark brown narrow bands on the secondaries.

United States.—Expands two inches.

Boisd.

5. H. sylvanus *Boisd.* Ann. Soc. Ent. 2me sér. X, 313.

Upper side fulvous, with yellowish spots, of which one is situated towards the base;*the others forming behind the middle a transverse and flexuous range. These spots are more apparent in the female; the male has on the primaries a black, wide, oblique streak.

Under side greenish fulvous, but more bright in the middle of the primaries and at the internal angle of the secondaries, with pale yellowish spots. Secondaries with five spots. Body above pale fulvous, below whitish. Antennæ, annulate with whitish; club, terminated with a black hook; ferruginous below.

California and Europe.

Boisd.

6. H. sylvanoides *Boisd.* Ann. Soc. Ent. 2me sér. X, 313.

Size and form of *H. sylvanus. Upper side* of the male like *H. sylvanus*, except that near the oblique black spot there is a blackish streak which appears to be a prolongation of it, and there are not at the extremity near the border the three or four points a little paler than the ground, which are found in *H. sylvanus*.

Under side of the female has on the disk a black triangular spot, followed by a small white transparent spot, the summit with three yellow points. Secondaries a little sinuous, with the border deep, the base widely blackish. *Under side* pale yellow, sometimes a little grayish on the secondaries, and not of a bright yellowish-green as in *H. sylvanus.*

California.

Boisd.

7. H. nemorum *Boisd.* Ann. Soc. Ent. 2me sér. X, 314.

Upper side of the male as in *H. sylvanoides*, the border a little wider, the mark of the primaries also wider, prolonged by a streak to the summit.

Under side deep yellow; that of the secondaries without spots; that of the primaries paler in the middle, with the impression of the mark of the opposite surface.

California.

Boisd.

8. H. agricola *Boisd.* Ann. Soc. Ent. 2me sér. I, 314.

Upper side blackish; that of the primaries having the mark prolonged to the summit by a blackish streak, a transverse row of
yellow points between the border and this mark. That of the
secondaries with the black border rather wide, and the base more
or less brown.

Under side of the primaries yellow, with the mark less definite
than above; that of the secondaries yellow, with a kind of transverse band, nearly median, of a paler tone.

California.

Boisd.

9. H. pratincola *Boisd.* Ann. Soc. Ent. 2me sér. I, 315.

Upper side bright yellow, nearly without border, having only in
certain males some blackish triangular streaks on the nerves; that
of the primaries with the mark as in *H. sylvanus*, ordinarily surmounted towards the summit with a blackish streak more or less
distinct.

Under side uniform yellow; that of the primaries having towards
the summit, on the edge, a small spot a little paler than the ground;
that of the secondaries without spots. Female larger, with a separate blackish border; that of the primaries having an oblique,
blackish ray, surmounted towards the summit by a spot of the
same color. Under side of the primaries nearly as in the male;
that of the secondaries with a transverse, irregular row of spots
paler than the ground color.

California.

Boisd.

10. H. ruricola *Boisd.* Ann. Soc. Ent. 2me sér. I, 315.

Wings a little sinuous, yellow, with a small brown border; primaries with the mark distinct as in *H. sylvanus*, marked longitudinally with a small whitish line.

Under side yellow, with all the surface of the secondaries and
the summit of the primaries greenish.

California.

Boisd.

11. H. campestris *Boisd.* Ann. Soc. Ent. 2me sér. I, 316.

This species is distinguished from all the other California species, by the large truncated spot, which forms the mark of the

primaries. Figure and size of *H. nemorum*. Wings yellow, with a rather wide brown border; fringe pale yellow. Primaries of the male marked at the summit, with two or three points of the ground color. Secondaries with the disk more or less marked with black in the middle.

Under side rather pale yellow, nearly uniform; that of the primaries marked at the summit with three small paler spots; that of the secondaries with a transverse line of similar small spots.

California.

BOIS.

12. **H. sabuleti** *Boisd.* Ann. Soc. Ent. 2me sér. X, 316.

Wings of nearly the same yellow as in *H. sylvanus*, with a rather wide brown border, serrate on the primaries; the latter having the mark shorter and more truncate than in *H. sylvanus*, joined to a grayish spot; under side paler yellow, with a row of brown streaks slightly sagittate; that of the inferiors with a row of similar streaks towards the base. Female larger. *Under side* paler; that of the primaries, between the border and the disk, with a row of spots paler than the ground color.

California.

BOIS.

13. **H. ? vestris** *Boisd.* Ann. Soc. Ent. 2me sér. X, 317.

Upper side rusvety brown; that of the primaries with four small white spots somewhat transparent, of which two are punctiform, near the upper edge; the two others larger, in the ramifications of the median nerve; that of the secondaries without spots. *Under side* duller, a little more grayish, with the same spots as above.

California.

BOIS.

14. **H. comma** *Lin.* Syst. Nat.

Resembles *H. sylvanus*, but the under side is more greenish and spotted with white. These spots are nine in number, three towards the base, the six others forming a bent row behind the middle. Fringe white, spotted with black below. Club of the antennæ terminated below by a large ferruginous point.

California and Europe.

BOIS.

[The following descriptions of new species have been kindly
furnished by Mr. Samuel Scudder, of Boston. They were found
among Dr. Harris' MSS., and are to appear in the new edition of
his work on the insects of New England injurious to vegetation.
Not having seen the species, I have placed them all provisionally
under this genus.—J. G. M.]

15. H. hobomok *Harris MS.* •

Dark brown above; on each of the wings a large tawny yellow
spot, occupying the greater part of the middle, four or five minute
spots of the same color near the tips of the fore wings, on which is
also a short brownish line at the outer extremity of the central
mesh; *under side* of the fore wings similar to the upper, but paler;
hind wings brown beneath, with a yellow dot near the shoulder,
and a very broad deep yellow band which does not attain the inner
margin, and has a tooth-like projection extending towards the
hinder edge. The male has not the usual distinguishing oblique
dash on the fore wings, which differ from those of the female only
in the greater size of the tawny portion, which extends to the front
margin.

Massachusetts.

HARRIS MSS.

16. H. leonardus *Harris MS.*

Dark brown above; fore wings of the male tawny yellow on the
front margin from the base to beyond the middle; behind this
tawny portion is a short black line, and behind the latter a row of
contiguous tawny spots extending from the middle to the inner
edge towards the tip, the spots at this extremity small and separated from the others; fore wings in the female without the tawny
front edge and black line; hind wings in both sexes with a central
curved, tawny yellow band; wings beneath bright red-brown; the
first pair blackish from the middle to the inner edge, and spotted
as on the upper side; hind wings with a yellow dot in the middle,
and a curved row of seven bright yellow spots behind it.

Massachusetts.—Expands inch and a half.

HARRIS MSS.

17. H. samacus *Harris MS.*

Dark brown above; all the wings with a tawny yellow spot occupying the greater part of the middle of each, and with two or three

little detached spots of the same color near the extremity of the first pair; beneath, ochre yellow, with small pale yellow spots near the tip, corresponding to those on the upper side of the fore wings, and on the hind wings seven small square pale yellow spots, namely, one before the middle and the others in pairs behind it.

Massachusetts.—Expands one and a quarter inch.

HARRIS MSS.

18. **H. metacomet** *Harris MS.*

Dark brown, slightly glossed with greenish-yellow above; the male with a short oblique black line on the middle of the fore wings, on both sides of which in the female are two yellowish dots on the middle, and two more near the front margin and tip; hind wings, beneath, with a transverse row of four very faint yellowish dots, which, however, are often wanting.

Massachusetts.—Expands one three-tenths of an inch.

HARRIS MSS.

19. **H. ahaton** *Harris MS.*

Dark brown above; fore wings in the male tawny before the middle from the base nearly to the tip, the tawny portion ending externally in three minute wedge-shaped spots; on the middle an oblique velvet black line, near the outer extremity of which are two or three small tawny spots; *under side* spotted as above; hind wings without spot above; of a greenish or dusky yellow tinge below, with a transverse curved row of four minute yellowish dots, which are often very faint or entirely wanting. In the female there is a tawny dash along the front margin of the fore wings, and the oblique black line is wanting, but the other spots are larger and more distinct.

Massachusetts.—Expands from one to one and one-tenth inch.

HARRIS.

20. **H. wamsutta** *Harris MS.*

Dark brown above; fore wings with a broken row of small tawny spots towards the tip, and in the males a large tawny patch, covering the whole of the fore part of the wings from the base to the middle, and an oblique curved black line behind it; hind wings with a small tawny dot before the middle, and an indented tawny band or row of contiguous unequal spots; *under side* of the fore wings light brown, and with larger yellow spots than on the other side; hind wings light brown, with two large irregular bright yellow spots, connected in the middle, and covering nearly the whole surface.

Massachusetts.—Expands nearly an inch.

HARRIS MSS.

GONILOBA Westwood.

Head occasionally clothed with red hairs; labial palpi as seen from above, forming two short square projections in front of the face. Antennæ with a long and slender club, the terminal half of which is reflexed, forming a slender hook, acute at the tip. Primaries long, triangular, generally marked on the disk with semi-pellucid spots. Apical margin entire, slightly convex towards the apex; discoidal cell long and narrow. Secondaries large, subtriangular; outer angle rounded, outer margin slightly scalloped, spotted with black. Anal angle produced into a short tail turned outwards or into an obtuse point. Upper disk of the wings often unspotted, but the base is yellowish or metallic-colored. Lower disk often varied with silvery patches.

1. G. tityrus F. Figured in Bolsd. et Lec. pl. 72. Sm. Abb. I, pl. 19.

Wings brown; primaries with a transverse semi-transparent band across the middle, and a few spots towards the tip, of a honey yellow color; secondaries, with a short, round obtuse tail on the anal angle.

Under side of primaries similar to that above; that of the secondaries has a broad silvery band, edged with black. Margin of all the wings below a little paler, with the nerves black. Fringe yellow and brown.

Larva, which feeds on *Robinia*, "is pale green, transversely streaked with dark green, with a red neck, a very large head roughened with minute tubercles, slightly indented or furrowed above, and of a dull red color, with a large yellow spot on each side of the mouth."

United States.—Expands two and a half inches.

HARRIS.

2. G. yucone *Boisd.* Figured in Boisd. et Lec. pl. 70.

Wings brown, lighter at the base; primaries, with a yellow spot near the centre, a broad irregular band and two oblong spots of the same color near the summit.

The *secondaries* have four square yellow spots or a macular ray. Fringe broad, yellow and brown, that of the secondaries brighter.

Under side of primaries bluish on the outer edge; the yellow band interrupted by brown, and a whitish spot near the anal angle. Upper edge with an ashy streak, one end of which is furcate.

The female is destitute of the spots on the secondaries; the band on the primaries is not so broad. Body paler than the wings.

Southern States.—Expands nearly three inches.
                                                              Boisp.

3. G. olynthus *Boisd.* Figured in Boisd. et Lec. pl. 75.

Wings blackish-brown, paler on the middle of the secondaries. Primaries with six or seven unequal white spots. Secondaries with three or four white spots or a macular white ray.

Under side ochry, except the lower part of the primaries; markings similar to those of the upper side. Secondaries without spots. Thorax greenish; abdomen brown above, whitish below; pectus pale green.

United States.—Expands two inches.
                                                              Boisp.

4. G. antoninus *Latr.* Encyc. Method. IX, 746.

Club of the antenna yellowish, abruptly terminating in a sharp hook. *Upper side* of the body and wings blackish. Primaries with six or seven yellowish transparent spots from the middle to the summit, of which the one near the middle of the upper edge and two or three others are in the form of small lengthened points near the summit; the others are below, and disposed in an oblique line.

Under side the disk is deeper black, and the upper edge from the base to near the middle is yellowish-gray. On the middle of the secondaries there is a transverse range of two small spots, sometimes square, sometimes nearly punctiform, yellowish and vitreous, sometimes obsolete.

Under side of secondaries is grayish or yellowish from the base

to near the middle; then, of a reddish-brown, with the portion of
the outer edge contiguous to the outer angle, paler or cinereous.
California—Brazil—Surinam.

Godt.

NISONIADES Hübn.

Head and thorax broad, abdomen elongated. Antennæ with
the club somewhat fusiform, elongate, curved, with the tip gradually acuminated; that of the males larger and more slender than
that of the females. Labial palpi very hirsute. Primaries divari-
cating and horizontally extended when at rest, with the costal
margin often recurved in the males. Apical margin entire, fringe
not spotted. Secondaries broadly triangular, with the outer and
anal angles rounded. Fringe not scalloped, nor spotted. Hind
legs with the middle spurs distinct.

1. **N. juvenalis** *Sm. Abb.* Figured in Boisd. et Lec. pl. 65. Sm. Abb.
1, pl. 20.

Wings deep brown; primaries with a number of black spots, a
white spot on the cellule, and an interrupted curved line of white
points, three or four of which are near the costal edge. Secondaries dull brown, with two or three curved rows of paler points.

Under side of the primaries very similar to the upper; secondaries with several spots near the upper edge.

United States.—Expands an inch and a half.

Boisd.

2. **N. brizo** *Boisd.* Figured in Boisd. et Lec. pl. 66.

Wings blackish-brown; primaries with two broad transverse
pale bluish lines, edged with black, serrated; on the outer edge, a
row of yellowish points. Secondaries with two curved rows of
similar points.

Under side of all the wings with two rows of yellowish spots
near the lower edge.

The female, besides the bands on the primaries, has a zigzag
yellowish transverse near the outer edge.

Southern States.—Expands an inch and a half.

Boisd.

3. N. catullus *Godt.* Encye. Méthod. IX, 777. Figured in Sm. Abb. I,
pl. 24.

Small; body black, head white. Wings deep black, with a
transverse line of white points near the posterior edge; primaries,
with other small points of this color, fewer in number on the under
side, and that of the secondaries.

Var. Wings without spots on the upper side; secondaries with
only one white point before the ray formed by the others; in some
specimens the spots fail entirely.

Southern States.

ABBOT.

4. N. l'herminier *Godt.* Encye. Méthod. IX, 777. *N. pygmœus?* Fab.

Antennœ black, with the rings and a part of the under side of
the club whitish; terminal hook brown. Wings blackish, but
paler below, inclining to ashy and without spots.

Carolina.—Expands nine lines.

GUÉRIN.

5. N. tristis *Boisd.* Ann. Soc. Ent. 2me sér. X.

Figure and size of *N. juvenalis.* Wings blackish-brown, with
the fringe of the secondaries white. Primaries with some black
undulations, on the middle a small whitish point, then a bent line
of six similar points, separated into two groups, the one of four
near the upper edge, the other of two, beyond the median nerve.

Under side paler than the opposite. In this species, as in *N.
juvenalis*, the small points are placed on the most obscure little
bands.

California.

BOISD.

CYCLOPAEDES Eus.

Head as broad as the thorax; labial palpi remote, hirsute, porrected, as low as the head; terminal joint very minute, conical,
nearly concealed by the hairs of the preceding joint. Antennœ
short, club stout, slightly curved, not hooked at the tip, which is
obtuse. Wings erect when at rest. Primaries long, fringe entire.
Disk dark brown, with orange-colored spots, alike in both sexes.
Secondaries short, entire; spotted on the primaries. Hind legs

with the tibiæ destitute of a pair of spurs in the middle. Abdomen, especially in the males, long and slender, with the tip slightly tufted.

1. C. coras *Cram.* C. *æsculapius* F. C. *otho?* Sm. Abb. Figured in Boisd. et Leo. pl. 77. Sm. Abb. pl. I, pl. 31. Cram. pap. 3, pl. 31, fem.

Small, blackish, with the body and base covered with yellowish hairs. Antennæ russety above, whitish or paler below, with the rings black. Wings traversed on both sides by a russety yellow band, formed by a suite of spots. *Upper side* of secondaries with a russety spot near the centre; *under side* with an arcuate band of spots. Male; the base of the primaries is russety yellow, which is divided in the form of striæ; the blackish line, in the form of a cicatrice, is bordered outwardly by a deep black line. On the *under side*, the spots are paler and mingle with the yellow. Along the posterior edge a row of small, round, indistinct spots.

Southern States.

GODART.

PAMPHILA Fab.

Head very broad in the males; thorax robust; abdomen as long as the secondaries. Labial palpi porrect, short, densely hairy, remote. Antennæ terminated by a thick, nearly straight club, generally with a short slender hook. Primaries alone erect in repose. Apical margin convex in males, fringe entire, not alternated in its colors. Disk in the males in many species marked with an oblique velvety patch of scales. Secondaries broadly triangular, outer and anal angles rounded, slightly truncated near the anal angle; margin entire. Discoidal vein nearly obliterated.

1. P. sabuleti *Boisd.* Figured in Boisd. et Leo. pl. 76.

Wings brown, but the color almost displaced on the primaries by ochre yellow; a yellow mark on the brown external border. Secondaries with a large circular yellow spot on the disk. *Under side* ochry, with irregular brown spots and streaks, the latter proceeding from the base.

Southern States.—Expands a little over an inch.

GODART.

2. **P. origenes** *F.* R. S. III, p. 329. *P. erynes* Boisd. Figured in Boisd. et Lec. pl. 76.

Wings greenish-brown; primaries pale orange at the base, extending along the costal and lower edges; a spot near the middle.

Under side of primaries similar to the upper; that of the secondaries greenish-yellow. Thorax greenish; upper side of abdomen ochry.

United States.—Expands a little over an inch.

BOISD.

3. **P. arpa** *Boisd.* Figured in Boisd. et Lec. pl. 68.

Wings blackish-brown, with half of the primaries lighter; a dark band commencing on the middle of the lower edge, and extending obliquely towards the summit, and forming an acute angle with an indistinct streak proceeding from the base.

The disk of the secondaries is lighter than the borders. *Under side* of all the wings ochry yellow, with darker lines proceeding from the base, contiguous on the primaries, forming a dark brown space, which bears two ochry spots.

Southern States.—Expands nearly two inches.

GODART.

4. **P. bulenta** *Boisd.* Figured in Boisd. et Lec. pl. 67.

Wings deep brown, occupying the whole extent excepting the half of the costal rim and the outer edge, with honey yellow. Near the summit, a curved streak of brown extending into the yellow field.

The *secondaries* have two long oval yellow spots; the lower one the smaller.

Fringes yellow; sides of the thorax and of the abdomen the same color.

Under side paler; summit of the primaries pale orange; lower edge blackish, interrupted by yellow.

The *primaries* of the female are traversed by an irregular yellow band, interrupted near the summit, where it forms a large round spot. The secondaries have but one large roundish yellow spot.

Southern States.—Expands nearly two inches.

GODART.

5. P. brettus *Boisd.* Figured in Boisd. et Lec. pl. 75.

Wings dark brown, greenish towards the base; primaries with seven or eight yellow irregular spots, forming a curved macular band.

Under side of primaries pale brown, clearer towards the outer edge, sprinkled with pale dots.

Under side of secondaries pale green, with irregular darker spots.

Southern States.—Expands one inch.

                                                                GODART.

6. P. avogos *Boisd.* Figured in Boisd. et Lec. pl. 76.

Wings blackish-brown; more than half of the primaries pale yellow, with a thin short line of brown near the centre. The secondaries, with a cuneiform spot on the middle. Fringe yellowish.

Under side of all the wings greenish, and destitute of spots.

The *primaries* of the female have five pale yellow streaks on the costal edge, below which there is a furcate streak. Secondaries without spots.

Southern States.—Expands an inch.

                                                                GODART.

7. P. phyleus *Boisd.* Figured in Boisd. et Lec. pl. 76.

Wings deep brown; primaries varied with yellow, forming an irregular, angular, interrupted band towards the outer margin of the primaries; a long club-shaped yellow mark proceeding from the base, with a brown streak in the centre of it, and a yellow line near the costal edge. Secondaries with five cuneiform spots, forming a curved row, the second of which is long and reaching to the base, besides a narrow yellow line extending from the base to near the anal angle.

Under side ochry yellow; primaries with sagittate brown spots near the outer edge, and a large irregular spot at the base.

The *female* is ochry yellow, with all the edges covered with cuneiform brown spots, as well as the disk of the primaries and the upper edge of the secondaries, some of which are furcate.

Southern States.—Expands over an inch.

                                                                GODART.

8. P. lineur *Godt.* Encyc. Method. IX, 748.

Wings black; ordinary spots of the primaries and those in the form of points on the secondaries of a transparent white; that of the four anterior spots of the primaries which is nearest the upper edge, is emarginate at each end; those of the secondaries are in the form of points, of which one is isolated, nearly central, and the four others below, in a transverse row; the antepenultimate is the largest; beyond the extremity of this series, there is a fifth, very small and indistinct. Wings finely bordered with white.

United States.

GODART.

9. P. thaumas *Fab.* R. S. III, 527. *P. origenes* Fab. Foemina?

Small, brownish-black; anterior half of the primaries, excepting the internal edge, fulvous. The black line of the middle, common to the males, is surmounted at its interior extremity with a fulvous point, and divided abruptly at its posterior edge from the adjacent portion of the surface by a linear incision, followed by a depression; between this depression and the edge and nearly in a transverse line, are four small fulvous points, of which the inferior is a little larger and isolated, and the others in a small line. The female has in this place some white and transparent points, varying from six to eight, but the three superior are constant.

United States.

GODART.

10. P. druzii *Godt.* Encyc. Méthod. IX, 767.

Very similar to *P. thaumas*. Primaries blackish, with a transverse row of fulvous spots. The male has only two, of which the interior is divided into two unequal parts; the black line and distinctive of the sex form only an oblong point; it is terminated behind by the lowest of the preceding spots. Between the nerves there are two spaces, of which the scales are elevated in the form of finely striated pencils. Secondaries of a glossy russety brown; under side more dull, traversed by a ray of small pale yellowish spots, obsolete in some specimens.

United States.

GODART.

This species approaches very nearly the *P. vitellius* Sm. Abb. I, pl. 17. It is also probably the same as *bion* Fab. Suppl. Ent. Syst. p. 432. Another species analogous to the preceding as well as to *P. thaumas*, Fab. names *exclamationis* Ent. Syst. tom. III, pars 1, p. 326, No. 932. Wings, as well as body, blackish; primaries with a yellowish linear spot, and a point of the same color on the under side.

GODART.

11. P. peckii *Kirby.* Faun. Bor. IV, 300. Figured in Kirby, Faun. Amer. Bor. IV, pl. 4.

. *Body* brown, paler on the under side. Antennæ rufous above ; below the joints a white patch. Knob fusiform, hooked ; wings above tawny brown, with an articulated angular band common to both wings, of pale yellow. Primaries striped and streaked with the same color near the base and in the costal area ; underneath, the wings paler. Primaries have nearly the same marks as above ; on the secondaries, the angular band is surmounted by another irregular spot, so as to form two contiguous spots, or rather one large irregular didymous one.

Canada.

KIRBY.

12. P. numitor *Fab.* E. S. III, 324. Figured in Hübn. Zutr. f. 275.

The smallest of the family. Antennæ black, rings white, terminating in a small point. Body black above, white below ; upper side of all the wings blackish, but glossed for the greatest extent, with shining yellow ; *under side* of primaries blackish, with the outer edge and summit yellowish ; *under side* of secondaries yellowish, with the outer edge blackish.

United States.

GODART.

13. P. vitellius *Sm. Abb.* Figured in Sm. Abb. I, pl. 17.

· *Head* and thorax of males clothed with greenish, fulvous hairs ; club of antennæ fulvous, stem brown ; primaries tawny above, with slender black veins ; in the centre of the disk a large black oval spot, the anterior part of which as well as the base within are velvety, and the remainder silky. Outer margin broadly brown and uninterrupted, although irregularly notched within ; two small connected, transverse, fulvous spots near the tip, separating a part of the dark border from the rest. Secondaries above darker tawny, with black veins and a broad irregularly notched dusky border all around the wings, broken near the anal angle by a longitudinal streak of orange, running to the margin. Wings beneath pale tawny ; base of primaries black, with brownish tips, preceded by two small transverse patches of paler buff color, the upper one farthest from the tip. Secondaries marked along the margins with some slight dusky spots, indicating the dark border of the upper side; a dusky spot in the middle of the disk; under side of the head and breast pale buff.

United States.—Expands an inch and a quarter.

STRICHTHUS Boisr.

Body robust; abdomen not extending beyond the anal angle of the secondaries; terminal joint of the palpi inclined; posterior tibiæ with two pairs of spurs. Usually dark brown, with numerous translucent angular and square whitish spots, either in rows or scattered.

1. S. oilus *Linn*. Syst. Nat. 1, 795. *S. tarrarus* Hübn. *S. syrichthus* Fab. *S. orchus* Cram. Figured in Westw. Brit. Butterflies, pl. 38.

Wings rounded; primaries varied with black and white. Secondaries beneath cinereous, with waved black streaks. Antennæ black, club cinereous beneath.

WESTWOOD.

2. S. ruralis *Boisd*. Ann. Soc. Ent. 2me sér. X, 311.

Wings black, with two white spots between the base and the transverse band of the primaries; secondaries with two bands of spots. *Under side* of the secondaries mingled with white and brown, the middle and the extremity having a kind of band or brownish shade, with obsolete spots between these two spaces.

California.

BOISD.

3. S. cæspitalis *Boisd*. Ann. Soc. Ent. 2me sér. X, 312.

Wings black, with two small white spots between the base and transverse bands of the primaries; secondaries have on the middle a small macular band. *Under side* of secondaries with a narrow median band, continuous, serrate; no white spots at the base.

California.

BOISD.

4. S. scriptura *Boisd*. Ann. Soc. Ent. 2me sér. X, 313.

Small; the white spots small; two white spots between the base and the transverse band of the primaries. *Under side* of secondaries whitish, with the white spots distinct.

California.

BOISD.

5. S. ericetorum *Boisd.* Ann. Soc. Ent. 2me sér. X, 313.

Upper side of the male white, a little sulphury, having no other markings than a festooned terminal line, forming a row of small sagittate spots, resting on a black line at the root of the fringe; at the summit of the superiors the small spots form two or three rows. *Under side* of the wings white; that of the secondaries with two brownish bands, the one covering a part of the base, and the other at the extremity. *Upper side* of the female blackish, with two white transverse bands; the first in the middle, wide, sinuous, irregular; the second, much more narrow, formed of small sagittate spots, except that which is on the upper edge of the primaries, which is quadrangular, and cut by the nerves.

California.

Boisd.

Sec. II. HETEROCERA.

Antennæ variable; prismatic, pectinate, serrate, moniliform or filiform. Wings never erect when at rest: the posterior pair frequently frenate. Ocelli generally present. Flight sometimes diurnal, sometimes crepuscular, more frequently nocturnal.   •

Fam. I. EPIALIDAE.

Proboscis short or none. Palpi obsolete. Antennæ moniliform, scarcely longer than the width of the head. Thorax not crested. Abdomen not barbate. Wings deflected, long, narrow, nearly equal. Primaries opaque, secondaries semi-hyaline.

EPIALUS *Fab.*

Antennæ shorter than the thorax, moniliform, inserted at the anterior and lateral part of the head, a little above the eyes. Palpi indistinct. Proboscis spiral, but slightly apparent. Wings elongated, rather narrow, tectiform. Body more or less pilose—the last abdominal segment of the female forming an elongated oviduct or sort of tail. Legs simple, more or less pilose. Tarsi composed of five articles, of which the last is terminated by two small hooks. The *larva* lives in the ground, and feeds on the roots of plants. It is white or reddish-white, soft and naked, or slightly downy, with a brown, horny head; a spot on the forepart of the body, brown and hard; sixteen legs. Cocoons imperfect, sometimes made of silk, sometimes of morsels of wood or grains fastened together by gummy silk.

1. **H. argenteo-maculatus** *Harris*. Figured in Agassiz' Lake Superior, pl. 7, fig. 6.

Superior wings, ashen gray, with silvery white spots near the base. Next to these are three or four brown spots, or an interrupted line of brown not extending across, terminating towards the inner angle in an oblong drab spot which extends to the edge. The centre is occupied by an oblique long spot of drab, with an indistinct touch of brown in the middle. On the upper edge there are four drab spots, the one nearest the tip being the largest and rounded below. There is a broad margin of the same color on the outer edge, gradually enlarging from near the tip and narrowing at its termination. On this margin there are three indistinct lines of silver white.

The inferiors are pale yellow, pilose at the base; an oblong drab spot on the edge near the tip, and below the tip a large spot of deeper yellow.

On the *under side* the markings are similar, but much less distinct.

Harris.

Fam. COSSIDÆ.

Body thick, rather densely pilose. Head small. Antennæ shorter than half the length of the wings. Palpi small, eyes naked. Proboscis short, or none. Legs short and robust, more or less pilose. Wings strongly veined. Flight nocturnal. Wings in repose, tectiform.

COSSUS *Fab.*

Body stout. Palpi very short or not visible. Antennæ serrated or pectinated, longer than the thorax. Abdomen extending more

or less beyond the hind wings. Legs stout, pilose; hind tibiæ
with four short spurs. Wings rather long, hardly broad. Primaries hardly convex along the costa, rounded at the tips, very
oblique along the exterior border; first and second inferior veins
almost contiguous at the base; third near the second and about
twice further from the fourth. Female with a serrated oviduct.

1. C. robiniæ *Peck.* Mass. Agric. Soc. Report, V, 67.

Male. Dark brown. Primaries paler brown, hoary along the
interior border, with irregular blackish reticulations, and with a
discal blackish stripe composed of five large irregular spots.
Secondaries pale luteous, black to about half the length from the
base and along the costa. *Female.* Hoary, shaded with pale
brown. Thorax with three slender black stripes. Primaries with
irregular blackish reticulations, and some discal and anterior black
streaks. Secondaries dark brown or blackish, paler towards the
margin, more indistinctly reticulated. Fringe with black dots.

The *larva* bores the locust tree (*Robinia pseud-acacia*).

United States.—Male expands 1¾ inch. Female 2 to 2¼ inches.

2. C. populi *Walker.* C. B. M., Part VII, p. 1515.

Female. Cinereous. Antennæ black, very minutely serrated, a
little longer than the thorax. Palpi black, extending as far as the
head. Legs with whitish bands. Wings slightly reticulated, with
very numerous minute transverse blackish streaks. Primaries with
two very slender irregular blackish bands; one at beyond one
third of the length; the other sub-apical and forked in front.
Length of the body 14 lines. Wings expand 28 lines.

Hudson's Bay.

WALKER.

3. C. plagiatus *Walk.* C. B. M., Part VII, p. 1515.

Male. Hoary. Palpi not extending so far as the head; third
joint very minute. Thorax with a slender black stripe along the
inner side of each scapula. Tarsi gray, with whitish bands. Primaries reticulated with gray, narrower and much more oblique
than those of *C. populi;* a brown patch with hoary dots on the
middle of the interior border, and an irregular, sub-apical oblique
band of the same hue. Secondaries gray, hoary and indistinctly
reticulated with gray along the borders; fringe of the four wings

whitish, with blackish intervals. Length of the body 11 lines, of the wings 28 lines. ·

United States.

WALKER.

4. C. querciperda *Fitch.* Fifth Report, No. 204.

"Smaller than *C. Robiniæ,* with thin and slightly transparent wings, which are crossed by numerous black lines, the outer margin only of the forward pair being opaque and of a gray color; the hind wings colorless, with the inner margin broadly blackish and the hind edge coal black."

New York.

FITCH.

ZEUZERA Latr.

Body stout. Palpi very short. Antennæ slender, shorter than the thorax. Abdomen extending far beyond the secondaries. Legs stout, almost bare; hind tibiæ with two very minute apical spurs. Wings narrow. Primaries slightly acuminated, straight along the costa, extremely oblique along the exterior border; discal areolet intersected by a forked veinlet; second superior vein forked at half its length; second inferior vein more than twice further from the third than from the first; third a little further from the third than from the second. *Male.* Antennæ deeply pectinated, bare from half the length to the tips. *Female.* Antennæ bare. Oviduct exserted.

1. Z. canadensis *Herr. Schæf.* Lep. exot. ser. I, 168.

Male. Straw color; primaries thickly covered with little transverse brown streaks; fore part of the disk white, hind part grayish. Secondaries white, with straw-colored veins.

Canada.

HERR. SCHÆF.

2. Z. pyrina *Fab.* E. S. 890.

Head white, front blue, thorax white, with twelve blue points disposed in the following order: 2, 4, 4, 2. Primaries white, with black points disposed in bands; outer edge ferruginous; anterior tibiæ blue below.

North America.

FAB.

Fam. CONCHILOPODIDAE.

LIMACODES Duncan.

Body rather stout, slender in some species. Proboscis not visible. Palpi porrect, rather stout, covered with scales, extending a little beyond the head; third joint conical, acute. Antennæ of the males simple, compressed, rather serrated, pilose at the apex; those of the females slender, a little serrated towards the apex, which is acute, extending a little beyond the head. Legs stout, pilose; hind tibiæ with four spurs. Wings moderately broad, deflexed; primaries elongate, posterior margin rounded. Abdomen a little tufted at the extremity in both sexes.

1. L. cippus *Cram.* L. *querceti* Herr. Schæf. Figured in Cram. Pap. Exot. I, 84, pl. 53. Sm. Abb. pl. 13. Nat. Libr., vol. 37, pl. 21, p. 177. Walker, C. B. M. V, 1144 (1855).

Brownish-red. Primaries with a curved dark brown band beyond two-thirds of the length and with some dark brown marks nearer the base; each wing with two green spots, which are divided on the outer side by a white and black border from two red spots; upper green spot transverse, smaller than the other, which is longitudinal and attenuated at its tip. Secondaries with testaceous borders and a dark brown spot on the interior angle.

WALKER.

Larva destitute of feet, properly so called, their place being supplied merely by a few protuberances; and along the under side of the body there is a soft pliable membrane, covered with a kind of glutinous matter, by means of which and the protuberances, it slides rather than creeps over the surface of a body. The back appears composed of three parts, the intermediate of which is separated from the others by a kind of keel, and is oval, a little pointed at both ends; the lateral parts projecting a little beyond the edges of the body. The head is entirely retractile.

NAT. LIB.

2. L. quercicola *Herr. Schæffer.* Lep. exot. I, t. 175. Walker, C. B. M. V, 1144.

Brownish-red. Primaries with a curved dark brown band, beyond two-thirds of the length, and with two dark brown discal

spots nearer the base; each wing with two small green spots,
which are contiguous on the outer side to two larger red spots;
fore green spot transverse, hind one triangular. Secondaries rather
paler than the fore wings.

Georgia.

WALKER.

3. L? pithecium *Sm. Abb.* Figured in Sm. Abb. pl. 74. Nat. Libr.
vol. 37, pl. 31, p. 185.

Primaries bluish, with transverse waved bands of yellowish-
brown, and more or less clouded with dusky; secondaries entirely
brown, with a narrow yellow line within the fringe; body of the
female rather thick, thorax and abdomen bluish, the former brown
on the side and the latter with brown rings. The body of the
male is wholly light brown, with clouds of a deeper color, and the
abdomen tufted at the apex. The female expands an inch and
three lines, the male somewhat less.

NAT. LIB.

Larva flat, with long projecting appendages on each side, covered
with hairs and two other projecting pieces of intermediate size
behind the head, and a larger pair over the tail.

4. L? spinuloides *Boisd.* Figured in Herr. Schaef. Lep. exot. sp.
ter. 1, f. 157. Walker, C. B. M., V, 1147.

Ferruginous. Primaries with an oblong black discal spot, a
row of black marginal dots, and a short white costal sub-apical
streak. Secondaries pale brown, with very pale borders. *Male.*
Antennæ slightly pectinated. Primaries with two oblique brown
bands, which are connected by the interior border. *Female.* Antennæ simple. Primaries dingy whitish along the costa near the
base, with an oblique dingy whitish band which includes the black
discal spot, with a short oblique white streak resting on the interior border, and with a short sub-apical band of black dots.

North America.

WALKER.

5. L? fasciola *Boisd.* Figured in Herr. Schaef. Lep. exot. sp. ser. 1,
f. 166. Walker, C. B. M., V, 1148.

Male. Fawn color. Antennæ hardly pectinated. Primaries
reddish, with a slightly oblique white band, which is forked behind
and hooked in front, with a white apical spot, and with a blackish

band which proceeds from the hook of the white band.   Secondaries testaceous.

North America.
WALKER.

6. L? textula *Boisd.*   Figured in Herr. Schael. Lep. exot. sp. ser. I,
    f. 364.   Walker, C. B. M., V, 1148.

Female.   Pale fawn color.   Wings with abbreviated transverse
whitish bands, whose borders are partly blackish.

North America.
WALKER.

7. L? pallida *Walk.*   C. B. M., V, 1148.

Testaceous.   Antennæ nearly simple.   Abdomen extending as
far as the hind wings.   Primaries with two curved gray slender
discal bands.

North America.
WALKER.

8. L? Gavula *Boisd.*   Figured in Herr. Schael. Lep. exot. sp. ser. I,
    f. 183.   Walker, C. B. M., V, 1149.

Male.   Primaries pale fawn color.   Antennæ simple.   Secondaries whitish.

Nova Scotia.
WALKER.

9. L. laticlavia *Clemens.*   Proc. A. N. S., Phil. 1860, p. 157.

Body and fore wings rather dark ochreous yellow.   Fore wings
with an oblique silvery band, inclined towards the base of the
wings, from the costa to the middle of the inner margin, and
toothed toward the base on the sub-median nervure or fold.   A
rather faint reddish-brown line extends from the costal origin of
the silvery band to the hind margin beneath the middle.   Hind
wings pale ochreous yellow.   Abdomen rather reddish ochreous.

Larva.   Outline elliptical, somewhat pointed behind ; body flattened, with the sides curving from a central ridge, flattened above.
The ridge has a vertical elevation at its sides, growing less and
less before and behind, and terminates in front in a rounded margin,
and behind in an obtuse short spine.   The body is smooth, with
no distinct spined papulæ, but the edges of the ridge and the outline of the body are thrown into folds, sub-crenated.   The body is
thickest in the middle, whence it curves anteriorly and posteriorly.

General color of the body is pale green and dotted with numerous yellow points. Central ridge is bordered in front with yellow.

The *larva* feeds on the under side of the leaf of maple in September, and the *imago* appears in the spring.—*Clemens*, Pro. A. N. S., 1860, p. 157.

PIMELA Clemens. Lagoa? Walker.

P. lanuginosa *Clemens*. Proc. A. N. S. Phila. p. 156, 1860.

Female? The wings of my specimen are badly worn and denuded. Antennæ pale brownish-yellow. Face dark brownish; head and tail dull yellow. The anterior tibiæ and all the tarsi are dark brownish. The undenuded portion of the fore wings at the base, is woolly and pale brownish-yellow.

Male? Antennæ yellowish-white. Face and the fore legs blackish-brown, the hairs white and all the tarsi blackish-brown toward the ends. Thorax white, very slightly tinted with yellowish. Abdomen rather deep, dull yellow. Wings white, slightly tinted with yellowish; fore wings woolly toward the base, with a dark brownish discoloration along the upper part of the disk and the costa adjoining it.

Clemens.

ADONETA Clemens.

A. voluta *Clemens*. Proc. A. N. S. p. 156, 1860.

Reddish-brown, somewhat paler in the ♀ than the ♂. Fore wings with a dingy yellow streak along the base of the inner margin, extended toward the disk above the middle of the wing, and on this portion are two or three blackish dots. On the hind portion of the disk is a short black streak. In the ♂ there is another short black streak along the median nervure and its last branch, with a curved row of three black submarginal spots. The lower streak and the spots are as distinct in the ♀ as in the ♂. In both sexes there is a subapical dingy yellow patch, lightly bordered behind with whitish. Hind margin spotted with black. Hind wing pale reddish-brown.

Larva. Body semi-cylindrical, tapering posteriorly, and rounded obtusely in front. Nearly smooth, but with a subvascular row of small fleshy, minutely spined papulæ on each side of the vascular line, three of which, placed anteriorly, are separated and distinct,

9

and three approximated on the last rings; the intermediate ones are minute. The outline of the body above the ventral surface is furnished with a row of minute spined papulæ.

Bright green, with a broad dorsal yellow band containing a reddish purple one, which is constricted opposite the second and third pairs of anterior papulæ and dilated into an elliptical patch in the middle of the body. This is almost separated from a smaller elliptical patch which is constricted opposite the third pair of posterior papulæ and ends in a small round patch. The anterior and posterior papulæ are crimson and the intermediate ones green. The superventral row of spined papulæ are green.

In September, on the leaf of apricot. Imago in March.

CLEMENS.

EMPRETIA CLEMENS.

E. stimulea *Clemens.* Proc. A. N. S. p. 158, 1860.

Body and fore wings uniform dark ferruginous, with two small subapical white spots, and in the ♂ two more near the base of the wing beneath the median nervure. Hind wings pale reddish-brown.

Larva. Body semicylindrical, truncated obliquely before and behind, with a pair of anterior long, fleshy, subvascular, slenderly spined horns and a pair smaller beneath them, above the head; a posterior similar pair and a smaller anal pair beneath them. The superventral row of papulæ are rather large and densely spined. After the last moulting the longer horns become moderate in length.

The portion of the body between the anterior and posterior horns is a fine bright green color, bordered anteriorly and superventrally by white, with a central, dorsal, oval reddish-brown patch bordered with white, which color is again edged by a black line. The horns, papulæ, and anterior portion of the body are reddish-brown, with a small yellow spot between the anterior horns, while the posterior pair are placed in a yellow patch.

The spines with which the horns are supplied produce an exceedingly painful sensation when they come in contact with the back of the hand, or any portion of the body on which the skin is thin.

On a great variety of plants; fruit trees, the rose, Indian corn (*Zea mays*), and a number of other plants.

CLEMENS.

D. penscolata *Clemens.* Proc. A. N. S. Phila. p. 159, 1860.

Body dark reddish-brown.   Fore wings dark reddish-brown
along all the borders, with a large central pea-green patch, extending from the base of the wing to the subterminal portion,
bordered narrowly on the inner side and behind with white, and
deeply indented opposite the middle of the inner margin, where
there is a bright brown patch in the reddish-brown border.   Hind
wings yellowish-brown.

I do not know the larval state of this species, and have only
two specimens, both apparently females.   I can perceive no difference in the structural characters of the imago of this and the pre-
vious species, and am quite sure that they belong to the same
generic group.   The discovery of the larval form will, however,
determine the question.

Illinois.

CLEMENS.

NOCHELLA CLEMENS.

N. tardigrada *Clemens.* Proc. A. N. S. Phil. p. 159, 1860.

Male. Body and fore wings rather dark reddish-brown, with a
small, nearly triangular pea-green patch narrowly bordered with
dark brown at the base of the wing, beneath the median nervure,
slightly excavated behind where it adjoins a bright brown patch.
Towards the hind end of the disk, in its middle, is a minute oval
dark brown streak; two small pea-green subapical spots, the one
nearest the costa minute.

Larva.   The body is elliptical, much flattened above.   There
is on each side a row of subvascular, minutely spined papulæ, of
which the three anterior and two posterior are more conspicuous
than the rest.   The superventral row of papulæ are moderate,
equal, and form the outline of the body.

General color very pale green, with dorsal patches of the general
hue beautifully margined by crimson lines, and crimson vascular
patches, of which those between the *fourth* and *fifth*, *seventh* and
eighth pairs of subvascular papulæ are most conspicuous, although
small.   All the papulæ are pale green.

On the apricot in September.   Imago in April.

The genera Pimela, Limacodes, Adonета, Empretia, and Nochelia belong to that most anomalous family Limacodidæ.   Per-

haps some of the groups described as new have been heretofore established, but I found the effort to identify them from meagre and unsatisfactory diagnoses of the imago an almost futile task.

CLEMENS.

Fam. IV. ZYGAENIDAE.

Front squamose. Palpi cylindrical, barbate, or hirsute; third article very distinct, sometimes naked. Antennæ fusiform, sometimes cylindric, and moniliform, often pectinate. Tongue long, convolute. Tibiæ armed at the apex with four more or less distinct spurs. Wings deflected, longer than the body; primaries more narrow; secondaries rounded, very rarely angular. Flight diurnal. Larva rather contracted, sluggish; head small, pubescent or pilose. Pupa folliculate.

ALYPIA Kirby.

Body short, rather robust. *Head* small; eyes moderate. Proboscis shorter than half the body. *Palpi* hairy, extending a little beyond the head; second article a little longer than the first; antennæ thicker in the middle than at the apex, nearly as long as the body; thorax thick; abdomen more slender. Wings rather wide, not elongate, rounded on the margins. Feet robust, rather hairy, with strong spines.

1. **A. octomaculata** *Fab. A. octomaculalis* Hübn. *A. quadriguttalis* Hübn. Figured in Sm. Abb. pl. 44.

Black, with two sulphur-yellow spots on the primaries and two white ones on the secondaries; shoulder-covers and front sulphur-yellow; fore and middle tibiæ thickly covered with orange hairs. *Larva* cylindrical, elongated, yellow, with transverse rows of black points, slightly hairy, without a caudal horn. Lives on the grape-vine, and incloses itself in a cocoon in the earth.

Northern States.

2. **A. guttata** *Boisd.* Ann. Soc. Ent. X, 2me ser. 320.

Upper side black; secondaries without spots; primaries with about eighteen pale yellow, mostly rounded spots, of which two or three, towards the upper edge, are small and punctiform. Body black, with the shoulders and shield pale yellow; end of the

abdomen fulvous, as well as the head. *Under side* of the primaries
like the upper.

  California.   Rare.

BOIS.

3. **A. McCullochi** *Kirby.* Figured in Kirby, Faun. Amer. Bor. IV, pl. 4,
   fig. 5.

  Body and wings very black; orbits of eyes externally clothed
with white hairs; tippets whitish; primaries with three white
spots, one near the base, oblique, obversely wedge shaped, divided
into two by a longitudinal black line; next, at a little distance from
the anterior margin, is a subtrapezoidal small white spot, between
which and the posterior margin is an articulated band, abbreviated
at each end, of the same color, consisting of six spots divided by
black lines; the same spots distinguish the under surface of these
wings, and besides, there is a whitish longitudinal one on the costal
area. The secondaries have three white spots on both surfaces,
viz., a large rectangular one near the base divided longitudinally
into four; a longitudinal band divided into five spots; the longitudinal costal streak may almost be regarded as forming a sixth.
The four anterior legs are covered with orange hairs.

  Canada.

KIRBY.

FAM. V. GLAUCOPIDIDAE HARRIS.*

PROCRIS Fab. *Aglaope* Latr.

  Wings narrow, elongated, opaque, immaculate. Antennæ slender, tapering at each end, and bipectinated beneath in the males.
Palpi small, short, pendent, and nearly naked. Tongue short, but
distinct and spirally rolled. Abdomen slender and nearly cylindrical in the males, thicker in the females, and tufted at the end.
Spurs of the hind tibiæ two in number, and very minute.

HARRIS.

* The succeeding descriptions by Harris will be found in Silliman's
American Journal of Science, vol. xxxvi.

L. P. americana *Boisd.* Figured in Guerin's Iconographie and Griffith's Cuvier.

Blue black, with a saffron colored collar and a fan shaped, somewhat bilobed black caudal tuft. Expands from ten lines to an inch. *Larva* hairy, green, with black bands. It is gregarious and devours the leaves of the grape vine, and undergoes its transformations in an oblong-oval, tough whitish cocoon, which is fastened to a leaf.

2. P? smithsoniana *Clemens.* Pr. A. N. S. p. 540, 1860.

The entire insect is greenish black; immaculate.

Texas.

CLEMENS.

3. P. (Acoloithus *Clemens*) falsarius *Clem.* Pr. A. N. S. p. 540, 1860.

Black. Prothorax fulvous, especially on the sides, with a point on the median line black. Hind wings rather thin.

Penna., Ill.

CLEMENS.

MALTHACA CLEMENS.

M. perlucidula *Clemens.* Proceedings Acad. Nat. Sci. Phila. 1860, p. 541.

Blackish-brown. Wings slightly transparent. Fore wings with the basal half luteous *above the fold.* Hind wings luteous along the costa from the base to the middle.

CLEMENS.

GLAUCOPIS FAB.

Wings narrow in some, broad in others, entire, for the most part opaque, and with the body more or less glossed with blue, sometimes spotted or partially transparent. *Antennæ* feathered or bipectinated in both sexes; the pectinations elongated in the males and short in the females. *Palpi* more or less elongated and recurved. Tongue moderate, spirally rolled. Caudal tuft minute or wanting. Posterior tibiæ with three or four spurs of moderate size.

HARRIS.

1. G. ipomoeae *Harris.*

Fore wings greenish-black, with three yellowish-white dots near the front margin and two others close together beyond the middle;

hind wings violet-black, with a transparent colorless spot at base; *body* tawny orange; *antennæ* and *head* black, the latter spotted with orange; a broad stripe on the shoulder-covers, a transverse spot on the thorax behind, and the incisures of the abdomen black; legs violet-black; coxæ beneath, and a spot on the thighs, orange colored.

Southern States.—Expands an inch and three-quarters.

HARRIS.

2. G. (Cosmosoma *Hubn.***) omphale** *Hübn.* (according to Say). *Ægeria omphale* Say. Figured in Say Amer. Ent. VII, pl. 19.

Scarlet? wings transparent, veined and bordered with black; the first pair with a small black subcostal spot, and the black border very much widened at tip; head azure blue; antennæ black, with the tips white; two terminal joints of the palpi, and a line on each shoulder-cover black; four azure-blue dots in a transverse row on the fore part of the thorax; last four segments of the abdomen black, with four azure blue spots on each side, and a dorsal black line extending from the middle of the second segment, including in it seven azure blue spots; belly and outside of the second pair of tibiæ black.

Florida.—Expands an inch and a half or more.

For a specimen of this beautiful insect I am indebted to Mr. Doubleday. It cannot belong to the genus *Ægeria*, to which it was referred by Mr. Say, in his American Entomology, where it is figured.

United States.

HARRIS.

3. G. (Lycomorpha *Harris***) pholus** *Fab.*

Blue-black or deep indigo blue; wings at base and shoulder-covers orange. Expands fourteen or fifteen lines. *Larva* pale green with yellowish spots running into the green; head black, covered with a few short whitish hairs; body sparingly clothed with rather long hairs, which are white at the sides and black on the back, the hairs arising singly from minute tubercles, those on the third segment the longest, and with the others before them directed forwards. It eats the lichens on stone heaps in shady places, and undergoes its transformation in a thin silky cocoon.

United States.

HARRIS.

4. G. semidiaphana *Harris. G. fulvicollis* Hübn.

Slate color. Wings rather narrow and subacute; first pair
brownish slate, with the anterior edge clay-colored; hind wings
semi-transparent in the middle; head and antennæ black; collar,
front edge of the breast, and base of the palpi orange. Expands
fifteen to sixteen lines.
Middle and Southern States.

HARRIS.

5. G. latrellana *Kirby. Faun. Amer. Bor.*

Fore wings dusky drab with a silky lustre, and the anterior edge
clay color; hind wings rusty black; fringes of all the wings white,
interrupted with black in the middle; top of the head, orbits behind, base of the palpi, front of the breast, and a spot on the fore
part of each shoulder-cover orange; thorax, abdomen, and coxæ
glaucous or greenish-blue, with a silky lustre; abdomen beneath
and legs light brown.
Northern States.

HARRIS.

6. G. latipennis *Boisd.   Ann. Soc. Ent. X, 2me ser. 320.*

Wings black, each marked on the disk with a very pale yellow
spot, divided into three unequal parts; primaries near the summit,
with an oblique band formed of four yellow spots of the same yellow.   Body bluish-black; pectus marked with fulvous.
California.

BOISD.

7. G. epimenis *Drury. Vol. III. 39.   Probably genus *Brepha.*

Brownish-black. Fore wings sprinkled in spots with light blue
scales, which form a narrow band near the hinder margin and
marked with a large yellowish-white patch beyond the middle;
hind wings with a broad dark orange red band behind the middle.
The white spot of the fore wings is indented toward the middle
of the wing, and on the under side there is a small triangular spot
near the base of the wing and a short transverse one beyond it,
which unites behind with the angular projection of the large white
patch. Expands rather more than one inch.
North America.

HARRIS.

Fam. VI. ÆGERIADÆ Harris.

With *false eyes* or *ocelli*. *Secondaries* wide, entire; fringe short, vitreous, with a *frenulum;* two or three nerves on the interior margin, besides five others without a costal. Hymenopterous like insects, whose primaries usually are vitreous to the margins, and secondaries altogether. Body large; eyes naked; antennæ longer than half the primaries, gradually enlarging and again diminishing at the tip; seldom filiform; usually ciliate in the male, more seldom lamellar or pectinate. Palpi strongly developed, erect, hairy below; terminal joint sharp, naked. For the most part a distinct spiral tongue; in *Trochilium* only two short soft pieces. Legs robust, covered with scales or hairs, with two pairs of long spurs. Abdomen extending far beyond the anal angle, with seven segments (the female has but six), with red, yellow, or white rings, usually with a caudal tuft. *Primaries* narrow, at least four times longer than wide; interior angle rounded. *Secondaries* shorter but much wider; anal angle rounded. In a state of repose the wings are usually about half erected. *Larva* usually whitish, with head dark. Lives in the bark or the interior of trees and shrubs, seldom in the roots or stalks of herbaceous plants.

TROCHILIUM Scop.

Antennæ gradually thickened nearly to the end, which is curved but not hooked; tip with a pencil of hairs. Two short soft processes instead of a tongue.

Hornet like in appearance. *Body* stout; *antennæ* of the males with a lamellar process at every joint; *palpi* strong, densely pilose; *legs*, especially the posterior, clothed with a sort of fur. Male only with a caudal tuft. *Primaries* often, *secondaries* always transparent.

Harris.

1. T. marginatum *Harris.*

Black. Wings transparent; first pair with a broad border, the tip and a transverse band beyond the middle pale brown; hind wings with a broad black fringe; *antennæ* black; two longitudinal lines on the thorax; hind margins of the abdominal segments, orbits, palpi, and legs, except at base, yellow. Expands rather more than one inch and a quarter.

New Hampshire.

HARRIS.

2. T. tibiale *Harris.*

Brownish. Wings transparent; first pair with a narrow border and an abbreviated band beyond the middle pale brown; hind wings with a narrow brownish fringe; antennæ black; orbits, two lines on the thorax, edges of the abdominal segments and tibiæ yellow; hindmost tibiæ covered with yellow hairs. Expands one inch and a half. The yellow bands on the abdomen are much narrower and less bright than in *marginatum.*

New Hampshire.—On *Populus candicans.*

HARRIS.

3. T. denudatum *Harris.*

Chestnut brown. Fore wings opaque, with a large triangular transparent spot adjacent to the outer hind angle, a rusty red spot at base, and another near the middle; hind wings transparent, with the margin and fringe brown, and a rust red costal spot; orbits, edges of the collar, incisions of the abdomen, tibiæ, and tarsi dull yellow; antennæ brownish above, rust yellow at tip and beneath. Expands from one inch and a quarter to more than one inch and a half.

HARRIS.

T. triciincta *Harris.*

Blue-black. Fore wings opaque; hind wings transparent, with the border, fringe, and a short transverse line near the middle black; palpi at tip, collar, a spot on each shoulder, and three bands on the abdomen yellow; antennæ short, black; four posterior tibiæ banded with orange; tarsi yellow, tipped with black; tail flat, with two longitudinal yellow lines. Expands from one inch to one inch and two lines.

This species seems to come near to the European *T. asiliformis;* but the male has only three yellow abdominal bands; while in the *asiliformis* there are five bands in the male sex. The antennæ are shorter and thicker than in the following species, and are furnished beneath with a double row of short pectinations or teeth, which are thickly fringed with hairs. The sexes were captured together upon the common tansy.

North America.

HARRIS.

T. cucurbitae *Harris.*

Fore wings opaque, lustrous olive brown; hind wings transparent, with the margin and fringe brown; antennæ greenish-black; palpi pale yellow, with a little black tuft near the top; thorax olive; abdomen deep orange, with a transverse basal black band, and a longitudinal row of five or six black spots; tibiæ and tarsi of the hind legs thickly fringed on the inside with black and on the outside with long orange-colored hairs; spurs covered with white hairs. Expands from thirteen to fifteen lines.

Larva similar in form and color to those of other species. Lives in the pith of squash and pumpkin vines. Forms in the ground a cocoon composed of grains of earth cemented by a gummy matter. *Pupa* almost entirely excluded from the cocoon during the last transformation.

North America.

HARRIS.

T. caudata *Harris.*

Brown. *Male* with the fore wings transparent from the base to the middle; hind wings transparent, with a brownish border, fringe, and subcostal spot; antennæ, palpi, collar, and tarsi tawny yellow; hind legs yellow; end of the tibiæ and first tarsal joint fringed with tawny yellow and black hairs; tail slender, cylindrical, nearly as long as the body, tawny yellow, with a little black tuft on each side at base. The *female* differs from the male in having the fore wings entirely opaque; the hind legs black, with a rusty spot in the middle of the tibiæ, and fringed with black; caudal tuft of the ordinary form and size. Expands from one inch to one inch and three lines. *Larva* inhabits the stems of our indigenous currant, *Ribes floridum.*

HARRIS.

T. syringae *Harris.*

Brown. Fore wings with a transparent line at base; hind wings transparent, with a brown border, fringe, and subcostal spot; antennæ, palpi, collar, first and second pairs of tarsi, and middle of the intermediate tibiæ rost red; middle of the tibiæ and the tarsi of the hind legs yellow. Expands one inch and two lines. *Larva* lives in the trunks of *Syringa vulgaris,* the common lilac.

HARRIS.

T. exitiosa *Say.* Figured in Say, Amer. Ent. VII, pl. 19.

Steel blue. *Male* with the wings transparent; the margins and fringes, and a band beyond the middle of the first pair steel blue; palpi, collar, edges of the shoulder-covers and of the abdominal segments, two bands on the tibiæ including the spurs, anterior tarsi, and lateral edges of the wedge-shaped tail pale yellow. *Female* with the fore wings opaque; the hind wings transparent, with a broad opaque front margin, and the fringe purple-black; antennæ, palpi, legs, and abdomen steel blue, the latter encircled in the middle by a broad saffron-colored band. Male expands from nine to thirteen lines; female from fifteen to seventeen lines. *Larva* inhabits the trunks and roots of the peach and cherry trees, beneath the bark. The larva is the well known peach-tree borer, which annually injures to a great extent or destroys numbers of these trees. For the means of preventing its ravages, see Say's Entomology, Vol. II, and my communication in the New England Farmer, Vol. V, p. 88. The insects above described, though very dissimilar, are really the sexes of one species. I have raised many of them from the larvæ, and have also repeatedly captured them, in connection, on the trunks of peach and cherry trees.

HARRIS.

T. fulvipes *Harris.*

Blue black. Wings transparent; margin and fringes, and a transverse band beyond the middle of the first pair blue-black; antennæ black, yellowish at the end; palpi beneath, a spot on the thorax under the origin of the wings, intermediate and hindmost tibiæ, all the tarsi, and the basal half of the under side of the abdomen orange colored; hindmost tibiæ somewhat thickened by a covering of tawny hairs. Expands thirteen lines.

HARRIS.

T. tipuliformis *Harris.*

Blue-black. Wings transparent, with the margin and fringes blackish; the first pair with a transverse blue-black band beyond the middle, and a broad one at tip streaked with copper color; antennæ black; palpi beneath, collar, upper edges of the shoulder-covers, a spot on each side of the breast, three narrow rings on the abdomen, ends of the tibiæ, and the spurs pale golden yellow; tail fan-shaped, blue-black. The male has an additional transverse yellow line between the second and third abdominal bands. Expands from seven and a half to nine lines. *Larra* lives in the pith of the currant bush. This destructive insect is not a native, but has been introduced from Europe with the cultivated currant bush.

HARRIS.

T. scitula *Harris.*

Purple-black. Wings transparent, with the margins golden yellow; the first pair with a narrow purple-brown band beyond the middle and a broad one at the tip ornamented with golden yellow lines; fringes blackish; front and orbits covered with silvery white hairs; antennæ black; palpi, collar, upper edges of the shoulder-covers, a narrow band at the base of the abdomen, a dorsal spot behind it, a broad band around the middle, the lateral edges of the fan-shaped tail, anterior coxæ, sides of the breast, tibiæ and tarsi, except at the joints, with the spurs golden-yellow. Expands about eight lines. This beautiful little species is easily distinguished by the prevalence of yellow on the under side of the body and legs.

HARRIS.

T. pyri *Harris.*

Purple-black. Wings transparent, with the margins, a narrow band beyond the middle of the first pair, and a broad one at tip, purple-black, the latter streaked with brassy yellow; antennæ blackish; palpi beneath, collar, edges of the shoulder-covers, a broad band across the middle of the abdomen, a narrow one before it, an indistinct transverse line at base, the posterior half of the abdomen beneath, the sides of the breast, anterior coxæ, legs except the joints of the tibiæ, and the lateral edges of the wedge-shaped tail golden yellow. Expands six lines and a half. *Larra* lives under the bark of the pear-tree. For some further particulars respecting this species, see my communication in the New England Farmer, Vol. IX, p. 9, 1830.

HARRIS.

THYRIS Illiger.

Wings broad, subtriangular, more or less angulated and indented, opaque, with small semi-transparent spots. *Antennæ* fusiform, but slender, and only slightly thickened in the middle; arcuated and simple in both sexes. *Tongue* moderate. *Body* short and thick; *Abdomen* conical and tufted at the end.

HARRIS.

T. maculata *Harris.*

Brownish-black, sprinkled with rust yellow dots; hind margins of the wings deeply scalloped, with the edges of the indentations white; each of the wings with a transparent white spot, which in the fore wings is nearly oval and slightly narrowed in the middle; in the hind wings larger, kidney shaped, and almost divided in two; palpi beneath, a spot before the anterior coxæ, the tips of the tarsal joints above, and the hind edges of the last three or four abdominal segments white. Expands from six to eight lines.

Massachusetts.

Harris.

Fam. VII. PSYCHIADAE.

THYRIDOPTERYX Steph.

Body of the male densely pilose. Antennæ deeply pectinated, not longer than the thorax. Abdomen extending beyond the wings. Legs pilose. Wings narrow, bare, vitreous, and colorless. Primaries about twice the length of the secondaries, rounded at the tips. Secondaries slightly truncated, with a long and stout frenulum. Female apterous.

T. ephemeraeformis *Harris.*

Black, pilose; wings vitreous; anterior margin of the primaries and interior of the secondaries squamous.

Harris.

PEROPHORA Harris.

Body stout, thickly clothed with short hairs. *Proboscis* obsolete, *palpi* short; *antennæ* of the *male* deeply pectinated to the tips; abdomen extending beyond the hind wings; legs rather short; femora and tibiæ thickly pilose; wings rather long, thickly clothed, opaque. *Female* winged; *antennæ* moderately pectinated.

P. melsheimerii *Harris.*

Pale ash red; wings irrorate with minute black points; a common oblique linear fuscous fascia bent backwards before the apex of the primaries, marked with a larger median blackish point.

Harris.

Fam. VIII. SPHINGIDAE.[1]

The perfect insects included in this group are characterized
by the absence of simple eyes on the vertex at the base of the
antennæ. The head is well developed, and well clothed with
hairs, that but rarely show a tendency to become tufted; the
antennæ are prismatic, and more or less thickened towards
the tip, where they are recurved in the form of a hook, and
surmounted by a ciliated seta; they are doubly ciliated in
the males, on the sides of the plates prolonged beneath from
the stalk, and nearly simple in the females: in some genera
the terminal seta is obsolete, but the stalk is distinctly prismatic, and the articles are ciliated or bear short pectinations
in the males. The eyes are usually large, hemispherical and
salient, and the palpi have the third article reduced to a mere
point, placed on the summit of the well developed second
article. The tongue is usually well developed, and nearly
equal to the length of the body; in some instances it is more
than twice longer than the body, and in others it is almost
obsolete.

The thorax is always well developed and large, containing
powerful muscles, that are attached to elongated, narrow and
dense wings, the inner border of which is much shorter than
the exterior, in consequence of the obliquity of the hind
margin, and are attached to each other by a bristle and hook.
They are characterized by the following peculiarities of structure. The basal portions of the marginal and costal nervures are thick and strong, and contiguous to each other and
the subcostal nervure; these and the subcosto-marginal nervules proceed towards the apex of the wing almost like a
bundle of rods, thus forming an external margin capable of
resisting rapid and strong vibrations upon the atmosphere.
In addition to the two marginal nervules, given off from
near the posterior-superior angle of the disk, the subcostal
divides into a subcosto-apical, post-apical and inferior nervules. At the origin of the subcosto-inferior, the discal-nerv-

---

[1] The following monograph of the Sphingidæ is the production of Dr.
Brackenridge Clemens, of Easton, Pa., and was published in the Journal
of the Acad. Nat. Sci. Phila., July, 1859. By his kind permission it is
inserted here. Everything is retained except the admirable paper on
Classification which precedes it, and some minor details, besides a few
Brazilian species.—J. G. M.

ure takes a transverse course, throwing off near its centre,
the disco-central, and joins the submedian at the origin of
the medio-superior nervule; in addition to this, the median
throws off more posteriorly the medio-central and posterior
nervules.   Lastly, near the inner margin is found the sub-
median nervure, which is simple and usually bifid at the base.

In the posterior wings, the costal nervure is simple and
prolonged to the hind margin, and is connected with the
subcostal towards the base, by a short intercostal nervule.
The subcostal nervure subdivides into two branches, the
apical and postapical; the discal nervure arises at the bifurcation of the subcostal, and emits the disco-central nervule
about its centre, and anastomoses with the submedian at the
origin of the medio-superior.   The median nervure is nearly
straight, but angulated at the origin of the medio-central,
and posterior to this point throws off the medio-posterior.
The submedian and internal nervures are both simple.

This pterogostic structure, without undergoing any essen-
tial variation whatever from the type, is found in all the
genera of the group.

The abdomen is usually cylindrico-conical, longer than the
posterior pair of wings, sometimes tufted at the tip, and each
of its segments are furnished on the posterior edges with a
row of acute spinules concealed by a covering of scales.

The legs are usually long and strong, and the under surface of the tarsi roughened with numerous, acute, rigid spinules and furnished with a pair of free, simple claws.   The
anterior tarsi have a long single spur on the inner surface,
the middle a terminal pair, and the posterior two pair.

The eggs of the perfect insect are deposited singly on the
food-plants of the larvæ, which are usually conspicuous in
size when full grown, and live a solitary life.   They have
naked, cylindrical bodies, varying slightly in form, and pre-
senting, usually, differences of ornamentation in the several
genera.   They possess eight pairs of feet, three of which are
thoracic, four abdominal, and one terminal; the latter are
large, strong, and almost square, with the plantæ situated at
the anterior angle.   On the dorsum of the eleventh segment
is placed a rigid spine, called the caudal horn, and when this
is absent it is replaced by a lenticular tubercle.

The pupæ are cylindrico-conical, with the extremity of the
abdominal case terminating in single, stout, acute spine, and
is contained in an imperfect cocoon, or near the surface in a
cell, or in a subterranean cell.

Synoptical Table of Genera.

A. ANTERIOR WINGS ENTIRE.

1.* Terminal margin obliquely convex.

† Antennæ clavate-prismatic or prismatic, with a short hook and seta.

‡ Abdomen long, cylindric-conical, not tufted at the tip.

1° *Tongue twice, or nearly twice, as long as the body.*

Macrosila.—Head large; eyes very large; wings rather broad, interior angle dilated.

2. Leucophæta.—Head large, eyes very large; wings narrow, interior angle rounded.

2° *Tongue nearly as long as the body, or somewhat longer.*

Sphinx.—Head rather long and narrow, eyes small; wings narrow and long.

Macrosila Forresan.—Head large and broad, eyes large; fore wings broad. Wings rather short and broad, hind margin in middle slightly dilated.

Dolba.—Tongue a little longer than the body, eyes small, head broad and obtuse.

3° *Tongue two-thirds as long as the body.*

Pachylia (*in part*).—Head large, prominent, eyes large; body thick and large.

Darapsa, Group II.—Tongue moderately long. Interior border of wings straight.

Lapara.—Tongue moderate; head small and short; palpi very short; abdomen linear.

4° *Tongue about one-third as long as the body.*

Ceratomia.—Body thick; head small, eyes small; thorax short, globose; abdomen long.

Daremma.—Body rather slender; tongue short, distinct; abdomen tapering.

5° *Tongue as long as palpi.*

Ellema.—Body subfusiform; head small, narrow, subtufted and sessile; eyes small.

|| Antennæ slender, minutely serrate-setose.

‡ Abdomen more or less tufted at the tip.

Œnosanda.—Head slightly crested; tongue moderate; palpi long and slender.

Perigonia.—Head rounded, smooth; tongue rather short; palpi very short and stout.

Macroglossa.—Head very broad; tongue one-half as long as body, eyes small; palpi broad beneath.

||| Antennæ subclavate or fusiform, with a minute hook.

‡ Abdomen not tufted at the tip.

Arctonotus.—Tongue obsolete or very short; body very pilose; abdomen hardly longer than thorax.

10

Deilephila.—Tongue as long, or nearly as long, as body; abdomen attenuated at tip.

    †† Abdomen tufted at the tip.

Sesia.—Wings hyaline in the middle.

Macroglossa.—Wings opaque; tongue as long as the body.

    II*. Terminal margin wavy between nervules.

Amceryx.—Tongue as long as the body; head broad and conical, eyes large; wings narrow.

    M. Antæus.—Tongue nearly twice as long as the body.

    S. Juglandis ♀.—Tongue nearly obsolete.

    III.* Terminal margin nearly straight or slightly sinuate.

Amceryx Caicus.—Body rather long and slender, wings narrow.

| Antennæ with a long hook tapering to the end, ciliferous in ♂, simple in ♀.

    ‡‡ Abdomen thick and large; wings deeply concave on inner border.

    Tongue two-thirds as long as the body.

Paohylia.—Interior angle of hind wings, covered with white scales; head broad, eyes large.

    Tongue as long as the body.

Philampelus.

    †† Antennæ somewhat fusiform, rather short, hook minute.

    ‡ Abdomen oblanceolate, body long and slender.

    Tongue as long as the body.

Anterior wings narrow, tip very acute, often somewhat hooked.

Chærocampa.—Head large, conical; eyes moderate; abdomen with a slender pencil of hairs.

    IV.* Terminal margin excavated by the tip, convex from the middle.

    ‡ Abdomen without apical tuft.

Ambulyx.—Wings narrow and very long; head prominent, conical, obtuse; tongue long.

    Tongue not quite as long as the body, or as long.

Pergesa.—Antennæ filiform, longer than thorax; body oblanceolate; wings slightly denticulated.

Chærocampa (in part).

    Tongue nearly obsolete.

    S. Juglandis ♂.—Antennæ subpectinated.

    Tongue about one-half as long as the body.

Darapsa.—Head subtufted, front nearly vertical, eyes small; antennæ with a long hook.

        ‡‡ Abdomen with apical tuft.

        Fore wings with silvery streaks.

Callionima, Group II.—Head prominent, conical; antennæ minutely serrate setose.

      B. ANTENNÆ WITHIN NOT ENTIRE.

    I.* Terminal margin angulated, denticulated, excised or indented.

    1. Fore wings with angular indentations above interior angle.

      ‡ Abdomen with apical tuft.

Proserpinus.—Antennæ clavate with minute hook; tongue as long as
    body; eyes minute.
        ‖ Abdomen without apical tuft.
Unxia.—Antennæ rather slender; tongue moderately long.
    2° Fore wings circularly excavated near the tip and interior angle,
        middle rounded.
Thyreus, Group II.—Head small, eyes very small; tongue equal to 3d
    abdominal ring.
    8° Fore wings truncated at the tips.
        ‖ Angulated and denticulated.
    † *Tongue nearly as long as the body.*
Thyreus, Group I. Abdomen with apical tuft; head broad and obtuse;
    eyes small.
                ‖† Angulated in the middle.
                ‖‖ Abdomen with apical tuft.
Enyo.—Antennæ subfusiform, short, with angular hook; tongue equal to
    3d abdominal ring.
Perigonia.—Antennæ slender, setaceous; tongue rather short; head ob-
    tuse; palpi short.
            ‖‖‖ Abdomen without apical tuft, or scarcely tufted.
Calliomma, Group V.—Fore wings with silvery lines (*in note*).
Smerinthus (*in part*).—Tongue about as long as palpi.
Deidamia.—Tongue two-thirds as long as body; body fusiform.
                ‖‖‖ Not angulated in the middle.
Perigonia.—Group II.
        4° Fore wings denticulated.
            † Without silvery streaks.
Smerinthus.—Tongue about as long as palpi or almost obsolete.
            †† With silvery streaks and angulated.
Calliomma.—Group IV.

SESIA Fabr.

The body is pilose, stout and more or less oval or elliptical in
outline, in the ♀, but more elongate and slender in the male. The
thorax is advanced and tapers anteriorly to the head, which is
small, but free and prominent, with the front broad; the eyes are
very small; the palpi exceed the front and terminate acutely in a
pencil of hairs; the tongue when unrolled extends to about the 5th
abdominal segment; the antennæ are longer than the thorax, slender at the base, clavate and furnished with a minute seta at the
extremity. The abdomen is tufted at the extremity, and about

twice as long as the thorax. The wings are transparent in the
middle; the fore wings with the hind margin entire, obliquely
convex, and the inner margin concave beyond the inner angle;
hind wings somewhat acuminated at the tip and short. The legs
are slender and the hind tibiæ with four moderate spurs. *Male*,
antennæ finely ciliferous. *Female*, nearly simple.

The *larva* tapers anteriorly, has a dorsal and stigmatical stripe,
and a short recurved horn. It undergoes its transformation in an
imperfect cocoon on the surface of the ground.

1. **S. diffinis** *Boisd.*   *S. fusiformis* Abbot & Smith.   Figured in Sm. Abb.
I, pl. 43.   Boisd. sp. gen. pl. 15.

Head and thorax pale yellowish-green; palpi blackish terminally
and pale yellow beneath; breast pale yellow, with blackish hairs
beneath the legs, *and all the legs black*. The abdomen adjoining
the thorax has the thoracic hue; the third and fourth segments,
sometimes only the fourth, are black or blackish along the sides of
the four first anterior rings, and the fifth and sixth are pale brownish mixed with yellow. The ventral surface is *bluish-black*, with
pale yellow patches corresponding to the tufts on the margins of
the fifth and sixth segments. The lateral anal tufts are black, the
central pale brown. The disk of the anterior wings is transparent
almost to the base, with a narrow, dark brownish border along the
costa, a patch on the inner margin tapering to the inner angle, and
a narrow terminal border in the ♂, but rather broad and dentate
between the nervules in the ♀, of the same hue; a ferruginous
patch on the apical interspace, sometimes followed by a smaller
one in the succeeding, in the ♀. The posterior wings are bordered
with dark brown on the costa near the base, broadly on the inner
margin, the terminal margin in the ♂ very narrow, and moderate
in the ♀.

There are variations in color; sometimes the thorax is fawn-
colored above and somewhat ochreous beneath; the abdomen fawn-
colored at the base, the two middle segments dark reddish-brown,
the ends and sides blackish and the two terminal rings fawn-color
above, with two large yellow patches on the ventral surface which
is black.

Mature Larva. Pale pea-green, reddish beneath, with a dark green dorsal line, a pale yellow stigmated stripe.

Canada; Northern and Southern United States.

CLEMENS.

2. **S. thysbe** Fab. *S. pelasgus* Cramer. *S. cimbiciformis* Steph. I. *S. ruficaudis* Kirby, Walker. Figured in Cram. pl. 248.[1]

Head, palpi above and thorax dark green, mixed with brown; palpi on the sides blackish, beneath of a light cream color; the breast and legs, except the tibiæ of the hind pair, which are brownish, have the same yellowish-white hue. The eyes are slightly encircled with white scales. The two basal segments of the abdomen above are yellowish-brown; the two middle are deep ferruginous or reddish-brown, and the terminal have small ferruginous patches in the middle, the rest of each being a dull, yellowish-brown. The ventral surface is bright ferruginous, with three or four small yellowish tufts between the segments on the line separating the dorsal and ventral surfaces; the lateral anal tufts are black, the central reddish-brown and ferruginous beneath. The anterior wings, the basilar space, especially towards the inner margin, is ferruginous, and olivaceous toward the base of costa; the disk is divided by a dark brown line; the costa is dark brown and the broad terminal band has the same hue, with a ferruginous patch in the apical interspace. The posterior wings have a bright ferru-

[1] *S. ruficaudis* of Kirby.—"Body yellow olive, underneath pale yellow. Antennæ black; fore wings reddish-brown, hyaline in the disk, with the hyaline part half divided towards the base, with a costal bar; covered with yellow olive hairs at the base underneath the costa, the posterior margin and the nervures are dark ferruginous; there is also a yellow stripe on the inner side of the base; hind wings hyaline in the disk, base externally and costa yellow; internally the base is ferruginous; underneath the dark part of the wings is ferruginous and the base pale yellow; two first segments of the abdomen yellow olive, two next black, the rest ferruginous, with pale yellow lateral spots."

S. ruficaudis of Walker.—Fawn-color. Head whitish about the antennæ and beneath, with a brown band in front. Pectus testaceous. Abdomen deep red, fawn-color at the base, with testaceous spots along each side; hind borders of segments black; apical tuft red, with some black hairs on each side. Wings limpid, deep red at the base, and with broad deep red borders. Fore wings deep red at the tips and with a blackish discal streak. Length of the body 9—12 lines; of the wings 18—24 lines.

ginous, broad inner border, a moderately broad duller terminal band, the nervules in which are blackish.

Mass.; Canada; New York; New Jersey; Pennsylvania.

CLEMENS.

3. S. fusicaudis *Walker*, C. B. M. p. 63.

Light fawn-color. Head beneath and pectus whitish testaceous. Palpi prominent. Abdomen deep red; basal part light fawn-color, bordered with white; a row of testaceous spots along each side. Apical tuft blackish-brown; middle third part deep red. Wings limpid, deep red towards the base, and with very broad deep red borders. Fore wings fawn-color at the base, deep red towards the tips. Length of the body 13—14 lines; of the wings 25—27 lines.

Georgia.

CLEMENS.

MACROGLOSSA Ochs.

The body is rather short, stout, and thick. The head is large, broad, and prominent; the antennæ with a minute seta and about as long as the thorax; the eyes small and rather flattened; the palpi thick and very broad beneath. The thorax is thick, well advanced in front of the anterior wings, and tapering but little to the head. The abdomen is flattened beneath, tufted at the tip, and about twice as long as the thorax. The legs rather slender; hind tibia with four moderate spurs. The wings are opaque; the length of the anterior is somewhat less than that of the entire body, rather more than twice longer than broad across the inner angle, and sometimes thrice; hind margin entire, very obliquely convex, and the inner margin concave above the inner angle.

Larva.—The European type of this genus has a small head and a caudal horn on the 11th ring, and tapers anteriorly; the skin is finely shagreened and is marked by a stigmatal and substigmatal line. It undergoes its transformation on the surface of the ground in an imperfect cocoon. The pupa is elongated, with the head-case very salient.

§ Antennæ subclavate; tongue as long as the body.(?)

1. *M.* flavofasciata *Walker*, C. B. M. p. 67.

Testaceous blackish beneath. Head with a blackish band in front. Abdomen blackish, with a testaceous tuft on each side at the tip. Wings blackish-brown, with a broad oblique luteous band. Fore wings somewhat luteous beneath toward the base. Length of the body 8 lines, of the wings 20 lines.

Albany River; Hudson's Bay.

CLEMENS.

§§ Antennæ slender, scarcely clavato-prismatic; tongue about one-half as long as the body; not pilose.

2. *M.* tantalus *Linn.* *Sphinx* Ixion Linn. *Sphinx* zonata Drury. *Sphinx* titan Cram. *M.* annulosum Swainson, pl. 132, f. 1. *M.* balteata? Kirtland. Figured in Cram. pl. 68. Drury, pl. 28. Swains. pl. 132.

Head, palpi above and thorax brown, but in the recent specimens tinged with deep olivaceous; palpi beneath whitish, and the breast and legs ash-colored or brownish-white in the male; in the female these parts have a more or less brownish hue. Abdomen brown or olivaceous brown, with the third segment banded above with white; beneath brown, the upper segments in the males having an ashy hue, with four white points on the lateral, hind portions of the ventral segments; lateral terminal tufts blackish-brown, the central testaceous. Anterior wings ferruginous-brown with a double row of whitish spots extending from the discal spot to the inner margin; discal spot blackish surrounded with white; with three white subterminal spots approximated in the subcosto-inferior, medio-superior, and central interspaces, and a terminal dull brownish band. Posterior wings blackish, costal border pale brownish-white, fringe above white and short.

South America; Mexico; West Indies; Texas; Ohio.

CLEMENS.

3. *M.* œnotus *Cramer* II, 80, pl. 148. *M.* fasciatum Swainson II, pl. 132.

Head, palpi and thorax obscure brown; palpi beneath and breast white. Thorax with a blackish patch above the base of the wings. Abdomen brown inclining to blackish posteriorly, with two orange-colored spots on each side of the second and third segments, a blackish-brown patch on the fourth and a pale yellow spot on the fifth, with a lateral tuft beneath it of the same hue. Terminal tufts dark brown. Abdomen beneath brown. Anterior wings obscure purplish-brown, varied with dark brown; a dark brown

patch at the base, with a line and band of the same hue crossing
the disk; a dark brown demi-line extending from the origin of the
medio-central nervule to the inner margin, and a line crossing the
base of the nervules furcate above, with a subterminal band also
furcate toward costa, of the same hue; a white spot in medio-
central interspace. Posterior wings blackish-brown, with a central pale orange-yellow band.

South America; Mexico.

CLEMENS.

4. M. aegra Pory. Cent. de Lep. de l'Ile de Cuba, Decade II, with figure.
Walker, C. B. M. p. 89.

Cinereous brown, testaceous beneath. Thorax with two ferruginous stripes on the sides, margined between with hoary. Abdomen ferruginous, tessellated with hoary, with two pale yellow spots
on sides of middle segments, and two rows of white spots beneath.
Wings rather broad, with a white line near the base and varied
with ferruginous bands, especially a broad interrupted one near
external border; a white spot toward the end of medio-central
interspace. Posterior wings blackish, with an oblique, central,
pale yellow band, and the exterior border margined with the same
hue.

South America; West Indies.

CLEMENS.

PROSERPINUS Hübner.

The body is rather long, slender and tapering. The head is
free, prominent and moderately large; the front broad, oval and
obtuse; the antennae subclavate, longer than the thorax, with a
minute terminal setigerous hook; the eyes minute and shaded with
hairs from above; the palpi are pilose, rather thick and equal to
the front; the tongue as long as the body. The thorax is advanced
and tapers in front to the head, and is smooth. The abdomen is
twice longer than the thorax, cylindrico-conical, with an abundant
terminal tuft in both sexes; very sparingly tufted on the sides.
The legs are slender and smooth, the posterior tibia with four
moderate spurs. The anterior wings are as long as the body without the the tuft; three times longer than wide across the inner

angle; tip acuminated, the hind margin entire and obliquely convex from the tip to the medio-posterior interspace, where it is angularly indented; the inner angle salient and the inner margin concave above it. Hind wings rather short, obtusely rounded at the tip and the hind margin entire. *Male.*—Antennæ finely cilliferous. *Female.*—Antennæ simple.

Larva tapers anteriorly from the third segment, body cylindrical, head small and the eleventh segment with a caudal horn. It is ornamented with rows of vascular round spots, and irregularly elliptical subdorsal and lateral spots. The metamorphosis takes place on the surface of the ground in an imperfect cocoon.

Duponchel describes the larva of this genus, under the name *Pterogon*, as having a lenticular tubercle instead of a caudal horn. The outline of the wings, as given in the diagnosis, differs also from the European type, in which the fore wings are slightly hooked, with two or three distinct dentations. Abbot and Smith represent the wings of *P. gaurae* with these peculiarities, but my specimens do not correspond.

CLEMENS.

1. **P. gaurae** *Abbot & Smith.* Figured in Sm. Abb.'1 pl. 31.

Antennæ brownish-green and whitish at the tips. Palpi beneath, white; the tips of the palpi, head and thorax greenish, with a greenish white line on the sides of the head and thorax. Abdomen greenish or brownish-green, and the apical tuft the same, with the hind portions of the segments paler. Anterior wings pale yellowish-green, with deep green shades; the basal portion pale yellowish-green, with a broad, median dark green band, the anterior edge of which is concave, and its posterior, beginning on the costa at the origin of the post-apical vein, inclines to about the middle of the inner margin. The median band is bordered posteriorly with pale yellowish-green, and the terminal border is shaded with bright greenish, deepened toward the costa and tip, with a pale streak at the tip and a pale line from the costa to subcostoinferior vein. The discal spot is dark green on a somewhat lighter ground. Posterior wings orange, with a narrow terminal blackish

band; sometimes the orange color is deepened to reddish above
the terminal band; fringes paler.

Texas.

Mature larva, head green. Body dark green; with the first
segment banded with white containing four black points; with a
row of vascular black dots, and two rows of semi-elliptical black
dorsal patches edged with white, and a row of lateral somewhat
oval patches, blackish and crimson behind, also edged with white;
a row of subdorsal dots between this and dorsal patches; prolegs
crimson, with crimson patches on the sides of the tenth and eleventh segments. Horn yellow at the base and black terminally.
(*Abbot & Smith*.)

Pupation.—The larva enters the pupa state in Georgia about
the latter part of May, and appears as a perfect insect during the
middle of June. (*Abbot & Smith.*) In Texas there are two broods
of perfect insects, according to the dates of capture, one during
the entire month of April and another in July.

Food-plants.— *Gaura biennis.*

Georgia; Texas.

CLEMENS.

2. **P. clarkiæ** *Boisd.* Ann. Soc. Ent. Fr. X, 2me ser. p. 318.

The appearance (port) and size of *P. gauræ* of Georgia. Superior wings of an olive-green, with the extremity faintly tinted with a
little greenish-white and a transverse whitish, nearly straight band.
Inferior wings of the same yellow color as the European (Œnothera
with a little black border. The four wings of an olivaceous green
beneath, with a whitish band on the inferior wings. Body olivaceous.

California.

CLEMENS.

UNZELA WALKER.

Body fusiform, rather stout. Proboscis moderately long. Palpi
as usual. Antennæ rather slender. Abdomen much less than
twice the length of the thorax. Legs moderately stout; hind
tibiæ with four rather short spurs. Wings moderately broad, not
long. Fore wings straight along the costa, rounded at the tips;
exterior border slightly oblique, forming a very obtuse and much

rounded angle in the middle, with a slight excavation in front and
two shorter and more distinct indentations behind. Hind wings
rounded at the tips; exterior border slightly denticulated, somewhat excavated toward the interior angle.

1. U. ? jæpyx *Cramer*, I, 137, pl. 87, f. C. Walker, C. B. M. 162.

Ferruginous brown. Abdomen purplish with testaceous bands
on the hind portions of the segments and a white transverse band
at the base of the abdomen. Thorax dark brown. Anterior
wings dark brown from the base to the middle, with two somewhat
roseate, separated, oblique lines crossing the middle of the disk
and a round spot at the base margined with roseate; terminal portion of the wing greenish with a black spot on costa at about the
origin of the post-apical nervule, another beneath the tip on posterior margin and a larger one at the inner angle, containing a
small blue spot. Posterior wings dark brown, somewhat roseate
on inner margin, with a black terminal line.

THYREUS Swainson.

The body is obtuse, broad and stout. The head is moderate,
the front obtuse, nearly vertical, uniformly broad and thickly
haired; the palpi very hairy, rather short and obtuse; the eyes
small : the tongue, when unrolled, reaches to about the fourth or
fifth abdominal segment; the antennæ taper at the extremity and
end in a long hook without seta. The abdomen is broad and
rather short, a little more than once and a half longer than the
thorax, semi-oval in outline, tufted with terminal and lateral tufts.
The thorax is thick, hairy, globosely rounded in front with metathoracic sub-tufts. The wings are narrow and rather long. The
anterior is length equal to that of the body, truncate at the tips,
angulated opposite the medio-superior nervule, excavated from
post-apical to superior and doubly excavated from the superior
nervule to the inner angle. Posterior wings, tip rounded, hind
border denticulated and the inner angle somewhat salient and
acute. *Male.*—Antennæ elliferous. *Female.*—Almost cylindrical
and simple.

Larva, the head is moderate and the body is naked, wrinkled transversely, and tapers gently from the fourth segment, and is furnished with a lenticular tubercle on the eleventh segment instead of a caudal horn. Its position when disturbed is not sphinx-like; it shortens the anterior rings and throws the head from side to side, making at the same time a crepitating noise. When on the ground, its motions under irritation are often violent. It prepares for pupation on or near the surface of the ground.

1. **T. abbotii** *Swainson*. Figured in Swains. pl. 60.

Head, palpi, and thorax, dull chocolate-brown; prothorax with a blackish-brown transverse line, and two others crossing the middle of thorax; abdomen dark-brown, lighter in the middle; terminal tufts dull yellowish-brown in the male, and female with a large light-yellowish central pencil, and small lateral brownish ones. Anterior wings dull-chocolate brown, lighter beyond the middle, even yellowish-brown in the female; an oblique dark-brown line passing behind and near to the minute dark-brown discal dot; several dark-brown lines on the inner margin, and curving obliquely to the lower part of medio-superior nervule, and proceeding thence to the costa as sharply-angulated lines, and long dark-brown dashes projecting upward in the interspaces; apical interspace grayish-brown, with a dark-brown sagittal dash on the margin, and others in the three following marginal interspaces: fringes dark-brown. Posterior wings sulphureous, with a dark-brown terminal band, breaking into a series of short lines in a slightly roseate space above anal angle; fringes brown.

Mature Larva. *Male*, head dark-brown, banded broadly at sides with light-green, and with a narrow central, short greenish band. Body reddish-brown, with numerous patches of light-green, oval on the dorsum, and irregularly triangular on the sides, with an interrupted, subdorsal chocolate-colored line. The lenticular tubercle on the eleventh segment is black, encircled at the base by a yellowish line and a blackish cordate patch; anal shield pale green terminally, and brown above, crossed by irregular brown lines. *Female*, body uniform reddish-brown, or blackish-brown, immaculate; with interrupted dark-brown subdorsal lines, and numerous transverse striae. Length about three inches. Swainson's figure of this larva is erroneous.

Pupation. The transformation of the larva takes place in a superficial cell. The pupa is dark-brown; the head case broad and rounded; the tongue case not apparent, and level with the breast. There is, I think, but one annual brood. The larva reaches its development about the latter part of July, and enters the pupa state to appear in the following spring as an imago.

Food-plants. The indigenous and cultivated grape-vines, and *Ampelopsis quinquefolia.*

New York; Pennsylvania; Georgia; Massachusetts; Ohio.
CLEMENS.

GROUP II.

The thorax tapers on the sides markedly to the head, which is small and prominent. The front is smooth and narrow, the eyes very small, the palpi acutely haired at the extremity, and exceeding the front, the antennæ with a moderate hook without seta; the tongue extends to about the third abdominal ring. The tip of the anterior wings is rounded, the hind margin circularly excavated beneath tip, and above the inner angle, the middle being convex. Posterior wings, hind margin scarcely denticulated, and slightly excavated near the inner angle.

1. T. nausica. Figured in Cram. pl. 107. Walker, C. B. M. p. 99.

The head, palpi, and thorax, dull ferruginous brown, palpi beneath and breast rufescent; a yellowish-white streak on the sides of the head and thorax, and a transverse ferruginous line on the hind part of metathorax. The abdomen a dark chestnut-brown, with the hind margins of fourth, or fourth and fifth segments, pale yellow, with three or four bright ferruginous, lateral spots, beginning on the fourth segment, and two very small pure white tufts on the segments adjacent to the triple apical tuft, which is deep chestnut; beneath rufescent, with three lateral white dots on the hind portions of the posterior segments. Anterior wings brown, with a purplish hue, costa grayish-brown; an indistinct dark-brown band and line in basilar space; a dark chestnut, broad median band, divided above the medio-superior nervule to the costa, and containing a lighter colored discal spot; a grayish-brown subterminal line interrupted by the central nervules, and edged anteriorly with brownish, with a long, dark-chestnut patch interposed in the medio-central interspace; a ferruginous patch at the base of apical interspace, with two dark-brown adjacent patches in the succeeding interspaces. The fringes dark-brown in the middle, pale yellow in the excavations, and bordered by dark-brown. Posterior wings bright-red, with a dark-brown terminal band; fringes from the tip to the centre brownish, and thence to anal angle pale yellow.

Canada; Massachusetts; New York; Pennsylvania; New Hampshire.

CLEMENS.

DIDAMIA CLEMENS.

Size moderate. The body is quite fusiform, and the inclination of the sides of the thorax to the head is quite abrupt. The head is small, almost impacted on thorax, but not depressed; it is compressed laterally and subtufted, the front vertical and moderately broad; the eyes small, and somewhat sunken; the labial palpi short and pilose; the tongue extends to the end of the third abdominal segment; the antennae taper at the end, slightly hooked, and without the terminal seta. The thorax is thick, and well clothed with long decumbent hair. The abdomen is long, rather slender and oblanceolate, with an exceedingly slight terminal tuft. The legs are rather slender, and moderately long, the anterior tibiae tufted at the sides; the posterior with two very short middle and terminal spurs concealed in the tibial hairs. The anterior wings are about equal in length to that of the body, and are a little more than twice longer than broad across the inner angle; the hind margin angulated in the middle, truncate at the tip, excavated from the post-apical nervule to the medio-superior, and angularly indented above the inner angle; the inner margin concave. The posterior wings are rounded at the tips, hind margin slightly denticulated. The submedian nerve is simple at the base. *Male*, antennae ciliferous. *Female*, antennae simple.

1. **D. inscripta.** *Pterogon? inscriptum* Harris. *Thyreus? inscriptus* Walker,
C. B. M. p. 308.

The head is grayish-brown, and whitish above the eyes; palpi
reddish-brown. Thorax grayish-brown, with a double, curved
white line crossing the prothorax, edged behind with brown, and
a brown sagittal dorsal patch, with a short whitish line across the
middle of tegulæ. The abdomen is dull brown above, with three
or four subdorsal, deep brown spots; beneath, a dull ferruginous
brown, with the hind portions of the segments of a lead color.
Anterior wings ash-gray at the base, in the middle, and towards
the tip, banded with brown; a short, obscure, brown costal streak
at the base; two brownish bands before the middle, united on the
inner margin by blackish-brown; discal spot ash-gray; a reddish-
brown band, arising on the costa at the origin of post-apical nervule, convex in the middle, and retreating thence to the inner margin; the subcosto-inferior and medio-superior interspaces pale-
brown, as well as the portions of the succeeding interspaces
exterior to the band, and marked by reddish-brown innules; a deep
brown apical patch encircled with white; and a subterminal one
similarly colored in post-apical interspace. Posterior wings dull
reddish-brown, with a dusky terminal border tapering to the inner
angle; fringes white.[*]

Indiana; Long Island; New York; Pennsylvania.

CLEMENS.

PERIGONIA Boisd.

Body broad, slightly fusiform. Head obtuse. Proboscis rather
short. Palpi very short and stout. Antennæ setaceous, slender,
a little longer than the thorax. Abdomen much longer than the
thorax. Legs rather slender; hind tibiæ with four moderately long
spurs. Wings opaque, moderately broad. Fore wings hardly convex
toward the tip of the costa, rather oblique along the exterior border,
which is slightly angular in the middle and behind the tip; fourth
inferior vein (posterior) remote from the others. Hind wings very
slightly denticulate along the exterior border. *Male*, antennæ
minutely serrate setose. *Female*, antennæ simple. (*Walker.*)

---

[*] *Paperism.*—Larva transformed in a cell. Tongue-case of pupa, an
elevated short ridge; at its cephalic end a short central spine, and on
each of the eye-cases, a spinous tubercle. Color, very dark brown.

1. P. Isaca *Fabr. Perigonia stula Boisd.*

Ferruginous brown, somewhat cinereous and testaceous beneath.
Fore wings with three grayish, diffuse bands, and transverse blackish lines. Posterior wings with variable luteous bands, and streaks
along the interior angle.

Mexico; South America; West Indies.

CLEMENS.

GROUP II.

Fore wings not angular in the middle of the exterior border, and
are excavated behind the sub-apical angle. The exterior border
of hind wings convex, and not denticulated. Head conical.

2. P. subhamata *Walkr, p. 102.*

Brown (male) or ferruginous (female), paler beneath. Wings
with oblique, undulating, pale ferruginous bands, which are most
numerous on the fore wings, and the latter have a discal dot of the
same hue, and a cinereous sub-apical spot. Length of the body
13—15 lines; of the wings 28—32.

Mexico and South America.

CLEMENS.

GROUP III.

Head rounded in front, not conical. Fore wings somewhat
rounded at the tips, slightly convex and not excavated along the
exterior border, which is very oblique.

3. P. glaucescens *Walkr, p. 103.*

Brown, testaceous beneath. Head with a white streak on each
side behind the eye. Antennæ tawny, very slender, not longer
than thorax. Thorax slightly tinged with green. Abdomen ferruginous, slightly glaucous; fifth segment whitish; sixth and seventh segment with a whitish tuft on each side; apical tuft blackish.
Wings reddish beneath. Fore wings with a glaucous tinge, and
with two oblique bands, the one dark brown and interior, the other
ferruginous and exterior, and bordered with dark brown on its
outer side. Hind wings dark brown, with a luteous spot by the
interior angle, and a white speck near the base of the interior border. Length of the body 12 lines; of the wings 28 lines.

CLEMENS.

4. P. undata *Walker*, p. 103.

Brown. Head beneath and pectus somewhat hoary. Thorax with a short, broad, posterior, dark brown stripe on each side. (Abdomen and hind wings wanting.) Fore wings cinereous, shining, with a white dot and a black discal streak at the base, with a white streak traversing the black discal spot, and with two broad, irregular, ferruginous bands, which are bordered, and the exterior one interlined with black. Length of the body 9(?) lines, of the wings 18 lines.

Jamaica. •

CLEMENS.

ENTO Hübn.

The body is long, thick and fusiform. The head large, prominent and broad; front nearly vertical, flattened, and smooth; eyes large and salient; palpi smooth, stout and closely applied to the front; tongue extends to the end of the third abdominal segment; antennæ rather short, not as long as the thorax, minutely ciliferous, fusiform and ending in an angular hook with seta. The thorax is crested in front, long from the base of anterior wings to the head, and rounded in front. The abdomen is oblanceolate, slightly more than twice longer than the thorax, and sparingly tufted at the apex. The legs are slender, the anterior and middle smooth, the posterior with femora and tibiæ pilose, with two short and two moderately long spurs. The anterior wings are very oblique, length much less than that of the body, and somewhat more than twice longer than broad across the inner angle; the posterior margin truncate at the tip, obtusely angulated opposite medio-superior nervule, excavated from post-apical to superior, and thence excavated and slightly wavy to the inner angle, which is hooked; inner margin deeply concave. Posterior wings rounded at tip; hind margin doubly excavated from the medio-central to inner angle, which is acute.

Larva. Head rather small; body tapers anteriorly, and is wrinkled transversely, with a long, straight, caudal horn. *Pupa*

11

rather slender; head case obtuse; tongue case not apparent. The larval transformation is subterranean.

1. **E. lugubris** *Drury*, I, 61, pl. 28, f. 2. Abbot & Smith, I, pl. 69, pl. 20. *Thyreus lugubris* Harris. *Sphinx fegeus* Cramer.

Head, palpi, thorax and abdomen brown, with an obscure purplish or reddish hue; palpi beneath pale reddish brown. Abdomen with an indistinct double row of dorsal, dark brownish spots; beneath as well as the thorax, pale rufescent brown, with a tawny line in the middle of ventral surface; yellow lateral dots on the hind portions of the segments, and a small lateral, pale yellow pencil of hairs at the base of the first segment. Anterior wings brown, with a rufous tinge in the middle and toward the tip; an oblique, pale brown line before discal spot, beginning near the origin of subcosto-inferior vein, margined on each side with darker brown; discal spot blackish, edged with pale brown; a broad, dark brown, subterminal shade, extending from post-apical vein to the hind margin, and bordered anteriorly by a curved, pale brown line; a ferruginous brown spot in apical interspace, with its basal portion and the middle of the next interspace pale reddish hue and three indistinct brownish lines crossing the nervules. Posterior wings brownish, deepening toward terminal margin, with indistinct lines above the inner angle, and dark brown marginal spots at the inner angle and on the ends of medio-posterior and central veins.

Mature Larva. Head dark green, with a yellow frontal band. Body pale green, with vascular dark green dashes, and a dark green subdorsal line bordered beneath with whitish; also short, lateral, pale yellow bands; horn dark green; stigmata reddish. (*Abbot & Smith.*)

Food-plants. Ampelopsis hederacea. (Virginian creeper.)

Georgia, West Indies, Mexico, South America.

CLEMENS.

2. **E. camertus** *Cramer.*

Mouse color; abdomen with a double row of blackish brown spots. Fore wings with a testaceous discal spot; with a blackish oblique interior line margined with hoary, and a large diffuse exterior blackish patch, with a sub-apical ferruginous spot and a blackish submarginal line edged with white. Posterior wings with dark oblique undulating lines and blackish marginal spots.

Mr. Walker's description does not correspond well to Cramer's

figure, pl. 595, which is dark brown, and the anterior wings lateous brown, with a broad dark brown median band tinged obscure
purple. The following individual from Brazil, in the collection of
the Academy of Natural Sciences, of Philadelphia, appears to me
to come nearer to Cramer's figure.

Dark brown; thorax distinctly crested. Abdomen dark brown
with a double row of spots on the sides, and a small lateral rufous
terminal tuft and a long central one dark brown, with a cinereous
ring just above them; beneath, a dull cinereous central line edged
with dark brown. Anterior wings dark brown varied with obscure
purplish; basal portion dark brown, with a dark median patch
chiefly beneath the median nerve and intersected by paler lines on
the inner margin, and bordered behind and above broadly with a
paler hue; a dark brown patch extending from the origin of subcosto-inferior vein to the tip of post-apical, excavated on each side
beneath, and extended as a line to the margin at the end of medio-
posterior vein, inclosing a lighter patch in the middle on the costa,
and at the tip mixed with rufous; a testaceous curved marginal
patch. Posterior wings dark brown, paler towards the hind margin. *Posterior legs hairy to the end of the tarsi.*

Mexico, West Indies, South America.

                                                            CLEMENS.

DEILEPHILA Ochs.

The body is usually stout and thick. The head moderate,
prominent; the front smooth, rather broad and long, semi-elliptical; the eyes moderate; the tips of the palpi level with the
front; the tongue as long or nearly as long as the body; the
antennae clavate, terminating suddenly in a minute hook and seta.
The thorax is thick, and tapers abruptly to the head. The abdomen is thick and cylindrico-conical, about twice as long as the
thorax, and tapers rather suddenly at the terminal segments,
having at the tip a more or less distinct, short pencil of hairs.
The wings are entire; the length of the anterior equal to that of
the body, rather more than twice and a half longer than broad,
the hind margin obliquely convex; the inner somewhat concave
above the interior angle. The posterior wings are rounded at the
tip and the hind border slightly excised near the interior angle.

The legs are long and the two exterior spurs of the hind tibiæ very short, the two interior long. *Male.* Antennæ cilfferous. *Female.* Antennæ simple.

Larva. Head small and elongate-globose, caudal horn rather short, nearly straight and rough. Without oblique bands, but with a row of subdorsal spots on each side. The anterior segments are much attenuated, and are capable of being withdrawn or shortened or much extended; none of the segments dilated. When disturbed, they fall from their food-plants, shorten the anterior segments and bend the head toward the terminal extremity. In repose, the anterior rings are merely shortened. The larval transformation takes place in a superficial cell excavated from the surface.

1. D. lineata *Fabr. Sphinx deucus* Cramer. Figured in Cram. pl. 123. Sm. Abb. pl. 39.

Palpi white beneath. Head and thorax dark olive with a white line on each side extending to the end of tegulæ, where it is edged above slightly with blackish; two white dorsal lines and one on superior edge of the tegulæ. Abdomen greenish-brown, tinged with reddish on the sides: a white dorsal line with a double row of black dorsal spots and lateral alternate white and black spots. Anterior wings deep olivaceous, with a straight buff-colored band from the inner margin of the base to the tip, and its basal and apical portion whitish; the olivaceous portions of the wing are bordered and shaded with black; a white discal line and all the nervules white except the apical; a marginal bluish-gray space and fringes dark buff. Posterior wings black, costa brownish, with a rose-colored central band, including a white spot near the inner margin and a marginal reddish line; fingers white.

Mature Larva. Head dark green, dotted with yellow dots. Body uniform yellowish-green; a dorsal patch on first segment darker and dotted with yellowish-white; a subdorsal row of elliptical spots, connected by an intermediate faint yellow line; the spots consist of two curved short black lines, inclosing superiorly an orange-yellow dash, and inferiorly the yellow subdorsal line. The stigmata are reddish-orange, black margined on a yellow base.

Shield and terminal prolegs roughened with white dots; caudal horn yellowish-orange toward extremity, and rough. Feet yellow. Length about three inches.

Pupation. The pupa is light brown, the head-case compressed laterally and prominent; tongue-case not apparent. In Pennsylvania the first brood of larvæ reach maturity about the latter part of July, and appear as imago about the middle of August. There is doubtless a second brood, but I have never seen them during autumn. In Texas, the first brood of perfect insects occurs from about March 10th to April, and there is another about the middle of July.

Food-plants. *Portulacca olsracca* (purslane) and the turnip. I have, however, fed the larva in confinement on the leaves of the *apple-tree.*

Mexico; West Indies; Canada; entire United States; the western plains to the Rocky Mountains, and California.

CLEMENS.

2. D. chamænerii *Harris. D. intermedia* Kirby, Faun. Bor. Am. p. 302. Figured in Agass. Lake Sup. pl. 7.

Palpi beneath whitish. Head and thorax olive-brown, with a white line on the sides, margined on the tegulæ above with blackish. Abdomen brownish-olive, with small dorsal white spots, with two lateral alternate white and black patches on the sides at the base, fourth segment immaculate and fifth and sixth white spotted. Beneath, the thorax is testaceous and the abdomen dark brownish with white lines on the hind portions of the segments. Anterior wings deep olivaceous, with a buff-colored band from the inner margin of the base to the tip, sinuous posteriorly and irregularly indented before; a black patch at the base and one at the origin of disco-central nervule, with an indistinct whitish discal spot. The terminal margin dull brown and black, margined before; fringes brown. Posterior wings black, with a rose-colored central band, deepening toward the inner margin and including a white spot; the hind margin is indistinctly marked with reddish, and the fringes white.

Mature Larva. Green, somewhat bronzed, dull red beneath; with nine round cream-colored spots encircled with black on each side, and a dull red caudal horn. *Harris.*

Food-plants.   Epilobium angustifolium (great willow-herb).
Canada—United States.

CLEMENS.

[Dr. Clemens regards this species, on the authority of Walker,
as identical with *D. galii* of Europe.—J. G. M.]

PERGESA WALKER.

Body moderately stout. Proboscis long. Palpi as usual.
Antennæ slender, rather longer than the thorax. Abdomen oblanceolate, more than twice the length of the thorax. Legs long,
slender; hind tibiæ with four long spurs. Wings rather long,
moderately broad, very slightly denticulated along the exterior
border. Fore wings hardly convex in front, acuminated; exterior
border rather oblique, very slightly undulating, its fore part very
slightly concave. Hind wings rounded at the tips.

In the European *Porcellus* the head is free, short, obtuse, and
broad. The body short and stout. The palpi project beyond the
clypeus; the eyes are quite small but salient; the tongue scarcely
as long as the body; the antennæ rather clavato-prismatic, with a
short hook and seta. The thorax is short and obtuse in front.
The length of the anterior wings about equal to that of the body,
and are a little more than twice longer than broad across the inner
angle. The hind margin of the posterior wings is slightly wavy.
The individuals were formerly part of the genus Chœrocampa.

Larva. Smooth, anterior segments retractile, with ocellated
spots on the sides of the fifth and sixth, and *without a caudal horn.*

1. P. thoratus *Hübner*, Exot. Schmett. f. 525.

Green, testaceous beneath. Head and thorax with a white line
on each side. Thorax and abdomen somewhat golden-hued on the
sides. Abdomen rufo-fawn color, with green along the dorsum
toward the base, and a row of yellow dorsal dots. Anterior wings
with interrupted whitish bands curving from inner margin to costa,
and tinged with rufescent; with brown lines at base of the nervules,
and a greenish patch over the middle of median nervules, with a
pale brown apical patch above it; marginal space rufo-brownish.

Posterior wings blackish at base, with a broad, median, luteous band, and a brown marginal band.

Var. β. Male. Fawn-color; anterior wings gray and brown mixed, with a silvery discal spot. Posterior luteous, interrupted with ferruginous along exterior margin.

Var. γ. Female. Anterior wings rufescent, banded with gray and brown mixed.

Mexico; West Indies.

CLEMENS.

DARAPSA WALKER.

Size moderate, body rather slender and tapering. The head is small, narrow, and almost sessile; the vertex subtufted, front vertical; the eyes small; the palpi short and rather slender; the tongue about *one-half* as long as the body; the antennæ a little longer than the thorax, slender and almost filiform, with a long hook without seta. The thorax is rather short, almost globosely rounded in front. The abdomen oblanceolate, thrice as long as the thorax. The anterior wings are as long, or somewhat longer than the body, twice and a half longer than broad across the interior angle; the tips acuminated, the hind margin excavated rather deeply from beneath the tip to medio-superior vein, and thence convex to the interior angle; the inner margin deeply concave above interior angle. Posterior wings with tips rather pointed and hind margin somewhat excavated before the interior angle. *Male.* Antennæ prismatic and cilliferous. *Female.* Antennæ slender and almost filiform.

Larva. Head very small and elongate-globose. The body tapers suddenly to the head, from the anterior portion of the third segment, which, together with the fourth and fifth, are much swollen. The anterior rings are retractile within the fourth. A caudal horn on the eleventh segment. It is ornamented with a subdorsal line and irregularly oval lateral patches. The larval transformation takes place on the surface of the ground in an imperfect cocoon, consisting of vegetable debris nailed by silken threads.

During the day the larva conceals itself beneath a leaf, stretching out the body on the midrib.

1. **D. chœrilus** *Cramer*, II, 91, pl. 247. *Sphinx azalea* Abbot & Smith. *Chœrocampa chœrilus* Harris. Figured in Sm. Abb. I, pl. 27.

Head, palpi and thorax ferruginous brown, with a spot at the base of anterior wings, and tegulæ behind tipped with brownish-gray. The abdomen fawn color, with the hairs of the hind portions of segments whitish. The anterior wings are fawn color, tinged with reddish from the base to the middle; a broad ferruginous brown shade crossing the nervules, and composed of three lines having between them two rows of indistinct, fawn-colored spots; marginal space grayish at the tip, and obscure purplish toward the interior angle; a ferruginous brown line across the middle of the disk, and another, rather indistinct, near the base. Posterior wings ferruginous, deepening to a ferruginous brown narrow border, on the excavated portion of the hind margin; fringes whitish.

Mature Larva. Head green, with a narrow, central, brownish line. Body green, deepening on the sides and whitish on the dorsal region, with six oblique, irregularly oval, lateral whitish bands; stigmatic orange; horn bluish-green. A variety is represented by Abbot & Smith in which the green color is replaced by pale ferruginous and the bands the same; horn dark brown. (*Abbot & Smith.*)

Pupation. Undergoes the larval transformation in an imperfect cocoon on the surface of the ground. Abbot & Smith represent that in Georgia the first brood enter the pupa state about the middle of May and appear as perfect insects during the middle of June; another became a pupa September 15th and an imago on April 16th following.

Food-plants. *Azalea nudiflora.* (Abbot.)

Georgia; Massachusetts; Connecticut; New York.

CLEMENS.

2. **D. myron** *Cramer*, III, 91, pl. 247. *Sphinx pampinatris* Abbot & Smith, I. *Otus cnotus* Hübn. *Chœrocampa pampinatris* Harris. Figured in Cram. pl. 247.

Head, palpi, prothorax and tegulæ dull dark green; a whitish patch at the base of anterior wings, the tegulæ beneath edged with whitish and a triangular whitish line on dorsum of thorax. Abdomen dull greenish. Anterior wings dull pale green from the base to about the middle, with discal spot and a moderate band across the middle of disk dark green; a broad dark green shade across the nervules, divided in the middle by an indistinct lighter line, and deeply excavated posteriorly, where there is a dull greenish cinereous marginal patch. Posterior wings ferruginous, with a dusky green patch near the interior angle.

Mature Larva. Head pale green, with an indistinct, lateral yellowish line. Body pale green, inclining to yellowish and deepening in color beneath the subdorsal lines, which are greenish-white, and curve on the sides from first segment to base of caudal horn, with seven irregularly oval, greenish-white patches inclosing orange-colored stigmata and bordered beneath with dark green. There are several small crimson vascular spots on the dorsum. Sometimes reddish-brown, and the subdorsal lines and lateral patches tinged with reddish. Horn reddish-brown, with black tubercles.

Pupation. Transforms on the surface in an imperfect cocoon. *Pupa* intense with the wing-cases brown and dotted with lines of black dots; eye-cases black; abdomen with the incisions between the segments black and round black lateral spots. The fall brood of larvæ enter the pupa state from the latter part of August to the middle of September.

Pennsylvania; Massachusetts; Georgia; New York.

CLEMENS.

3. D. pholus *Cramer.* Figured in Cram. I, pl. 67.

Imago. Fore wings blackish-brown, with a gray triangular discal patch; a fawn-colored patch on the median nervules and a red submarginal line, with two marginal brown bands, one arising on the costa at about the origin of post-apical vein, and the other near the margin itself. Posterior wings red, paler towards the base.

West Indies.

Tongue scarcely one-half as long as the body. Anterior wings excavated behind the tip.

CLEMENS.

4. D. versicolor. *Chærocampa versicolor* Harris, p. 303, 8.

Pale green varied with olive and whitish. A white line on each side of the head, a dorsal white line, tinged with reddish and extending from the head to the tip of the abdomen; prothorax and edges of tegulæ above and beneath margined by white lines. A metathoracic spot on each side, and the middle of the abdominal segments tinged with dark buff, with the hind margins of the segments dark green from the base to the middle and thence to the tip reddish-brown. Anterior wings slightly ferruginous at the base, with narrow olive-green and dull white bands, the latter slightly tinged with ferruginous, arising at the inner margin of the base and curving to the costa from the basal portion of the disk to beyond the origin of post-apical nervule; an oblique whitish apical line with an olive-green patch adjoining and before it, in the post-apical interspace, and the line edged with olive-green in the apical interspace. Hind wings rust colored, with an indistinct, greenish terminal margin. *Under surface* of anterior wings pale sulphureous; toward the base pale ferruginous, with an olive streak along the costa from the base widening toward the tip. Posterior wings olive-green powdered with white at the base.

Massachusetts.

CLEMENS.

GROUP II.

Proboscis moderately long. Wings long, rather narrow. Fore wings slightly acuminated, convex in front toward the tips; exterior border slightly convex, very oblique; interior border slightly concave from half its length to the interior angle. Hind wings hardly acuminated.

5. D. rhodocera *Walker*, p. 184.

Fawn color, paler beneath. Sides of the head and of the thorax whitish. Antennæ rose color above. Abdomen paler than the thorax, with a blackish spot on each side at the base. Fore wings with a cinereous tinge, with an oblique exterior line, with a brownish discal dot, and with two diffuse ferruginous spots, one in front, the other behind; cilæ ferruginous. Hind wings blackish, whitish about the interior angle; cilæ mostly whitish. Length of the body 17 lines; of the wings 86 lines.

St. Domingo.

CLEMENS.

CHŒROCAMPA Dup.

The body in this group is slender, long and tapering. The thorax is smooth, rather short, advanced in front of the base of the anterior wings and tapers on the sides to the head. The head is rather large, prominent and moderately broad; the front smooth, conical and broad; the eyes moderate and salient; the palpi ascending to a level with the front; the tongue extends to the end of the abdomen; the antennæ are short, but longer than the thorax, clavato-prismatic, terminating suddenly in a short hook and seta. The abdomen is quite long, more than twice longer than thorax, oblanceolate, tapering very much to the tip, which is acute. The wings are narrow, the anterior three times longer than broad across the inner angle, and the length much less than that of the body; the tip very acute, the hind border very oblique and nearly straight or slightly excavated beneath the tip. Hind wings, the tip somewhat acuminated, hind border very oblique, and interior angle well marked. The legs are long and slender, the anterior tibiæ hairy, and hind tibiæ with four moderate spurs.

Larva. The head is small and the anterior segments very much attenuated from the third, and retractile; third and fourth swollen, with a large subdorsal ocellus on the latter, followed by a row of ocelli, similar; eleventh segment with a caudal horn (*Abbot & Smith*). The larval transformation takes place in an imperfect cocoon spun on the surface of the ground.

1. **C. teres** *Drury. Therstra teres* Hübner. *Chærocampa teres. Metopsilus teres* Duncan. Figured in Drury, I, pl. 28, Nat. Libr. vol. xxxvi. pl. 5.

Palpi pale ferruginous beneath; head and thorax brownish olive, with a lateral whitish line inclining to roseate on the sides; tegulæ slightly edged above with ferruginous. Abdomen with a broad, dorsal, dusky band, containing five indistinct darker lines and lateral band on each side, rusty yellow. Anterior wings greenish brown, slightly glaucous toward the base, with a minute discal spot, dark brown, and with numerous oblique, alternate, dark brown and yellowish lines, extending from near the base and middle of inner margin to the tip, with a straight, brownish, submarginal line. Posterior wings black, with a row of subterminal yellow spots.

Mature Larva. Light green, with a large, subdorsal, crimson ocellus on the fourth segment, containing a blue ring and edged with black and white rings, with six others smaller and similar, placed on a white subdorsal line, which begins on the second segment and extends to the crimson caudal horn. The dorsum is dashed with brown points; stigmata yellow dotted with black points above and below. (*Abbot & Smith.*)

S. America; Mexico; W. Indies; Southern States; Illinois; Ohio; Texas.

CLEMENS.

2. C. chiron *Drury,* I, 50, pl. 26. *Sphinx nechus* Cramer. *Thyreus nechus* Hübner.

Green, sometimes ferruginous fawn-color; a line on the sides of head and thorax and body beneath whitish testaceous. Fore wings dark green; with a pale yellow streak at the base of the inner margin, and an irregular, oblique brown, or testaceous band traversing the lower part of the nervules, enlarging toward the inner margin and extended above on it as a line. Posterior wings black, with a band of pale yellow spots. Abdomen green, slightly gilded on the sides, with a double row of black dorsal dots. Legs very long.

S. America; Mexico; West Indies.

CLEMENS.

§§ *Fore wings very acute and somewhat hooked.*

3. C. falco *Walker,* p. 132.

Fawn-colored, whitish testaceous beneath. Head and thorax with a whitish stripe along each side. Disk of the thorax cinereous brown. Abdomen brown, with a fawn-colored stripe along each side, and a double dorsal whitish line. Fore wings with blackish speckles, with a blackish discal dot and with several blackish, slightly oblique, posterior lines, slightly hooked and more acute at the tips than in the other species of this genus. Hind wings with two blackish stripes; exterior border slightly emarginate. Length of the body 15—19 lines; of the wings 30—40 lines.

Mexico.

CLEMENS.

§ *Hind border of anterior wings nearly straight.*

4. C. procne *Clemens.*

Head and thorax dull brown (if not faded), with a broad whitish stripe on the sides, extended to the lower edge of tegulæ. Abdomen brownish testaceous, with faint dark brown dorsal marks in atoms. Anterior wings rather pale brownish, punctated with dark atoms and with obscure dark brown lines extending from the base to the tip; discal spot dark brown and small. Posterior wings uniform blackish-brown. Under surface of the wings brownish, somewhat tinged with rufous, and with two rows of brown spots in the middle of the posterior.

California.

CLEMENS.

§§ *Fore wings very acute and somewhat hooked.*

5. C. drancus *Cramer,* II, 55, pl. 132. *Xylophanes drancus* Hübner.

Blackish-brown; sides of head and thorax with a white line, and a white dorsal line extending from the head to tip of the abdomen; tegulæ edged above with reddish-brown, beneath with white. The base of abdomen with two reddish-brown bands. Anterior wings blackish-brown, discal spot black; several lines extending from the inner margin to the tip, three of which in the middle of the wing arise from a blackish patch on the inner margin placed on a fawn-colored ground and a single black, subterminal line placed between two dark brown lines. Posterior wings uniform dark brown. (*Cramer's figure.*)

West Indies.

CLEMENS.

§§ *Anterior wings acute and somewhat hooked.*

The following species resembles in some respects Mr. Walker's *crotonis*, but I think it is not the same.

6. C. nitidula *Clemens.*

Head and thorax with a rufo-whitish line on each side. Head and anterior portion of tegulæ dark brown, tinged with greenish, with the disk brown. Abdomen brown, paler on the sides, with a double row of dorsal dark brown dots and a black patch on the sides at the base. Anterior wings dull greenish-brown, with a

large black spot on the inner margin near the base; discal spot
small and black; *a single brownish line from the inner margin to
the tip;* with two rows of indistinct brownish dots on the nervules
before it, and a more decided row behind, near the posterior margin. Posterior wings black, with a row of central, pale testaceous,
triangular spots, and a narrow terminal border of the same hue.

Under surface of the wings, disk of the anterior blackish, and
thence rufescent brown; posterior wings rufescent brown, with two
lines of dark brown dots.

Mexico.

CLEMENS.

§ *Hind border of anterior wings nearly straight.*

7. C. vermnia *Clemens.*

Head and thorax brown. Abdomen brown, with black rings
between the basal segments and a black spot on each side of the
basal segment. Anterior wings brown with a faint wavy line and
narrow band across the middle of the disk, somewhat deeper brown;
discal spot small and dark brown; an oblique brownish band extending from the origin of subcosto-inferior vein toward the inner
angle, followed by two short lines of the same hue; a blackish-
brown, irregular, wavy line, extending from the costa near the origin of the post-apical vein to inner margin above the angle, and
another of the same hue joining it by an angle on the disco-central
vein, and extended very irregularly from near the tip to the inner
angle, and shaded toward the hind margin of the wing with dark
brownish. Posterior wings dark brown, dull greenish at the base,
with an irregular, central, luteous band, tinged with orange.

Mexico.

CLEMENS.

AMBULYX Boisd.

Body rather slender or hardly stout. Head prominent, conical,
obtuse. Proboscis long. Antennæ minutely serrated. Abdomen
long, oblanceolate. Legs slender; hind tibiæ with four very long
spurs. Wings narrow and very long, especially in the typical species, *A. strigilis.* Fore wings slightly curved in front toward the
tips, which are acuminated; exterior border excavated by the tip,
nearly straight, and extremely oblique from thence to the interior

angle, where the interior border forms an inward curve; second inferior vein (*superior*) nearly twice farther from the third (*posterior*) than from the first (*disco-central*); third more than twice farther from the fourth than from the second. Hind wings somewhat emarginate along the exterior border. *Walker.*

1. **A. strigilis** *Linn.* *Manl.* I, 658.

Pale fawn color, luteous beneath. Head with a furcate ferruginous brown spot between the antennæ and thorax, with two large lateral patches of the same hue. Antennæ white. Abdomen with a brown dorsal line and oblique brown lateral streaks, edged with testaceous. Anterior wings fawn color, with separated, oblique ferruginous streaks on the costa, four abbreviated, wavy blackish-brown lines crossing the middle of the nervules, a few spots on the inner margin, and a marginal black line (bordered above in Cramer's figure with blue). Posterior wings luteous or pale orange, with three angulated brownish lines and brownish terminal margin.
South America; West Indies.
CLEMENS.

2. **A. gnaamma** *Stoll, Cramer,* V, 157, pl. 35, f. 3.

Fawn color; head with a band between the antennæ, the tegulæ and a band at the base of the abdomen dark greenish-brown. The antennæ white. Abdomen fawn-color, with brown or ferruginous dorsal spots. Anterior wings brown, with a glaucous hue; a rectangular spot on the base of the inner margin dark greenish-brown, edged with testaceous; a small round one at the base, two in the disk, another near the tip on costa, one in medio-posterior interspace and a small one above the interior angle of the same hue and edged with greenish. Posterior roseate, with three angulated blackish-brown bands sometimes dilated and somewhat connected.
South America; Mexico; West Indies.
CLEMENS.

PHILAMPELUS HARRIS.

The body is large and thick. The head rather large, free and prominent, with the front long, smooth, conical and rather broad; the eyes large or moderate; the palpi ascending and pressed closely to the front; the tongue as long as the body; the antennæ long, exceeding the thorax, slender and tapering at the extremity into an ample hook with seta. The thorax is thick, moderately advanced in front of the base of anterior wings and rounded. The abdomen large, thick, cylindrico-conical and acute at the tip, more than twice the length of the thorax. The wings are moderately long; the length of the anterior somewhat more than that of the body, and about twice and a half longer than broad across the inner angle; the hind border entire, slightly excavated from the tip to medio-superior vein, and thence convex to interior angle, or very oblique and almost straight, with the inner margin deeply concave. The posterior are somewhat acuminated at the tips and the hind margin slightly excavated before the inner angle. The legs are long but strong, and the hind tibiæ with two short and two long spurs. *Male.*—Antennæ cilliferous. *Female.*—Antennæ simple.

Larva. The head is small and globose, and the segments of the body anterior to the fourth much attenuated to the head; these and the head are capable of being retracted within the fourth, which is much swollen. Instead of a caudal horn on the eleventh segment there is a shining lenticular tubercle, and the body at this part is rounded, and descends very abruptly to the anal shield. It is ornamented with irregularly oval, stigmatal patches and a faint subdorsal line.

In repose, or when disturbed, the anterior rings are retracted within the fourth, causing it to appear truncated and bulbous anteriorly, and at the same time the body is thrown into a sphinx-like posture. The larval transformation is subterranean.

The pupa is cylindrico-conical; head-case distinct and prominent; tongue-case not apparent.

§ *Eyes moderate. Fore wings undulating.*

1. **P. satellitia** *Linn.* Ins. II, 146, 36. *Sphinx lycaon* Cramer. A. *Pholus lycaon* Hübner. *Daphnis pandorus* Hübner. Figured in Drury, 1, pl. 20.

Head, tips of the palpi and middle of thorax pale green, basal articles of palpi brownish; tegulæ dark olive, forming a triangular patch; a dorsal line on prothorax and two metathoracic patches dark olive. Abdomen pale brownish tinged with green, with a dark olive patch on dorsum at the base and a lateral blackish patch on each side. Anterior wings pale green, with deep olive shades; a sub-median nearly square patch on inner margin, with a shade extending to the base, a patch above the interior angle, with a spot in the medio-posterior interspace separated from it by the nervule, and almost bordered by a faint line which is angulated on the medio-central, a sub-apical patch and a broad disco-median shade, all deep olive; a double blackish discal spot. The medio-central and posterior nervules and the space between the patches on the inner margin, tinged with roseate; a few olive-colored dashes across the disk and two lines of the same hue, sometimes faint, crossing the nervules from the hind portion of sub-median patch. Posterior wings pale green, with a large, round black patch toward the middle of inner margin, and a broad sub-terminal black demi-band terminating in blackish lines and a row of spots toward inner margin, on a roseate ground.

Mature Larva. Head green. Body pale green on dorsum, deepening on the sides, with minute dark green rings, which become on the dorsum dark green dots. Six short, irregularly oval patches on the sides, margined with a black line, inclosing the stigmata, which are bordered with pale crimson. The lenticular tubercle black and contained in a yellow patch bordered with black.

Food-plants. Indigenous and exotic grape-vines and *Ampelopsis.*

South America; Mexico; West Indies; United States.

CLEMENS.

2. P. achemon *Drury. Sphinx crantor* Cramer. *Pholus crantor* Hübner. Figured in Drury, II, pl. 20.

The head, tips of the palpi and disk of the thorax fawn-color with a grayish hue; basal articles of the palpi dark reddish-brown; tegulæ deep ferruginous brown, forming a triangular patch margined with whitish. The abdomen pale reddish-brown with a cupreous lustre, and the hind portions of the segments tipped with white. Anterior wings dusky fawn-color, sometimes pale-fawn color, with a ferruginous brown dot at the base, a square sub-median patch on the inner margin, a patch above the inner angle divided toward its apex by the medio-posterior nervule and a large sub-apical patch, ferruginous brown ; from the sub-median patch two faint brown lines are thrown off posteriorly to the costa, the most exterior being angulated on the medio-central vein, and from its anterior portion are two other diverging brownish lines, with a faint line above them near the base of the wing ; the disco-median shade is rather faint and brownish.   The posterior wings are pink, deepening in intensity toward the middle of inner margin, and above the interior angle is a reddish-brown streak ; a subterminal row of ferruginous brown spots from the middle to the interior angle, and a broad dusky terminal band.   The under surface of the wings is roseate.

Young Larva.   Green, with yellow lateral stripes edged with black, and a long, recurved, slender reddish horn.

Mature Larva.   Head reddish-brown.   Body pale reddish-brown on the dorsum, with a darker vascular line, and pale-reddish subdorsal line on each side, and the general color deepened laterally.   Six lateral, short, irregularly-oval white patches bordered with black, containing the stigmata.   The anterior rings are dotted with blackish.   The lenticular tubercle is black, and contained in a brown patch edged with adjacent black and white lines.

Food-plants.   The grape.

New York ; Pennsylvania.

CLEMENS.

3. P. typhon A?rg, Neue Schmett. pl. 3, t. 1.

Cinereous, reddish beneath.   Palpi red.   Thorax with two dark-brown abbreviated stripes.   Abdomen with dark-brown bands, red on the sides.   Anterior wings glaucescent and testaceous mixed, with several blackish-brown sub-trigonate patches.   Posterior wings red, with a denticulated black band varied with glaucescent, with the exterior margin brown, and the cilia white.

Closely allied to *P. acheron.*

Mexico.

CLEMENS.

4. P. labrusca. — *Madam Merian, Ins. Sur. pl. 34.*

Green, testaceous beneath.   The abdomen sometimes, and rarely the whole body and anterior wings, testaceous.   Abdomen with a black spot at base on each side, beneath and at sides spotted with white. Anterior wings green, with two darker bands margined with white, one of which crosses the disk, and meets an oblique one on the inner margin. Posterior wings blue, with a black angulated band edged interiorly with red, and a sub-terminal black band breaking into black lines toward interior angle on a reddish ground; terminal margin testaceous.

S. America; Mexico; West Indies.

CLEMENS.

§§ Eyes large. Fore wings nearly straight.

5. P. vitis Linn. Merian, Ins. Surin. Philampelus hornbeckiana Harris, p. 299, note. (?) Figured in Drury, I, pl. 28. Cram. pl. 267. Sm. Abb. I, pl. 46.

Head and thorax grayish tinged with greenish. Thorax with a dorsal dark olive line, tegulæ dark olive, edged with white. Abdomen dark olive, paler on the sides, with a pale dorsal line; a blackish patch on the sides at base, and a dark olive dorsal patch at the base. Anterior wings deep olive, with a double whitish transverse line toward the base, a pale buff-colored band (in faded specimens white or whitish), extending from the base to the tip, crossed by another of the same hue from the lower third of inner margin to costa, beyond the origin of post-apical vein, and containing posteriorly a dark olive line; the nervules of the median nerve pale flesh color, or whitish, when faded; discal spot double and black. Posterior wings pale-green, pale-yellowish along the costa, with a central black line terminating in a black patch, near the middle of inner margin, and a sub-terminal black band tapering to interior angle; the inner margin rose-red, inclosing above the interior angle a whitish spot; terminal margin cinereous.

Mature Larva. Head reddish, with two black lines in front. Body flesh color mixed with yellow, and with short, transverse black lines. The lateral semi-oval bands are yellowish-white, edged with black. Body beneath the stigmata is greenish, with black lines and stigmatal blackish dots on the three anterior segments; lenticular tubercle blackish with dorsal black lines. *Abbot and Smith.*

Pupation. According to *Abbot and Smith*, it enters the pupa state August 14th, and appears as an imago September 7th. Another became a pupa September 29th, and appeared July 18th following.

Food-plants. Jussiæa erecta (decurrens)?

S. America; Mexico; West Indies; Southern U. States.

CLEMENS.

The following species approaches *P. vitis* so nearly in its ornamentation, that I am much disposed to place it as a variety. But for the present, perhaps, it is better to represent it as distinct.

6. P. jussieum *Hübner.* Sphinx fasciatus Sulz.

Pale buff, tinged with reddish. Head and thorax with a dorsal olivaceous green line. Thorax with two broad olivaceous green stripes. Abdomen with two black spots at the base on the sides, and two dorsal olivaceous green stripes. Anterior wings olivaceous green, costa reddish-brown, with a discal mark, a transverse streak near the base, with two connected bands along the middle, and the veins pale buff; exterior margin reddish-brown. Posterior wings pale-green, rosy along the inner margin and exterior half of terminal border, with two black spots near the middle of inner margin, and a sub-terminal black band ending in short lines, and a dusky patch at inner angle.

S. America; West Indies; Mexico.

CLEMENS.

PACHYLIA Walker.

The body is large and thick. The head is large, free and prominent; the front smooth, long, broad and elliptical: the palpi ascend to its level; the eyes are large or very large, salient and hemispherical; the tongue strong and thick, but when unrolled extends only to about the third abdominal segment; the antennæ are about as long as the thorax, with a long hook, compressed laterally. The thorax is smooth, immaculate, thick and cylindrical, well advanced in front of the base of anterior wings, and tapering on the sides to the head. The abdomen is large, nearly cylindrical or oblanceolate, generally rather more than twice the length of the thorax. The wings are about equal in length to that of the body, or somewhat longer, and about twice and a half longer than broad across the inner angle; the hind margin of the anterior entire,

almost obliquely convex, but slightly excavated near the tip and
above inner angle, or more decidedly excavated and rounded in
the middle, with the tip acuminated; the inner margin deeply concave above inner angle. The posterior wings are suddenly curved
above the tip, and the hind margin slightly denticulated, or almost
straight. The legs are strong and moderately long, the posterior
tibiæ having two very short external and two long internal spurs.
Male, antennæ prismatic and well ciliated.   *Female*, antennæ
simple.

The specimens of the perfect insects of this genus in my
possession most undoubtedly show strong affinities to that of *Philampelus*. I am at a loss to conceive wherein Mr. Walker can
perceive any affinity to *Macroglossa*, unless it be in *resumens* and
inconspicua. These species I have never seen, and the generic
diagnosis given above cannot, therefore, include any structural
peculiarities which may characterize them.

1. P. ficus *Merian*, pl. 33.

Pale luteous brown, varied with dark brown. Head, thorax
and palpi dark brown. Abdomen pale brown on the sides and
between the basal segments; the two basal segments banded with
blackish-brown. Anterior wings luteous-brown, with dark brown
markings; a patch at the base and a single line nearly joining it,
three wavy lines crossing the middle of the disk, a conspicuous
discal spot, a patch near the origins of medio-superior and central
nervules, a small patch on the inner margin beneath it, consisting
of three short lines, the most posterior of which is the continuation of the upper of three separated, denticulated lines curving
across the middle of the nervules. A semi-oval, apical, pale,
greenish-brown patch, pointed on the tip and bordered beneath by
a dark brown triangular shade, the tip of which reaches the medio-
central nervule on the margin. Posterior wing pale luteous, with
a broad central black band and a broad marginal band of the same
hue tapering towards the inner margin, with an indistinct line of
the same hue above it; inner angle covered with oliveous scales.

Mexico; West Indies; S. America.

CLEMENS.

I think the following is the male of *P. ficus*. Should the conjecture be wrong, I would propose for it the name *P. ignwea*.

Bright pure brown somewhat tinged with ferruginous. Thorax with a purplish reflection. Palpi beneath white. Abdomen paler than thorax, pale yellowish on the sides and between the basal rings. Anterior wings with a paler rather broad stripe near the base containing a dark brown line and indistinct lines of the same hue crossing the middle of the disk; discal spot conspicuous, ferruginous brown, with three separated, denticulated, rather indistinct dark brown lines crossing the middle of the nervules; a semi-oval, apical, pale lutecus patch, bordered beneath by a triangular ferruginous brown shade, with a pale purplish patch at the interior angle. Posterior wings ochraceous, with a central black band not extended to costa, and a marginal blackish band tapering toward the inner angle, bordered above by a series of black dots on the nervules continued as a line toward the inner margin; the inner angle covered above with olveous scales. The wings beneath ochraceous, both anterior and posterior with a row of sub-terminal blackish dots and the latter with a faint central dark line.

From the Smithsonian Institution. Capt. Pope's collection in Texas.

                                             CLEMENS.

Anterior wings rather narrower than the preceding, more pointed at the tip and the hind border more distinctly sinuous.

2. P. inornata *Clemens. Sphinx ficus Cramer.*

Dull greenish-brown or dark reddish-brown. Abdomen rusty brown on the sides. Anterior wings in the ♀ with an olivaceous hue toward the base and somewhat purplish posteriorly. A pale brownish nearly semi-circular patch on the middle of costa extending beneath to the medio-superior and behind to the post-apical nervule; this is bordered by a broad umber brown band, which sends off to the middle of inner margin a short band of the same hue. There is only one distinct denticulated umber-brown line crossing the middle of the nervules, and is sometimes obsolete. A semi-oval, apical pale brown patch, tinged with dull greenish and bordered beneath by a triangular umber-brown shade. Posterior wings nearly concolorous umber-brown, or deep reddish-brown, deepened to an obscure marginal blackish band. The inner angle curved above with niveous scales.

Honduras and Brazil.

CLEMENS.

3. P. resumens *Walker*, p. 190.

Fawn color, paler beneath. Abdomen with a black band on each of the three basal segments; the four following segments with two black spots on each. Fore wings with several undulating transverse brown lines, with a brown discal dot, and with three brown dots near the interior angle; exterior border cinereous. Hind wings paler, with a black discal stripe, which is connected at the tip of the wings with a black marginal stripe. Length of the body 17—18 lines; of the wings 40—42 lines.

Var. β.—Cinereous brown. Hind wings dull pale fawn color, greenish toward the base.

S. America; Honduras; West Indies.

CLEMENS.

4. P. inconspicua *Walker*, p. 190.

Fawn-color, testaceous beneath. Abdomen with two rows of black dots, and toward the base with two interrupted black bands. Fore wings with three undulating oblique blackish lines, a little darker between the third line and the exterior border. Hind wings a little paler than the fore wings, with two dark brown stripes, the one discal, the other marginal; a brown undulating line between them. Length of the body 21 lines; of the wings 48 lines.

Jamaica.

CLEMENS.

MACROSILA Walker.

Size large, or very large, body thick and long. The head is large, free and advanced; the front very broad and long, tapering but little to the tips of the palpi; the eyes very large and salient; the antennæ clavato-prismatic, with a short hook and seta; the palpi very thick and ascending, and pressed against the front; the tongue twice or nearly twice the length of the body, or about *one-third* longer. The thorax is large and thick, somewhat rounded in front, and tapering moderately on the sides to the head.   The abdomen is tapering and cylindrico-conical,· at least twice the length of the thorax.   The wings are long, entire; the anterior rather broad across the inner angle, which is dilated, the hind margin obliquely convex, sometimes slightly wavy, and the interior margin with a long concave excision.   The legs are long and strong, the posterior tibiæ having four very long spurs.

This group is very closely allied to Sphinx by the characters of the perfect insect, and I have hesitated much whether to restrict its limits as described by Mr. Walker, or to extend it.   The general agreement in the length of the tongue of such individuals here included as I have been able to examine, has led me to take the latter course.   This will doubtless be regarded as objectionable, but I think a greater degree of clearness of arrangement is attained.   Under any arrangement portions of the two groups as compared to each other do not present well-marked or decided differences, and if some of the members of the present one strongly recall that of Sphinx, one member of the latter reproduces in its structure most of the peculiarities of Macrosila.

CLEMENS.

1. M. collaris *Walker*, p. 201.

Hoary, white beneath.   Thorax dark-brown in front, and with some brown marks on each side.   Abdomen with a much interrupted, middle, brown line, and with transverse, brown spots along each side.   Wings brown beneath.   Fore wings with a white discal dot, and with oblique, undulating, transverse, brown lines; also with a testaceous streak which extends from the base to an oblique, undulating, testaceous band.   Hind wings brown, whitish at the base and along the anterior border, and with two hoary bands. Length of the body 18—19 lines; of the wings 42—46 lines.

West Indies.

CLEMENS.

2. M. hasdrubal *Cramer*, pl. 246, f. P.

Somewhat hoary.   Head and thorax grayish-brown, the latter with a black streak on the upper edge of tegulæ.   Abdomen with indistinct, lateral, blackish patches, edged before with whitish.

Fore wings with a black streak at the base, with two wavy, black lines crossing the posterior part of the disk; black marks on the costa, and marginal black spots and a series of dots on the median nervures. Hind wings blackish-brown, white along the interior angle, with brown undulating lines. *Male.*—The anterior wings principally brown. (Smaller than the ♀ with the black lines more distinct. The under surface in both ash-gray, with two brown bands.—*Poey.*)

Mature Larva. Gen. Char.—Head large. Body nearly uniformly cylindrical, with anal shield, broad and truncate at the extremity. Caudal horn *extremely long, slender, and membranous.*—Head reddish-brown. Body black, with nine or ten bright yellow, transverse bands on the middle of the segments. The first segment, the prolegs and a spot, whence rises the caudal horn, reddish-brown, dotted with black. (*Poey's fig.*)

Pupation. The larval transformation takes place on the surface, where the pupa is covered simply by the superficial debris. The pupa is represented without the detached tongue-case. (*Poey.*)

Food-plants. The larva feeds on a species of *Plumieria.*

South America and Central; West Indies.

CLEMENS.

I think it doubtful whether Cramer's *M. hydraspus* and *medor* are the same species, but having no specimen of the former, I am unable to determine the question. The general markings of the anterior wings are very similar, but *hydraspus* has *three white spots* on each side of the posterior abdominal segments, besides the three yellow spots on the basal rings. This is a peculiarity neither of the male nor female *medor* of Cramer.

Prof. Poey regards his *M. duponchel* as differing specifically from *medor* of Cramer, and *antaeus* of Drury. His figure, however, does not differ from a specimen in the Acad. Nat. Sciences from Jamaica, nor from a Mexican specimen in my own collection, except that the latter is much larger than either, and the subterminal line in Poey's figure is more distinctly edged with white.

The third article of palpi a small terminal hook; anterior wings
slightly wavy.

3. M. antaeus ——. *Merian, I. 2. Sphinx hydraspus* Cramer, I. A.(?)
Sphinx modor Cramer, I. A. *Sphinx jatrophae* Fabr. 18; Mant. Ins.
II. 94, 21; Ent. Syst. III, 1, 362, 23. Gmel. Syst. Nat. I, 5, 2376,
63. *Cocytius jatrophae* Hübner. *Amphonyx duponchel* Poey.

Palpi blackish-brown, beneath yellowish-white. Head, thorax,
and abdomen, blackish-brown, intermixed with gray atoms; tegulae with a black streak, edged beneath with whitish; abdomen
with a dorsal row of black spots, and three large yellow spots on
each side at the base edged with black, and black spots from the
last to the tip of abdomen. Anterior wings blackish-brown,
sprinkled with grayish scales; a grayish spot at the base, with a
double, angular, black line crossing the middle of disk to the upper
third of inner margin, and two or three serrated lines of the same
hue on the middle of the nervules, and a subterminal black line
curving from the costa, near the origin of post-apical to near the
lower angle, and edged anteriorly rather broadly with brownish-gray;
black circlets on the ends of posterior nervules, and a broad black
apical streak; black streaks in medio-central and posterior interspaces, and two discal whitish spots, one near the sub-median
nerve, and the other near the sub-costal. Posterior wings transparent in the middle, with black nervules and a broad, terminal,
black border, with indistinct, grayish spots above inner angle; yellow at the base. Beneath, the body is whitish, with abdominal
blackish spots; and the wings yellowish toward the base.

South America; Mexico; West Indies.

CLEMENS.

4. M. cluentius *Cramer*, I, 124, pl. 78, f. B.

Grayish-black, testaceous beneath; antennae testaceous. Thorax fawn-color on the sides. Abdomen black, with a broad cinereous stripe, and several luteous spots on the sides. Anterior
wings with numerous black spots or marks on the costa and inner
margin, and semicircular black marks on the ends of the nervules,
with a subapical streak and stripe behind, fawo-color. Posterior
wings black, with an interrupted median stripe, and the interior
margin luteous.

South America; West Indies.

CLEMENS.

5. **M. rustica** Cram. IV, 21, pl. 301. *Acherontia chionanthi* Hübner. Figured in Sals. pl. 20. Cram. pl. 301. Sm. Abb. pl. 34.

Head and ends of palpi blackish-brown, with a short white dash on the vertex, and white spots at the base of the antennæ; palpi beneath white. Thorax blackish with white spots on the disk, and tegulæ at the base of anterior wings. Abdomen blackish-brown, with a narrow blackish dorsal line, and three round orange-yellow spots margined with black on each side, and two rows of dorsal white spots. The under surface of the thorax and abdomen is white. Anterior wings blackish-brown, or ferruginous brown, when faded, mottled with white; a few white spots at the base; the middle of disk crossed by two black lines and a brown one, which is margined on both sides with white, with serrated black lines traversing the nervules, margined broadly behind with brownish-white; discal spot white, an irregular sub-terminal blackish line, with white marginal spots and a short, oblique, apical streak, edged above with white; cilia white spotted. Posterior wings blackish, costa and disk yellowish, with a white spot near the base, and one above the inner angle crossed by black lines.

Mature Larva. Head and body dark-green, the latter becoming yellowish on the dorsum and sides, with faint greenish lines; thoracic rings with wavy, reddish dorsal lines. Seven oblique lateral blue bands edged with purple, and beneath this a white band colored yellowish on its lower part. Horn yellow, with reddish tubercles. (*Abbot & Smith.*)

Pupation. Enters the ground to transform. Pupa dark reddish-brown, with long detached tongue-case applied to the breast by its point. It becomes a pupa in Georgia in July.

Food-plants. The fringe tree.

S. America; Mexico; West Indies; Texas; Georgia; Virginia.

CLEMENS.

6. **M. instita** *Clemens.*

Head and palpi blackish-brown. Thorax concolorous, rather rusty brown, with a small metathoracic black tuft. Abdomen black, with dispersed bluish scales along the dorsum, with the basal segment banded with brown, and three large orange yellow spots on the sides of the basal segments; beneath and between

these spots are short white marks. The legs and under surface of
thorax blackish-gray, and whitish in the middle. Anterior wings
are brown in the greater part, separated by an exceedingly irregular outline from a black costal portion covered with dispersed pale-
blue scales, and which is dilated from the costa into an angular
basal, a large nearly square median, and an apical irregularly-oval
patch; the brown portion has two broad dilations toward the
costa, both extending to the sub-costal nerve. The median black
patch contains a small white discal dot, and is edged beneath and
behind by pale-brownish. The post-apical nervule and sub-costo
inferior are pale-colored, and toward the termination of medio-
central and posterior nervules are four small black spots, two on
either side of each. The fringes are brown, broadly spotted with
black. Posterior wings are pale-brownish and grayish from the
middle to the base, with a large black patch at base, two central
black bands, and between the latter and the former an oblique
demi-line; a moderate, black marginal band, having a bluish one
in its centre. The fringes black, spotted with brown.

Honduras.

CLEMENS.

7. M. cingulata *Linn. Sphinx drurei*, Donovan. *Sphinx convolvuli*,
Drury. Figured in Drury, 1, pl. 25. Cram. pl. 228. Sm. Abb. 1,
pl. 32.

Head, ends of palpi and thorax cinereous, with a brownish tinge;
palpi white beneath, prothorax with two blackish lines and tegulæ,
with one central and one on superior margin of the same hue; metathoracic tufts black, with a few bluish scales. Abdomen brownish cinereous, with large rose-colored lateral patches, separated by
black bands. Anterior wings grayish-brown, with a grayish spot
at base, irregular dark-brown angulated lines crossing the disk,
and discal spot whitish, ringed with blackish; three dark-brown
lines curving across the middle of the nervules, and bordered posteriorly with brownish-gray, in which the last line is produced into
points on the nervules; a row of dark-brown circlets on the posterior nervules, with a line of the same hue in post-apical interspace
extended to the tip, and streaks of the same hue in the central and
posterior interspaces. Posterior wings rosy toward the base, with
a central black band and black demi-line above it, a grayish space
posteriorly, and a broad marginal cinereous band, bordered above
with black. Legs cinereous, thorax and abdomen beneath white.

Mature Larva. Head yellowish, with two brownish dashes on each side. Body blackish-brown, with a crimson vascular line containing anteriorly diamond-shaped blackish-brown patches; a crimson sub-dorsal line, and a wavy, yellowish stigmatical line, sending off just above the stigmata short-curved processes. Horn short, brownish, and white on the sides. (*Abbot & Smith*.)

Pupation. Pupa reddish-brown, with a detached cylindrical tongue-case that makes one turn and a half, and is applied to the breast. The larva transformation is subterranean. In Virginia, pupation began October 3d, and the imago appeared May 30th; in Georgia, it began August 20th, and the imago appeared September 11th. (*Abbot & Smith*.)

Food-plants. The sweet potato.

Mexico; West Indies; Texas; Georgia; Virginia; Pennsylvania.

CLEMENS.

6. **M. carolina** *Linn.* Figured in Drury, I, pl. 25.

Head, palpi, and thorax blackish-gray or brownish-gray; thorax grayish on the sides, with short black lines on prothorax, the middle and upper edge of tegulæ; metathoracic tufts black tipped with bluish, followed by two large black patches. Abdomen blackish-gray, with a double row of dorsal white spots, five nearly round orange-yellow spots on each side, with black bands between and intermediate white spots below. Anterior wings cinereous or brownish-gray, with a white spot at base; angulated, somewhat indistinct, blackish lines crossing the middle of the disk to the basal portion of the inner margin; discal dot white, with parallel, rather approximated, black lines crossing the middle of the nervules, an irregular subterminal black line and marginal whitish line; with a black line hooked below in post-apical interspace, and a short one at tip edged above with whitish and blackish shades toward the base of medio-central and posterior interspaces. Posterior wings gray, with a black spot at base, an oblique black demi-line, a double black central band, and a broad marginal blackish-gray band, having a black band in the middle and edged above with black. Under surface of thorax and abdomen gray, with a reddish-brown tinge.

Mature Larva. Downy, wrinkled transversely. Head and body dark green, the latter paler on the dorsum, with whitish dots;

lateral oblique white bands, edged above with bluish and short transverse black lines. Stigmata black, with a yellow point above and below, except the *first* and *last*, which are orange-yellow with a black central point, and all edged with blue. Shield and terminal prolegs edged below with yellow; caudal horn rust-colored terminally. Feet white, ringed with black.

Pupation. The larval transformation takes place in a subterranean cell. The pupa is dark reddish-brown, with a detached, cylindrical, rather thick, tongue-case, not as much arched nor as long as that of *5-maculata*.

Food-plants. The tobacco and tomato plants.

South America; Mexico; West Indies; and generally throughout the United States.

CLEMENS.

9. M. quinquemaculata *Steph. Philogethontius celeus* Hübner. *Sphinx carolina* Donovan, XI, pl. 381.

Head, palpi, and thorax ash-gray; prothorax with three obliquely transverse black lines; tegulæ with a superior and short central black line; the lateral metathoracic tufts bluish in the middle, followed by a large black patch on each side. Abdomen gray, with a slender black dorsal line, with four or five orange-yellow spots on the sides separated by black bands, having white spots above and beneath. Anterior wings gray, varied with brownish in the middle and toward the tip, with oblique black lines on the inner margin beneath median nervure, and three of the same hue arising about the middle of inner margin and curving toward the inner angle within the submedian, and thence continued across the nervules toward the costa; a sub-terminal black and marginal white line, both limited anteriorly by the disco-central nervule; a short apical black line, one in post-apical interspace hooked below, a slender recurrent one in disco-central interspace, a double one in medio-superior and blackish shades in the central and posterior. Posterior wings whitish, with a black spot at base, a black demi-line, two central, separated, serrated black lines, and a broad brownish-gray marginal band, bordered broadly above with black. Under surface of the thorax and abdomen red-ash color.

Mature Larva. Head green, with a black stripe on each side. Body very dark green, with a black patch on first segment, and lateral oblique greenish-yellow bands, each meeting a stigmatal stripe of the same hue, thus forming a series of angular bands on the sides. The stigmata are all black, except the *first* and *last*, which are orange-yellow. The feet and caudal horn black. Body dotted with numerous yellowish-green dots, and marked with short black lines above the lateral bands.

Pupation. The larval transformation is subterranean. The pupa dark reddish-brown, with a cylindrical, long and much-arched, detached tongue-case.

Food-plants. The tomato and potato plants.

Throughout the United States.

CLEMENS.

10. **M. brontes ?** *Sphinx brontes* Drury, II, 52, pl. 29, f. 8.[1] Walker.

"The insect here described differs much from Drury's figure, and may be a distinct species."

Cinereous. Antennæ white. Thorax margined with black, with white on the sides. Abdomen with a median black line, and two angulated black streaks on the sides. Anterior wings with a white discal spot, with transverse angulated interior brown and exterior black lines, with an exterior undefined white band and streak behind, sometimes obsolete, and with exterior black streaks. Hind wings brownish, with three blackish streaks.

United States.

CLEMENS.

11. **M. forestan** *Cramer*, IV, 216, pl. 894.

Tongue *one-third* longer than the body.

Head and tips of palpi brownish gray, the latter beneath gray

---

[1] *Brontes* Drury. "The antennæ are white inwardly, but brown outwardly. The eyes large and black. The head and neck dark brown. Thorax and abdomen gray ; on the hind part of the former are two small black spots, and on each ring two small black streaks. Anterior wings gray, with a white discal spot and a small white cloud next the tips ; having several curved and indented black lines crossing them from the anterior to the posterior edges, some being faint and others very distinct. The fringes are brown, spotted with white. The inferior wings are of a very dark brown, but along the abdominal edges and corners are gray. Fringe like that of the superior wings. *Beneath*, breast white ; abdomen white with four central reddish spots ; anterior wings uniform, dark grayish-brown, with a narrow white streak at the tips. Inferior wings crossed by two faint lines and also of a dark grayish-brown."

From New York.

or whitish. Thorax with a black line in front extended on the sides to tegulæ, where it is bordered below with whitish. Abdomen brownish gray, with a lateral black angulated band on each side, sometimes a black stripe with dull yellowish spots. Anterior wings gray or hoary, more or less varied with green and pale brownish, with a black streak along the base of inner margin, several black angulated lines crossing the disk and angulated black lines crossing the base of the nervules; discal spot grayish, adjacent to which is a greenish-brown median patch; black streaks at the base of medio-central and posterior interspaces and blackish circlets on the ends of posterior nervules, with a black curved subapical line. Posterior wings nearly uniform blackish brown, with a whitish patch above the interior angle crossed by two or three black lines; sometimes with faint blackish transverse bands.

Collection Acad. Nat. Sciences, Philadelphia, and Mr. W. H. Edwards, of Newburg.

South America; Honduras. *

CLEMENS.

SPHINX Linn.

The size is very large, large, or moderate. The body is long, tapering, and cylindrical. The head free and prominent, the front broad, long, and conical. The antennæ prismatic, a little longer than the thorax, with a short hook and seta. The tongue variable. The thorax advanced and tapering on the sides to the head. The abdomen somewhat more than twice longer than the thorax and sometimes nearly thrice. The wings are long and narrow; the length of the anterior exceeding that of the body, and about one-third as long as they are broad across the inner angle, with the tip acuminated, the hind margin entire and usually very obliquely convex, with the inner angle rounded and the inner margin nearly straight or slightly concave. The legs are moderately long and stout, the hind tibiæ with four very long spurs.

Larva. The head is large, semi-oval, and flattened in front. The body is almost uniformly cylindrical, smooth, and obliquely banded on the side, with an arching caudal horn, and the thoracic segments somewhat folded. The tongue-case of the pupa is short and detached, but reposes upon the breast. It is contained in a subterranean cell.

GROUP I.

Size very large. Head large. Eyes large and salient. Tongue nearly twice as long as the body. Palpi thick, ascending and pressed against the front.

1. S. leucophæata *Clemens.*

Head, palpi, and thorax gray; tegulæ with a black line on the superior margin. Abdomen grayish, with a black patch on each side at the base and alternate black and whitish demi-bands. Anterior wings gray, with a small black patch about the middle of the base; an indistinct blackish double line arises at the base of the inner margin and extends to the origin of medio-central vein, and two lines of the same hue cross the lower portion of disk obliquely to about the anns point; a blackish wavy line, curved toward the costa, and bordered beneath with pale gray, arises about the middle of the inner margin and extends to the lower part of disco-central nervule, whence it retreats indistinctly to the costa; a subterminal, angulated, abbreviated black line, bordered irregularly with pale gray. A deep black streak in post-apical interspace continued to the tip, and conspicuous black streaks at the base of medio-central and posterior interspaces; discal spot obscure and whitish; fringes gray. Posterior wings grayish, with a black median band and broad black marginal band, with a space on terminal margin from the middle to the lower angle, gray. Beneath, thorax ash gray, abdomen white, with a few brownish ventral spots.

Texas.

CLEMENS.

GROUP II.

Size large or moderate. The head moderate. The eyes small and but moderately salient. The tongue one-third longer than the body, or about as long or somewhat shorter. The palpi are thick and slightly exceed the front, with which the hairs of the lip are scarcely identified.

13

2. S. cinerea *Hübner.*   *Lethia cherais* Hübner.

Head, palpi and thorax dark gray; tegulæ tipped with whitish
terminally, with a black line on the superior edge and a short indistinct one above and parallel to it, and a metathoracic spot on
each side. Abdomen dark gray, with a black dorsal line and
alternate black and white lateral demi-bands. Anterior wings
dark gray, with a black spot at base, a delicate black discal line;
a black streak at the tip and in post-apical interspace, bordered
above with pale gray, in sub-costo inferior, medio-central and posterior interspaces, and a slender black line in sub-median sulcus;
a sub-terminal blackish line and one near the margin bordered
below with pale gray and both abbreviated toward costa. Posterior wings sordid gray, with a broad median and a terminal black
band.

Massachusetts; Wisconsin; Southern States.

                                        CLEMENS.

3. S. sordida *Hübner.*   *Agrius eremitus* Hübn.   *Sphinx ingens* Walker,
   p. 219 ? [1]

Dark brownish cinereous. Head and thorax paler on the sides,
with a rather broad blackish-brown stripe on the middle of tegulæ,
extending to prothorax and edged above with two lines of the
same hue, and with a brownish dorsal line on the disk of thorax;
metathoracic spots, black. Abdomen with a dorsal black line and
alternate black and whitish demi-bands on the sides; beneath
white, with central blackish spots. Anterior wings brownish cinereous, with a black margined white discal spot, through which
passes a short blackish discal dash, and a smaller one above it;
with blackish-brown costal marks over the disk, the two most
posterior of which reach to the discal spot and are joined or nearly
joined at an angle by two more or less distinct lines from the inner

---

[1] *S. ingens.*—Blackish-gray, paler beneath. Head and thorax paler on
each side. Thorax with two black stripes. Abdomen with interrupted
white and blackish bands. Fore wings slightly tinged with brown, with
black costal marks, and with discal and exterior streaks; two whitish
discal dots, the fore one occasionally obsolete. Hind wings black, with
two whitish undulating bands; cilia white. Length of the body 17—19
lines; of the wings 42—46 lines.
   Mexico.

margin of the base; a broad diffuse blackish-brown apical streak with a costal line above it in apical interspace, and blackish-brown streaks in the interspaces, except the medio-superior; an abbreviated blackish-brown line edged exteriorly with grayish near the terminal margin. Posterior wings yellowish-white, with a black spot at the base, a median and broad marginal band black. Length of the body 16 lines; expansion of the wings 35 lines.

Var. A. a male.—Brownish, with two distinct dark brown lines from the inner margin of base and the middle of the costa, angulated on the disk; over the median nervules the wing is dark brown, with faintly indicated irregular lines crossing the middle of the nervules to the costa and grayish spots exterior to them. Length of body 23 lines; expansion of the wings 54 lines.

Near Jalapa, Mexico.   Acad. Nat. Sciences, Philadelphia.

Var. B. a male.—Blackish cinereous; two distinct black angulated lines crossing the posterior portion of the disk from the inner margin of base; with a band of blackish-brown lines crossing the middle of the nervules.   Length of the body 20 lines; expansion of the wings 47 lines.

Near Jalapa, Mexico.   Acad. Nat. Sciences, Philadelphia.
CLEMENS.

Mr. Walker's *Ingens* is probably one of these varieties of *sordida*. Mexico; Texas; Massachusetts.

4. S. plebeia *Fabr.* Sp. II, 146, 31.

Head and thorax dark gray, with a transverse black line on prothorax continued to the tegulæ, which are pale grayish beneath it. Abdomen gray, with a slender black dorsal line and a black stripe on each side containing whitish spots. Anterior wings gray, with a short black stripe at the base of the inner margin, two very oblique, short black lines from the basal portion of costa to the disk, sometimes uniting with the line from the base on the disk, and two distinct serrated black lines crossing the middle of the nervules from about the origin of post-apical to the lower third of inner margin; black streaks in all the interspaces, that is medio-superior contained in a white streak, and short white streaks on the terminal portion of medio-central and posterior interspaces; discal spot white and the nervules tipped with blackish at their

ends. Posterior wings blackish-brown, grayish towards the base
and the inner border, and sometimes faintly grayish in the middle.
Pennsylvania ; Connecticut ; Massachusetts.

CLEMENS.

5. S. kalmiae *Abbot & Smith*. Figured in Sm. Abb. I, pl. 37.

Head and thorax ferruginous brown, paler on the sides; tegulae
with a central and upper black line, metathoracic patches black.
Abdomen ferruginous brown with a central black line and alternate whitish and black demi-bands. Anterior wings ferruginous
brown, paler in the middle, with two oblique blackish streaks at
the base of inner margin and very oblique ferruginous streaks from
the costa to disk; a pale streak in post-apical interspace, margined
on each side with ferruginous, and ferruginous and brownish streaks
in the remaining interspaces, with a whitish line near the margin
edged above with blackish; discal spot small and ferruginous ;
fringes reddish-brown.   Posterior wings brownish-white, with a
broad central and terminal black band ; exterior margin reddish-
brown and fringes of the same hue.

Mature Larva. Head green, with a lateral black stripe.   Body
fine pale green, deepening on the sides, with pale yellow, lateral,
oblique bands edged above with black, which is again bordered
with pale blue; first and second prolegs with a black spot on the
sides; stigmata orange-yellow; shield and terminal prolegs dotted
with numerous brown dots on a pale brownish patch ; caudal horn
blue, but thickly covered with black tubercles.   Length about
three inches.

Pupation. The larval transformation is subterranean.   The pupa
dark-brown ; the tongue-case half as long as the breast and applied to it, with the extremity bulbous.   The larva enters the pupa
state during the latter part of August or in September, and appears as an imago in the following June or early in July.

Food-plants. I have found the larva nearly full grown on the
lilac about the middle of July.   Also feeds on the leaves of *Kal-
mia latifolia*. (*Abbot & Smith*.)

Canada ; New York ; Pennsylvania ; Massachusetts ; Georgia.

CLEMENS.

6. S. drupiferarum *Abbot & Smith*. Figured in Sm. Abb. 1, pl. 36.

Head and thorax blackish-brown, whitish fawn-color on the sides. Abdomen brown, with a slender dorsal line and a lateral black band on each side containing brownish-white spots. Anterior wings dark brown, with costa from base beyond the disk, and to median nervure below, whitish fawn-color, with wavy, separated dark brown lines crossing lower portion of the nervules, the last bordered above with whitish; a fawn-colored marginal space tapering to the tip and containing a whitish line. A black discal dash, and two delicate black discal lines continued singly on the disco-central nervule, with black streaks in submedian sulcus and all the interspaces except the medio-superior. Posterior wings whitish, with a broad median black band enlarged towards the costa and sub-terminal black band, with the terminal margin fawn-color.

Mature Larva. Head green, with a lateral blackish band. Body pale green, with lateral, oblique purple bands, edged beneath with white; caudal horn dark reddish-brown, yellow on the sides at base; stigmata orange-yellow. Length about 8½ inches.

Pupation. The larval transformation takes place in a subterranean cell. The pupa is dark brown, with reddish-brown between the segments and the tongue-case short, reposing on the breast and truncate at the extremity. The perfect insect from the full larva appears early in June.

Food-plants. The larva feeds on the leaves of the various varieties of *Plum.*

Pennsylvania; Massachusetts.

CLEMENS.

7. S. insolitosa *Clemens.*

Antennæ blackish-brown. Palpi blackish-brown. Head and thorax blackish-brown or blackish and white on the sides. Abdomen brown, with a black stripe on each side. Anterior wings pale brown, with a ferruginous hue; the inner border fuliginous, a terminal fuliginous band tapering to the tip of the wing, with a wavy outline anteriorly, and the costa and a patch on the costa above the tip of the same hue; a slender black discal line, with black lines and streaks in all the interspaces and sub-median sulcus. Fringes blackish. Posterior wings yellow or stramineous, with a broad terminal black band and the fringes whitish.

Wisconsin; New York.

CLEMENS.

8. S. gordius *Cramer*. Figured in Cram. III, pl. 247.

Head and disk of the thorax blackish-brown or black and reddish-gray on the sides. Abdomen dark gray, with a dorsal black line and alternate black and grayish demi-bands. Anterior wings blackish-gray, with a roseate hue; discal spot conspicuous and white, a discal black line bifid toward the discal spot, with the usual lines and streaks in interspaces and submedian sulcus, black; a blackish-brown marginal shade, with pale grayish on the portion of the wing above it, at the base and the tip of the wing. Fringes dark brown spotted with white. Posterior wings gray, with a black median band, and a broad, black marginal band; the fringes white.

Mature Larva. Apple green, with seven oblique white lateral bands, slightly edged above with violet, a rusted caudal horn, and a brownish line on each side of head. (*Harris.*) There is almost too much resemblance in this description to the larva of *drupiferarum.*

Pupation. The larval transformation is subterranean; pupa with a very short detached tongue-case. (*Harris.*)

Food-plants. The larva feeds on the leaves of the apple-tree. (*Harris.*)

Maine; Massachusetts; Connecticut.

CLEMENS.

9. S. jasminearum *Le Conte*, Sr. Wilson, Treat. Ent. in Ency. Brit. pl. 236, f. 5, 6.

Palpi gray-brownish on the sides. Head and thorax pale gray, with a transverse black line on prothorax extended to the middle of tegulæ, with a black dash in the middle of the disk and metathoracic black streaks on each side of median line. Abdomen dull gray, with a black stripe on each side containing whitish spots. Anterior wings gray, with blackish-brown markings; a blackish streak at the base of inner margin, with two brownish lines from the disk to its lower end; two blackish-brown oblique lines or a broad oblique streak from the costa to the disk at the origin of median nervules; discal spot white, with a brownish discolored patch just posterior to it, extending from costa at the origin of subcosto inferior nervule to medio-posterior interspace, where it becomes a black spot, and continued thence to inner margin as two brownish lines; two doubly curved lines of connected spots crossing the middle of the nervules from near the origin of post-apical to the lower third of the inner margin, with an irregular brownish line near the terminal margin; a long, decided black streak in medio-central interspace, with a blackish spot on the terminal margin of the medio-central nervule. Posterior wings nearly uniform blackish brown, with a faint grayish central band and a grayish patch above the interior angle.

Pupation. Larval transformation subterranean. The pupa is dark brown, with a very short cylindrical tongue-case bulbous at the extremity, and applied to the breast.

Food-plants. Mr. Newman, of Philadelphia, found a pupa of this insect beneath an isolated ash tree, under such circumstances as to render it probable that this is one of the food-plants of the larva.

Long Island; New York; Pennsylvania.

CLEMENS.

Length of tongue unknown.

10. S. coniferarum *Abbot & Smith.* Figured in Sm. Abb. I, pl. 42.

Cinereous; white beneath. · Thorax with a brown stripe on each side. Abdomen cinereous without bands. Anterior wings, with a brown basilar, wavy line, a brown costal spot above the discal spot, which is blackish; with a crenated brown line crossing the middle of the nervules edged anteriorly with whitish. A long black streak in medio-central interspace, and a shorter one in the posterior, with the ends of the nervules tipped with blackish. Posterior wings brown. (*Abbot & Smith's figure.*)

Mature Larva. Head yellow with two black lines. Body gray, with three rows of dorsal, square, dark-gray spots, one of which is vascular, having a black dot at each angle, and a slender, whitish, vascular line, with whitish striæ between the square spots. First segment with two dashes and one subdorsal on each side. The larva is full grown about August 27th and Nov. 10th, which latter produces an imago in April following. (*Abbot & Smith.*)

Food-plants. Pinus palustris.

Georgia; Canada.

CLEMENS.

N. B. The specimen Dr. Harris described under this name, as I have ascertained from a photograph, was *E. harrisii.* This is probably likewise identical with *S. coniferarum.* The discovery of the larva of *harrisii* will remove any doubt respecting the identity of the insects.—D. CLEMENS.

ANCHETA Walker.

Body rather long and slender. The head large, free and prominent; the front broad, subconical, the vertex pilose or subtufted; the eyes large and salient; the tongue as long as the body; the palpi rather slender, scantily pilose and pressed against the front, with the terminal article *exposed*. Antennæ as long or somewhat longer than the thorax, with a short hook and seta. Thorax well developed anterior to the base of the fore wings, but rounded anteriorly, usually with a slight double crest on the fore part of the dorsum. Abdomen slender and oblanceolate, at least twice the length of the thorax. Legs long and slender, hind tibiæ with moderate spurs. The wings narrow and moderately long; the length of the anterior less than that of the body, and about three times longer than broad across the inner angle, the tip acuminated, the hind border obliquely rounded, but wavy between the nervules, the inner angle rounded and the inner margin moderately concave. Posterior wings rather acute at the tip, with the hind margin entire.

Head smooth, thorax scarcely crested.

1. A. ello Linn. Figured in Drury I, pl. 27. Cram. IV, pl. 301.

Head and thorax gray; the front of thorax and the vertex discolored with blackish, without distinct markings, with a black line on sides of thorax extending from the eyes to the base of anterior wings. Abdomen gray, with a dorsal gray band, containing a slender blackish line, and banded with alternate black and gray bands in both sexes. Anterior wings pale grayish, varied with blackish; with a blackish stripe extending irregularly from the base to the tip, and consisting chiefly of streaks between the nervules; base of the wing blackish, with a patch in costa over disk, and at the origin of subcosto-inferior nervule, and with a row of marginal black spots in the interspaces. Posterior wings rust red, with a broad, blackish brown, terminal band and a cinereous patch at the anterior angle.

The anterior wings of the specimens described are unfortunately worn.

Mature Larva. Head purple; body obscure brown, with a black dorsal line, and spotted irregularly with white on the sides; caudal horn purple. (*Merian.*)

Food-plants. The leaves of a species of *Psidium* or Guava. (*Merian.*)

South America; West Indies; Mexico; Texas; Southern United States; California.

CLEMENS.

Vertex and thorax with distinct double crests.

2. A. obscura Fab. sp. II, 142, 14. *Erinnys sibeno* Hübner.

Hoary and somewhat bluish gray. Head and thorax dark gray and paler on the sides, the latter with a few short black lines, or with the disk before blackish brown, and a stripe of the same hue on the sides. Abdomen dusky gray *without bands*, and two brownish dorsal lines. Anterior wings hoary, or gray tinted with bluish, with blackish markings; a blackish streak extending from base to the tip, and a short, nearly parallel blackish streak above the interior angle; a blackish-patch on costa at the posterior extremity of the disk, a fainter one about the middle, and another at the origin of the post-apical nervule; a row of black dots on the lower third of the nervures and another about the middle, each series being connected by a faint acutely angled line; a row of marginal, black dots in which terminate faint, slender, blackish lines in the interspaces from the post-apical to the medio-central. Posterior wings rust-red or reddish fawn-color, with a dark-brown patch on the terminal margin, about the interior angle, and a series of indistinct dots above the nervules.

In the markings of the anterior wings this species bears a very striking resemblance to *A. ello*.

Mexico; West Indies; Texas.

CLEMENS.

3. A. noyron *Cram.* IV, 23, pl. 301.

Hoary, cinereous. Thorax with a broad, anterior, blackish band, and two blackish, posterior, abbreviated bands. The segments of the abdomen with interrupted, blackish bands, separated and whitish. Fore wings dark brown, varied with yellowish, with a few brown bands more or less definite and branched, sometimes almost obsolete. Posterior wings luteous, broadly margined with black, with a somewhat hoary patch along the interior angle.

South America; West Indies.

CLEMENS.

Thorax doubly crested.

4. A. alope *Drury*, 1, 58, pl. 27.

Brown. Abdomen blackish, with hoary interrupted bands and a dorsal stripe. Anterior wings with a series of angular black lines about the middle of the nervures, with a paler streak near the middle of the inner margin, more or less bent backwards, sometimes blackish brown. Hind wings luteous or orange yellow, with a broad brown terminal margin.

Var. β. Female. Brown, cinereous beneath. Head and thorax with a blackish stripe. Abdomen hoary, with three slender black stripes and with broad black bands; tip fawn-color. Fore wings with indistinct blackish lines and streaks, and with some exterior fawn-colored streaks. Hind wings luteous, with very broad dark brown borders; exterior margin somewhat fawn-colored. Length of the body 20 lines; of the wings 39 lines.

S. America; West Indies.

CLEMENS.

5. A. guttularis *Walker*, p. 227.

Hoary, whitish beneath. Head and fore part of the thorax with a brown middle line. Abdomen with a slender whitish stripe, and with a slight lilac tinge. Wings beneath pale brown, white at the base and along the interior border of the hind wings. Fore wings with a black streak along the middle, and with several black dots. Hind wings brown, ferruginous at the base; cilia white. Length of the body 10 lines; of the wings 18 lines.

St. Domingo.

CLEMENS.

Thorax doubly crested.

6. A. canotrus *Cramer*, IV, 22, pl. 301.

Cinereous, beneath white. The head is whitish, with the sides of a dirty rose color. The segments of the abdomen whitish, and white beneath, with black points towards the sides. Anterior wings reddish brown toward the base, with slightly fawn-colored

lines and streaks, sometimes with the margins brown in part.
Posterior wings rufescent or reddish brown, with a terminal blackish
brown band and a small cinereous patch at the interior angle.

S. America; Mexico; West Indies.

CLEMENS.

Hind margin of fore wings not denticulated, entire?

7. **A. calous** *Cramer*, II, pl. 125.

Cinereous. Thorax with three blackish brown stripes. Abdomen with two dorsal black lines and broad interrupted black bands.
Anterior wings with pale brownish and blackish brown lines in the
interspaces, a blackish brown line on the inner margin and a white
discal line. Posterior wings red, with black radii from the hind
margin.

South and Central America; West Indies.

CLEMENS.

DOLBA WALKER.

Size moderate or small. The body is stout, and rather short.
The head rather small, but free and moderately prominent; the
front broad, vertical, rounded and obtuse; the eyes quite small
and scarcely salient; the palpi nearly horizontal and equal to the
front; the tongue somewhat longer than the body; the antennæ
rather slender, with a short hook and seta, and about as long as
the thorax. The thorax but little advanced anterior to the base
of fore wings, tapering but little to the head and rounded in front.
The abdomen rather conical, and about twice the length of the
thorax. The length of the anterior wings rather more than that
of the body, somewhat more than twice longer than broad, the tip
rounded, the hind margin entire and oblique, somewhat prominent
in the middle and slightly concave above the inner angle; inner
margin slightly concave. Posterior wings obtusely rounded at the
tip, hind margin entire and somewhat concave before the inner
angle.

1. **D. hylæus** *Drury*. Figured in Drury II, pl. 25. Sm. Abb. 1, pl. 35.
Sphinx prini Abbot & Smith. *Hylaicus dyarus* Hübner.

Palpi white beneath. Head and thorax brownish ferruginous,
and whitish on the sides, with two white dots on the disk of thorax

and two black metathoracic spots. Abdomen brownish ferruginous, with a row of dorsal brown spots and a double row of white spots, and with lateral alternate black and narrow white demi-bands. Anterior wings dull ferruginous, or dark brownish varied with white and blackish; a white spot at the base, with a blackish band, white margined towards the base, crossing the middle of the disk; discal spot white and black margined, a band of blackish lines crossing the middle of the nervules, margined posteriorly broadly with whitish, and black circlets on the posterior ends of median nervules; apical line black, white margined toward costa. Posterior wings whitish, with an indistinctly double, median blackish band, joined near inner margin by a blackish patch from the base and a broad terminal dark brown band edged above with blackish. Sometimes the wing is blackish brown, with a central white line and a fainter one above it, with white at the base.

Mature Larva. Head green, with a pale blue line on each side. Body pea green, with lateral oblique pink bands edged below with white; caudal horn crimson. (*Abbot & Smith.*)

Pupation. Pupa reddish brown; tongue-case not apparent. Pupation began May 17th, and the imago appeared June 19th. Another entered the pupa state August 25th, and appeared April 26th, in Georgia. (*Abbot & Smith.*)

Food-plants. Prinos glaber; Winterberry.

Mexico; Georgia; Massachusetts; Connecticut.

CLEMENS.

CERATOMIA Harris.

Size large. Body usually thick and long. The head small, nearly sessile, and somewhat depressed; front broad and almost vertical, pilose or sub-tufted; the eyes small and scarcely salient; the palpi rather short and slender, nearly horizontal and not identified with the front; tongue about one-third as long as the body, not as long as the thorax; the antennae longer than the thorax, ending in a short hook with seta. The thorax is thick, sub-globose, but little advanced anterior to the base of the fore wings. The abdomen is cylindrical, tapering near the extremity, and nearly thrice or full thrice the length of the thorax. The legs stout and the hind tibiae with two long internal and two short

external spurs. The wings are rather broad, the anterior with the
tip rounded, the hind margin entire, obliquely convex, and the
inner margin somewhat concave above the interior angle. *Male*,
antennæ cilliferous. *Female*, antennæ simple.

Larva. Head large, semi-oval, somewhat flattened in front.
Body wrinkled transversely and granulated, with a vascular line of
fleshy serrations and a thoracic dorsal line of granulations on each
side, and with four thoracic fleshy granulated horns; caudal horn
rather short, straight, and roughened. The pupa is smooth;
tongue-case not apparent. Transformation subterranean.

1. C. quadricornis *Hübn.* *Agrius emynitor* Exot. Schmett.

Palpi brown. Head grayish or whitish-fawn color. Thorax
with the disk fawn color or greenish brown and whitish on the
sides, a short transverse dark-colored line before and the tegulæ
with a central and superior blackish line on each side, with black
metathoracic spots. Abdomen fawn colored or brownish, with a
slender black dorsal line and two black stripes on each side. Anterior wings fawn color, varied with blackish brown, or dull greenish brown varied with black; costa grayish at the base, with wing
of a pale hue above the median nervure and dusky beneath it;
three dark brown irregular lines advance from the basal portion
of the inner margin to the disk beyond its middle, and thence
retreat to the costa; diurnal spot white, with a short black discal
dash resting on median nerve; several subterminal blackish lines
arise above the interior angle and run nearly parallel to the hind
margin to disco-central nervure, whence they retreat to the costa;
black streaks in all the interspaces, with the fringes brown, spotted
with white. Posterior wings pale brownish, with a subterminal
blackish or dark-brown band and shaded with blackish in the middle or forming indistinct dark-colored lines.

Mature Larva. Head pale green, with an indistinct whitish
lateral stripe. Body pale green, becoming just before pupation
in one of the sexes more or less reddish brown, dotted with obscure
granulations; lateral stripes pale greenish, with whitish granulations and two thoracic dorsal white granulated lines; caudal horn
greenish; stigmatæ black encircled with yellow and divided by a
yellow line. Feet reddish or tipped with reddish. Length about
3 inches.

Pupation. The larval transformation is subterranean. Pupa dark brown, smooth cylindrico-conical, tongue-case not apparent. The larva reaches maturity about the beginning of September, and appears as an imago during the following May or June.

Food-plants. The larva feeds on the leaves of *Ulmus americana*, the American Elm.

Massachusetts; Pennsylvania; Michigan.

CLEMENS.

2. C. repentinus *Clemens.*

Head and thorax dark gray, paler on the sides; prothorax with two black transverse lines, the first edged above with luteous scales; tegulæ with a central black stripe. Abdomen dark gray, pale gray on the sides, with a slender dorsal black line and with two black stripes on each side. Anterior wings pale or rather deep cinereous, varied with black and white; two black lines arise near the basal portion of the inner margin and cross the disk to the costa, sometimes indistinct or obsolete in the middle; a blackish costo-discal patch containing a short black discal streak; discal spot white and black margined; two distinct sets of double, serrated, undulating black lines cross the middle of the nervules, and are separated by pale grayish or whitish, with an irregular whitish line near hind margin; a black apical line margined with whitish, and black streaks in the two last median interspaces; fringes white, spotted with dark brown. Posterior wings blackish gray, with three parallel, narrow undulating black bands; fringes white, spotted with dark brown.

Food-plants. I have been assured by various collectors that the larva feeds on the ash; none of them, however, were able to describe it from recollection.

Michigan; Connecticut; New York; Pennsylvania.

CLEMENS.

N. B. This insect is probably *Sphinx brontes* of Drury. See page 191. (D. CLEMENS.)

SMERINTHUS Latr.

Size moderate or large. The body is robust and thick, with the tip of the abdomen turned upward in the males. The head is small, sessile, sometimes sunken and depressed; the front moderately broad, vertical, pilose or subinflated: the eyes small scarcely prominent or visible from above; the palpi thick and short, but equal to the front; the tongue almost as long as the palpi; the antennæ usually without the terminal hook, without distinct seta, and about as long as the thorax. Thorax short, almost globose and but little advanced. The abdomen cylindrico-conical, more than twice longer than the thorax. Wings without bristle and hook. The anterior are longer than the body, and about twice as long as broad; the hind margin angulated opposite the post-apical vein and the medio-central, truncate at the tip and excavated between the angles, or denticulated along the hind margin; the inner margin is deeply concave above the interior angle, which is somewhat prominent. *Male*, antennæ densely ciliferous or subpectinated, with the articles produced beneath. *Female*, antennæ simple.

Larva. The head is semi-oval or pyramidal, with vertex acute. The body granulated, with a caudal horn, and obliquely banded with dorsal thoracic lines on each side. Transformation subterranean. The pupa of Group I. smooth and cylindrico-conical, and the position of the larva, when at rest or when disturbed, sphinx like.

GROUP I.

§ *Hind wings dilated on the costa at the tip.*

† *Fore wings angulated and excavated on the hind margin.*

1. S. myops *Abbot & Smith.* *Smerinthus rosacearum* Boisduval. Figured in Sm. Abb. I, pl. 26, Boisd. Sp. Gen. pl. 15.

Palpi, head and thorax chocolate brown and the two latter portions with a purplish or rosy tinge; the sides of palpi and a stripe in the middle of the thorax tawny yellow. Abdomen brownish luteous, with irregular tawny yellow spots, and the hind portions of the segments dark brown. Anterior wings chocolate brown, with a faint purplish or reddish gray tinge towards the base; a small blackish spot at the base, between median and sub-median nerves; an indistinct brownish curved line crosses the basal portion of the disk, with a large, median, chocolate brown patch, with

Its anterior margin darkest, inclined towards the anal angle, and joined at an acute angle by a patch of the same hue about the middle of sub-median nervure; one or two wavy sub-terminal brown lines, with an irregular chocolate brown band near the hind margin, extending from the tip to about the middle of the wing and thence to anal angle indistinctly; a dull yellow patch above anal angle, with blackish spots above it in sub-median spices, and another about the middle of apical interspace, with an angular, narrow, bluish line at the tip. Posterior wings dull yellow, with the costa and outer portion from near the middle, chocolate brown, and one or two short bluish lines above the tip and a dull yellow spot upon it; ocellus black, with a large pale blue pupil.

Nature Larva. From Abbot & Smith's figure; head bluish green, with a bright yellow line on the sides. Body bluish green with a row of sub-dorsal and stigmatal reddish brown spots; six oblique lateral bright yellow bands, with two thoracic sub-dorsal yellow (?) lines; caudal horn yellow on the sides.

Pupation. The larva enters the earth to transform. In the Southern States the first brood enters the pupa state about the middle of June, and becomes imago early in July; pupation begins with the second during the latter part of October, and they appear as perfect insects during the following spring. The pupa is smooth, abdomen cylindrico-conical and acute; color deep brown. (*Abbot & Smith.*)

Food-plants. The leaves of the wild cherry.

CLEMENS.

†† *Fore wings denticulated on hind margin, with a denticulation opposite disco-central nearly obsolete.*

2. S. exnnoatus *Abbot & Smith.* Figured in Sm. Abb. 1, pl. 25.

Palpi, head and thorax fawn-color, with a roseate tinge, with a chestnut-colored thoracic dorsal stripe tapering to the head and metathoracic transverse patch of the same hue. Abdomen fawn-color with a dark brown dorsal line. Anterior wings fawn-color, with dark brown shades, with a small blackish spot at the middle of base and two brown lines crossing the basal portion of the disk; a large, median, brown patch, with its anterior margin darkest and inclined towards the inner angle, and the posterior margin concave in the middle, tinged with purplish towards the centre, containing a brown discal dot, and joined at an acute angle by a patch of the same hue about the middle of the submedian nervure; two or three brown lines crossing the middle of the nervules and following the outline of median patch, succeeded by an irregular brownish band; the marginal space brown; a small brown spot at inner angle, with two or three black spots above it in sub-median sulcus, with faint blackish streaks in the post-apical, subcostal and costo-inferior and medio-superior interspaces. Posterior wings rose-color in the middle, with a brownish patch at the tip crossed by two or three short whitish lines; ocellus black, pupil pale blue, with two short whitish lines between the ocellus and the inner margin.

Var. A male. Brownish olivaceous. Thoracic streak dark brown. The median shade of the fore wings brownish olivaceous with a purplish tinge, and a deep brown streak at the base of posterior interspace; discal spot blackish.

Egg. Spheroids much flattened above and beneath, almost like narrow sections of a cylinder; smooth, white, with an equatorial, reddish brown band, having a slender, central, white line. Investing tunics thick and resisting.

Young Larva, on first emerging from the egg is green, without granulations, and oblique, lateral stripes; a long reddish caudal horn; without thoracic subdorsal lines.

Mature Larva. I regret I have no description of the mature larva. The following is that of Harris: Apple green, with two short, pale lines before, seven oblique, yellowish white lines on each side and a bluish caudal horn. According to Abbot & Smith's figure, the head is green with a crimson line on each side; the body yellowish green, lateral bands and caudal-horn yellow, with a subdorsal and double stigmatal row of crimson spots.

Pupation. The larva enters the ground to transform; the pupa is chestnut-brown, smooth, with a short, obtuse, terminal spine.

Food-plants. The leaves of the apple tree and those of the *Rosa carolina.*

Pennsylvania; Massachusetts; Georgia.

CLEMENS.

§§ *Costa of superior wings rounded and entire from the base to the tip, which is rounded.*

　† *Fore wings denticulated on hind margin, with that opposite disco-central nearly obsolete.*

14

3. S. modesta *Harris.* Figured in Agas. Lake Sup. pl. 7.

Palpi, head, thorax and abdomen olivaceous. Anterior wings
from the base to nearly the hind end of the disk very pale olivaceous, with an indistinct, irregular, darker streak across the middle, and margined towards the base of the wing with a still paler
hue; a broad, deep, olivaceous, median band, undulating anteriorly and crenated or undulating posteriorly, containing a pale,
angular, discal spot and darkest towards the base of the wing; a
deep, olivaceous band across the middle of the nervules crenated
posteriorly and bordered with a paler hue; the remainder of the
wing is deep olivaceous with a paler band from the middle to the
inner angle. Posterior wings purplish-red in the middle, with a
transverse, black spot above inner angle and a blackish, olivaceous
patch beneath it; in the male the wing is olivaceous exteriorly and
along terminal border.

Pupation. Mr. Ashton, of N. Y., has taken the perfect insect in
July.

Food-plants. Mr. Crist, of Nazareth, Northampton Co., Pa.,
informed me he found a larva of this insect several years ago on
the Lombardy poplar.

Massachusetts; Lake Superior; Pennsylvania; Sonora, Mex.,
New York.

CLEMENS.

†† *The hind margin of fore wings angulated and excavated.*
  Articles of the antennæ with single short pectinations in ♂,
  simple in the ♀.

4. S. geminatus *Say. Sphinx œdiatus jamaicensis* Drury. *Smerinthus ce-*
    risii Kirby. Figured in Drury II, pl. 25. Kirby Faun. pl. 4. Say's
    Amer. Ent. 1, pl. 12.

Palpi reddish-brown; head thorax in front and tegulæ whitish
or pale gray, with a large, thoracic, dorsal, deep chestnut, semi-
oval patch. Abdomen brownish-gray. Anterior wings gray,
tinged with rosy and with dark brown streaks and patches; two
curved, brownish, basal lines bordered with rosy-gray; the basal
half of medio-posterior interspace filled by a dark brown or a ferruginous brown patch, joined by a line of the same hue crossing
the disk from the costa and obliquely by another from the upper
third of inner margin, shaded posteriorly with brownish, through
the centre of which passes the sub-median nervule; discal spot

pale, margined with brown; a brownish band, margined before with darker brown, crosses the base of the nervules, and is followed by two or three more or less distinct rosy-gray and brownish, undulating, subterminal lines; a deep brown, semi-oval patch at the tip edged with whitish, and a ferruginous brown spot above inner angle, usually with two smaller spots above it; the middle of terminal space dark brown. Posterior wings rosy, along exterior and terminal border yellowish-gray; ocellus black, emitting a short, broad line to inner angle, and with two or three blue pupils.

Food-plants. I have secured numbers of the pupæ from the middle of October to the beginning of November at the base of willows.

Canada; Illinois; Massachusetts; Pennsylvania; Jamaica.

CLEMENS.

‡‡ *Structure unknown.*

5. S. ophthalmicus *Boisduval.* Ann. Soc. Ent. t. III, 3me ser. xxvii.

La *S. ophthalmica* assez rapproché de notre *ocellata*, plus voisin de *geminatus* de Say, mais l'oeil n'est pas double et il diffère de toutes les espèces du même groupe par sa large bande brune, anguleuse, qui traverse le milieu des ailes supérieures.

S. ophthalmicus is nearly related to the European *ocellatus*, and more intimately to *geminatus* of Say, but the pupil is not double, and it differs from all the species of the same group by having a large, angular, brown band traversing the middle of the superior wings.

This description of M. Boisduval is almost too indefinite to authorize even a conjecture respecting this species, but it will possibly prove to be merely a variety of *geminatus*.

CLEMENS.

‡‡‡ *Antennæ ciliferous in the ♂, simple in the ♀.*

6. S. astylus *Drury.* Sphinx is Boisd. Figured in Drury II, pl. 26.

Reddish-brown or cinnamon-colored. Thorax with a dorsal ferruginous stripe attenuated before. Tegulæ tinged with rosy white in the ♀. Abdomen fawn-color, with a faint dorsal brownish line and the sides in the ♂, somewhat tawny yellow, in the ♀ rosy white. Anterior wings very white toward the base in the ♀,

with a bluish-black stripe along the inner margin, and a line of the
same hue along the medio-posterior nervule, joining it near the
inner angle, with sub-terminal whitish bands faintly tinged with
roseate, and a tawny yellow spot at the tip and inner angle. Posterior wings tawny yellow or lutescent, intermixed with brownish
toward the costa, and a black ocellus above the inner angle, with
a bluish pupil. Under surface of anterior wings tawny yellow,
somewhat reddish-brown exteriorly, with yellow spots and white
bands corresponding to those on the upper surface. Posterior
wings reddish-brown, with two parallel, irregular rosy white central lines. Length of the body 45 lines; expanse of the wings 80
lines in the ♂, 33 lines in the ♀.

Massachusetts; New York.

CLEMENS.

GROUP II.

The hind margin of the anterior wings somewhat excavated from
the tip to medio-central nervule, and thence rounded to the inner
angle, entire in the ♂, crenated in the ♀. Posterior wings emarginate at the tip, hind border entire in the ♂, crenated in the ♀.
Antennæ with the stalk ciliferous, and the articles produced beneath the stalk each bearing four short pectinations in the ♂, and
simple in the ♀. Palpi short in the ♀ and scarcely exceeding the
front; in the ♂ exceeding it, divergent, almost attaining the level
of the vertex, the development being in the second article and the
third rudimental; the tongue about as long as the palpi.

Larva, is granulated on transverse wrinkles, tapers anteriorly,
the thoracic rings being slender. The head is pyramidal and
granulated, the vertex elevated above the dorsum and bifid; caudal
horn densely spined. The pupa is rough, with the terminal segments of abdomen flattened.

The position of the larva at rest is not sphinx-like; it is extended along the mid-rib of a leaf, and when disturbed, throws its
head from side to side, making a crepitating noise.

This group has its European representative in *Smerinthus populi*,

7. B. juglandis *Abbot & Smith*. Figured in Sm. Abb. l, pl. 29.

Palpi reddish brown or dark brown; head and thorax pale fawn color or pale grayish, with a more or less distinct thoracic dorsal, brownish stripe. Abdomen fawn color or unicolor. Anterior wings, from the base to about the middle of disk, pale gray, with a faint lilac tinge or pale fawn color, and a brownish line crossing the basal part of the disk; a broad median shade, with its posterior margin commencing on the costa midway between the origin of post-apical vein and the tip, and inclined to about the middle of inner margin, darkest at the edges and ochraceous brown, dark brownish or ferruginous brown, and sometimes almost obsolete above the medio-posterior vein, whence are emitted two lines which mark the outline of the shade; a line of the same hue parallel to posterior margin of median shade, with an intervening paler space and a light-colored shade near hind margin, extending from disco-central vein to the inner angle; the marginal space dark colored, with a small light-colored costal spot extended to the tip. Posterior wings ochraceous brown or dull fawn color, with a central light-colored band edged on each side by dark lines, corresponding to the posterior edge of median shade and its parallel line.

Mature Larva. Head pale reddish brown, with a pale yellow lateral stripe and granulations. Body pale green or yellowish green, with oblique lateral crimson streaks, edged beneath with pale yellow; body tinged with crimson above the prolegs and behind the horn; granulations pale yellow; horn brownish, with blackish spinules. Feet dark reddish brown. Length about 2½ inches.

Pupation. The pupa is blackish brown, roughened, with four little prominences on the front of the head-case, and the terminal segments flattened on the ventral surface. The larva attains its full growth about the middle of September, and undergoes its transformation in a cell just beneath the surface.

Food-plants. The leaves of the black walnut and the hickory.

Massachusetts; New York; Pennsylvania; Georgia.

CLEMENS.

DAREMMA WALKER.

Body rather slender. Proboscis short, distinct. Antennæ setaceous, serrated, a little longer than the thorax. Abdomen tapering, full thrice the length of the thorax. Legs rather short and

stout; hind tibiæ with four long spurs. Wings long, moderately
broad. Fore wings very slightly convex in front, hardly acuminated, entire, slightly convex and very oblique along the exterior
border. Hind wings hardly acuminated.

1. D. undulosa *Walker*, p. 231.

Cinereous, hoary beneath. Thorax with a black testaceous-
bordered band in front and another behind, where there is also a
white band; a black stripe on each side. Abdomen with slight
testaceous bands, with a brown stripe in the middle, and with brown
spots along each side. Wings with white brown spotted cilia.
Fore wings with slender undulating blackish bands, three toward
the base and four beyond the middle, where there is a white black-
ish-bordered discal spot; a blackish apical streak. Hind wings
with three brown bands.
    Length of the body 13 lines, of the wings 36 lines.
    Orillia, West Canada.

                                                    CLEMENS.

CHROSANDA WALKER.

Male. Size small. Body moderately stout, subfusiform. Head
slightly crested. Proboscis moderately long. Palpi a little longer
and more slender than in the other genera; third joint minute,
conical, apparent. Antennæ setaceous, very minutely serrate, much
longer than the thorax. Abdomen less than twice the length of
the thorax, slightly tufted at the tip. Legs rather slender; hind
tibiæ with four moderately long spurs. Wings rather short, moderately broad. Fore wings rounded at the tips, moderately oblique
and slightly convex along the exterior border; first, second, and
third inferior veins somewhat approximate; fourth remote.

1. CH. noctuiformis *Walker*, p. 232.

Hoary, whitish beneath. Head with a brownish crest. Thorax
with a brownish stripe along each side. Abdomen with a black
dot on each segment. Fore wings with several slender undulating
or angular, dark brown bands, and with a transverse more distinct

streak by the interior angle, near which there is a brown spot. Hind wings brown, yellow towards the base.

Length of the body 6 lines, of the wings 14 lines.

St. Domingo.

CLEMENS.

LAPARA Walker.

Male. Body rather slender. Head small, short. Proboscis moderately long. Palpi very short. Antennæ slender, subclavate, hardly longer than the thorax and attenuated but hardly hooked toward the tips. Abdomen linear, full twice the length of the thorax. Legs slender; hind tibiæ with four moderately long spurs. Wings rather narrow, not long. Fore wings almost straight in front, slightly rounded at the tips, straight and very oblique along the exterior border; interior border straight; second inferior vein far nearer to the first than to the third; fourth very remote. Hind wings rounded at the tips.

This genus has much outward resemblance to the *Bombycidæ.*

1. L. bombycoides *Walkr,* p. 233.

Cinereous. Fore wings with a zigzag, oblique, black line, and with several lanceolate, black marks. Hind wings brownish, paler towards the base; ciliæ white.

Length of the body 10 lines; of the wings 24 lines.

Canada.

CLEMENS.

ELLEMA Clemens.

Size small. Body rather slender, diameter nearly equal, but slightly fusiform in the ♂. The head is quite small, sessile and somewhat depressed, being but partially visible from above; the front moderate, vertical and subinflated; the palpi rather short and slender, but equal to the front; the tongue equal to palpi; the eyes very small; the antennæ terminating in a short hook and seta, and longer than the thorax. The thorax is very short and pilose, but little advanced anterior to the base of the fore wings and rather globosely rounded in front. The abdomen is cylindrical, or nearly so, and about thrice the length of the thorax. The anterior wings are equal to the length of the entire body, and are a little more than twice longer than broad, with the tip rounded, and the hind margin entire and obliquely convex, the inner angle rounded and the inner margin straight. Hind wings rounded at the tips.

Male. Antennæ prismatic and ciliferous. *Female.* Antennæ fusiform and finely ciliated.

L. B. barrisi. *Sphinx coniferarum* Harris, p. 297.

The palpi, head and thorax moderately pale umber, with the sides of the thorax at the base of the anterior wings and lower portion of tegulæ grayish. Abdomen brownish-gray. Anterior wings umber colored, varied with pale gray, with two blackish-brown lines from the inner margin crossing the disk to the costa, and a series of blackish lunules in the interspaces, extending from the costa a little beyond the origin of post-apical nervule to the lower third of the inner margin and bordered interiorly with pale gray; the mark in medio-central interspace is lanceolate, and sometimes that in the posterior interspace; the ends of the nervules tipped with dark brownish; fringes brown, spotted with white. Lighter towards the base. *Female,* the pale gray less abundant on anterior wing, with long black dashes in the basal portion of medio-central and posterior interspaces, and blackish in the middle of submedian sulcus.

Mature Larva. Mr. George Newman, a collector in Philadelphia, assures me he has taken the larva of this insect near maturity on the pines of New Jersey about the latter part of September. He could describe it only in general terms. It was without a caudal horn, and in general color green.

Maine; New Jersey; New Hampshire; North Carolina.
                                                        CLEMENS.

ARCTONOTUS Bond.

Male. Body thick, very pilose. Proboscis very short, obsolete. Palpi stout, very short and pilose. Antennæ thick, serrate, very pubescent, much longer than the thorax. Abdomen elongato-obconical, hardly longer than the thorax. Legs stout, pilose;

hind tibiæ with four rather short spurs. Wings moderately broad, not long, hardly denticulated, rather deeply ciliated. Fore wings straight in front, slightly acuminated, rather oblique and slightly convex along the exterior border; second inferior vein (medio-superior) nearer to the third (medio-central) than to the first (disco-central); third rather further from the fourth (posterior) than from the first. Hind wings much rounded at the tips.— *Walker.*

This genus appears to connect *Smerinthus* with the *Bombycidæ.*

1. **A. lucidus** *Boisd.* Walker, p. 264.

Male. Gilded, tawny. Palpi brown. Antennæ testaceous with ferruginous branches. Lappets of the thorax (*tegulæ*) with a darker border, which has a whitish edge. Fore wings with two oblique, purplish bands, which are connected along the interior border. Hind wings red, with gilded borders, and with a ferruginous submarginal band.

"Size of our *cnotheræ.* Wings quite entire; the superior dim yellowish-gray, with a brilliant yellow reflection, marked with two or three very obscure transverse bands, the most decided of which is sinuous and placed near the extremity. Inferior wings violet, with the extremity of an obscure purple and the fringe paler.

Body very short; corselet very hairy, of the color of the superior wings. Antennæ very robust (*très fortes*). Under surface of the wings of a grayish tint, with the disk of the superior ferruginous." *Boisduval, Ann. Soc. Ent. Fr.,* 2me ser. X, p. 319.

California.

CLEMENS.

Fam. IX. DREPANULIDAE.

Appearance geometriform. Proboscis often none, sometimes conspicuous. Palpi very short. Antennæ of the male usually pectinated, of the female, simple. Abdomen not extending beyond the secondaries. Legs slender; wings wide; primaries *often falcate.* Flight nocturnal; wings extended in repose. Larva naked, with fourteen feet, gibbous on the back, attenuated behind, no anal feet.

The following genus is the only representative of this family as yet discovered in this country.

DREPANA Schr.

Body very slender. Proboscis not visible. Palpi very short, not extending beyond the head. Antennæ longer than the thorax. Abdomen not extending so far as the hind wings. Legs slender, bare, hind tibiæ with four rather short spurs. Wings broad. Primaries falcate, slightly convex along the costa, undulating or indented along the exterior border; interior angle rounded; discal areolet intersected by a secondary vein; second inferior vein more than twice further from the third than from the first; third not further from the fourth than from the second. *Male.* Antennæ moderately pectinated. *Female.* Antennæ very minutely pectinated, much longer than those of the male.

1. D. fasciata *Steph.* *Uncula* Hav.

Wings brownish-yellow; anterior with two oblique brown striæ, bent towards the costa; the posterior one with a brown cloud attached towards the outer margin; between these streaks is a small black dot towards the anterior edge of the wing; posterior wings with a single streak.

WALKER.

2. D. arcuata *Walk.* C. B. M. VIII.

Male. Pale testaceous. Antennæ with brown branches. Fore wings very falcate, with brown oblique streaks along the costa; with two slender zigzag brown bands near the base, with two dark-brown discal dots, and with three exterior brown bands; the first and the third of the latter slight and undulating; the second darker, more distinct, and nearly straight, ending at the tip of the wing, which is pale brown in front and gray behind, excepting the extreme tip, which is wholly dark brown. Hind wings with several indistinct tawny undulating bands, and with two minute brown discal dots. Length of the body 4 lines; of the wings 15 lines.

This species closely resembles *D. falcataria* in form and color and markings, but may be distinguished by its more falcate fore wings, by the more oblique second exterior band, by the less numerous and less distinct bands of the hind wings, and by other differences.

Nova Scotia.

WALKER.

The two following species differ from the European groups of *Drepana* by the outline of their fore wings, which are convex in the middle of the exterior border.

WALKER.

3. D. rosea *Walk.* C. B. M. VIII.

Male. Pale dull rose-color. Head bright rose-color. Antennæ with rather short and thick-set branches. Hind tibiæ with the apical spurs rather long. Wings partly yellow towards the base, with a yellow oblique and slightly undulating band, which in the hind wings is dilated, and occupies the whole apical half of the wing, with the exception of a spot in front of the exterior border. Fore wings nearly straight along the costa, slightly falcate at the tips; exterior border undulating, convex in the middle, third inferior vein thrice farther from the fourth than from the second. Length of the body 4 lines; of the wings 12 lines.

Nova Scotia.

WALKER.

4. D. marginata *Walk.* C. B. M. VIII.

Male ? Like *D. rosea* in the form of its wings. Yellow. Head rose-color. Antennæ like those of *D. rosea* in structure. Legs partly red, more pilose than those of *D. rosea*; hind tibiæ with very minute spurs. Wings with some slender indistinct oblique and undulating pale-reddish bands. Fore wings nearly straight in front, slightly falcate at the tips, undulating along the exterior border, which is convex in the middle; costa with a slight reddish tinge towards the base; exterior border with a red band, which contains some black marks, and is continued to the fore part of the exterior border of the hind wings; two white discal dots; second inferior vein about twice farther from the third than from the first; third twice farther from the fourth than from the second. Length of the body 4 lines; of the wings 12 lines.

WALKER.

FAM. X. SATURNIDAE.

Antennæ bipectinated in the male; much longer than the width of the head. Tongue often obsolete. Palpi very short. Legs robust, hairy; hind tibiæ with two small apical spurs. Abdomen pilose, sometimes not reaching the ends of the wings. Wings wide and sometimes fenestrate; fore wings often falcate, interior margin with only one vein. No *frenulum.*

SATURNIA Schrank.

Palpi distinct, rather short, clothed with scales, compressed, triarticulate, terminal joint short, ovate; maxillæ obsolete. Antennæ short; those *of the male* bipectinated, each joint bearing a simple pectination, the latter diminishing in length towards the apex of the antennæ; those of the female with each joint unidentate, *not pectinated;* head moderate; thorax rather short and pilose; abdomen moderate, pilose, tufted at the apex; wings entire, broad, horizontally expanded.—*Stevens' Illust. Brit. Ins.*, Vol. II, p. 86.

L. B. to *Smith & Abbot.* Figured in Vol. I, pl. 49. Naturalists' Lib. XXXVII, p. 156, pl. 16, fig. 8.

Antennæ, head, and thorax yellow, the two latter hairy; superiors, yellow in the male, with several undulating brown streaks; reddish-brown in the female, with three waved continuous yellow lines across the surface and a cluster of small yellow spots towards the centre. Superiors, yellow beneath, with a black ocelliform spot in the middle, with a white pupil, behind which is a transverse reddish ray. Inferiors, yellow above, with a large central ocelliform spot, which is black, with a white elongated pupil; behind this eye there is a black semicircular band, succeeded by another parallel one which is ferruginous; the inner margin of the wing is likewise ferruginous. On the under side yellow, with a transverse ferruginous ray.

The male expands two and a half inches; the female is larger. Thorax and legs ferruginous, abdomen ochre-yellow, with a narrow purple line on each segment.

Larva, clear green, with a lateral brown stripe, edged below with white, beginning on the fourth segment and ending at the anus. Each segment has five or six tufts of green prickles, terminated by minute black points, which occasion a smarting sensation if they penetrate the hand. There is a triangular brown spot on the under side of each segment, beginning with the fourth. Feet brown.

The cocoon is spun between several dry leaves.

It feeds on sassafras (*Laurus sassafras*), dogwood (*Cornus florida*), and poplar (*Liriodendron*).

United States.

2. S. maia *Drury*. Figured in Sm. Abb. pl. 50. *Proserpina* Fab. Sat. Library XXXVII, p. 154, pl. 16, fig. 1. Drury II, pl. 42. Cram. Pap. Exot. II, 3 pl. 95. Pal. Beauv. Ins. Afr. et Amer. pl. 24.

Head and antennæ black; the latter strongly pectinated. Thorax in front whitish. Top of head black and hairy, behind ferruginous. Abdomen above black, terminated by a tuft of ferruginous hairs in the males; below gray, with white spots on the sides. Wings black, thin and translucent; they are crossed by a whitish band, which expands on the inferiors. On each there is a black spot, with a whitish streak on it. Under side similar. Legs black; femora ferruginous. Expands two and a half inches.

The larva varies much in color, according to age. When full grown, it is yellow, with a broad dark stripe on each side and two reddish tubercles on the top of each segment. The head, posterior segment, and legs, purplish red. Each segment has several hairy spines.

Feeds on various species of oak.

United States.

3. S. hera *Harris*, Ins. of New England, p. 284. Fig. on pl. 359, IV of Audubon's Birds of America.

Resembles *S. maia* in form and size, but the wings are more opaque. Color pale yellow. On each of the wings there is a reniform black spot between two transversely undulating black bands; outer margin black; the veins, from the external black band to the edge are marked with broad black lines, and there is a short black line at the base of the superiors. The head, forepart of the thorax, and upper side of the legs are deep ochre yellow. The rings of the abdomen are transversely banded with black at the base and with ochre yellow on their hinder edges. The reniform spots on the superiors have a very slender central yellow crescent, and those on the inferiors touch the external black band.

Expands three inches.

, The other moth figured on the same plate in Audubon is probably the female of *hera*.

Southern States.

HARRIS.

4. S. eglanterina *Boisd.* Ann. Soc. Ent. 2me ser. X, 322.

Size and form of *Proserpina*. Upper side of primaries yellowish-white, slightly flesh color, powdered with a little blackish at the base, with the upper edge and two transverse bands black; the one, near the base, uniting with a large longitudinal streak of the same color; the other, near the extremity, bent, but not sinuous. Between these two bands there is a black rounded spot, or kind of eye, marked with a small whitish crescent; fringe widely black, uniting with some sagittate streaks of the same color, situated on the nerves. Secondaries of a beautiful ochry yellow, marked in the middle with a large black point, in place of an eye; beyond the middle a black curved band, in a line with that of the primaries. Fringe black, forming some sagittate spots of the same color. Head and prothorax ferruginous; thorax mingled with yellow. Abdomen of the same color as the secondaries, paler below and a little annulated with black. Under side like the upper. Antennæ black, pennated in the male, a little ciliate in the female.

California.

BOISD.

5. S. pica *Walker.* C. B. M. 1315.

Male. White. Head, thorax in front and behind, pectus and femora luteous. Antennæ, tibiæ and tarsi brown. Abdomen above luteous, with a whitish spot and a brown band on each segment. Wings with black borders, with two curved black bands, with a large curved discal black spot, and with marginal black streaks. Fore wings with a black basal streak. Length of the body 11 lines; of the wings 30 lines.

United States.

WALKER.

6. ♀ megæra *Fab.* Ent. Syst. III, 1. Walker, C. B. M. pt. v, 1378.

Primaries bluish spotted with white; secondaries white at the apex, blue with yellow waves.

North America.

WALKER.

7. S. galbina *Clemens.* Proc. A. N. S. for 1860, p. 156.

Antennæ luteous. Body and head rather dark brown. Fore wings yellowish-brown, with a rather faint, whitish, angulated band at the base. On the discal nervure is a round, black ocellus having

a central subvitreous streak, containing a yellow circle, and toward
the base of the wing a slender blue crescent. A whitish band
crosses the middle of the nervules, with a faint wavy one between
it and the hind margin. In the apical interspace is a black spot,
with a crimson streak to the tip of the wing. The marginal portion of the wing is whitish and is tinged in the terminal edge with
pale yellowish-brown. Hind wings similar in color and ornamentation to the fore wings, the ocelli being somewhat smaller. On
the *under surface*, which is similar in hue to the upper, the faint
wavy bands of the fore and hind wings are very distinct.

Texas.

CLEMENS.

ATTACUS LINN.

The *Attaci* are distinguished from the *Saturnians* by their superior size—the wide, strongly pectinated antennæ *in both sexes;*
the horizontal and widely extended wings, which are marked with
vitreous, diaphanous spots, and by the tubercles on the backs of the
larvæ.

1. **A. cecropia** *Linn.* Drury, I, pl. 18. Figured in Sm. Abb. pl. 43.
Nat. Lib. XXXVII, p. 132, pl. xl.

Antennæ brown and broadly pectinated. Body fulvous. Thorax
very hairy, with a white band before. Abdomen annulated with
alternate white and dark brown, the latter edged behind with black;
primaries falcate at their extremity. They are brown and covered
with a white dust; a fulvous spot at the base, bordered with whitish. On the disk, a semi-transparent reniform spot, bordered with
black, with a white centre. A fulvous band crowned with white
crosses both wings; a sinuous whitish band on a grayish ground
crosses the posterior edge; towards the inferior angle there are
two or three irregular round black spots in a series; near the upper angle there is an ocellated black spot, nearly surrounded with
green; between this and another oblong black spot on the tip,
there is a mark similar to an inverted W.

Secondaries similar, excepting the lower edge, which has a narrow brown band; above it a series of spots of the same color, on
a grayish ground, which is surmounted with a broad band of brown.
The discoidal spot is larger and the transverse band broader.

Expands from five and a half to six inches.

Larva, light green; the second segment, surmounted with two red tubercles, having a number of short black hairs; the third segment has two larger tubercles; the others are crowned with oval yellow warts with hairs at the end; the last segment has but one of a larger size. On the side, two series of long, light blue tubercles, and a shorter series over the first five segments.

Feeds on apple, cherry, wild plum, currant, barberry.

It spins an oval cocoon, which is often as large as a hen's egg, which it attaches to the side of a stem. Externally it is brown and wrinkled; inside of this outer covering there is paler brown silk; this covers an inner cocoon closely spun, within which the chrysalis reposes.

United States.

2. A. promethea *Drury*. Figured in Drury II, pl. 11. Sm. Abb. I, pl. 44. Nat. Lib. XXXVII, p. 134, pl. 12.

Eyes and antennæ dark brown; the latter broadly pectinated in the males. Thorax and abdomen dark brown. Legs and under side of the body reddish-brown. Wings same color, falcate on the outer edge. A sinuous, grayish line crosses both in the middle; outer margin drab, through which passes a sinuous, dark reddish line; an ocellate black spot, surmounted by a blue crescent near the tip, between which and the tip there is a zigzag whitish line. The wings near the upper angle are of a rich flesh color.

The secondaries are similar, except the drab margin, on which, besides the sinuous line, there is a series of oblong dark brown spots between the line and ground color of the wings.

The under side is similarly marked, but the color approaches to a crimson tint. In the middle of the superiors there is a small sagittate spot of dark red; the inferiors have an indistinct, short, white line in the middle. Expands three inches and a half.

The female differs considerably from the male. The body is reddish-brown. The upper surface of the wings is bright ferruginous. They have the ocellated spot and the zigzag line near the tip as well as the sinuous line on the drab margin as in the male, but the oblong corresponding spots on the inferiors are ferruginous instead of brown.

Both lower wings are crossed by an undulating yellowish-white line, the inner edge of which is black and the outer gray. At the

base there is a large fulvous spot, bordered with white and black.
On the middle of the superiors there is an oblong yellowish-white
spot, broadest at the upper extremity, bordered with black. On
the middle of the inferiors there is a spot of similar color, but
more square and emarginate below.

The under surface is similar, but the color is brighter and the
ocellated spot on the superiors is brownish. Expands four inches.

Larva green; feet yellow. Each segment except the posterior
has six blue spots, mounted with black tubercles. In the second
and third segments the two middle tubercles are supplanted by two
red processes of a third of an inch in length. The last segment
has but five tubercles; the central one has a yellow process.

It feeds on *Laurus sassafras*, spice wood, *L. benzoin*, and swamp
buttonwood, *Cephalanthus occidentalis*.

In preparing for its transformation, it selects a leaf and covers
the upper surface of it with a yellowish-brown silk, extending this
coating over the footstalk of the leaf and attaching it firmly to the
branch. It next draws the edges of the leaf together, thus covering itself with a mantle, in which it spins a strong cocoon. It
soon assumes the pupa form, in which state it remains suspended
with the leaf during the winter and is disclosed the next summer.

United States.

8. A. luna *Fabr.* Figured in Sm. Abb. pl. 46. Drury, 1, pl. 4. Cram.
Clerck, Icon.

Antennæ brown; head white and small. Thorax white, sometimes yellowish or greenish, with a reddish-brown band at the
anterior part, which extends the whole length of the upper edge
of the superior wings.

Body of the same color with the thorax, but usually whitish.
Both pairs of wings are clear green. On each there is an ocellate
spot, of which a small part is transparent, encircled with yellow,
before which there is a semicircle of black and blue, and in that
of the primaries a purple line between the semicircle and the transparent part. On one side of each there is also a whitish line. The
nervures on all the wings are very distinct and pale brown. The
wings near the body are densely pilose.

The secondaries are terminated by a spatular tail, nearly two
inches long; all the wings are edged with pale yellow or ochre.

The under side is similar to the upper, except an indistinct un-

16

dulating line running along the margin of both wings. Feet ferruginous or purple-brown. Body covered with white hairs having the appearance of wool. Expands about five inches.

Larva pale bluish-green. A yellow stripe on each side of the body. Between each segment of the back a line of yellow. On each segment five or six small pearly protuberances, tinged with purple or red, having a few hairs. At the posterior end three brown spots, edged above with yellow. Length, when at rest, about two inches; about three, when in motion.

It spins its cocoon of whitish silk about two inches long, between two or three leaves it has previously drawn together with silken threads. The moth is disclosed in June.

It feeds on walnut (*Juglans*) and hickory (*Carya*).

United States.

4. A. polyphemus *Fab*. Figured in Nat. Lib. XXXVI.

Antennæ ferruginous; body of the same color; head cinereous. Superiors falcate, especially in the male. Upper margin cinereous, or dull ochre yellow. Base and outer edge russety. About half from the centre to the tip they are sprinkled with dark brown. Towards the base an irregular band of pale white and carmine. An obsolete ferruginous band crosses the middle. Towards the margin a band of pale purple and brownish, terminated at the tip with a black spot interrupted by the nervure, on a whitish ground nearly surrounded with purple. Near the centre there is an ocellate, transparent spot, bordered with a double ring of yellow and black, and a whitish semicircle towards the base.

Inferiors, fulvo-cinereous; posterior border russety; a broad band, half pale violet and half blackish, surmounts this border. In the centre, a large black ocellate spot, with a yellow iris and a transparent oval point in the middle. Above the transparent part there is a blue dust that insensibly mingles with the black.

On the under side the ground color is paler, but the bands are more distinct. The outer border of the superiors is deep brown. The base of the inferiors is brighter ferruginous, resting on a brown band crossing both inferiors horizontally. The black part of the ocellate spot on the upper side is not discernible, and instead of the band there is a row of indistinct semicircular spots. Expands nearly six inches.

Larva, somewhat similar to that of *A. luna*, but it is destitute of the lateral yellow stripe and the bands between the segments. It has pearly tubercles tinted with purple. Head and feet brown. Posterior end bordered by a brown mark similar to the letter V.

It forms its cocoon similar to *A. luna.*

United States.

5. **A. paphia** *Fab.* Figured in Petiv. Gazoph. tab. 29.

Nearly the size of *A. cecropia.* Primaries with the extremity subfalcate; ferruginous yellow, with the anterior edge cinereous. A yellowish white band, an ocellated spot, white, of which the middle is gray. The iris brown and the pupil transparent; edge ferruginous, on which there is a black violet ray. A little before the extremity there is an indistinct blackish marginal spot. Secondaries yellow, rounded, an ocellated spot similar to the preceding placed in the middle; paler towards the posterior edge, with indistinct undulated rays. Under side ferruginous yellow, with the same spots as on the upper side. The ocellated spots of the male are oblong; those of the female round.

North America.

Godt.

6. **A. angulifera** *Walker.* C. B. M. 1224.

Male and female. Wings with a blackish zigzag band, which extends from much beyond the middle of the costa of the fore wings to three-fourths of the breadth of the interior border of the hind wings. This band is diffuse on the inner side, and is bordered with a diffuse whitish line on the outer side. Discal spot whitish, forked, with a black border; larger in the fore wings than in the hind wings. Exterior border pale testaceous, curved, outwardly black bordered band between the base and the discal spot, and with a black subapical ocellus, which is bordered with white on the inner side. Hind wings with a row of elongated spots near the exterior border.

Male. Brown. Antennæ very deeply pectinated; branches in pairs, which are of equal length. Abdomen extending to much less than half the breadth of the hind wings.

Female. Ferruginous or reddish. Antennæ moderately pectinated; the alternate branches black and rather longer than the others. Abdomen extending to much more than half the breadth

of the hind wings.   Length of the body 7—12 lines; of the wings
42—48 lines.

North America.

WALKER.

7. A. didyma *Palis de Beauv.* Figured in Palis of de Beauv. pl. 20.

Body very thick, very hairy; wings saffron yellow. Primaries
with some vinous spots; sprinkled above with numerous, small,
irregular dots; a large vinous spot at the base; external edge with
a deeper band, nearly ferruginous, bordered with the same color
as the base. Each wing has two round, ocelliform spots towards
the middle; ring vinous; centre white; these two are contiguous
on the primaries. Those on the secondaries are a little separated,
the upper one is browner. Under side paler yellow, edges above
a little ferruginous and somewhat more spotted than the rest. The
ocelliform spots have their edges nearly violet; upper spots entirely
violet.

North America.

DE BEAUVOIS.

8. A. splendida *De Beauvois.* Ins. en Afrique et en Amer. p. 133, pl.
22, f. 1, 2

Dull reddish-brown. Thorax banded with white before and behind.
Abdomen with a white stigmatal band, edged above and beneath
with black, and containing reddish-brown spots. Fore wings with
a basal white streak extending from the costa to the base of medio-
posterior nervule and thence to the inner margin at the base of the
wing, bordered toward the base with orange-yellowish and externally by black. The breadth of the disk is occupied by a large
trigonate vitreous patch, extended behind so as to interrupt a white,
wavy, narrow band crossing the middle of the nervules, and which
is bordered internally with black and externally with orange-yellowish. The trigonate patch is edged within by white and externally by black behind and before. Beyond the transnervular band
the wing is brown dusted with blackish and powdered with whitish
roseate in the medio-posterior and submedian interspaces behind
the band. At the tip is a large whitish roseate patch, three contiguous black spots at the end of the postapical interspace, with a
wavy, black, submarginal line. Hind margin luteo-testaceous.
Hind wings, trigonate vitreous patch somewhat larger than in fore
wings, continued around the costa to the base of the wing and the

medio-posterior interspace and those adjoining it, powdered with
whitish roseate behind the band. Hind margin luteo-testaceous,
with a row of black spots and a dark brown line.

Texas.

CLEMENS. Proc. A. N. S. for 1860 p. 160.

CERATOCAMPA Harr.

Body thick. Proboscis short, hardly visible. Palpi very short,
not exceeding as far as the head. Antennæ a little shorter than
the thorax. Legs stout, rather long, hind tibiæ with two very
minute apical spurs. Wings rather long, moderately broad. Fore
wings acuminated, very slightly convex in front; exterior border
almost straight, very oblique; second inferior vein twice or more
than four times further from the third than from the first. *Male*.
Antennæ deeply pectinated, merely serrated for more than one-
third of the length from the tips. *Female*. Antennæ simple.

(The name of the genus is founded on the character of the larva,
that being armed with horns.)

C. R. M.

1. C. regalis *Fab*. F. *regia* Sm. Abb. *Lucewa* Cram. Figured in Sm.
   Abb. p. 121 pl. 61. Nat. Lib. XXXVII, p. 161, pl. 18. L. Drury,
   pl. 9.

Antennæ pectinated half their length, and setaceous at the end ;
head orange-red ; thorax same color, with a yellow band in front,
extending round each side, and two longitudinal broad yellow lines
on the top; abdomen red, with a yellow band across each segment
except the last. Superiors olive, with about six large yellow spots
in a series crossing them, the two largest near the tip; two or
three other irregular yellow spots further towards the base; two
yellow spots at the base; nervures thick and red. Inferiors orange-
red, with large irregular patches of yellow and a series of six or
seven olive-colored sagittate spots between the veins towards the
anal angle. The under side of the superiors is yellow at the base, red
in the centre, and olive on the margin. The series of yellow spots
and the red nervures similar to the upper side. Under side of
inferiors bright yellow, with a red spot in the centre. A pale red
transverse band which expands and covers the whole of the outer

angle, where there are a few sagittate olive spots. Body beneath
yellow, with some red spots; legs red. Expands five inches.

Larva green, with pale blue across each segment; on the side
of each segment a large bluish spot nearly square; head and feet
orange. On the first segment two long curved spines; on the
second, four, and an equal number on the third. They are yellow,
except at the tip, and are beset with small sharp points. On each
of the other segments there are six shorter spines, except the eleventh, on which there are seven, the longest one in the middle, and
on the last segment there are eleven. Length from five to six
inches.

Feeds on black walnut (*Juglans*), persimmon (*Diospyros vir-
giniana*).

Chrysalis short and thick, with a small macro at the posterior
part and edges of the segments without spines.

United States.

2. C. Imperialis *Drury. Imperatoria* Sm. Abb. Figured in Sm. Abb. II,
pl. 55. Jardine's Nat. Lib. XXXVII, pl. 17.

Antennæ and head yellow or reddish-brown; thorax brown in
front, yellow on top, purple on the sides; abdomen yellow, shaded
with purple.

Primaries yellow, sprinkled with purple, a large purple spot at
the base, a double round spot, with a yellow centre on the disk, a
sinuous purple band, commencing at the tip and crossing the wing,
a broad purple patch on the external border.

Secondaries of the same color, a smaller purple cloud at the
base, a purple band with a round spot, having a yellow centre
resting on it. Under side paler, the sprinkled dots not so numerous, and the bands indistinct. Expands four and a half inches.

Larva varies in color; sometimes tawny, again orange and
tawny, occasionally green. It has two short rugose horns on each
of the second and third segments, and some minute sharp points
on the others, crowned with tufts of long rigid hairs. There is a
small yellow spot, surrounded with a black ring, on the sides of all
the segments except the first three.

Feeds on the plane-tree (*Platanus occidentalis*), the oak (*Quercus*), sweet gum (*Liquidambar*), and pine (*Pinus*).

Chrysalis narrow, elongated, tail bifid at the extremity, edges
of the segments armed with a regular series of spines.

United States.

DRYOCAMPA Harris.

Body stout. Proboscis not visible. Antennæ shorter than the thorax. Abdomen hardly extending beyond the hind wings. Legs stout; hind tibiæ with two minute apical spurs. Wings moderately broad, thinly pilose. Primaries straight along the costa, acuminated at the apex, hardly convex, and very oblique along the exterior border.

Male. Antennæ deeply pectinated to much beyond half the length, minutely serrated from thence to the tips. *Female.* Antennæ simple.

1. D. stigma *F.* Figured in Smith & Abbot, p. 111, pl. 56.

Reddish-ochreous. Superiors purple on the outer border and internal side, thickly sprinkled with blackish dots; a small white spot in the centre and crossed from the tip with a narrow purple band. Body deep yellow; the under side similar though paler and not having so many black spots. Inferiors with a narrow transverse purple red band; border sprinkled with a few black dots. Expands from one inch and three-quarters to two inches and three-quarters.

Larva yellow, with black thorns on the back. Feeds on the oak. United States.

2. D. senatoria *F.*

Ochre-yellow. Wings faintly tinged with purplish-red, especially on the front and hind margins, and crossed by a narrow purple-brown band behind the middle. Superiors sprinkled with blackish dots; a small white spot near the middle. The male is much smaller than the female; its wings are thinner and more tinged with purple-red. Expands about an inch and three-quarters; the females two and a half or more.

Larva black, with four narrow ochre-yellow stripes along the back and two on each side. On each segment about six short thorns or sharp points, besides two on the top of the second segment, which are long and filiform, but not flexible. United States.

3. D. pellucida *Abb.* *Virginiensis* Drur. Figured in Smith & Abbot, p. 115, pl. 58.

Resembles *D. senatoria*, but is smaller and more delicate.

Body ochre-yellow. Superiors of the male purple-brown, with a large colorless transparent space in the middle, near which is a small round white spot, and towards the hinder margin a narrow oblique very faint dusky stripe. Inferiors purple-brown, nearly transparent in the middle, and margined with pale purple. Under side similar.

Larva rust-yellow; body pea-green, shaded on the back and sides with red; striped with very pale yellowish-green, and armed with black spines.

United States.

HARRIS.

4. D. rubicunda *F.* Harris, Ins. of Mass. p. 293.

Superiors rose-colored, crossed by a broad pale yellow band. Inferiors pale yellow. Abdomen and legs rose-colored.

United States.

HARRIS.

5. D. bicolor *Harris,* Ins. of Mass. p. 293.

Upper side of the fore wings and under side of the hind wings are brownish-gray, sprinkled with black dots, and with a small round white spot near the middle, and a narrow oblique dusky band behind it on the fore wings; the upper side of the hind wings and the under side of the fore wings, except the front edge and hinder margin of the latter, are crimson-red, and the body is brownish-gray. The male expands two inches and a quarter.

United States.

HARRIS.

BOMBYCIDAE Steph. *Bombycina* Harr.-Boh.

The difficulty of distributing this family into consistent genera has been acknowledged by all who have studied it. Various synopses have been proposed, but none, as yet, have been generally adopted. Most of them have been founded more or less exclusively on the perfect insects, but such cannot stand as the larvæ and transformation become better known.

The *Bombycidæ*, so called from *Bombyx*, the ancient name for silkworm, inclose themselves in cocoons of silk in the larval state, and hence are called *spinners* by the Germans. They are mostly thick-bodied moths, with the antennæ generally pectinated in both sexes. The organs of the mouth are in an undeveloped state, the thorax woolly, and the anterior legs often very hairy. The larvæ for the most part have tubercles mounted with tufts of hair, and live exposed on plants.

GASTROPACHA Ochs.

Body thick. Head prominent. Proboscis obsolete. Palpi stout, porrect, pilose, extending some distance beyond the head; third joint less than half the length of the second, rounded at tip. Antennæ curved, a little shorter than the thorax. Abdomen generally extending more or less beyond the hind wings. Legs stout, very pilose, hind tibiæ with two very minute apical spurs. Wings moderately broad, denticulated along the exterior border. Fore wings nearly straight in front, slightly acuminated at the tips, moderately oblique along the exterior border; first and second inferior veins almost contiguous at the base; third rather remote from the second, more remote from the fourth. *Male*. Antennæ rather deeply pectinated. *Female*. Antennæ moderately pectinated.

1. G. americana. Figured in Smith & Abbot, p. 101, pl. 51.

Color, reddish-brown; margins of anterior and posterior wings notched; notches white; behind the middle of each of the wings is a pale band, edged with zigzag dark-brown lines, and there are also two or three short irregular brown lines running backwards from the front edge of the fore wings, besides a minute pale crescent edged with dark brown, near the middle. In the female, the pale bands and dark lines are sometimes wanting, the wings being almost entirely of a red-brown color.

United States.

HARRIS.

2. G. laricis *Fitch*. (*Pinara Fitch laricis*.) Figured in Fitch's Second Report.

Male. Head densely clothed with white hairs in front, blackish ones about the eyes. Palpi minutely concealed by fine long hairs. Antennæ short, abruptly bent near the middle, pectinated to the bend, and then shorter to the end. Thorax clothed with long hairs of dark gray; an oblong crest of glossy scales on the posterior part. Tongue short, not coiled. Abdomen with blackish hairs above, whitish beneath, the end with a dense pure white tuft. Wings semitransparent, thickly covered with brown scales, which are denuded; veins robust and white, with darker irregular bands; unemarginate. Legs densely covered with long white tufts; forward shanks have a tuft of blackish hairs.

Female. Much larger, and differently colored. Wings thin, translucent; hind edge with a slender white band; before this there is a narrow pale dusky band abruptly widened near its middle to double its width; this band is margined on its anterior side by a white line, by which it is separated from a much broader and more dusky band which is waved in its middle; forward of this the wings are milk-white, crossed by four very faint equidistant wavy bands of the same delicate pale dusky hue with those behind. Hind wings of the same dusky tint as the bands of the fore wings, but paler; a white line on their hind margin. Body white, with a tuft of pale brown at the apex. Thorax crested blackish. Antennæ shorter than those of the male. Expands an inch and a half.

New York.

Fitch.

3. G. velleda *Stoll*. Figured in Smith & Abbot, p. 103, pl. 51.

Body thick and woolly, white, variegated or clouded with blue-gray. On the fore wings are two broad dark-gray bands intervening between three narrow wavy white bands, the latter being marked with an irregular gray line; the veins are white, prominent, and very distinct; the hind wings are gray, with a white hind border on which are two interrupted gray lines, and across the middle there is a broad faint whitish band; on the top of the thorax is an oblong blackish spot, widening behind, and consisting

of long black and pearl-colored scales shaped somewhat like the
handle of a spoon.   Great disparity in the size of the sexes.

HARRIS.

4. O. occidentalis *Walk.   Ricifolia* Sm. Abb.   *Americana* Harris.   Figured in Smith & Abbot, II, pl. 51.

Ferruginous; cilia of the wings marked with white; primaries
with oblique blackish fascia, testaceous at the base, cinereous at
the exterior margin; secondaries with the disk partly testaceous.
North America.

HARRIS.

CLISIOCAMPA Curtis.

Body stout or thick.   Palpi short, hardly extending beyond the
head; third joint slightly acuminated.   Antennæ a little longer
than the thorax.   Legs stout, pilose; hind tibiæ with two very
minute apical spurs.   Wings more or less broad.   Fore wings
straight in front, slightly rounded at the tip, somewhat oblique along
the exterior border; first and second inferior veins almost contiguous at the base; third twice further from the fourth than from the
second.   *Male*, antennæ deeply pectinated.   Abdomen robust,
hardly extending beyond the hind wings.   *Female*, antennæ very
slightly pectinated.   Abdomen thick, extending for one-third of
its length beyond the hind wings.   (*C. B. M.*)

1. C. decipiens *Walk.   Castrensis* Smith & Abbot.

Color rust or reddish-brown, variegated with gray, especially on
the middle and base of the fore wings.   Anterior wings crossed
obliquely by two dingy white parallel lines; margin ciliate and
whitish.   Hind wings without lines or spots; a portion of the
costal margin whitish.   Beneath darker.   Length of the body 5—6
lines; of the wings 10—12 lines.
United States.

WALKER.

Harris, Ins. of Mass., has called this species *Americana*, but
that name is preoccupied by Fab.

2. O.? americana *Fab.*

Male. Antennæ strongly pectinate. Wings whitish; primaries with some fuscous costal streaks.

PAB.

3. O. sylvatica *Harris.* Ins. of Mass. p. 271.

Brownish-yellow or nankin color. The hind wings, except at base, are light rusty brown. On the fore wings are two oblique rust-brown and nearly straight parallel lines. A variety is sometimes found with a broad red-brown band across the fore wings, occupying the whole space, which, in other individuals, intervenes between the oblique lines. The wings expand from one inch and a quarter to one and three quarters.

Larva. Light blue, clear on the back, and greenish at the sides. Head blue, without spots. Two yellow spots and four black dots on the top of the first segment. Along the top of the back a row of eleven oval white spots, beginning on the second segment, and two small elevated black and hairy dots on each segment, except the eleventh, which has only one of larger size. On each side of the back is a reddish stripe bordered by slender black lines; and lower down on each side is another stripe of yellow color between two black lines. The under side of the body is blue-black. Lives in communities of three or four hundred under a common web or tent, which is sometimes made against the trunk of the walnut, oak, and more rarely of apple-trees.

Northern States.

HARRIS.

ARTACE WALKER.

Body moderately stout. Proboscis obsolete. Palpi stout, porrect, pilose, not extending beyond the head; first joint short; third minute, conical. Abdomen extending a little beyond the hind wings. Legs stout, pilose; hind tibiæ with two minute apical spurs. Wings rather narrow. Fore wings straight in front, rounded at the tips, very oblique along the exterior border; interior angle somewhat rounded and very obtuse; first and second inferior veins contiguous at the base; third about twice farther from the fourth than from the second.

Male. Antennæ rather deeply pectinated to beyond one-third of their length, slightly pectinated from thence to the tips. *Female.* Antennæ moderately pectinated.

1. A. punctistriga *Walker*, C. B. M. pl. 5, 1491.

White. Antennæ with tawny branches. Tarsi with black bands. Fore legs very thickly clothed with long hairs. Fore wings with four oblique bands of black dots on the veins; these bands form each an angle near the costa, and there the dots are largest, and the space between them is occasionally blackish; a row of black dots (which are occasionally obsolete) between the veins on the exterior border. Hind wings with a transverse more or less indistinct brownish mark near the interior angle. Length of the body 8—10 lines; of the wings 16—24 lines.

Georgia.

WALKER.

2. A. albicans *Walker.* C. B. M. 1492, pl. v.

White. Palpi rose color, blackish towards the base. Antennæ with brown branches. Legs with black bands; fore tibiæ partly clothed with rosy hairs. Wings with a row of black dots between the veins on the exterior border, near which there is a parallel row of brownish dots. Fore wings with a rosy tinge towards the base of the costa; veins with black dots, which form four or five oblique bands. Length of body 5—6 lines; of the wings 12—16 lines.

Georgia?

WALKER.

3. A. punctivena *Walker.*

Male. Tawny, shining, paler beneath. Middle tarsi black, with testaceous bands. Fore wings with five oblique bands of black dots; the dots on the veins, with the exception of those of the exterior marginal band which lie between the veins. Hind wings with an indistinct interrupted submarginal grayish band. Length of the body 6 lines; of the wings 12 lines.

WALKER.

Fam. XI. NOTODONTIDAE Herr.-Sch.

Body usually robust, pilose, abdomen extending beyond
the wings, sometimes nearly double the length. Proboscis
often none or very short, sometimes rather long. Palpi
moderate, rarely very long. Antennæ of the male usually
pectinate, rarely simple; of the female, simple, rarely sub-
pectinate. Eyes usually naked. Legs densely pilose or
scaly. Primaries not wide. Wings entire, often long.

CERURA Schr.   Harpya Hübn.

Body stout, pilose. Proboscis very short. Palpi very short.
Antennæ pectinated to the tips, longer than the thorax. Abdomen
extending beyond the hind wings. Legs stout, pilose; hind tibiæ
with two minute apical spurs. Wings rather long. Fore wings
almost straight along the costa, rounded at the tips, very oblique
along the exterior border; anterior angle much rounded; discal
areolet intersected by a secondary forked vein; three inferior veins,
second about four times further from the third than from the first.
C. H. M.

1. C. borealis *Harris. Furcula Sm. Abb.* Figured in Griffith's Règne
Animal, Smith & Abbot, p. 141, pl. 71.

Antennæ feathered in both sexes, but narrow and tapering, and
bent upwards at the point; the legs, especially the first pair, which
are stretched out before the body when at rest, are very hairy;
wings thin and almost transparent. Ground color, dirty white;
the fore wings are crossed by two broad blackish bands, the outer
one of which is transversed and interrupted by an irregular wavy
whitish line ; the hinder margins of all the wings are dotted with
black, and there are several black dots at the base and a single one
near the middle of the fore wings; the top of the thorax is blackish, and the collar is edged with black.
United States.

HARRIS.

NOTODONTA Ochs.

Body stout. Proboscis distinct, very short. Palpi short, porrect, pilose, not extending beyond the head; third joint very minute. Abdomen extending for one-third or one-half of its length beyond the hind wings. Legs stout, femora and tibiæ densely pilose; hind tibiæ with four rather long spurs. Wings somewhat long, rather narrow or moderately broad. Fore wings nearly straight in front, rounded at the tips, very oblique and slightly denticulated along the exterior border; interior angle very oblique; interior border tufted in the middle; discal areolet intersected by a secondary forked vein; three inferior veins, second thrice further from the third than from the first. *Male*. Antennæ moderately pectinated. *Female*. Antennæ simple.

1. **N. angulosa** Sm. *Abb*. Figured in Smith & Abbot, pl. 83.

Male. Crested; primaries fawn-color, with black flexuous lines and streaks, back porrect; secondaries whitish. *Female*. Primaries fawn-color, with white spots and three fulvous bands; secondaries pale testaceous, with a fuscous subapical costal spot.

Georgia.

C. B. M.

2. **N. basistriens** *Walk*. C. B. M. 1000.

Male. Cinereous, hoary beneath. Head, thorax, and fore wings partly clothed with black hairs. Proboscis testaceous. Antennæ tawny. Thorax with a slender black band between the fore wings. Abdomen slightly testaceous. Fore wing, with a testaceous patch, which occupies the basal third part of the wing, is bordered with black and has a brownish disk; the adjoining part of the wing has a whitish tinge, which is widest in front, and beyond it is a slender undulating oblique brown band, which is obsolete towards the costa; the wings beyond are indistinctly mottled. Hind wings whitish for about two-thirds from the base, with a slight discal undulating grayish band, which corresponds to the band of the fore wings. Length of the body 8 lines; of the wings 19 lines.

New York.

C. B. M.

The following are placed by Walker in Doubleday's genus *Heterocampa*, which differs from *Notodonta* in the deeper pectination of the antennæ of the males, in the dilation of the fore tibiæ, and in the more slender legs.

1. **H. astarte** *Doubleday*, C. B. M. 1023. Figured in the Entomologist, 57, pl. 6, 1, 2.

Primaries ash-green, with ferruginous transverse streaks and central crescent; apex with a white lunate spot.

East Florida.
C. B. M.

2. **H. umbrata** *Walk.* C. B. M. 1023.

Ferruginous. Thorax with a black band in front. Fore wings with several indistinct transverse slightly oblique undulating blackish lines. Hind wings hoary, grayish along the border, and with a slight discal curved grayish band. Length of the body 9 lines; of the wings 20 lines.

East Florida.
C. B. M.

3. **H. varia** *Walk.* C. B. M. 1023.

Female. Cinereous. Thorax with blackish marks. Fore wings with some whitish marks along the costa, with a costal subapical short oblique whitish band, and with three discal whitish spots; five irregular undulating black double bands. Hind wings pale gray, with broad brown borders. Length of the border 10 lines; of the wings 24.

New York.
C. B. M.

4. **H. manteo** *Walk.* C. B. M. 1029.

Primaries fuscous-cinereous, with numerous transverse more obscure streaks, a marginal series of black points, a central white line, in which there is a geminate black point.

New York.
C. B. M.

5. **H. biundata** *Walk.* C. B. M. 1025.

Male. Cinereous. Head, thorax, and fore wings slightly tinged with green. Pectus, abdomen beneath, and legs, whitish. Fore wings with some blackish marks at the base, and with a double

undulating blackish band at one-fourth of the length; two slight
oblique and undulating brown bands beyond the middle, and towards the exterior border a more oblique and undulating band of
blackish spots; under side grayish, whitish about the borders.
Hind wings brownish, whitish towards the base and beneath.
Length of the body 9 lines; of the wings 20.

New York.

WALKER, C. B. M.

6. E. ipomææa *Doubleday*, Entomologist, 60.

Primaries fusco-ferruginous, sprinkled with cinereous, an indistinct middle band, a stigma pupilled with ashy-ferruginous, veins
towards the apex black.

Florida.

WALKER, C. B. M.

EDEMA WALK.

Body moderately stout. Proboscis short. Palpi slender, pubescent, extending beyond the head; second joint more than twice the
length of the first; third lanceolate, nearly half the length of the
second. Abdomen extending a little beyond the hind wings. Legs
slender; hind tibiæ with four long apical spurs. Wings moderately broad. Fore wings straight along the costa, almost angular
at the tips; exterior border oblique and slightly convex; three inferior veins; first and second contiguous at the base; third remote.
Male. Palpi ascending. Antennæ minutely pectinated to beyond
five-sixths of the length, more than half the length of the body.
Female. Palpi porrect, shorter than those of the male. Antennæ
simple, less than half the length of the body.

1. E. unicornis *Sm. Abb.* Figured in Sm. Abb. II, pl. 83.

Anteriors, light brown, variegated with patches of greenish-
white and with wavy dark brown lines, two of which inclose a small
whitish space near the shoulders; there is a short blackish mark
near the middle; the tip and outer hind margin are whitish, tinged
with red in the males; and near the outer hind angle there are one
small spot and two black dashes; posterior wings of the male are
dirty white, with a dusky spot on the inner hind angle; those of
the female are sometimes entirely dusky; body brownish—two

16

narrow black bands across the forepart of the thorax.   Wings expand one and a quarter to one and a half inches.

Larva. The top of the fourth ring rises in the form of a long horn, sloping forwards a little; the tail, with the hindmost feet, which are rather longer than the others, is always raised when the larva is at rest, but it generally uses these legs in walking; head large, brown; sides of the second and third ring, green; rest of the body brown, variegated with white on the back—a few short hairs hardly visible.

United States.

HARRIS.

2. B. concinna Sm. *Abbott*. Figured in Sm. Abb. pl. 64.

Color, light brown; forewings dark brown along the inner margin are more or less tinged with gray before; a dark brown dot near the middle, a spot of the same color near each angle, a very small triangular whitish spot near the shoulders, and several dark brown longitudinal streaks on the outer hind margin; the hind wings of the male are brownish or dirty white, with a brown spot on the inner hind angle; those of the female are dusky brown; body light brown, with the thorax rather darker. Expands from one to one and three-eighth inch.

Larva. Yellowish brown, paler on the sides, striped with slender black lines; head red; on the top of the fourth ring there is a hump, also red; along the back, several short black prickles; hinder extremity tapering, and is always elevated at an angle with the rest of the body, when not crawling.

United States.

HARRIS.

3. B. albifrons Sm. *Abb*. Figured in Sm. Abb. pl. 60.

Male. Hoary. Palpi brown above. Thorax with a tawny band near the fore border. Forewings with various small brown marks, white along the costa for half the length from the tips; the outline of this white part is very irregular, and the adjoining part of the wing behind it is dark brown; a row of short undulating blackish streaks along the exterior border. Length of the body six lines, of the wings fifteen lines.

Female. Cinereous. Fore wings thinly covered with black flecks; a brown zigzag band at a little before one-third of the length, and extending from the costa to rather beyond half the breadth of the wing; a large white patch on the fore half of the

breadth of the wing between the first band and a second, which is
brown, oblique, complete and slightly undulating; beyond the
latter there are two slight whitish oblique bands, the first incomplete, the second marginal and intersected by a blackish band.
Hind wings pale brown, partially and very thinly flecked with
brown, with a brown discal spot, and with a brown oblique slightly
undulating band, which is composed of flecks, and corresponds to
the second brown band of the fore wings.   Length seven lines—
wings twenty lines.

United States.
WALKER, C. B. M.

4. B. producta *Walk.*   C. B. M. 1031.

Male and Female. Cinereous.   Palpi above blackish-brown.
Antennæ brown.   Thorax with two brown bands.   Legs whitish;
fore legs above blackish-brown.   Fore wings slightly mottled with
brown, and with two irregular black slender bands; the first emitting a branch from its middle towards the base of the wing; the
second emitting two branches to the fore part of the exterior border; a white apical spot, a whitish spot at the base and some black
streaks along the exterior border.   Hind wings brown, with a
whitish fringe; under side whitish, with two or three bands of
brown dots.   Length of the body 5—6 lines; of the wings 11—12
lines.

East Florida.
C. B. M.

ICHTHYURA Hüb.   *Pygæra* Ochs.   *Clostera* Hoffmansegg.

Body moderately stout.   Proboscis very short.   Palpi short,
porrect, not extending as far as the head; third joint, small, conical.   Antennæ less than half the length of the body.   Abdomen
extending for about one-third of its length beyond the hind wings,
tufted at the tip.   Legs stout; fore tibiæ very densely pilose;
hind tibiæ with small apical spurs.   Wings moderately broad.
Fore wings straight along the costa, rounded at the tips, slightly
oblique along the exterior border; interior angle much rounded;
discal areolet intersected by a secondary vein; three inferior veins,
second nearly contiguous to the first, rather remote from the third.
Male. Antennæ rather deeply pectinated.   *Female.* Antennæ minutely pectinated.

1. L. inclusa *Hübner.*   *L. americana* Sm. Abb.   *L. americana* Har.

Antennæ pectinated in both sexes; the thorax has an elevated crest in the middle; tail tufted and turned up at the end in the males; the fore legs thickly covered with hairs to the end, and are stretched out before the body when at rest; color brownish-gray; fore wings faintly tinged with pale lilac, and more or less clouded with rust-red; they have an irregular row of blackish dots near the outer hind margin, and are crossed by three whitish lines, of which the first nearest the shoulders is broken and widely separated in the middle; the second divides into two branches, one of which goes straight across the wing to the inner margin, and the other passes obliquely till it meets the end of the third line, with which it forms an angle or letter Y; across the middle of the hind wings there is a narrow brownish band, much more distinct beneath than above; on the top of the thorax there is an oblong chestnut-colored spot, the hairs of which rise upwards behind and form a crest. All the whitish lines on the fore wings are more or less bounded externally with rust-red. It expands from one inch and one quarter to one inch and five-eighths.

WALKER.

2. L. alboaigma *Fitch.*   Fifth Report, p. 64.

Grayish-brown; fore wings crossed by three faint paler streaks, the two first parallel, the hind one with its outer half silvery white and strongly waved in the shape of the letter S; width 1.50.
United States.

FITCH.

3. L. vau *Fitch.*   Fifth Report, p. 65.

Similar to *inclusa*, but darker colored and smaller, with the bands more slender and distinct, and may be readily distinguished from that species by its having the first band not dislocated but in its middle strongly curved backwards, the apex of the curve usually forming an acute point. The last band also is much more strongly undulated near its outer end, curving backwards almost in a semi-circle, and is of a much more vivid white color and broadly bordered on its hind side with bright rust-red. Its hind wings also are destitute of the paler band across their middle; width about 1.20.
United States.

FITCH.

EUDRYAS Hübn.

Wing structure similar to that of the Noctuina. In the hind wings the costal and subcostal veins do not run adjacent and parallel to each other, as is usual amongst the genera of the family, but arise from a short, common stalk. In the fore wings the structure is precisely that of the Noctuina, showing the secondary or subcostal cell, and the subdivision of the nervules characteristic of this group.

The head is smooth, rather short, with ocelli. The antennæ setaceous, minutely ciliated. The labial palpi slightly ascending, but little exceeding the clypeus, smooth, rather thick; middle and basal joints nearly equal, the terminal minute and ovoid. Tongue rather slender, and about as long as the anterior coxæ.

Thorax and basal segment of the abdomen tufted. Breast woolly. Abdomen smooth. Legs tufted; fore legs especially, which have a large globose tarsal tuft, one on the tibiæ and one on the coxæ. In repose, the fore legs are held in advance.

I. E. grata *Fab.* Ent. Syst. III, 457.

Fore wings pure white, with a broad stripe along the front edge, extending from the shoulder a little beyond the middle of the edge and a broad band around the outer hind margin, of a deep purple brown color; the band is edged internally with olive green and marked towards the edge with a slender wavy white line; near the middle of the wing and touching the brown stripe, are two brown spots, one of them round and the other kidney-shaped; and on the middle of the inner margin there is a large triangular olive-colored spot; the under side of the same wings is yellow, and near the middle there is a round and kidney-shaped black spot. The hind wings are yellow above and beneath; on the upper side with a broad purple-brown hind border, on which there is a little wavy white line, and on the under side with only a central black dot. Head black. Along the middle of the thorax, a broad stripe of black and pearl-colored glittering scales. Shoulder covers white. Upper side of the abdomen is yellow, with a row of black spots on the top, and another on each side; under side and the large muff-like tufts on the fore legs, are white; other legs, black.

Larva. Blue, transversely banded with deep orange across the middle of each ring; bands dotted with black; head and feet orange; top of the 11th ring somewhat bulging, and the forepart of the body hunched up when at rest. Feeds on the grape.

United States.

HARRIS.

2. D. unio *Hübner.*

Smaller than *E. grata;* differs in having the stripe and band on its fore wings of a brighter purple brown color, the round and kidney-shaped spots contiguous to the former also brown, the olive-colored edging of the band wavy with a powdered blue spot between it and the triangular olive-colored spot on the inner margin, and a distinct brown spot on the inner hind angle of the posterior wings; all the wings beneath are broadly bordered behind with light brown, and the spots upon them are also light brown.

United States.

HARRIS.

DATANA WALK.

Body rather stout, pilose; hairs rather smooth. Proboscis short, not exceeding the breadth of the head. Palpi short, porrect, not extending beyond the head; second joint very much longer than the first; third acute, very minute. Thorax somewhat convex. Abdomen extending for one-fourth of its length beyond the hind wings. Legs stout, pilose; hind tibiæ with four rather long spurs. Wings broad or rather broad. Fore wings nearly straight along the costa, hardly angular at the tips; exterior border more or less oblique; three inferior veins; first and second united at the base; third rather remote. *Male.* Antennæ minutely pectinated; the branches successively but very slightly decreasing in length. *Female.* Antennæ minutely serrated.

1. D. ministra *Drury.* Figured in Drury, pl. 14. Sm. Abb. pl. 61.

Luteous-tawny. Thorax rather darker towards the hind part, which is pale testaceous. Pectus, abdomen and legs pale testaceous. Fore wings tawny, with four slender ferruginous bands; first band at one-fourth of the length, curved outward; second, third and fourth bands oblique; second curved backward towards the costa, beyond the distal spot or spots, the space between it and the first a little darker than the wing elsewhere; third and fourth bands very slightly undulating; a more or less distinct streak between them, very near to the fourth; under side without bands. Hind wings a little paler than the fore wings; under side pale testaceous. *Male.* Fore wings with one discal brown spot. *Female.* Fore wings with two discal brown spots, the outer one larger than the other. Length of the body 10 lines; of the wings 26—27 lines.

United States.

WALKER.

2. D. contracta *Walk.* C. B. M. 1062.

Much resembling the preceding species, but with narrower fore wings. Luteous-tawny. Thorax brown towards the hind part, which is whitish testaceous. Pectus, abdomen and legs testaceous. Fore wings tawny, whitish testaceous about the base and along the outer side of the second, third and fourth bands; four slender brown bands; first much like that in *D. ministra*, but rather less convex; second more oblique, more retracted towards the costa, and nearer the first on the hind border; third and fourth also rather more oblique than in the preceding species; cilia brownish. Hind wings whitish, with testaceous borders. Length of the body 7 lines; of the wings 19 lines.

North America.

WALKER.

3. D.? anguina *Sm. Abb.* Figured in Sm. Abb. pl. 54.

Female. Pale luteous; thorax cinereous; abdomen and secondaries fawn color; primaries subferruginous, spotted with black; band and exterior margin whitish, base pale luteous.

Georgia.

Sm. Abb.

4. D.? aurora *Sm. Abb.* Figured in Sm. Abb. pl. 57.

Yellow; thorax rosy before; abdomen rosy at the apex; primaries rosy at the base and margin; secondaries of the *male* rosy, of the *female* white.

Georgia.

Sm. Abb.

NADATA Walker.

Body moderately stout, pilose; hairs rather smooth. Proboscis distinct, shorter than the breadth of the head. Palpi porrect, rather slender, not extending beyond the head; second joint full twice the length of the first; third minute conical. Thorax highly crested; the crest terminating in an acute cone. Legs rather slender, pilose; hind tibiæ with four long spurs. Wings rather broad. Fore wings with slight undulations along the exterior border, slightly acute at the tips; three inferior veins; first and second connected at the base; third rather remote. *Male.* Antennæ moderately pectinated, more than half the length of the body. Abdomen not extending beyond the hind wings. Fore wings almost straight along the costa, exterior border less oblique than in the female. *Female.* Third joint of the palpi more acute than in the male. Antennæ simple, hardly more than half the length of the body. Abdomen extending for one-fourth of its length beyond the hind wings. Fore wings slightly convex along the costa.

1. N. gibbosa *Sm. Ab.* Figured in Sm. Abb. pl. 52.

Tawny, whitish testaceous beneath. Fore wings very minutely covered with ferruginous flecks; a slightly oblique ferruginous band at one-third of the length, and another more oblique, at a little beyond two-thirds of the length; the outer border of the latter is more or less paler than the rest of the wing; two white discal dots, one behind the other, exterior border with whitish marks. Hind wings testaceous, whitish towards the costa, and with a slender indistinct tawny somewhat undulating discal band; exterior margin slightly tawny. Length of the body 7½—10 lines; of the wings 20—24 lines.

United States.

WALKER.

FAM. ARCTIIDAE Herr.-Schaff. *Chelonides* Boisd.

Stature robust; ocelli conspicuous; maxillæ short sub-membranaceous, sometimes obsolete. Antennæ moderate, of the female, when not nearly obsolete, bipectinate or ciliate, sometimes serrate or simple. Palpi small, pilose, often triarticulate. Abdomen stout, maculate. Wings entire, deflexed, variegated in color. Frenulum conspicuous. *Larvæ* with coarse hairs, growing in clusters or tufts from the tubercles in transverse rows on the body.

OROYA Ochs.

Male. Body slender. Proboscis very short. Palpi short, stout, very hairy; third joint very small. Antennæ very deeply pectinated. Legs slender; hind tibiæ with two rather short apical spurs, or with four moderately long spurs. Wings broad. Fore wings with the first, second and third inferior veins near together. Hind wings extending beyond the abdomen.

1. O. leucostigma *Sm. Abb.* Figured in Sm. Abb. pl. 29.

The males have large ashen-gray wings, crossed by wavy darker bands on the upper pair, on which, moreover, is a small black spot near the tip, and a minute white crescent near the outer hind angle. The body of the male is small and slender, with a row of little tufts along the back, and the wings expand one inch and three-eighths. The females are of a lighter gray color than the males, their bodies are very thick, and of an oblong oval shape, and, though seemingly wingless, upon close examination two little scales, or stinted winglets, can be discovered on each shoulder.

Larva of a bright yellow color, sparingly clothed with long and fine yellow hairs on the sides of the body, and having four short and thick brush-like yellowish tufts on the back, that is on the fourth and three following rings, two long black plumes or pencils extending forwards from the first ring, and a single plume on top of the eleventh ring. The head, and the two little retractile warts on the ninth and tenth rings are coral red; there is a narrow black or brownish stripe along the top of the back, and a wider dusky stripe on each side of the body.

United States.

HARRIS.

2. O. antiqua *Linn.* Figured in most European works.

The male is of a rust-brown color, the fore wings are crossed by two deeper brown wavy streaks, and have a white crescent near the hind angle. They expand about one inch and one-eighth. The female is gray, and wingless, or with only two minute scales on each side in the place of wings, and exactly resembles in shape the female of the foregoing species. The *larva* is yellow on the back, on which are four short square brush-like yellow tufts; the sides are dusky and spotted with red; there are two long black pencils or plumes on the first ring, one on each side of the fifth ring, and one on top of the eleventh ring; the head is black; and the retractile warts on top of the ninth and tenth rings are red.

United States and Europe.

HARRIS.

8. O. leucographa *Walk.* C. B. M.

Male. Obscurely fuscous; primaries paler, with a sub-basal streak, a costal ante-apical spot, two bands, the first wide before the middle, the second arcuate dark fuscous, and a white posterior spot. *Female.* Apterous.

Georgia.

WALKER.

4. O. vetusta *Boisd.* Am. Soc. Ent. 2me sér. X, 322.

Primaries fuscous, a paler band at the base and a white anal spot; secondaries fusco-rufescent.

California.

BOISD.

APANTESIS WALKER.

Female. Body fusiform, clothed with close smooth hairs. Head small. Head and thorax clothed with short hairs, lying close and smooth. Proboscis short. Palpi hairy, porrect; third joint conical, small. Antennæ minutely pectinated. Abdomen with very short hairs, extending to one-third of its length beyond the hind wings. Fore wings narrow, subfusiform, slightly convex along the costa; outer border slightly oblique and convex; hind angle very obtuse and much rounded; first, second and third inferior veins very near together at the base; fourth twice further from the third than the third from the first. Hind wings rather broader than the fore wings and hardly two-thirds of the length. Legs moderately stout; hind tibiæ with four spurs of middling length.

1. A. radians *Walk.* C. B. M. 632.

Female. Dark brown. Head clothed above with luteous hairs. Proboscis testaceous. Antennæ black. Thorax in front luteous with two brown stripes; middle part with two luteous stripes. Abdomen above testaceous towards the base and with two luteous stripes. Fore wings with testaceous borders, excepting the apical third part of the costal margin; a discal testaceous streak, extending from the base along one-fourth of the length of the wing, forked at its tip. Hind wings red towards the base; the outline of the red part very angular. Fore femora with a luteous spot on each. Length of the body 5 lines; of the wings 12 lines.

Georgia.

                                        WALKER.

DEIOPEIA *Curt.* *Eyprepia* Ochs. *Euchelia* Boisd.

Palpi elongate, above recurved subsquamous; first article stout, second long; third short, ovate. Maxillæ much longer than the head. Antennæ simple in both sexes, rather short, those of the male subpilose below. Primaries oblong, subelliptic, truncated; secondaries subdiaphanous, strongly plicate. Legs moderate; tibiæ very short, hind tibiæ with four spurs at the apex.

1. D. bella *Linn.* Figured in Cram. Pap. Exot. II, 20, 109. Drury 1, pl. 24. Nat. Lib. vol. XXXVII, pl. 24.

Primaries fine yellow, traversed with several irregular white bands, with a series of black dots in each and a regular row of black dots on the outer margin; fringe pure white. Secondaries scarlet, irregularly margined with black behind; fringe white, thorax nearly white, spotted with black; abdomen whitish; antennæ black, naked, setaceous.

Expands from an inch and a half to an inch and three-quarters.

United States.

                                        HARRIS.

2. D. aurea *Fitch.*

Fore wings bright marigold yellow, with four bands of round pale sulphur-yellow spots upon a brilliant steel blue ground, the hindmost band almost upon the apex, its outer half abruptly widened and slightly united with the third band, which is the broadest and towards its outer end is abruptly narrowed and almost interrupted. Its hind wings are transparent, with a dusky margin and blackish veins. Width one inch.

Georgia.

FAM. LITHOSIIDAE STEPH. *Lithosina* Her.-Schaef.

Body slender, elongate, no ocelli. Proboscis often longer than the head. Palpi not extending beyond the head, cylindrical, third article shorter than the second or not longer. Antennæ usually ciliate or simple. Thorax not crested. Abdomen not extending beyond the wings or very little. Wings often subelliptical; primaries narrow, with rounded apex; secondaries often twice as wide as the primaries. Frenulum conspicuous. Color yellow or gray, seldom black, sometimes with cross bands or rows of black points, occasionally confluent. In repose, the primaries are plicate; the secondaries folded close to the abdomen. *Larva* herbivorous, usually with hairy tubercles. *Pupa* very short, with segments immovable.

EUSTIXIA WALKER.

Male. Body moderately long and wide. Palpi short. Antennæ setaceous, simple. Abdomen extending a little beyond the secondaries. Feet slender; wings not long; primaries nearly straight on the costal edge, oblique at the apical margin, the posterior angle subrotund.

1. E. pupula *Hübner.*

Male. Brownish-black, below whitish; wings whitish; primaries with four bands, secondaries with two, composed of black spots.

United States.

WALKER, C. B. M.

EUBCPHE Herr.

Male. Body slender. Palpi short. Antennæ slender, setaceous, simple, a little shorter than the body. Abdomen extending a little beyond the secondaries. Feet slender. Wings narrow, rather long ; primaries oblique at the apical margin ; secondaries rounded, not angulate.

1. H. aurantiaca *Hübner.*

Orange ; secondaries paler towards the base.
United States.

Hübn.

MIOZA Walker.

Body slender, rather short. Palpi straight, slender, a little shorter than the head ; third joint linear, conical at the tip, a little shorter than the second. Antennæ slender, setaceous, very minutely pubescent. Abdomen extending as far as or a little beyond the hind wings. Legs slender ; hind tibiæ with four long spurs. Wings long, narrow. Fore wings very slightly convex in front, conical at the tips, with a somewhat rounded angle behind ; the three inferior veins approximate at the base. Hind wings with four inferior veins ; third approximate at the base, fourth remote.

1. M. igninix *Walk.*

Pale red or saffron-color. Head white above, pale red on the vertex. Palpi with black tips. Antennæ black. Thorax white, with six black spots, one on the disk, two on each side, and one on the scutellum. Fore tibiæ and fore tarsi brown. Fore wings above white with black streaks on one-third of the breadth from the costa and on one-third of the length from the tips ; in the rest of the wing there are five elongated black spots, two before the middle and three beyond the middle. Length of the body 8—8½ lines ; of the wings 10—11 lines.
St. John's Bluff, E. Florida.

WALKER, C. B. M.

2. M. subterrena *Walk.*

Male. Pale red or saffron-color. Head and thorax white above. Antennæ white towards the base. Fore wings white above with many elongate brown points, and with two oblique bands of brown dots, one at one-fourth of the length, the other before two-thirds of the length. Length of the body 3 lines ; of the wings 10 lines.
United States.

WALKER, C. B. M.

3. M. ? **pupula** *Hübner*.

Orange; thorax white; primaries above marked with black, pale green, subroseous towards the apex.

United States.

WALKER, C. B. M.

PITANE WALKER.

Male. Body linear, moderately long and stout. Palpi pilose, very short; third joint very small. Antennæ moderately deeply pectinated, little more than half the length of the body. . Abdomen not extending beyond the hind wings. Legs rather stout; hind tibiæ with four long spurs. Wings moderately broad, not long; fore wings straight along the costa, slightly oblique at the tips; hind angle somewhat rounded.

1. P. ? **medinstina** *Hübner*.

Male. Black; disk of the thorax and abdomen at the end, luteous; primaries with a clavate postmedian band and seven white bands; secondaries luteous with a band and margins black.

Georgia.

WALKER, C. M. M.

CISTHENE WALKER.

Male. Body rather short, moderately stout. Palpi much shorter than the head; third joint conical, acuminated, less than half the length of the second. Antennæ stout, setose, setaceous, rather more than half the length of the body. Abdomen not extending so far as the hind wings; tip forcipated. Legs moderately stout; hind tibiæ with four rather long spurs. Wings moderately broad, not long. Fore wings very slightly convex in front, oblique at the tips, rounded and not angular behind; third inferior vein full twice farther from the second than the second from the first; fourth nearly twice farther from the third than the third from the second.

1. C. **subjecta** *Walk.*

Rose-color. Head black, rosy about the eyes. Palpi and antennæ black. Proboscis testaceous. Thorax with a black disk.

Legs mostly whitish, partly brown. Fore wings aeneous gray, with a fusiform rosy streak beyond the middle of the costa, and with a rosy discal stripe along more than half the length from the base, dilated and joining the hind border at each end. Apical third part of the hind wings aeneous gray. Length of the body 2½—2½ lines; of the wings 7—8 lines.

Var. a. Costal streak of primaries wanting, discal stripe appearing only at its tip.

Var. b. Discal stripe of primaries replaced by a slender streak, which extends along the hind border and is slightly dilated at the tip.

United States.

WALKER.

CROCOTA HÜBNER.

Male and Female. Body moderately stout, not long. Palpi stout, porrect, pubescent, as long as the head; third joint slender, acuminated, not half the length of the second. Antennae setaceous, slightly setose, rather stout, hardly or not more than half the length of the body. Abdomen not extending so far as the hind wings. Legs rather slender; hind tibiae with four long spurs. Wings rather broad, not long. Primaries very slightly convex in front, slightly angular at the tips, oblique along the apical border, indistinctly angular behind; first, second and third inferior veins approximate at the base; fourth remote from the third.

1. C. ferruginosa Walk.

Ferruginous, paler beneath. Abdomen pale ferruginous, with a row of dorsal black dots. Secondaries pale ferruginous, with a blackish dot in the disk and two or three blackish spots along the border. Length of the body 3½—4 lines; of the wings 10—11 lines.

Hudson's Bay.

WALKER.

2. C. brevicornis Walk.

Fawn color, or luteous fawn color. Antennae black, short. Abdomen rose-color. Primaries rosy beneath. Secondaries rose-color, with an indistinct and sometimes quite obsolete brown stripe

on the hind border, and a brown dot in the disk. Length of the
body 2½—8½ lines; of the wings 8—10 lines.
United States.

                                     WALKER.

8. C. rubicundaria *Hübner.*

Fulvous; wings sometimes with a discal fuscous spot; secondaries rufous, margined with black.

Var. a. Primaries tawny, with a slight brown dot in the disk. Secondaries red with a black discal spot and a broad black hind border.

Var. b. Secondaries partly red on the hind border.

Var. c. All the wings without discal spots.
Massachusetts.

                                     WALKER.

GNOPHRIA Stırs. *Setina* Schr. *Atolmis* Hübner.

Palpi moderate, recurved, subsquamous; maxillæ as long as the antennæ; antennæ simple; of the *male,* setaceous. Primaries narrow, of nearly equal breadth; secondaries opaque. Feet short, rather robust; tibiæ short, robust, hind tibiæ with four spurs.

1. G. vittata *Harris. Lithosis miniata* Kirby.

Deep scarlet; primaries with two broad stripes and a short stripe between them at the tip, of a lead color; secondaries with a very broad lead-colored border behind; the middle of the abdomen and joints of the legs of the same color.

Larva feeds on lichens, and may be found under loose stones in the fields in the spring. It is dusky and thinly covered with stiff, sharp, and barbed black bristles, which grow singly from small warts. Early in May it makes its cocoon, which is very thin and silky, and twenty days afterwards is transformed to a moth.

                                     HARRIS.

DASYCHIRA Stırs. *Orgyia* Ochs.

Body generally stout. Palpi porrect, pilose, extending very little beyond the head; first joint short; third slender. Abdomen not or hardly extending beyond the hind wings. Legs stout; fore legs with very long hairs; hind tibiæ with four moderately long spurs. Wings moderately broad, generally rather long. Fore wings slightly convex along the costa, hardly angular at the tips, oblique along the exterior border; interior angle more or less rounded; first and second inferior veins nearly contiguous. Antennæ of the male deeply pectinated; of the female, minutely. Female winged.

1. D. aphatina Sm. Abb. Figured in Sm. Abb. pl. 77.

Crested; primaries cinereous, with a white streak before, intersected behind with a black arc terminating in an angular white point.

Georgia.

WALKER.

2. D. rossii Curtis.

Transparent gray. Fore wings with two blackish waved lines, forming a fascia across the middle, with a spot between them and a sinuated, abbreviated band beyond them. Hind wings cream-color, ochreous along the hind border, with a broad blackish margin.

Arctic America.

WALKER.

LAGOA WALKER.

Male. Body stout, short, very pilose. Proboscis obsolete. Palpi very short. Antennæ deeply pectinated, rather less than half the length of the body. Abdomen extending a little beyond the hind wings. Legs stout, thickly clothed with long hairs; hind tibiæ with short apical spurs. Fore wings moderately broad, not long, straight along the costa, rounded at the tips; second inferior vein as far from the first as from the third; fourth proceeding from the base of the wing.

1. L. opercularis Sm. Abb. Figured in Sm. Abb. pl. 63.

Male. Pale luteous. Head whitish on the vertex, brown in front. Antennæ white; branches brown, with white tips. Abdomen and hind wings testaceous. Legs partly clothed with

17

whitish hairs; tarsi black.   Fore wings woolly, especially towards
the base.   Length of the body 6 lines; of the wings 18 lines.
   Georgia.

                                                    WALKER.

2. L. pyxidifera *Sm. Abb.*   Figured in Sm. Abb. pl. 54.

   Testaceous; primaries with some fuscous and black flexuous
discal streaks.
   Georgia.

                                                    WALKER.

APPENDIX.

By BRECKENRIDGE CLEMENS.

SPHINGINA (IN PART).
FAM. ZYGAENIDAE.

The present family, together with *Glaucopidiude, Ægeriidae* and *Sphingidae*, form the great group known as *Sphingina*. *Lithosidee* forms another group of families, and should precede the family *Arctiidae*.

I am convinced that the limit of the family under consideration is much more restricted than is usually represented. It is made to include a variety of incongruent forms, which it is extremely difficult to unite under a common and satisfactory definition. And hence it may be, that the diagnoses to which I have had access are indefinite, and that the characters drawn from the most important parts of structure are modified by numerous exceptions. The family is therefore restricted here to two genera, one of which displays some of the characters of the succeeding family group.

In the fore wings the subcostal vein at its posterior end is curved downward so as to form, in connection with the median vein, a fusiform disk, and gives rise to *five nervules, two of which run to the costa, one to the tip, and two to the hind margin beneath the tip*. In *Zygæna*, the subcostal vein is not attenuated at the posterior end giving rise to the two lower nervules, but in *Procris?* (Clem.) it is attenuated from the third subcostal branch. The discal vein is short, angulated and rather attenuated, and receives the discal fold at its angle. The median vein is 4 branched and curves upward from the origin of the posterior branch. The fold of the wing is thickened and the submedian is simple.

In the hind wings the subcostal branch is bifid, *the lower branch being angulated at its base*, and from the angle arises an angulated, more or less oblique discal vein which receives the discal fold. The median vein is 4-branched and curves upward from the posterior branch. *Procris?* (Clem.) is without a costal vein, and *Zygaena* has a costal vein bifid at the base, and is connected with the subcostal by an intercostal branch.

The antennæ are fusiform, sometimes pectinated, with branches shorter in the ♀ than in the ♂. The palpi are short, cylindrical and hairy, or very short, almost rudimental. The tongue is as long as the thorax beneath or almost wanting. Flight of the *imago* diurnal.

ZYGAENA Fabr.

Anthrocera *Scop.* Intr. Hist. Nat. I, 414; Steph.: Westw.

Fore wings rather narrow and elongated; their length exceeds that of the body somewhat; the tip of the wing is rounded and the hind margin obliquely rounded; the inner angle rounded and nearly opposite the middle of the costa. The subcostal nervure, or vein, and the median are adjacent in the basal third of the wing and diverge thence to form a markedly fusiform disk, placed above the middle of the wing, and which reaches to the apical third. There are five subcostal nervules, the first arising near the middle of the disk, and the two others adjacent to each other at the posterior-superior angle of the disk; the third nervule, viz., the apical, is bifid from its middle, and from its origin the subcostal curves downward throwing off two nervules to the hind margin. The discal vein is short and angulated, and receives the discal fold. The median nervure is 4-branched, and curves upward from the medio-posterior branch, which arises at a point about midway between the first and second subcostal branches, to join the discal at the angle which receives the discal fold. The fold of the wing is thickened, and the submedian nervure is simple.

The hind wings are somewhat more than one-half the length of the fore wings; irregularly ovate, dilated at the inner angle. The disk is broad, irregularly fusiform, and extends to the apical third of the wing. The costal nervure is bifid at the base of the wing, and is connected with the subcostal at its middle by a *minute intercostal branch*; from this point the subcostal departs obliquely and divides into two branches at the end of the disk, the lower one being angulated. An oblique angulated discal nervure at the angle of the lower branch, receives the discal fold. The median is 4-branched, curving upward to join the discal from the origin of the posterior nervule.

Fore wings marked with spots or blotches.

Head and face pilose; without ocelli. Eyes rather large, round. Antennæ claviform, one-third less long than the fore wings, the tip without hairs or seta. Palpi short, scarcely ascending beyond the front, cylindrico-conical, pilose beneath, acute. Tongue corneous, and about as long as the thorax beneath.

Body moderately stout, hairy; the fore wings when closed extending beyond the tip of the abdomen. Legs slender; tarsi roughened with spines. The fore tibiæ with a rather long internal spine; the tibiæ of the posterior legs with four very small spines.

Larva fat, contracted, subcylindrical, slightly pubescent. *Pupa* inclosed in a tough cocoon, pointed at both ends. The larvæ feed exclusively on papilionaceous plants.

L. E. onobryobia *Fabr.* **Walker 98–7. Var. 1.**

Fore wings shining blue, with six yellow spots margined with white, the posterior one red and semilunar. Hind wings yellow. Georgia.

WALKER.

PROCRIS? PASS.

Fore wings somewhat fusiform. The subcostal vein *with two distinct, rather long* marginal nervules, with apical vein *simple,* with *two disco-central* nervules. The median 4-branched, the medio-posterior opposite the first marginal nervule and the two upper branches on the line of the discal vein, which is straight. The fold of the wing is thickened from the base to the tip. Submedian simple. Hind wings not as broad as the fore wings at their broadest part, ovate. The subcostal vein is bifid, the lower branch giving rise to a decided rather oblique discal vein, which is angulated above the medio-superior nervule, where it receives the discal fold. Median vein with four, equidistant nervules.

Head moderate, advanced, but without decided neck; with rather large ocelli. Face moderate, oblique and *projecting tubercularly* at the base of the antennæ, and in the middle. Eyes small. Antennæ *incrassated at the tip, as long as the thorax beneath,* with rather deep pectinations in the ♂, serrated or minutely pectinated in the ♀. Palpi *rudimental, tubercular*. Tongue rudimental.

Body rather thick, short. Patagia rather elevated, consisting of two transverse plates rounded above, making the prothorax more than ordinarily wide above. Abdomen ovate, without apical tuft, less long than the thorax beneath. Legs short and slender; fore tibiæ unarmed; hind tibiæ with two very minute apical spurs.

1. P.? smithsoniana *Clemens*. Proc. Acad. Nat. Sci., 1860, 640.

The entire insect is greenish-black; immaculate.

Texas. Capt. Pope's collection. From the Smithsonian Institution.

FAM. GLAUCOPIDIDAE.

Wings narrow, often limpid or with limpid spots. Fore wings equal in length to that of the body. Hind wings short, scarcely more than half as long as the fore wings, rounded, rarely angulated. In the fore wings the subcostal vein is only slightly arcuate from the base to the tip of the wing and subdivides into five or six branches, the two first of which, sometimes contiguous and sometimes separated, run to the costa. The origin of the discal and subcosto-inferior nervule *is a common one*, and the marginal nervules arise contiguous to each other and interior to it, or one interior and the other exterior. After the origin of these, the subcostal continues to the tip of the wing, and about midway subdivides into an apical and post-apical branch, the former of which is sometimes bifid at its tip. The median is 4-branched and curves upward from the 2d (medio-inferior); the 1st (medio-posterior) is separated at its origin from the others, and is curved. The discal fold is distinct, and the discal nervure extends nearly across the disk.

The hind wings are *without the costal nervure*. The subcostal is bifid, sometimes sending a nervule to the costa from the disk. *The median is usually likewise bifid, sometimes with the lower branch forked near its end.* In some genera, however, it is 3-branched. The discal vein is usually much curved and oblique, usually without a nervule to the hind margin, but sometimes with a medio-discal nervule, that is, with one on the side of the median system.

The antennæ are pectinated. Palpi usually curved, smooth and cylindrical. Tongue moderate, usually as long as the thorax beneath.

Flight of the *imago* diurnal.

TABLE OF GENERA.

Hind wings without a discal nervule;
    Median vein of hind wings bifid;
        Wings usually hyaline.   GLAUCOPIS.
    Median vein of hind wings trifid;
        Subcostal vein with a marginal branch, discal vein vertical.
                                    ORMETICA.
Hind wings with a discal nervule;
    Median vein of hind wings bifid.   ECCHÆMOSIA.
    Median vein 3-branched.   CYANOPLEURA.

GLAUCOPIS FABR.

Wings most frequently narrow, sometimes ample; hyaline or limpid, with black borders or tips, and the veins covered with scales.

In the fore wings the subcostal nervure subdivides into two marginal nervules, a bifid apical branch and a post-apical branch; *the subcosta-inferior branch is usually the only one proceeding from the disk*, when it arises at its posterior-superior angle. Sometimes, however, the disk emits from four to six nervules(?). The median nervure is 4-branched.' Hind wings without costal nervure. The subcostal is bifid from the disk, and the discal is without branches to the hind margin.(?) The median is bifid or bifid with the lower branch forked near its tip.

Head with ocelli. Antennæ most frequently bipectinated. Palpi moderate, generally ascending, usually longer than the clypeus.

Body linear, most generally slender, subcylindrical and more or less metallic. Patagia small. Legs with the tibiæ roughened with spines.

This genus is of considerable extent, and its limits are very undecided. I have only a single specimen belonging to it, and

hence cannot venture on making a more definite diagnosis than
that given above. Systematists have divided it, however, into a
number of groups, some of which may prove hereafter to be true
genera, and the subdivision will assist the student in recognizing
individuals.

Group Isanthrene.

Isanthrene *Hübner*. Verz. Schmett. 126.

Body cylindrical. Palpi rather long; second joint rather short
and slender. Antennæ slightly pectinated beneath, serrated near
the tips. Wings hyaline, more or less bordered with black, and
in some species with a black band on the base of the disk. *The
disk emits five veins*, discal fold distinct along the whole length.
Abdomen linear. Legs rather stout; median and apical spines of
the hind tibiæ of moderate length. Especially distinguished by
the cylindrical abdomen.

WALKER.

1. G. chalciope *Hübner*. Samml. Ex. Schmett. 23, 236, f. 469, 470.

Blue Antennæ luteous. Abdomen with lateral white dots.
Wings limpid, margined with black. Fore wings with a black
band.
Havana.

WALKER.

Group Pœcilosoma.

Pœcilosoma *Hübner*. V. S. 126.

Body stout, convex, cylindrical, partly metallic. Antennæ
slender, minutely pectinated to the tips. Wings hyaline, metallic
at the base; fore wings with black tips; discal fold distinct.
Legs moderately stout; median and apical spurs of the hind tibiæ
very small.

WALKER.

1. G. multicincta *Walker*. C. B. M. 163.

Male. Dark brown; linear, cylindrical, partly covered with blue
scales. Head with some white hairs above and thickly clothed
with white hairs beneath. Palpi white beneath, straight, rather
short; third joint very small. Antennæ black, moderately deeply

pectinated. Thorax with two white bands in front, and with a
crimson stripe on each side of the wing ; a few scattered blue
hairs. Breast with white hairs. Wings limpid, rather broad.
Fore wings with black tips and borders, on the latter some blue
scales; a black band across the end of the discal areolet where the
veinlets hardly form an angle; no trace of the discal fold: Borders of the hind wings mostly black. Abdomen with two crimson
spots at the base, and with a row of crimson spots along each side;
a slender white band on the hind border of each segment ; under
side white, with short crimson and black bands along the apical
half, and with a tuft of crimson hairs at the tip. Legs brown,
mostly clothed with white; coxæ blue beneath ; fore tibiæ with
long spines beneath ; middle and apical spurs of the hind tibiæ
rather long.   Length of the body 6 lines ; of the wings 16 lines.
  St. Domingo.

WALKER.

Group Laemocharis.

Laemocharis *Baird*. Herr.-Schaeff. *Erraca* Walker. C. B. M. 161.

  Body linear, cylindrical, rather slender. Palpi not rising to
the vertex ; third joint slender, more than half the length of the
second. Antennæ minutely pectinated. Wings moderate, limpid ;
fore wings with black tips ; discal fold distinct. Legs slender ;
hind tibiæ with four small spurs.

WALKER.

1. G. partyi *Baird.* Herr.-Schaeff. Lep. Ex. Nov. Ser. 1, t. 249.

  Black. Head with two white dots. Abdomen with four basal
luteous dots, and two lateral interrupted white stripes. Wings
limpid, margined narrowly with black.
  Georgia.

WALKER.

Group Cosmosoma.

Cosmosoma *Hübner*. Harris, Descr. Cat. N. Amer. Sphing. 37.

  Wings mostly hyaline. The subcostal vein of the fore wings
is adjacent to the external margin, with two subcosto-marginal
nervules, one from the disk arising at a point midway between the
origin of the medio-posterior branch and its penultimate, the other
exterior to the disk, midway between it and the origin of the post-

apical nervule. The apical branch beyond its middle sends off the
post-apical nervule, and near its tip an apical nervulet to the costa.
Median vein 4-branched. Hind wings about half as long as the
fore wings; without costal vein; subcostal bifid from the origin of
the discal vein, which is very obliquely inclined towards the base
of the wing and abruptly curved above the median, where it receives the discal fold. Median vein bifid exterior to the disk, with
the lower branch furcate at the tip.

Head moderate, smooth, neck not distinct; with ocelli. Face
smooth and vertical. Eyes moderately prominent. Antennæ
rather more than half as long as the body, pectinated to the tips
in the ♂, less so in the ♀. Palpi rather stout, curved, exceeding
the face, smooth, but hairy at the base; basal and middle joints
nearly equal; terminal small and conical. Tongue equal to the
thorax beneath.

Body scarcely equal in length to the fore wings, rather slender,
nearly linear. Patagia small. Legs moderately stout, smooth;
fore tibiæ with a moderate, concealed spur from the base; hind
tibiæ with four rather small spurs.

CLEMENS.

1. G. omphale *Hübner*. *Ægeria omphale* Say, Am. Ent. II, pl. 19, lower fig.

Bright red. Antennæ black, with white tips. Head blue.
Thorax most frequently striped with black. Abdomen with a
black dorsal stripe, and the tip black, varied with blue. Wings
margined with black and with black veins.

Florida; Mexico near Jalapa.

CLEMENS.

2. G. impar *Walker*. C. B. M. 169.

Black. Head bright blue in front. Thorax luteous, which hue
extends over the basal part of the borders of the wings; an interrupted blue band in front of the thorax. Wings limpid; a black
stripe extending along the borders, and very broad at the tips of
the fore wings; a large slightly curved black spot at the tip of the
disk. Abdomen luteous at the base, near which are two dorsal
blue spots; three rows of blue spots at the tip. Legs dark testaceous. Length of body 7 lines; of the wings 20 lines.

-Mexico.

WALKER.

3. **G. tyrrhene** *Huber.* Ex. Schmett. 23, 242, f. 433–4.

Orange-colored. Head blue. Antennæ black. Abdomen with two blue stripes (interrupted in the ♀), and the tip blue. Wings limpid, with the base orange-colored, tip ferruginous. In the male the fore wings have a discal orange-colored spot.

Jamaica.

WALKER.

Group MARIANA.

Mariana *Walker.* C. B. M. 174.

Body short. Palpi rising above the head; third joint long, linear, shorter than the second. Antennæ of the male very broadly pectinated. Wings ample, limpid, with black borders; fore wings about twice the length of the hind wings, with the discal fold distinct. Legs slender; hind tibiæ with four minute spurs.

1. **G. columbina** *Fabr.* *Eurowia columbina* Hübn. Ex. Schmett. 6, 8, f. 9, 10.

Bright red. Antennæ black. The disk of the thorax black, with a white line. Abdomen with a dorsal black stripe, with transverse white lines. Wings limpid, margined with black; fore wings with a spot near the disk and the tip red.

Jamaica.

WALKER.

EUCHROMIA *Hübn.*

Wings more or less narrow and elongated, opaque or marked with a few hyaline or limpid spots. The wing structure and outline of the fore wings are more markedly sphingiform than in the genus *Glaucopis*. The subcostal vein gives rise to two marginal branches from the hinder part of the disk to the post-apical branch midway between the origin of the subcosto-inferior branch and the tip of the wing; the subcosto-inferior and discal vein arise from the subcostal at a common point. There is no disco-central branch. The median is 4-branched, with the medio-posterior remote from the other branches. The submedian simple. The hind wings are rather more than half as long as the fore wing; *without costal nervure;* subcostal bifid from the origin of the discal, which is obliquely curved towards the base of the wing and gives rise to a disco-central branch below the middle. The median is two-branched(?) from the insertion of the discal.

Head with ocelli. Antennæ of the males most frequently pectinated, sometimes plumose, of the females sometimes unpectinated or serrated. Palpi of moderate length, sometimes short, generally curved and cylindrical.

Body rather slender, cylindrical and smooth. Abdomen, with a prominent tubercle on each side of the basal segment, generally smooth, sometimes tufted along each side. Legs usually slender and rather long.

The same uncertainty is connected with the present limits of this genus as with the preceding one. In general structure, the species included in it are sometimes allied to the *Lithosidæ* and again to the *Bombycidæ* or to the European genus *Syntomis*. It has been divided into a number of groups so as to indicate their special peculiarities with accuracy.

Synopsis of Species.

.1. Discal areolet not narrow.
B. Antennæ of the ♂ pectinated or plumose.
C. General structure like that of *Syntomis*.
D. Abdomen not inflated along each side.
E. Palpi not porrect.
F. Body and wings more or less metallic.
G. Hind tibiæ not ciliated.
  i. Hind wings rounded or hardly angular.
  j. Body hardly hairy.
  k. Wings unspotted.
    l. Wings bright red.   llchas.
  K. Wings very generally spotted or wholly blackish with green or blue
    reflections.
    l. Allied to the *Lithosidæ* in structure. Antennæ pectinated to the
      tips. Wings broad. Abdomen rather short, extending very little
      beyond the hind border of the hind wings.
  m. Abdomen more or less metallic.
    n. Hind wings partly red.   fustuosa.
  nn. Hind wings bluish at the base.   bella.
  P. Body narrow, cylindrical. Wings long and narrow, covered with
    opaque or limpid spots. Abdomen long, extending for half its
    length beyond the hind wings. Resembles *Syntomis*.

m. Wings with luteous or yellow spots.
   n. Fore wings not marked with blue.
   o. Abdomen not metallic.
   p. Abdomen with many bands.
   q. Fore wings with two spots and a streak.   ferox.
   qq. Fore wings with five dots.   ipomaeas.
mm. Wings with white or limpid spots.
   o. Hind wings limpid, black margined.   semistriata.
   oo. Hind wings with two or more spots.
   p. Fore wings with six white spots.   vulcanus.
   pp. Fore wings with three white spots.   euboyanes.
   l'. General color black, with golden green stripes or rows of spots. Antennae pectinated.
   m. Thorax with green streaks and dots.
   n. Legs black.   interrupta.
   l'. Body short. Antennae pectinated. Wings shorter and broader than preceding groups and opaque.
   m. Hind wings with a hyaline stripe.
   n. Abdomen banded with yellow.   ventralis.
   nn. Abdomen with glittering green spots.   quadrigutta.
GG. Hind tibiae ciliated.
    i. Color black.   plumipes.
    ii. Color pale.   pretus.
CC. General structure like that of *Bombycidae*.
   d. Body not metallic.
   f. Wings with various shades of brown and white or fawn color.
   g. Hind wings blue.
    h. Abdomen luteous.   dryas.
   gg. Hind wings not blue.
   h. Abdomen brown or black.
   i. Hind wings not or hardly limpid towards the base.
   j. Fore wings with cuneiform marks.   sylvius.

Group Empyreuma.

Empyreuma *Hübner*. Vers. Schmett. 120.

Body metallic, rather long, spotted, and scarcely hairy. Antennae setaceous, much more than half the length of the body, thickly and rather deeply pectinated to the tips. Wings long, moderately broad, wholly opaque and squamose, not spotted. Hind wings not angular. Abdomen nearly linear, not petiolated. Legs stout, not plumose. Tibiae with short spurs. This group approaches nearest to *Zygaena* in its form and in the color of its wings.

                                           WALKER.

1. R. Hebas *Fabr.* Hübn. Samml. Ex. Schmett. 12, 21, f. 41, 42.

Black, with shining green reflection.   Wings bright red, with a median green streak and white punctures.   Abdomen black, with two golden bands.

Cuba, St. Domingo.

WALKER.

Group Belemnia.

Belemnia *Walker*, 211.

Body rather long and narrow.   Body and wings brilliantly metallic.   Antennæ setaceous, more than half the length of the body, thickly and rather deeply pectinated to full three-fourths of the length in the male.   Fore wings long, moderately broad, opaque and squamose, with red or yellow semi-hyaline spots towards the tips.   Hind wings angular on the hind border near the base.   Abdomen linear, not petiolated.   Legs slender, not plumose.   Tibiæ with short spurs.

WALKER.

1. R. eryx *Fabr.* *Sphinx insurata* Cram. Pap. III, 67, pl. 140, f. E, F.

Wings black.   Fore wings golden towards the base, with a discal spot and the abdomen beneath, blood-red.

In this species the following varieties of color occur:—

Var. a. Head and thorax with gilded or golden green spots. Fore wings gilded towards the base, with a red spot in the disk. Abdomen with a cupreous stripe, bright green towards the base and bright blue towards the tip on each side.

Var. b. Like *Var. a.* Abdomen with gilded green spots on each side along the whole length.

Var. c. Spots on the fore wings yellow.   Red beneath the abdomen extending partly over the sides above on the hinder half.

West Indies, South and Central America.

WALKER.

Group Automalis.

Automalis *Walker*, 213.

Approaches the *Lithosiidæ* in structure.   Body more or less metallic.   Third joint of the palpi very short.   Antennæ pectinated to the tips.   Wings broad, opaque, more or less spotted, metallic at the base.   Abdomen rather short, extending very little beyond the bind wings. Fore tibae dentate beneath; middle and apical spurs of the bind tibiae small.

WALKER.

1. E. instrucom *Walker*, 215.

Black. Head, palpi, thorax in front and three dorsal stripes bright green. Antennae minutely pectinated beneath to the tips. Fore wings dark brown, golden green at the base, and with two bright red spots, one near the base, the other in the middle near the fore border, the last also appears beneath where there is another spot beyond it. Hind wings deep purplish blue, bright red along the middle part of the bind border; this red stripe widens in breadth towards the tip of the wing. Femora and tibiae mostly golden green; fore coxae and fore tibiae white on one side. Length of the body 5—6 lines; of the wings 18—20 lines.

Jamaica.

WALKER.

2. E. bella *Gefr.* Icon. Reg. An. Ins. Texts, 502.

Shining violet-blue. Antennae black. Wings black. Fore wings with a yellow streak at the base and a spot in the disk of the same hue, and a blue streak near the base towards the bind border.

Mexico.

WALKER.

Group Hippola.

Hippola *Walker*, 223. *Syntomida?* Harris, N. A. Sphing. 34.

Male. Body cylindrical, slender. Palpi very hairy at the base, moderately long; third joint small, conical at the tip, not more than one-fourth of the length of the second. Antennae rather deeply plumose. Wings long and narrow, mostly opaque; discal areolet-veinlet forming a right angle; discal fold distinct along the whole length. Abdomen long, linear; appendages small. Legs moderately long; fore tibiae furrowed beneath; middle and apical spurs of the bind tibiae rather small.

1. D. ferox *Walker*, 223.

Male. Dark purple. Head with tawny hairs in front and with a short orange band behind. Palpi with black hairs towards the base. Antennæ dark blue, white above towards the tips. Thorax orange with two purple stripes on each side. Fore wings dark bluish-green, purple along the hind borders, with two small yellowish white spots between the first and third inferior veinlets, and with a very short yellowish-white streak before the middle of the discal areolet, and only visible beneath. Hind wings purple, partly bluish-green, with a broad white streak near the base and towards the hind border. Abdominal segments above and beneath with orange bands which are connected on each side; appendages testaceous. Legs bluish-purple; coxæ beneath with orange tomentum, which also appears, but much more slightly, on the femora. Length of the body 7 lines; of the wings 23 lines.

United States.

WALKER.

2. E. ipomææ *Harris*. *Sesia ipomææ* Œmler. *Glaucopis* (*Syntomrida*) *ipomææ* Harris, N. A. Sphinx, 36. Var.? *E. ferox*?

Body tawny orange. Antennæ and head black, the latter spotted with orange. Thorax with a broad black stripe on the shoulder covers and a transverse spot of the same hue behind. Fore wings greenish-black, with three yellowish-white dots near the front margin and two others close together beyond the middle. Hind wings violet-black, with a transparent colorless spot at the base. Abdomen with the incisures black. Legs violet-black; coxæ beneath and a spot on the thighs orange-colored. Expands one inch and three-quarters.

Georgia.

HARRIS.

3. E. fenestrata *Stoll*. Cram. Pap. Exot. V, 140, pl. 30, f. 8. Drury, Ins. 1, 54, pl. 25, f. 3. Westw. ed. Drury, I, 53, pl. 25, f. 3.

Black. Fore wings with two limpid, approximated spots before the middle of the wing, and behind the middle a short, indented limpid band curved externally. Hind wings limpid, margined with black. Feet red.

Jamaica.

WALKER.

Group Emdera.

Emdera *Walker*, 23.

Color partly metallic. Body nearly linear, not broad. Palpi moderately long; second joint rather short. Antennæ pectinated

to the tips. Wings long, rather narrow, with limpid spots. Hind
wings not angular. Legs rather long and slender; hind tibiæ
with two moderately long spurs; first at three-quarters of the
length; second at the tip.

1. E. vulcanus *Walker*, 228.

Black, clothed with black hairs. Thorax with a white spot on
each side, and with a white band in the hinder part beneath. Fore
wings with a white dot on each side at the base and with eight
limpid spots; two near the base; two in the disk, and four forming
a short band nearer the tip. Hind wings with three limpid spots;
two near the base, and one beyond the middle. Abdomen with
two rows of white spots along each side, and with a few red hairs
at the tip. Fore femora clothed with red hairs. Length of the
body 9 lines; of the wings 24 lines.

Mexico.

WALKER.

2. E. subcyanea *Walker*, 230.

Black, clothed with black hairs. Fore part of the thorax
blackish-green on each side in some aspects, and with six white
dots, two on each side and two nearer the disk; a white dot behind the scutellum. Fore wings very narrow, with three large
white hyaline spots which have a slight opaline lustre, and form a
very slightly curved stripe on the disk; third spot intersected;
under side brilliant blue towards the base and along the hind
border. Hind wings brilliant blue in front and wholly so beneath,
with three hyaline white spots; basal spot of moderate size; the
other two small. Femora and tibiæ with blue scales; a white
streak on each of the posterior femora, and a larger one on each
of the fore coxæ. Length of the body 9? lines; of the wings 25
lines.

Mexico.

WALKER.

Group Calonota.

Calonotos *Hübner*. Verz. Schmett. 123.

Color partly metallic. Body rather slender. Palpi moderately
long; second joint small. Antennæ pectinated to the tips.
Wings long and narrow. Hind wings not angular. Legs rather

18

stout; median and apical spurs of the hind tibiæ of moderate
length.

WALKER.

1. M. interrupta *Walker*, 1621.

Male. Black, with a metallic green tinge. Thorax with white
or green marginal dots in front, and with two dorsal streaks of
the same hue. Abdomen with a white dot at the base, and with
interrupted gilded green bands; under side with two lateral rows
of white spots, which decrease in size hindward. Legs piceous.
Wings black, narrow. Fore wings with four elongated limpid
spots, the hind one of the first pair nearer the base of the wing
than the fore one, which, like the exterior pair is intersected by
the black veins. Hind wings with the disk limpid towards the
base, and with an exterior intersected limpid spot. Length of
the body 7½ lines; of the wings 18 lines.

Mexico.

WALKER.

Group Antichloris.

Antichloris *Hübner.* Verz. Schmett. 124.

Body rather narrow. Palpi moderately long; second joint
small. Antennæ rather deeply pectinated, serrated towards the
tips. Fore wings opaque, unspotted, rather broad, slightly pointed
at the tips, obtusely angular on the hind border. Hind wings
obliquely truncated and slightly angular at the tips; hind border
a little sinuated. Peculiar in the form of the hind wings.

1. A. eriphia *Fabr.* A. *phæmenes* Hübn. Samml. Ex. Schmett. 9, 8, f. 15—8. A. *caca* Samml. Ex. Schmett. 34, 57, f. 133, 4.

Var. Male. Gilded green. Head crimson behind. Tongue and
antennæ black. Palpi black, white beneath. Thorax crimson on
each side in front. Pectus with white spots on each side. Abdomen above black, with three rows of triangular gilded green spots;
under side with two lateral interrupted white stripes, which extend
from the base to the middle. Fore coxæ white beneath. Wings
dark brown. Hind wings whitish in front.

Mexico, West Indies.

WALKER.

Group Heramia.

Heramia *Hübner*. Vers. Schmett. 124.

Wings narrow. Fore wings much longer than the body. The subcostal vein is adjacent to the external margin, with two marginal nervules from the hinder end of the disk, the first opposite the penultimate branch of the median, the second forked at about its middle. The apical branch gives rise at about its middle to the post-apical. The subcosto-inferior and the discal vein arise at a common point, the latter slightly curved. Median vein 4-branched, the posterior remote from the penultimate. Hind wings equal to the length of the body. Without costal vein. Subcostal vein bifid from the margin of the discal vein, which is very obliquely inclined to the base and suddenly curved about the middle of the disk, where it receives the discal fold; immediately beneath this arises a medio-discal nervule. Median vein bifid from the disk.

Head rather large, smooth, free; with ocelli. Face narrow. Eyes rather large, prominent. Antennæ shortly pectinated or serrated to the tip, whence it is moniliform, and more or less dilated or fusiform about the middle. Palpi curved, ascending to the middle of the face; basal joint hairy beneath; middle and terminal joint smooth and cylindrical. Tongue about as long as the thorax beneath.

Body cylindrical, smooth. Patagia small. Abdomen obtuse, with a prominent tubercle on each side of the basal segment. Legs slender and long; fore tibiæ with a moderate spur from the base; hind tibiæ towards the ends and the hind tarsi plumose. Hind tibiæ with two short spurs.

CLEMM.

1. **H. plumipes** *Drury*. *Agiaope plumipes* Westw. ed. Drury, II, 61, pl. 27, f. 3.

Blackish. Thorax marked with white. Abdomen banded with white. Hind tibiæ plumose.

Var.? Palpi short; third joint small. Black, indistinctly tinged with blue. Head, thorax, base of the wings, and abdomen towards the base with white dots. Wings blackish-brown. Abdominal segments with white bands. Legs partly covered with white scales; hind tibiæ with a white band before the middle, beyond which they are deeply plumose with black hairs to the tip; hind tarsi white, black and plumose towards the base.

Mexico.

WALKER.

2. B. protus Cram. *Sphinx adscita protus* Cram. Pap. Exot. II, 121, pl. 175, f. E, F. *Heranio protus* Hübn. Samml. Exot. Schmett. Addend. pl. f. 1—4. *E. plumipes* Clemens, Proc. Ac. Nat. Sci., Nov. 1860, 546.

Fawn-colored. Antennæ banded with black. Prothorax and basal portion of the abdomen whitish. Hind wings brownish. Fore wings testaceous. Femora and tibiæ black at the tips.

West Indies.

Var. Bluish-black. Antennæ with orange-yellow tips. Palpi orange-yellow; face, orbits and a spot between the antennæ of the same hue, the former with a central blackish stripe. Thorax with four spots on the disk orange-yellow or yellow, and four on the prothorax, one on each side and two central, and a stripe along the upper edge of the tegulæ, of the same hue. Abdomen banded with more or less decided orange-yellow, with a short, transverse white stripe at the base above between the tubercles, and with two white bands at the base beneath, the first of which is extended on the sides. Breast with three white marks on each side. Wings concolorous dark brownish, with a white spot on the costa at the base. The fore coxæ with an orange-yellow stripe and fore tibiæ striped externally with the same hue. Hind coxæ orange-yellow; femora black; tibiæ orange yellow banded with black at the tips, and ciliated with long hairs; tarsi orange-yellow and plumose to the tips.

This species was erroneously described in the Proceedings of November, 1860, as *plumipes*. Mr. Walker, on page 1632, describes varieties that approach this very nearly, but in making up the paper for the Proceedings, I overlooked them.

Cuba, West Indies.

CLEMENS.

Group Amycles.

Amycles *Walk-r*, 253, 1633.

Male. Body rather long. Palpi rather short; third joint very small. Antennæ rather deeply pectinated for nearly two-thirds of the length, setaceous and abruptly simple thence to the tips.

Wings rather short, very narrow. Fore wings distinctly angular on the hind border. Abdomen slightly tapering from the base to the tip. Legs moderately stout; spurs of the hind tibiæ rather long.

Female? Antennæ simple and beset with short bristles along the whole length. Wings short, extremely narrow, less distinctly angular.

WALKER.

1. **E. anthracina** *Walker*, 253, 1833.

Male. Purplish black. Prothorax with a red dot on each side beneath. Fore wings towards the tips dingy white, between which and the black there is a slight brown interval; fringe black. Hind wings dark brown, dingy white in front. Abdomen with an oblong oblique shining white spot on each side at the base.

Female? Fore wings with a whitish band of three-fourths of the length, blackish thence to the tips. Length of the body 5—6 lines; of the wings 12—14 lines.

Mexico.

WALKER.

Group Euceren.

Euceron *Hübner.* Verz. Schmett. 123.

Body rather stout, nearly cylindrical. Palpi moderately long, curved; third joint very minute. Antennæ slender, minutely pectinated to the tips. Wings opaque, spotted. Legs moderately stout; median and apical spurs of the hind tibiæ rather long. This group connects the *Glaucopididæ* with the *Bombycidæ.*

1. **E. sylvius** *Stoll.* Cram. Pap. Exot. V, 65, pl. 14.

Fore wings brown or fawn-color, with many blackish streaks. Abdomen in part red or luteous or yellow.

Var. a. Fore wings brown; areolets full of blackish marks of various size and shape, but mostly cuneiform. Abdomen partly red.

Var. b. Fore wings fawn-color, their spots less large and less numerous. Abdomen partly red.

Var. c. Like *Var. b,* but abdomen partly luteous.

Mexico.

WALKER.

2. E. dryas *Cram.* *Phalama dryas* Cram. Pap. Exot. I, 119, pl. 70, f. C.

Black. Abdomen luteous, with dots on the sides and the tip, black. Fore wings dark brown. Hind wings blue, broadly margined with brown.

West Indies.

WALKER.

　·

Group ———— ?

1. E. bimaculata *Fabr.* Mant. Ins. II, 100, 51 ; Ent. Syst. III, 1, 402, 54. *Sphinx sygaena bimaculata* Gmel. ed. Syst. Nat. I, 5, 2398, 148.

Wings concolorous black. Fore wings with two yellow spots. Hind wings with two white spots.

America, North ?

WALKER.

2. E. achemon *Fabr.* Sp. Ins. II, 162, 24 ; Mant. Ins. II, 104, 29 ; Ent. Syst. III, 395, 31. *Sphinx sygaena achemon,* Gmel. ed. Syst. Nat. I, 5, 2396, 131.

Wings brown, with two white spots. Abdomen blue, banded with yellow.

Jamaica.

WALKER.

3. E. dares *Cram.* *Sphinx adscita dares* Pap. Exot. I, 76, pl. 48, f. F.

Blackish-brown. Fore wings white, with a large brown spot on the disk, and a smaller one of the same hue on the margin.

West Indies.

WALKER.

Group Mastigocera.

Mastigocera *Harris.* N. A. Sphinges, 35, note.

Dr. Harris' description of the characters of this group is so indefinite that it is scarcely possible to determine its relationships. I think, however, it belongs to the genus *Euchromia* and to the group *Horamia.*

1. M. vespina *Harris.* Cat. N. A. Sphinges, 35.

Light rust-brown. Wings immaculate. Collar, first abdominal segments above, third below, and a triangular spot on each side, white. Head, thickened part of the antenne, edge of the thorax behind the collar, and a large triangular spot on each side of the second abdominal segment, black. Breast black, spotted with white. First and second pairs of thighs, except at the base, middle of the hind pair, and extremity of the tibiæ, black. Expands 1¼ inch to 1¾.

St. Thomas, W. I.

EARM.

ORMETICA CLYTEM.

Wings opaque. Fore wings rather narrow, equal in length to that of the body; hind margin very obliquely rounded, with the inner angle opposite the middle of the costa. The subcostal vein is adjacent to the costa, and gives rise to a marginal nervule from the disk nearly opposite the penultimate branch of the median vein, and another exterior but near to the disk. The post-apical arises just exterior to the second marginal nervule, and the apical is bifid at its posterior third. The discal vein and the subcosto-inferior arise at a common point, the former very obliquely inclined to the base, but straight. The median is 4-branched. Hind wings extremely short, not one-half as long as the anterior; without costal vein; subcostal vein arched, with a marginal nervule from the point of origin of the discal, and bifid at the tip much exterior to the cell. Discal vein vertical. Median 3-branched.

Head rather large, smooth, free; with small ocelli. Face tapering, smooth, vertical. Eyes rather large, prominent. Antennæ wanting. Palpi curved, cylindrical, ascending to the middle of the front, stout, smooth; basal joint short, rather hairy beneath; middle joint smooth, rather thickened in the middle and about four times as long as the apical joint; terminal joint very short, ovate. Tongue as long as the thorax beneath.

Body not metallic, rather stout, equal in length to the fore wings, smooth. Patagia moderate, decumbent, and overlapping the meso-thorax. Abdomen tapering at the tip, more than one-half as long as the body beneath. Legs smooth, rather stout; tarsi roughened with spines; fore tibiæ with a stout internal spur from the base; hind tibiæ with four spurs.

[G. sphingiformis *Clemens.*

Bluish-black. Face with a blue band. Body with a yellow stripe on each side extending from the head to the tip of the abdomen. Palpi blackish, whitish at the base and on the second joint beneath. Fore wings with the extreme costa from the base to beyond the middle yellow, with a broad stripe of the same hue from the base to the hind margin beneath the tip, somewhat contracted behind. Hind wings, exterior half yellow, interior half black. The under surface of the wings the same as above. Abdomen beneath with a central yellow stripe. Legs black; fore coxæ each with a yellow spot; femora white internally; tibiæ striped with white. Length of the body 9 lines; of the wings 19 lines.

The structure of this insect shows marked affinities to the group of *Sphinges.*

Mexico, near Jalapa.

CLEMENS.

CYANOPEPLA CLEMENS.

Female? Fore wings much longer than the body, moderately broad, rounded at the tip, and very oblique along the margin. The subcostal vein adjacent to the external margin, with a single marginal nervule from near the hind end of the disk, and a second marginal nervule just exterior to it. The apical branch near its exterior third sends off a post-apical nervule, and near the tip a nervulet to the costa. The subcosto-inferior nervule and the discal vein arise at a common point, the latter angulated. Median vein 4-branched, with the posterior nervule rather remote from the others, and the origin of the first subcosto-marginal nervule. Hind wings rather more than one-half as long as the fore wings, nearly equal to the length of the body. Without costal vein. Subcostal bifid at the origin of the discal vein, which is much curved. Median vein 4-branched, the superior branch is medio-discal, the two middle ones from a common base, the posterior remote.

Head moderate, smooth, without distinct neck; without ocelli. Face rather narrow, smooth. Eyes rather small, moderately prominent. Antennæ more than one-half as long as the body, minutely

pectinated or serrated beneath. Palpi curved, ascending rather
above the middle of the face, smooth, slightly hairy at the base;
middle joint rather more than twice longer than the basal joint;
terminal joint very minute, ovate. Tongue equal to the thorax
beneath.

Body metallic, cylindric, scarcely slender, smooth. Patagia
rather small, somewhat erected. Abdomen less than one-half as
long as the body beneath. Legs rather slender, smooth; fore
tibiæ with a short, concealed middle spur; hind tibiæ with four
rather short spurs. Tarsi minutely spinous.

1. C. cruenta *Clemens.*

Black. Palpi blue. Head and body metallic blue. Fore wings
with a large crimson spot at the base, extended to the middle of
the disk and to the fold beneath, and another of the same hue,
oval and obliquely placed in the median nervules; inner margin
at the base and a streak along the submedian vein metallic blue;
cilia at the tip white. Hind wings dark bluish-black, immaculate.
Length of the body 7 lines; of the wings 20 lines.

Mexico, near Jalapa.

CLEMENS.

LITHOSIDES.

Antennæ most frequently moderately long, slender, setaceous.
Tongue very often longer than the head. Ocelli very often absent. Palpi not longer than the head, cylindrical, third joint
shorter than the second, or not longer. Body slender, elongated.
Thorax not crested. Wings very often subelliptical, posterior
often folded and slightly enfolding the abdomen. Fore wings
rounded at the tips.

The wing structure of the species included in this group is so
diverse that I have been unable to draw up a diagnosis which will
apply to it. The insects arranged under this group, comprise
beyond doubt more than one natural family, but with the limited
number of specimens at my command I cannot undertake the division of it.

Fam. I. CTENUCHIDAE.

Group I.

Hind wings without costal vein. The subcostal vein blind from the origin of the discal, or posterior to it (*Acoloithus*), the lower branch more or less angulated towards its base. Discal vein simple, angulated usually beneath the middle of the disk, receiving a more or less thickened discal fold. Median vein 4-branched, with the posterior sometimes remote from its penultimate. In the fore wings the subcostal vein is not remote from the costa and its branches are decumbent, except in *Acoloithus*.

ACOLOITHUS Clemens.

The following insect greatly resembles *Americana* in appearance and almost exactly in ornamentation. It must, however, be very distinct from it. The wings are extremely narrow. Hind wings broader than the fore wings, less ovate than in *Americana*, and rounded at the interior basal angle; *length rather more than that of the body*. The disk of the fore wings is closed by a rather faint, irregularly oblique vein, *with one disco-central nervule*, and angulated at the medio-superior nervule, where it receives a rather faint discal fold. The subcostal vein with three equidistant, moderately erect marginal nervules *from the disk*, with the apical vein *simple*. Median vein 4-branched, with the posterior nervule and the marginal opposite at their origins. The fold is thickened and the submedian vein simple. In the hind wings the subcostal vein shows a tendency to separate into two veins from its point of bifurcation towards the base of the wing and resembling two veins crossing each other; exterior to the point of bifurcation and a little behind the middle of the lower branch arises a decided, curved discal vein which receives, just above the medio-superior nervule, a decided or thickened discal fold. The median vein is 4-branched, with the two posterior branches equidistant from the second one.

Head moderate, free, smooth; with large ocelli. Face broad, rounded. Eyes rather small, round and scarcely prominent. Antennæ nearly as long as the body, moderately pectinated in the ♂, minutely pectinated in the ♀. Palpi equal to the front, filiform, porrected, distinctly 3-jointed and with joints nearly equal; terminal joint obtuse. Tongue about one-half as long as the thorax beneath.

Body short, rather slender, not metallic. Patagia very minute. Abdomen *as long as the thorax beneath*, not tufted at the tip and scarcely tufted along the sides, with a minute, lateral tubercle on the basal segment. Legs extremely slender and rather short; fore tibiæ with a slender tibial spur from the middle; hind tibiæ with two minute apical spurs.

L. A. **falsarius** *Clemens.*

Black. Prothorax fulvous, especially on the sides, *with a point on the median line black*. Hind wings rather thin.

Pennsylvania; Illinois, from Mr. Kennicott.

CLEMENS.

AGLAOPE Latr.

Wings extremely narrow. Hind wings ovate-lanceolate, narrower than the fore wings; length much less than that of the body; length of the fore wings somewhat more than that of the body. The disk of fore wings closed by a very faint, irregular vein, with *two disco-central nervules;* subcostal vein with a single marginal nervule from the posterior end of the disk and with the apical branch *trifid* near the tip of the wing or *bifid* with a long fork. Median vein 4-branched, with the posterior scarcely remote from the penultimate. Fold of the wing thickened from the base to the tip. Submedian with a short fork at the base of the wing. Hind wings without costal nervure; subcostal bifid, with an oblique discal vein arising near the base of the lower branch, and angulated above the medio-superior nervule, where it receives the discal fold. Median vein 4-branched, with nervules nearly equidistant.

Head rather small, free, smooth; with large ocelli. Face smooth, rounded, rather narrow. Eyes rather small, scarcely pro-minute. Antennæ with bases approached, much shorter than the body, rather deeply pectinated in the ♂, less pectinated in the ♀. Palpi very minute, filiform, drooping, with only two distinct joints; terminal joint acute. Tongue about as long as the thorax beneath.

Body extremely slender, cylindrical, not metallic. Patagia cylindrical, minute. Abdomen without lateral tubercle, tufted at the tip and along the sides. Legs extremely slender; fore tibiæ without tibial spur; hind tibiæ with two very minute apical spurs.

1. **A. americana** *Boisd.* Griff. An. Klugd. Lep. *Procris americana* Boisd., N. G. Lep. I, pl. 16, f. 7; Guer. Icon. Règ. An. Ins., pl. 84, bis, f. 11. *Procris dispar* Har., Cat. *P. americana* Har., Cat. N. A. Sphin., p. 85. *Ctenucha americana* Walker, 286.

Blue-black. Prothorax above entirely fulvous or orange. Massachusetts, New York, Pennsylvania, Georgia.

Subcostal vein exterior to the disk, trifid; apical branch with a long fork.

2. **A. coracina** *Clemens.*

The specimens are imperfect and denuded. The entire insect is black, without the orange-colored prothorax of *Americana*.

Texas. Capt. Pope's collection. From Smithsonian Institution.

CTENUCHA Kirby.

Wings broad, or narrow, elongate-trigonate. Fore wings with the subcostal vein giving rise near the posterior end of the disk to a single marginal nervule, and another exterior to the disk and nearer to it than to the post-apical nervule, which is given off near the apical nervulet. The subcosto-inferior nervule and discal branch from a common stalk, the latter straight and the discal fold received by the medio-superior nervule. The median vein 4-branched, the posterior much behind the marginal branch, and rather remote from the penultimate. Hind wings without costal vein; subcostal bifid, with the discal given off from the fork and receiving the discal fold at its angle. Median vein 4-branched, with the posterior remote from the other branches, which are aggregated.

Head moderate, free, neck distinct, slightly hairy above; with ocelli. Face smooth, rather narrow. Eyes moderately large, prominent. Antennæ about one-half as long as the body, deeply pectinated in the ♂, slightly pectinated in the ♀. Palpi porrect, exceeding the front somewhat, squamose; basal joint slightly hairy; the basal and middle joint nearly equal; the terminal shorter, acuminated. Tongue as long or nearly as long as the thorax beneath.

Body cylindrical, slender, more or less metallic. Patagia scale-like. Hind wings equal to the body in length. Abdomen with a lateral tubercle on the basal segment. Legs rather slender; fore tibiæ with a short tibial spur; hind tibiæ with four moderately long spurs.

Wings broad; palpi porrect; post-apical nervule interior to apical nervulet.

1. **C. latreillana** *Kirby.* Fauna Bor. Am. IV. 306, 1.

Dark brown or blackish-brown. Palpi pale orange, tips blackish. Face dark blue. Head above, prothorax beneath and the tegulæ in front pale orange. Thorax and abdomen dark metallic blue. Wings with whitish cilia, except in the middle. The fore wings in the ♀ have the extreme costa luteous.

United States, Canada.

CLEMENS.

Wings moderately broad; antennæ moderately pectinated.

2. C. rubriceps *Walker*, 283.

Dark brown, black beneath. Head and palpi towards the base clothed with bright red hairs. Wings fringed with white. Fore wings with blackish veins. Hind wings bluish-black. Abdomen of the ♂ sericeous green above.

New Grenada.

WALKER.

Wings moderately broad; post-apical nervule interior to apical nervulet.

3. C. venosa *Walker*, 284.

Dark brown, black beneath. Head above, prothorax beneath, clothed with bright red hairs in the ♂, and with yellow hairs in the ♀. Face dark blue. Palpi blackish, base bright red. Patagia and tegulæ in front striped with yellow, the latter likewise on the superior edge. Wings fringed with white. Fore wings with four yellowish-white stripes; the first costal, second on the subcosto-inferior nervule, third on the median vein, extended to the two middle branches; fourth on the submedian vein. Hind wings and abdomen of the ♂ dark bluish-black, of the ♀ blackish.

Mexico, Texas. Capt. Pope's collection. Smithsonian Institution.

CLEMENS.

4. C. ruficeps *Walker*, 284.

Blue. Head above and thorax in front beneath clothed with crimson hairs. Palpi black, with crimson hairs towards the base. Thorax with a lappet on each side and a white spot on each shoulder. Legs white beneath. Wings blackish-brown, blue at the base. Fore wings with a white costa and a white interrupted stripe extending from the base to near two-thirds of the length in the disk. Hind wings with a white discal stripe tapering from the base to half the length.

Mexico.

WALKER.

*Wings long, narrow; fore wings opaque, post-apical exterior to
apical nervulet; hind wings hyaline in the middle. Palpi curved.*

5. C. fulvicollia *Heberr. Gleucopis (Ctenorha) semidiaphana* Harris,
      Cat. N. A. Sphin. 38, 4.

Slate-colored or blackish-brown. Antennæ blaish-black. Palpi,
basal joint ochreous, the other joints blackish. Head above, patagia, prothorax beneath, tegulæ in front and a stripe beneath the
fore wings ochreous or orange. Fore wings with a luteous stripe
along the extreme costa. Wings with cilia of the general hue.
Abdomen blaish-black, scarcely metallic.

Illinois. Mr. Kennicott.

                                                    CLEMENS.

GROUP II.

Hind wings without costal vein. Subcostal vein bifid, the lower
branch strongly angulated and parallel to the upper, the angle
giving rise to a doubly angulated discal vein, which sends off a
disco-central branch from the upper angle and receives the thickened discal fold at the lower one. Median vein 4-branched. In
the fore wings the subcostal vein is rather remote from the costa
and its marginal branches are erected; the discal with two central
nervules.

MALTHACA CLEMENS.

Fore wings rather broad, obovate; the discal cell broad behind,
fusiform. The subcostal vein sends two short nearly erect marginal
nervules to the costa, and from the superior angle of the disk arise
two long nervules, on a short common stalk, the lower one of which
is the apical, but delivered rather above the tip. The discal vein
is rather faint and gives rise to two disco-central nervules, the
upper one rather on the costal side of the wing. Median vein 4-
branched, the posterior nervule arising a little behind the first
marginal branch. The fold is thickened and the submedian shortly
forked at the base. Hind wings ovate; as broad as the fore wing
and in length equal to that of the body. Without costal vein.
Subcostal is furcate, the lower branch giving rise at an obtuse

angle to a thickened discal vein, which is angulated above the medio-superior nervule, where it receives the discal fold, and above this is given off a single disco-central nervule. Median vein 4-branched, with branches equidistant, except the two superior ones.

Head moderate, free, vertex rather elongated, smooth; ocelli large. Face moderately broad, rounded, slightly protuberant. Eyes rather small, scarcely prominent. Antennæ with bases almost united, rather thick, but tapering at the tips, pectinated. Palpi extremely short. Tongue about one-half as long as the thorax beneath.

Body slender, cylindrical. Patagia minute, rolled. Abdomen not tufted at the tip or on the sides, about one-half the length of the body beneath. Legs slender; fore tibiæ with a short concealed spur on its middle; hind tibiæ with two extremely minute apical spurs.

L. M. perinoidnia *Clemens.*

Blackish-brown. Wings slightly transparent. Fore wings with the basal half luteous *above the fold.* Hind wings luteous along the costa from the base to the middle.

Illinois, Mr. Kennicott. Maryland, Dr. Morris.

CLEMENS.

FAM. II. LYCOMORPHIDAE.

Hind wings without costal vein. Subcostal bifid, the lower branch slightly angulated near its base, giving rise to an oblique, simple discal vein. Median vein 3-branched, with branches equidistant, the medio-superior branch receiving the discal fold. In the fore wings is rather remote from the costa and its marginal branches rather erect.

LYCOMORPHA Harris.

Wings narrow. Fore wings nearly fusiform. Near the posterior end of the disk the subcostal vein gives rise to two marginal nervules and two nearly equidistant exterior to the disk. Without post-apical nervule. The subcosto-inferior nervule and the discal

arise on a common stalk, the latter angulated in the middle and
receiving the discal fold. The median vein is 4-branched, the
posterior arising at a point opposite the middle of the space between the first and second marginal nervules. Hind wings without costal vein. Subcostal bifid near the tip, the lower branch
giving rise to an oblique discal. Median vein 3-branched, the
superior nervule receiving the discal fold.

Head smooth, free, without ocelli. Face rounded. Eyes moderate. Antennæ a little shorter than the body, biserrated or very
minutely pectinated. Palpi short, little exceeding the clypeus,
cylindric, porrected; the basal joint long, nearly equal to the front;
the middle and terminal joints equal, very short and ovate. Tongue
a little longer than the thorax beneath.

Body slender, nearly cylindrical, not metallic. Patagia scale-
like. Hind wings equal in length to the body. Legs rather
slender; fore tibiæ with a short concealed tibial spur; hind tibiæ
with one middle spur and two moderate apical spurs.

1. L. pholus *Fabr.* Sp. Ins. II, 166, 43.

Bluish-black. The tegulæ and the basal fourth of the wings
luteous.

Nova Scotia, Massachusetts, Pennsylvania.

CLEMENS.

2. L. dimidiata *Herr.-Schaeff.* Pyromorpha dimidiata Lep. Ex. Sp. Nov.
Ser. I, t. 223.

Black. Fore wings yellow at the base. [Is it distinct from *L.
pholus*?]

Georgia.

Fam. III. MELAMERIDAE.

This family has much affinity to the *Glaucopididae* and
also to the *Pyralites*. The wings are very generally more
or less black, occasionally with a metallic hue, very frequently adorned with bright colors or partly limpid.

19

JOSIA Hübner.

Body generally nearly linear and cylindrical, varying in length and stoutness.   Palpi variable as to length; in some species much shorter, in others a little longer than the head; third joint varying from one-eighth to one-half of the length of the second.   Antennæ of the male generally more or less pectinated, sometimes simple; of the female generally simple, occasionally serrated.   Abdomen extending as far as the hind wings, or beyond them.   Legs mostly slender; hind tibiæ very generally with four spurs of various length; middle pair wanting in a few species.   Wings black, generally narrow, adorned with yellow, luteous, or white stripes, bands or spots.

Group Thyrgis.

Thyrgis *Walker*, 316.

Fem. Body cylindrical, nearly linear, moderately long and slender.   Palpi a little longer than the head; third joint linear, more than half the length of the second.   Antennæ minutely serrated. Abdomen obconical towards the tip, not extending beyond the hind wings.   Legs slender; hind tibiæ with four short spurs. Wings broad, moderately long.

1. J. tribuna *Hübner*. *Ephialtes tribuna* Exot. Schmett. 24, 246, f. 491, 2.

Luteous.   Head, disk of the thorax and abdomen, with a dorsal black stripe.   Wings black.   Fore wings with a luteous stripe at the base and an oblique luteous band behind the middle of the wing.   Hind wings with a broad luteous stripe.
Cuba.

WALKER.

DIOPTIS Hübner.

Body cylindrical, slender, generally long and linear.   Palpi varying in length, not longer than the head; third joint more or less shorter than the second.   Antennæ of the male generally pectinated, occasionally serrated or simple; of the female sometimes pectinated, more often simple.   Abdomen extending as far as the

hind wings, and most often beyond them. Hind tibiæ with four
spurs of various length, very rarely with two spurs. Wings mostly
limpid, generally long and narrow, broad in some species.

Group Euagra.

Euagra *Walker*, 323.

Body cylindrical, slender, linear, rather long. Palpi ascending,
as long as the head; third joint conical, very small, about one-
sixth of the length of the second. Antennæ minutely pectinated
to seven-eighths of the length in the male, simple in the female.
Abdomen extending from one-fourth to one-half its length beyond
the abdomen. Legs slender; fore tibiæ not dentated; hind tibiæ
with four moderately long spurs. Wings rather long and narrow.

1. D. hæmanthus *Walker*, 324.

Bright blue. Prothorax beneath and head-clothed with crimson
hairs. Head white in front. Palpi crimson towards the base.
Abdomen and legs white beneath. Abdomen with a tuft of black
hairs at the tip; sexual appendages large, testaceous. Wings
deep black, blue towards the base. Fore wings with an oblique
elongato-triangular white hyaline band in the disk beyond the
middle; this band is attenuated towards the hind border and
approaches nearer to it than to the fore border, and contains no
apparent veins. Hind wings with a narrow white hyaline discal
stripe which extends from the base nearly to the hind border and
is traversed obliquely by a black vein near its tip. Length of the
body 5 lines; of the wings 15 lines.

Mexico.

WALKER.

Group Hyrmina.

Hyrmina *Walker*, 331.

Body cylindrical, linear, very slender, rather long. Palpi
ascending, curved, shorter than the head; third joint pointed, not
one-fourth of the length of the second. Antennæ of the male
rather deeply, of the female minutely, pectinated. Abdomen extending a little beyond the hind wings of the male, and nearly as
far as them in the female. Legs slender; fore tibiæ of the male
slightly channelled and not dentated beneath; hind tibiæ with four

small spurs. Wings moderately long, rather broad; fore wings
with three inferior veins.

1. D. vinosa *Drury*. Ex. Ins. I, 47, pl. 23, f. 4.   *Sphinx vinosa* Drury
    App. 4.

Wings grayish-diaphanous. Fore wings with the anterior and
posterior margin reddish-yellow, with a large external spot, white
in the middle margined with black. Hind wings, *fem.*, with a
submarginal reddish-yellow band.
    Jamaica.
                                                    WALKER.

Group LAURON.

Lauron *Walker*, 833.

Body cylindrical, linear, slender, rather long. Palpi straight,
porrect, as long as the head; third joint acuminated, nearly one-
third of the length of the second. Antennæ closely pectinated;
branches of moderate length in the male, very short in the female.
Abdomen extending a little beyond the hind wings in both sexes
or not extending beyond them in the females of some species.
Legs very slender; fore tibiæ not dentated; hind tibiæ with two
very minute apical spurs. Wings long, rather broad, more or less
hyaline; three inferior veins.

1. D. ergolis *Walker*, 335.

Black. Thorax and the costa of the fore wings along the basal
half and a short, oblique band, red. Fore wings with the disk at
the base subhyaline, an abbreviated, oblique band near the tip,
white.
    Jamaica.
                                                    WALKER.

CHRYSAUGE Hübner.

Group FLAVINIA.

Flavinia *Walker*, 369.

Body slender, of moderate length, nearly linear and cylindrical.
Palpi porrect, shorter than the head; third joint acuminated, less
than one-third of the length of the second. Antennæ of the male
deeply pectinated, of the female simple. Abdomen hardly extend-

ing beyond the hind wings in the male, shorter in the female.
Legs slender; hind tibiæ with two small apical spurs. Wings of
moderate length, rather narrow.

1. C. dimas *Cram*. Pap. Exot. I, 91, pl. 59, f. C.

Whitish. Head, thorax in front and hind wings, red. Fore
wings with the costa red, with a median, oblique thickly spotted
black band.
West Indies.

WALKER.

URAGA WALKER.

Male. Body nearly linear and cylindrical, moderately stout and
long. Palpi longer than the head; third joint lanceolate, a little
shorter than the second. Antennæ moderately pectinated. Abdomen extending a little beyond the hind wings. Legs slender;
hind tibiæ with four small spurs. Wings of moderate length,
rather broad. Fore wings rounded and not angular on the hind
border.

1. U. hæmorrhoa *Walker*, 445.

Black. Head and prothorax clothed with crimson hairs. Palpi
crimson, with black tips. Abdomen blue, crimson towards the tip
beneath and with a slender crimson stripe on each side. Femora
blue. Fore wings with a narrow, linear, straight, slightly oblique
whitish band with testaceous borders at two-thirds of the length.
Hind wings bluish beneath towards the base. Length of the body
6½ lines; of the wings 15 lines.
Jamaica.

WALKER.

FAM. IV. PERICOPIDAE.

This family is composed of large species, which often have
pale dots on the head and thorax, and whose wings are ample
and frequently more or less vitreous. It is connected with
the *Melameridae*, and has some affinities with the *Arctiidae.*

PERICOPIS Walker.

Body nearly linear and cylindrical, moderately long and stout. Head and thorax of the male hairy, the latter thick. Palpi more or less ascending, hairy in the male; third joint acuminated in the male, conical in the female, about one-third of the length of the second. Antennae little or not more than half the length of the body, pectinated moderately or minutely in the male, very slightly or serrated in the female. Abdomen of the male slightly compressed, much narrower than the thorax, extending for one-third of its length beyond the hind wings; of the female obconical at the tip, extending for one-fourth of its length or less beyond the hind wings. Legs moderately stout; hind tibiae with two minute apical spurs. Wings long, rather broad, more or less semihyaline; four inferior veins.

WALKER.

1. P. eurocilia *Cram.* Pap. Exot. II, 128, pl. 178, f. C.

Ferruginous. Head, thorax in front and abdomen spotted with white. Thorax and abdomen on the sides striped with yellow. Wings with marginal white dots. Fore wings with a black stripe near the base, with a short, oblique black band in front, and the tip of the wing black; also a broad median yellow band, surrounding a black spot, abbreviated and inclined behind. Hind wings black, red at the base, with ferruginous discal streaks.

West Indies.

WALKER.

2. P. leucophaea *Walker*, 352.

Wings quite opaque in the female.

Blackish-brown. Antennae very minutely pectinated. Thorax with several white dots in front. Fore wings with a crimson dot on each at the base. Hind wings with a row of crimson spots near the hind border, close to which there is a row of white dots. *Male.* Abdomen with a luteous tip. Fore wings with two gray slightly oblique irregular nearly connected semi-hyaline bands, the subapical one clearer than the first. *Fem.* Last abdominal seg-

ment with a luteous margin. Length of the body 9—10 lines;
of the wings 24—28 lines.

Mexico.

WALKER.

COMPOSIA Hübner.

Body nearly cylindrical, rather stout, of moderate length. Palpi
vertical, shorter than the head; third joint less than half the length
of the second. Antennæ of the male slightly pectinated, of the
female minutely pectinated. Abdomen oblanceolate in the male,
fusiform in the female, extending as far as the hind wings. Legs
rather slender; fore tibiæ excavated beneath; hind tibiæ with two
minute apical spurs. Wings long, rather narrow with semihyaline
spots.

L. C. sybaris *Cram.* Pap. Exot. I, 112, pl. 71, f. H.? De Beauv. pl. 24,
f. 7. *Composia credula* Hübn. Samml. Ex. Schmett. II, Lep. III,
Phal. II, Var. viii. Coll. B, Var. II, f. 1—4.

Black, white beneath. Body and wings thickly dotted with
white. Fore wings with four nearly square crimson spots.

West Indies.

WALKER.

EUCYANE Hübner.

Body nearly cylindrical and linear, rather stout, moderately long.
Palpi ascending as long as the head; third joint linear, rather
more than half the length of the second. Antennæ of the male
moderately pectinated, of the female serrated. Abdomen hardly
extending to the hind border of the hind wings in the male, a little
shorter in the female. Legs moderately stout; hind tibiæ with
four small spurs. Wings ample; fore wings with a semi-hyaline
band; four inferior veins.

Wings very broad.

L. E. pylotis *Drury.* Ins. Exot. II, 9, pl. 5, f. 3. *Callimorpha? pylotis*
Westw. ed. Drury II, 11, pl. 5, f. 3.

Blackish-blue. Abdomen luteous beneath, with the hind borders black. Fore wings with a broad, white median band; cilia at the tip white. Hind wings with white cilia.

Mexico.

WALKER.

FAM. V. NYCTEMERIDAE.

Some of the genera, like a few of the *Periopidae* and of the *Chalcosiidae*, have much resemblance to the *Rhopalocera*. The body is slender and the wings ample, and they have likewise a general resemblance to some of the *Geometridae*.

CARALISA WALKER.

Male. Body hardly stout. Tongue elongate. Palpi porrect, extending far beyond the head; third joint elongated, acuminated, much more than half the length of the second. Antennae moderately pectinated, much more than half the length of the body. Abdomen extending as far as the hind wings. Legs slender; hind tibiae with four rather short spurs. Wings moderately broad. Fore wings straight in front, rounded at the tips, very oblique along the exterior border; first, second and third inferior veins nearly contiguous; fourth remote.

1. C. editha *Walker*, 1861.

Male. Deep blue. Head crimson beneath, white about the eyes. Palpi crimson at the base. Disk of the abdomen with a short broad crimson stripe, which tapers in front; under side crimson. Wings with broad black borders; cilia white. Length of the body 6 lines; of the wings 18 lines.

West Indies.

WALKER.

BUDULE HÜBNER.

Body slender, nearly linear and cylindrical, rather long. Palpi porrect, rather shorter than the head; third joint conical, not more than one-fourth of the length of the second. Antennae of the male minutely pectinated, of the female serrated. Abdomen generally extending beyond the hind wings. Legs slender; hind tibiæ with four spurs of moderate length. Wings long and narrow; fore wings with four inferior veins.

1. D. variegata *Walker*, 350.

Crimson. Head black, white about the eyes and with white dots above. Antennæ and palpi black, the latter black beneath. Abdomen black, with a white band which is widest beneath on each segment. Legs black, white beneath. Fore wings with black-bordered veins towards the base, in the middle with a black oblique band which does not extend towards the fore border, but is dilated and contains a white dot towards the hind border; apical fourth part black with three or four white dots in a transverse line. Hind wings veined with black, and with broad white dotted black borders. *Male*. Hind wings black, streaked with white beneath.

West Indies.

WALKER.

PSYCHOMORPHA Harris.

Body slender, hairy at the tip. Palpi slender, nearly horizontal, extending a little beyond the clypeus, covered with loose hairs so as to conceal the joints. Tongue moderate, spirally rolled. Antennæ in the male pectinated on both sides, the pectinations rather short, simple in the female. Wings short, somewhat triangular, with the outer margins rounded; discal areolet of the hind wings short, closed by a sinuous vein. Abdomen not extending beyond the hind wings. Legs short, hairy; spurs of the hind tibiæ three, slender, nearly concealed by the hairs.

1. P. epimenis *Drury*, App. III. Exot. Ins. III, 39, pl. 29, f. 2. See p. 136.

MELANCHROIA Hübner.

Body slender, of moderate length, nearly linear and cylindrical. Palpi porrect, hairy, shorter than the head; third joint conical, nearly half the length of the second. Antennæ closely pectinated; branches long or of moderate length in the male, very short in the female. Abdomen not extending as far as the hind wings. Legs slender; hind tibiæ with four spurs. Wings broad, not long, generally black with semi-hyaline white spots.

Spurs short, near together.

1. M.? cephise *Cram.* Pap. Exot. IV, 182, pl. 381, f. R. Hübner, Samml. Exot. Schmett. II, Lep. II, Phal. II, Ver. vii. Byp. A. Sphing. 17, f. 1—4.

Deep black. Head, prothorax, sides of the thorax in front and breast clothed with luteous hairs. Palpi, legs and hind borders of the abdominal segments whitish beneath. Wings fringed with white, and with an elliptical white spot on each tip; veins somewhat cinereous. Length of the body 5 lines; of the wings 18 lines. Mexico, West Indies, Central America.

WALKER.

2. M. incœnstans *Grey.* Samml. Exot. Schmett. V, 17, 431, f. 861-2.

Male. Black. Thorax with luteous spots. Wings bluish-black, at the base beneath luteous or red. Fore wings with white borders. Mexico.

WALKER.

FAM. ———— ?

VIRBIA WALKER.

Allied to the *Noctuidae.* Body rather short, moderately stout, nearly linear and cylindrical. Palpi stout, straight, porrect, a little shorter than the head; third joint very small. Antennæ simple in both sexes. Abdomen not extending beyond the hind wings. Legs rather stout; hind tibiæ with two very minute apical spurs. Wings rather short and broad. Fore wings distinctly angular; third superior vein trifurcate; first and second inferior veins near together at the base.

1. V. lutallinea *Walker.* C. B. M. 471.

Brown. Palpi at the base and tongue testaceous. Antennæ black. Abdomen on each side with a slight luteous stripe which tapers from the base towards the tip. Fore wings ferruginous above and luteous beneath for more than half the length from the base, and with a reddish line along the costa. Hind wings luteous with broad black borders which are of equal breadth from the tip of the fore border to the tip of the inner border. Length of the body 4 lines; of the wings 11 lines.

Mexico.

FAM. VI. LITHOSIIDAE.

In the hind wings the costal and subcostal veins have a common origin in the posterior third of the wing. The subcostal is bifid beyond the origin of the discal, which is sometimes doubly angulated, giving rise to a disco-central branch from the lower angle, and sometimes simple and curved. Median vein 8-branched. In the fore wings the subcostal vein is remote from the costa, and the marginal branches rather erect.

NUDARIA ? Haw., Steph.

Wings rather broad, semi-diaphanous, rounded. In the fore wings the subcostal vein forms a large subcostal cell over the discal vein, giving rise about the middle of the cell above to a marginal nervule, and beneath to the subcosto-inferior and discal vein, the latter having a disco-central nervule. At the apex of the cell behind, the vein becomes trifid, dividing into a marginal, post-apical and apical nervules, the latter with a nervulet from its middle. Hind wings about equal to the body in length; without costal vein; subcostal vein with a marginal nervule arising from the disk near the discal vein, and becoming bifid exteriorly at a point remote from the discal vein; with a disco-central nervule. Median 8-branched, with the posterior nervule somewhat inferior to the origin of the marginal nervule.

Head free, rather small, smooth; without ocelli. Face smooth, rather narrow, clypeus prominent. Antennæ setiform, moderately

long, scarcely ciliated in the males. Palpi slender, slightly curved,
but little exceeding the clypeus, slightly hairy at the base; the basal
joint twice larger than the middle; terminal joint minute, ovate.
Tongue as long as the thorax beneath.

Body slender. Patagia nearly obsolete. Legs rather long and
slender; fore tibiae unarmed; hind tibiae with four spurs, the
middle pair short.

Eggs globular, pale yellow; producing larvae one week after
deposition. The larva on escaping from the egg is geometriform,
with ten legs. This refers to the species described below which
differs sufficiently in structure from the European *N. mundana*, it
appears to me, to authorize the separation of our species from the
group containing the European species. It may belong to the
Geometrina.

1. N. mundica *Walker*, 576.

Pale yellowish. Fore wings with the costa at the base frequently touched with ochreous, with two irregular oblique blackish,
sometimes pale gray, bands, composed of large spots; one on the
middle of the disk, and the other crossing the nervules, and a
single spot of the same hue near the hind margin in the medio-
central interspace, sometimes connected with the posterior band.

Pennsylvania, New York.

WALKER.

LURINA Walker.

Male. Body short, thick, very hairy. Palpi thick, very short,
hairy; third joint very small. Tongue very short. Antennae
rather deeply pectinated. Abdomen extending as far as the hind
wings. Legs moderately stout; hind tibiae with two rather long
middle spurs and two minute apical spurs. Wings narrow, rather
long. Fore wings straight in front, slightly rounded and not
angular behind; first and second inferior veins almost contiguous
at the base; third about six times nearer to the second than to
to the fourth.

1. L. incarnata *Walker*, 477.

Black, clothed with black hairs. Head above, thorax and abdomen towards the tip thickly clothed with crimson hairs. Palpi, antennæ and legs black. Thorax with a black dorsal stripe, not extending to the front. Wings metallic bluish-green, not hairy. Length of the body 5½ lines; of the wings 10 lines.

Mexico.

WALKER.

APISTOSIA Désm.

Male. Body nearly linear, rather stout, moderately long. Palpi stout, very much shorter than the head; third joint conical, very small. Tongue of moderate length. Antennæ moderately pectinated. Abdomen extending a little beyond the hind wings. Legs stout; hind tibiæ with four long spurs. Wings moderately long and broad. Fore wings very slightly convex in front, obtusely angular behind; first and second inferior veins united at the base; third rather more than four times nearer to the second than to the fourth.

WALKER.

1. A.? terminalis *Walker*, 478.

Body bluish purple. Head, fore part of the thorax, tip of the abdomen and fore coxæ crimson. Palpi shorter than the head; third joint conical, less than one-fourth of the length of the second. *Antennæ wanting.* Abdomen extending for one-third of its length beyond the hind wings. Legs purplish-black, moderately stout. Wings black, tinged with green and purple, rather long and narrow; first and second inferior veins of the fore wings near together at the base; third full twice further from the fourth than from the second. Length of the body 6 lines; of the wings 19 lines.

Mexico.

WALKER.

The characters of this and of the following species, of which the specimens described are deprived of their antennæ, partly differ from those of *Apistosia.*

2. A.? multifaria *Walker*, 479.

Allied to *Euchromia?* Metallic blue. Head, prothorax and sides of the thorax clothed with rosy hairs. Abdomen extending very little beyond the hind wings. Fore coxæ, knees and tips of the tibiæ white. Palpi red, very much shorter than the head; third joint conical, very small. Wings black, rather long and narrow, tinged with blue towards the base; costa and fringe mostly white; first and second inferior veins very near together at the base; third full four times further from the fourth than from the second. Length of the body 7 lines; of the wings 20 lines.

California.

WALKER.

ARDONEA WALKER.

Male. Body rather slender, nearly linear, moderately long. Palpi hairy, much shorter than the head; third joint conical, not more than one-fourth of the length of the second. Antennæ moderately pectinated. Abdomen elongate-fusiform, extending for one-fourth of its length beyond the hind wings, forcipated at the tip. Legs rather slender; hind tibiæ with four long spurs. Wings rather long and narrow. Fore wings hardly convex in front, slightly angular behind; first and second inferior veins united at the base; third very near the second; fourth twice further from the third than the third from the second.

1. A. munda *Walker*, 1650.

Female. Deep blue. Head, and fore part of the thorax and of the breast crimson. Palpi crimson, with black tips. Antennæ black. Abdomen extending for about one-third of its length beyond the hind wings. Wings moderately broad; fringe white, with a black interval on the middle of the exterior border of each wing, and another towards the interior angle of the hind wings.

St. Domingo.

WALKER.

HYPOPREPIA HUEBNER.

Female. Body stout, rather short, elongato-subfusiform. Head rather small. Palpi stout, very much shorter than the head; third joint acuminated, not half the length of the second. Tongue short. Abdomen oblanceolate, not extending quite so far as the hind wings. Legs moderately stout; hind tibiæ with two minute apical spurs. Wings moderately broad, not long. Fore wings slightly convex in front; the hind-angle somewhat rounded; first and second inferior veins almost contiguous at the base; third about eight times nearer to the second than to the fourth.

1. **H. fucosa** *Hübner*. Exot. Schmett. 21, 236, f. 471-2.

Rose-colored. Abdomen with a broad dorsal gray band. Wings gray. Fore wings with the borders and a furcate stripe, rose-colored. Hind wings with the basal half rose-colored.
Georgia.

　　　　　　　　　　　　　　　　　　　　WALKER.

LYMIRE WALKER.

Female. Body stout, elongate-fusiform. Head large. Palpi stout, slightly curved, a little shorter than the head; third joint conical, very small, not one-fourth of the length of the second. Tongue of moderate length. Antennæ setaceous, moderately pectinated, rather more than half the length of the body. Abdomen extending for nearly half its length beyond the hind wings. Legs slender, rather long; hind tibiæ with four minute spurs. Wings very narrow, somewhat pointed. Fore wings straight in front for two-thirds of the length, conical towards the tips, very oblique along the apical border, very obtusely angular behind; first and second inferior veins united for a short space from the base; third very near the second; fourth remote from the third.

1. **L. melanocephala** *Walker*, 490.

Hoary. Head, antennæ, and palpi black. Head, palpi, and fore coxæ thickly clothed beneath with pale luteous hairs. Prothorax clothed with pale luteous hairs. Abdomen blackish, pale luteous beneath. . Anterior legs brown, with testaceous femora;

hind legs testaceous. Fore wings with testaceous fore borders.
Hind wings limpid, with hoary fore borders and tips.
Jamaica.

WALKER.

PERCOTE WALKER.

Male. Body rather thick and long. Palpi curved, ascending,
as long as the head; third joint slender, linear, not more than
one-fourth of the length of the second. Tongue short. Antennæ
minutely pectinated. Abdomen extending for nearly half its
length beyond the hind wings. Legs rather stout (mutilated in
the specimens described), with four? spurs of moderate length.
Wings narrow, not long. Fore wings straight in front, conical
towards the tips, rounded and not angular behind; first and
second inferior veins contiguous at the base, third about thrice
further from the fourth than from the second.

1. P. signatura *Walker*, 493.

Brown. Head with a luteous spot on each side behind the
vertex. Palpi luteous beneath towards the base. Thorax with a
luteous spot on each side. Abdomen luteous above, pale testaceous beneath. Coxæ luteous. Fore wings with a short oblique
limpid streak near the fore border and before the middle of the
length. Hind wings grayish hyaline with broad brown borders.
West Indica.

WALKER.

LITHOSIA FABR.

Fore wings rather elongated, subelliptico-truncate. Disk rather
narrow, closed by a very faint vein. Subcostal vein *remote from
the costa*, with two marginal nervules from near the middle of the
disk rather erected, and another exterior to the disk, between it
and the forecæ apical nervule. The subcosto-inferior and discal
from a short common stalk. Median 4-branched, the posterior
remote from the others, arising interiorly to the first marginal
nervule. Hind wings much broader than the fore wings; with

the costal and subcostal veins from a common stalk, the latter bifid beyond the disk, which is closed by a faint vein. Median vein 3-branched, the two superior on a common stalk, which becomes bifid opposite the fork of the subcostal.

Head rather small, free, smooth; without ocelli. Face moderate, flat, smooth. Eyes moderate, prominent. Antennæ simple, setose in both sexes? Palpi moderate, recurved, but little exceeding the clypeus, squamose; the basal joint tumid, and about equal to the middle joint, which is cylindric; the terminal joint slender and nearly equal to the middle joint. Tongue slightly more than one-half as long as the thorax beneath.

Body moderately thick, rather less than the length of the hind wings. Patagia small, nearly cylindrical. Abdomen beneath one-half the length of the body. Legs rather stout; fore tibiæ with a short spur at the base; hind tibiæ with four moderate spurs.

1. **L. miniata** *Kirby.* Faun. Bor. Am. IV, 305, 1. *Gnophria vittata* Harris. Ins. Mass. 2d ed. 262. *Atolmis? miniata* Clemens, Proc. Acad. Nat. Sci., Nov. 1860, 543.

Scarlet or yellow tinged with scarlet. Antennæ black. Palpi tipped with black. Fore wings with three broad slate-colored or lead-colored stripes, the first near the costa; the third near inner margin; the second short in the middle of the wing posteriorly. Hind wings blackish slate-colored, scarlet or pinkish at the base. Abdomen black with a broad scarlet stripe beneath.

CLEMENS.

2. **L. longipennis** *Walker,* 510.

Yellow. Palpi brownish towards the tips. Tibiæ and tarsi brownish. Fore wings long, narrow, conical at the tips, with a very long narrow brown border which is slightly widened at the tips, and does not extend farther than the tips of the hind wings towards the base behind. Hind wings with a brown fringe at the tips.

Mexico.

WALKER.

EUSTIXIA Hübner. See p. 252.

30

EUBAPHE Hübner. See p. 253.

The following genus is one of a group that appears to connect the *Lithosiidae* with the *Tineina*. It probably differs from the *Lithosiidae* in structure, and cannot be regarded as a member of the family.

MIEZA Walker. See p. 253.

2. M. subfervens *Walker*, 528. See p. 253.

3. M.? pupula *Hübner*. *Eustixis pupula* Hübn., Samml. Exot. Schmett. III, 24, 245, f. 469, 490. See p. 254.

Fam. VII. HYPSIDAE.

In the structure of the palpi, this family much resembles some of the groups of the *Noctuites quadrifidae* of Guenée.

PITANE Walker. See p. 254.

1. P.? mediastina *Hübner*. *Dysauxes mediastina* Hübner, Samml. Exot. Schmett. III, 27, 253, f. 505–6. See p. 254.

Male. Black. Disk of the thorax and abdomen at the tip luteous. Fore wings with a postmedian elevate band and seven bands, white. Hind wings luteous, bordered with black, and with a black band.

Georgia.

WALKER.

Fam. ————— ?

CROCOTA Hübner.

Fore wings rather broad, trigonate. The subcostal vein almost above posterior end of the disk, gives rise to a single marginal nervule, and the apical branch is trifid at the tip; and sometimes with a second short marginal branch from about the middle of the apical nervule. The subcosto-inferior and the discal arise on a short common stalk, the latter vein angulated. The median is 4-branched, with the posterior remote from the others. Hind

wings rounded, broader than the fore wings, with the costal and
subcostal veins from a common stalk, the former simple and the
latter bifid, with an angulated discal vein from the point of bifurcation. Median *with three branches*, the posterior remote.

Head moderate, free, smooth; ocelli small. Face moderate,
flat, smooth. Eyes rather large, prominent. Antennæ not more
than half as long as the body, rather stout, setaceous and slightly
setose. Palpi rather slender, porrected, exceeding the clypeus by
at least one-half their length, and pubescent; the terminal joint
pointed and slender, about one-half as long as the middle joint.
Tongue slender, about one-half as long as the anterior coxæ, or
rudimentary.

Body smooth, rather slender; length less than that of the hind
wings. Patagia scale-like. Abdomen smooth, beneath one-half
as long as the body. Legs rather slender; fore tibiæ with a short,
concealed, middle spur; hind tibiæ with four short spurs.

Closely allied to the *Arctiidæ*.

TABLE OF SPECIES.

Wings with a discal dot.
  Abdomen ferruginous, with dorsal and black dots.   **ferruginosa.**
  Abdomen rose color.   **brevicornis.**
  Abdomen reddish-brown or fulvous.   **rubicundaria.**
Wings without discal dot.
  Abdomen red, with a black stripe.   **lacta.**
  Abdomen testaceous; wings subhyaline.   **cupraria.**

1. C. rubicundaria *Hübner*. Samml. Ex. Sch. III, 28, 256, f. 511, 5, 12.
    Arctia rubricosa Harris, Ins. Mass. 2d ed. 374. See p. 256.

Fulvous or reddish-brown. Antennæ fulvous, blackish on the
sides. Fore wing sometimes with a brown discal spot. Hind
wings more or less red, with a more or less distinct marginal black
band, sometimes absent, and sometimes with a dark brown discal
dot. Fore wings with a second marginal nervule on the middle
of the apical.

Pennsylvania.

CLEMENS.

Variety? Yellowish. Fore wings without discal dot. Hind

wings with a discal dot and rather broad, distinct dark brown
marginal band.

Pennsylvania.

CLEMENS.

2. C. brevicornis *Walker*, 536. See p. 256.

Fawn color or luteous fawn color. Antennæ black, short.
Abdomen rose color. Fore wings rosy beneath. Hind wings rose
color, with an indistinct and sometimes quite obsolete brown stripe
in the hind border, and a brown dot in the disk. Body 2½—3½
lines long; wings 8—10 lines.

WALKER.

I have specimens which correspond very nearly to the above
description. The anterior portion of the body is luteous, as are
the fore wings, but combined with a reddish hue. Hind wings
cinnabar red, without marginal band or discal spot, and in one
specimen the terminal joint of the palpi is blackish.

Illinois, Mr. Kennicott.

CLEMENS.

3. C. ferruginosa *Walker*, 536. See p. 255.

Ferruginous. Abdomen pale ferruginous, with a row of dorsal
black dots. Hind wings pale ferruginous, with a blackish dot in
the disk, and two or three blackish spots along the border. Length
of the body 3½—4 lines; of the wings 10—11 lines.

Hudson's Bay.

WALKER.

It is possible this insect may be the *rubricosa* of Harris. I
have specimens which agree in general with Mr. Walker's description, but they possess noticeable differences in structure as compared with the others described previously. In these the *tongue is
rudimentary; fore wings with a second marginal branch in the
middle of the apical nervule.* In every other particular the structure conforms to that of the genus. These differences may be
sexual. In ornamentation they are reddish-brown, scarcely ferruginous, and in addition to the discal dot, have a rather faint dark
brownish band crossing the nervules. Hind wings rather paler
than the fore wings, one specimen with a blackish discal spot, the
other without it, and faint blackish spots along the margin near
the inner angle.

My own impression is that *rubicundaria* of Hübner and *rubricosa* of Harris is a variable insect, and that *ferruginosa* of Walker, and perhaps *brevicornis*, are not true species. I am much more uncertain, however, respecting the latter than the former.

4. *C.* cupraria *Walker*, 636.

Testaceous. Fore legs mostly brown. Wings slightly rosy testaceous, subhyaline, with a slight cupreous tinge towards the tips. Length of the body 3—4 lines; of the wings 9—11 lines. Jamaica ? S. America.

WALKER.

5. *C.* laeta. *Lithosia laeta* Boisd. Guer. Icon. Reg. An. Ins. pl. 88, f. 6, p. 619. *C. laeta* Walker, 637.

Grayish-black. Tongue testaceous. Abdomen red, with a black stripe which is broader beneath than above. Fore wings red along the costa. Hind wings red, with a broad grayish-black border. Length of the body 8 lines; of wings 9 lines.

N. America ?

WALKER.

CISTHRENE WALKER. *See* p. 234.

FAM. —————— ?

TRICHROMIA Hübner.

Body slender, rather long. Palpi short. Antennæ setaceous, simple, slender. Abdomen exceeding the hind wings by one-third. Feet slender, hind tibiæ with four long spurs. Wings rather narrow, scarcely elongated. Fore wings slightly convex along the costa, somewhat oblique along the apical border, posterior angle rounded.

1. *T.* trigemmis *Hübner*. Exot. Schmett. III, 22, 239, f. 477, 478.

Dark brown. Fore wings with a yellow median band, and a spot of the same hue at the tips. Hind wings white, the hind margin and more than one-third of the tip gray.

St. Domingo.

WALKER.

FAM. ——————— ?

CINCIA Walker.

Female. Body short, stout, linear. Palpi straight, much shorter than the head; third joint linear, conical at the tip, much shorter than the second. Antennæ slender, serrated, pubescent, a little more than half the length of the body. Abdomen not extending beyond the hind wings. Legs slender; hind tibiæ with four moderately long spurs. Wings rather broad, not long. Fore wings slightly convex in front, oblique along the apical border, angular behind; first, second and third inferior veins approximate at the base; fourth remote from the third.

1. C. consperma *Walker*, 539.

Whitish or hoary. Palpi blackish towards their tips. Thorax with black dots. Anterior tibiæ with black bands. Fore wings sprinkled with black points and with full twenty-four black dots, of which there is a row across each tip; under side and hind wings blackish.

Jamaica.

Walker.

FAM. ——————— ?

BRITHALES Poey.

Tongue distinct. Palpi cylindrical, produced beyond the head, with the third joint oriform. Antennæ of the males strongly pectinated. Wings exceeding the abdomen.

1. B. guacolda *Poey*. Cent. Lép. Cuba.

Wings brown; fore wings partly paler, with many black dots. Abdomen yellow. Body and feet dotted with black.

Cuba.

Poey.

FAM. —————— ?

Wings with tinceform structure. Hind wings with the costal nervure straight; with the subcostal *simple, attenuated interiorly to the discal, but joining the costal near its basal third.* Discal vein nearly straight, *with two disco-central nervules.* Median with three equidistant branches.

Fore wings with the disk extending beyond the apical third of the wing. About the middle of the disk the subcostal vein sends off a strong marginal branch, beyond which is a secondary cell, from the hinder end of which arise two marginal and an apical branch; discal vein nearly straight, with three disco-central branches; median 8-branched, the posterior very remote from its penultimate; the fold is thickened and the subcostal is forked at its base.

POECILOPTERA Clinxis.

The wings are longer than the body. The anterior rather narrow, enveloping the body when folded; apex obtusely rounded and hind margin slightly oblique. The subcostal nervule gives rise to a marginal nervule, about its middle, and within the disk forms a large secondary cell, from the hind end of which arise three distinct marginal nervules, the lower one reaching the costa rather above the tip. The disk extends rather beyond the apical third of the wing, and the discal vein gives rise to three nervules. The median is 8-branched, the posterior branch being remote from the others and arising opposite the origin of the subcostal branch, which forms the secondary cell. The fold is thickened, and the submedian forcate at its base. The hind wings are rather broader than the fore wings; obliquely rounded along the hind margin from the tip to the base; costa nearly straight. The costal nervure distinct and simple; the subcostal simple and rather attenuated from the discal vein towards the base. The discal vein gives rise to two nervules, and sends a false nervule through the disk towards the base of the wing. The median subdivides into three equidistant nervules.

Head rather small, smooth, free; without ocelli. Face rather narrow, tapering, vertical. Eyes small, salient. Antennæ slender, with joints closely set, *serrated beneath with scales.* Palpi slender cylindrical, curved, ascending rather above the middle of the front; basal joint squamose; middle and terminal joints smooth and equal in length. Tongue about one-half as long as the body.

Body slender, scarcely equal in length to the fore wings. Patagia scale-like. Abdomen slender, more than one-half as long as the body beneath. Legs smooth and slender; fore tibiæ with a long, concealed internal spur; hind tibiæ with a pair of apical spurs.

The wing structure of the insect included in this genus resembles most strikingly that of the *Tineina,* and must form a group connecting the *Lithosides* directly with it.

1. P. compta *Clemens.*

Palpi pale yellow, with the ends of the second and third joints black. Head yellow, with a black spot between the antennæ and a black band across the face. Thorax reddish orange, with two black spots in front; neck yellow, edged behind with blackish. Fore wings reddish orange, with four bluish-black patches placed transversely on the wing and containing yellow spots; the first at the base; the second interior to the middle of the wing; the third exterior to the middle, constricted toward the costa and connected behind with the subterminal patch, which is constricted in the middle. The hind wings are slightly hyaline; dark brown.

Texas. Capt. Pope's Coll. From the Smithsonian Institution.

CLEMENS.

FAM. ARCTIADAE.

Group Callimorphides.

Body slender, smooth or nearly smooth, much shorter than the wings, either when folded or extended. Head small, smooth, with ocelli. Fore wings elongate-trigonate; hind wings slightly diaphanous, ample, length equal to that of the body, folded when at rest.

Hind wings neuration arctiæform; costal and subcostal veins with a common origin near the middle of the disk;

subcostal bifid usually beyond the origin of the discal vein, sometimes from the origin of it; discal vein simple angulated. Median 4-branched, with the three upper branches more or less aggregated, and the fourth very remote from them. *Fore wings with a secondary cell* in the subcostal system.

DEIOPEILA Stph.

Fore wings elongate-trigonate, length exceeding that of the body by at least one-third; subcostal vein with a narrow cell above the discal vein, with a single marginal branch arising interiorly to it and one from its hinder apex; the subcostal vein continues towards the tip of the wing from the apex of the subcostal cell subdividing into post-apical and apical branches, the latter furcate. Discal vein, simple, angulated. Median 4-branched, the posterior very remote from the other branches.

In the hind wings the subcostal vein is bifid from the origin of the discal.

Head small, smooth, with ocelli. Eyes prominent. Antennæ simple in each sex, rather short and slightly pilose beneath in the males. Palpi curved, ascending nearly to the middle of the face, squamose, basal joint tumid, middle joint long, terminal joint short, ovate. Tongue about equal to the thorax beneath.

1. **D. bella** *Linn.* Syst. Nat. 1, 2, 864, 348, 399. *Tinea bella* Drury, 1, 61, pl. 24, f. 3.

Palpi white, with black tips. Head and thorax white, spotted with black. Thorax with an orange-yellow spot on each side in front. Fore wings orange-yellow, with five or six white bands, spotted in the middle with black, the last one furcate towards the costa and the hind border spotted with black. Hind wings bright red, with the hind margin bordered with a black, white-bordered, indented band, which is furcate at the tip of the wing. The under side of the wings is red; along the costa of the fore wings are three equidistant black spots, an angulated black band, sometimes interrupted, near the hinder margin, and a row of marginal black spots; along the costa of the hind wings, beginning on the middle,

are two white-bordered black spots, and a forcate, white-bordered
black band on the margin similar to that on the upper surface.

Illinois, Texas (from Smithsonian Collection, Capt. Pope),
Florida, Nova Scotia.

CLEMENS.

2. D. speciosa *Walker*, 569.

White. Head and thorax with black spots. Thorax with a
red spot on each shoulder. Fore wings with alternate black and
red bands, the former macular, the latter angular and very variable as to breadth; under side deep red, with a few black spots.
Hind wings red; with two or three variable black white-bordered
spots in front and with a black border.

West Indies.

WALKER.

SUPPLEMENT.

While the present compilation of the published North American Lepidoptera has been passing through the press, additional species have been announced by authors, and others have been detected that had been previously overlooked ; some important rectifications of synonymy have also been found necessary. With the view, therefore, of making the work as complete as I can, to the end of the year 1861, I propose to combine in a Supplement everything I can find bearing on the subject, not already presented in the preceding pages. This will include some species belonging to families elaborated by Dr. Clemens, and which he has omitted from their not having come under his observation, or from his not being satisfied with their exact position in the system.   J. G. M.

Fam. II. PIERIDAE, p. 15.

By S. H. Scudder (*in Proc. Boston Soc. Nat. Hist.* VIII, 1861, 178).

PIERIS Schr., p. 16.

P. oleracea *Boisd.* (p. 19 of the present work). *Pontia casta* Kirby, *F. Bor. Am.* IV, 289, pl. 3, fig. 1 (p. 19). *Pontia oleracea* Harris, N. Eng. Farmer, VIII, 402, Ibid. Ins. Inj. Veg., 1st ed. 213 ; 2d ed. 233, Ibid. Agass. L. Sup. 386, pl. 7, fig. 1. *Pieris crucifrarum* Boisd. Spec. Gen. 519.

The butterflies described by Harris, Boisduval, and Kirby, under the above-mentioned names, are one and the same insect. It is found inhabiting the northern and eastern portions of North America, reaching south but rarely as far as Pennsylvania, and extending to the east to Nova Scotia, west at least as far as Lake Superior, while to the North it is found up to Great Slave Lake, in the Hudson's Bay Company's Territory, and even according to Kirby, to lat. 65° N. on McKenzie River.

I have examined many specimens obtained by Mr. R. Kennicott at different points in British America, from Lake Winnipeg to the Great Slave Lake, and by Mr. Drexler upon the southeastern

shore of Hudson's Bay, all of which were kindly placed in my hands
for examination by W. H. Edwards, Esq., of Newburgh, N. Y.
I have also had before me in my comparisons specimens in the
Museum of Comparative Zoology at Cambridge, from various
points in the northern United States, among which are those collected by Professor Agassiz, on the north shore of Lake Superior;
besides these, I have availed myself of my opportunities of study-
ing the specimens contained in the cabinet of the late Dr. Harris,
now in possession of this Society, and have, in addition, compared
with them specimens in my own collection, obtained in various
portions of the New England States.

I have never seen a perfectly white specimen of this insect; the
most immaculate ones I have examined had a few gray scales scattered about the base of the primaries and along the basal half of
the costal border, while beneath, the whole surface of the secondaries was bathed with a scarcely perceptible tint of a pale-yellowish color; from this limit every possible intermediate variation
may be found, in males and females equally, till it comes to have
an upper surface with obsolete spots similarly situated to those on
the upper surface of *P. Rapæ* of Europe, and the line along the
costal border extending sometimes, with much distinctness, beyond
the tip, nearly half way down the outer border; the upper surface
is also sometimes faintly tinged with pale-greenish yellow, the extremities of their nervules tipped with black, and the grayish scales
of the base extended into the secondaries; but upon the under
surface are found the widest limit of variation, for not only may
the tips of the primaries become distinctly greenish or lemon-
yellow, and the nervules at the apical portion, together with the
medial nervure, be somewhat heavily bordered with grayish scales,
but also the whole surface of the secondaries may have its ground
color distinctly greenish or lemon-yellow, and all the nervures,
from origin to tip, very broadly and thickly bordered with grayish
scales, while a slender line of grayish scales—the continuation of
the third superior nervule—crosses the cell longitudinally; the
costal border also at base is colored with orange, and the inner
border at base with grayish scales; at the same time specimens are
found with the under surface of the secondaries having broadly bordered nervures combined with a basal color of nearly pure white.

No possible step in the gradation from one extreme to the other
is wanting, and both extremes are found equally among numerous

examples from as widely distant places as Massachusetts and the Great Slave Lake, though the suite of specimens with which I have made my comparisons would seem to indicate that the paler forms are more commonly met with in the more southern localities, and the more heavily marked ones are the characteristic forms of the north. It may be noticed in this connection that Kirby, by a comparison between a single specimen from Massachusetts with three from lat. 65° N., separated the northern from the southern as being *less* heavily marked.

SCUDDER.

P. protodice *Boisd.* (p. 17). Scudder, Pr. Boston N. H. Soc. VIII, 1661, 160.

An examination of a large number of specimens in the collection of the late Dr. Harris, in that of the Museum of Comparative Zoology, and in my own, has shown me that this butterfly also enjoys a wide geographical range, extending from Texas on the southwest, Missouri on the west, and the mouth of the Red River of the North on the northwest, as far as Connecticut, and the southern Atlantic States on the east.

Coincident with these widely separated geographical limits is its wide range of variation, especially to be noticed on the under surface of the secondaries, wherein it corresponds remarkably with *P. oleracea*. On the one hand, we have secondaries which are immaculate, save some scarcely perceptible yellow scales on the discal nervule, bordered by a very few scattered gray scales, a cluster of a few distant gray scales near the border, between the first and second superior nervules, and a dozen or so, more widely separated, similarly situated between the second and third, and the edge of the wing light greenish-gray, with the fringe white. On the other hand, we find greenish-gray scales spread quite heavily along the borders of all the nervures, with the exception of the basal half of the superior and first inferior nervules, which being clustered together toward the border into arrow-head spots, and uniting together at their widest portion, form a transverse zigzag bar; in the place of the few grayish scales, between the first and second superior nervules, we have a large spot of greenish-gray extending across the first superior nervule to the border; a few scales only border the anterior half of the third superior and first inferior nervules, and the yellow scales of the discal nervule are

only slightly increased in number, though the scales which border
it make a large spot, and are generally deficient in the greenish
tinge ; the narrow border is interrupted by the darker scales which
form the swollen tips of the arrow-head spots.

These extremes of variation I have found most generally in the
male; in the other sex, I have not seen any specimens which had
these wings so nearly immaculate as that first mentioned, the
nearest approach to it being in specimens which discover a few
scattered scales along the borders of the nervures, the cross-bar of
arrow-head spots, reduced to an indefinite indistinct zigzag band,
and the central spot of yellow, bordered with gray scales quite indistinct.

It may also be said of this species, as of *P. oleracea*, that these
differences are observable equally in any locality in which the insect may be found, and the gradation is complete, though I have
not as yet seen any heavily marked males from the extreme western
limit of their range, but all I have examined have been nearly
immaculate.

P. protodice is the American representative of the European
daplidice, the Alpine *callidice*, the Siberian *leucodice*, the South
American *autodice*, the Arabian *glauconome*, and the South Afri-
can *hellica*.   We have in temperate North America no representative of the European *P. chlorodice*.

In eastern Labrador there is a white butterfly, very closely allied
to, but yet distinct from *P. oleracea*.   It was considered by Boisduval to be the same (see Spec. Gen. I, 518).   Four specimens
were obtained by an expedition sent out in the summer of 1860,
by the Lyceum of Natural History in Williams College, to Labrador and Greenland ; they were collected by Mr. A. S. Packard,
Jr., on Caribou Island, Straits of Bello Isle, and have been sent
me for examination with numerous other insects.—It may be called
SCUDDER.

8. P. frigida *Scudder*.   Proc. Bost. Soc. N. H. VIII, Sept. 1861, 181.

Two of the specimens obtained were males and two females;
the shape of the secondaries of the male of *frigida* is as in the
female of *oleracea*, those of *frigida* being proportionally narrower
across the hind margin, and broader across a line parallel to it,
near the base of wing, than in the same sex in *oleracea*; or in
other words, the secondaries of *frigida* are relatively more quad-

rate, and those of *oleracea* more triangular; the outer half of the
costal border of the secondaries is slightly more docked in *frigida*
than in *oleracea;* the dark narrow line which follows the costal
border of the primaries extends around over rather more than half
the outer border of the wing, while in *oleracea* it seldom extends
beyond the tip, and very rarely half way round the outer border;
the nervures on the under surface are more heavily marked than
in the darkest individuals of *oleracea*, though the markings are in
the same locality, such as the outer and uppermost nervules of the
primaries, the median nervure, the nervures of the secondaries,
except the discal, the inner margin next the base, and a band
crossing the cell, which is the extension of the third superior nervule; the markings of the primaries are heaviest towards the outer
border, those of the secondaries away from it; the costal border
of the secondaries at base is slightly tinged with saffron; the color
of the under surface of the wings is slightly dirty white, tinted with
very pale greenish-yellow, especially noticeable on secondaries and
upper half of primaries; when any color is present on the primaries of *oleracea* it is confined to the tip; it differs further from
oleracea in having the black scales at base of both wings above
more profuse and widely spread, frequently bordering the nervures
quite broadly; indeed grayish scales are more or less scattered
over the whole of the upper surface, giving the insect a grim appearance, increased rather than diminished by the slightest possible
yellowish tint.

By this description it would be exceedingly difficult to distinguish this species otherwise than by immediate comparison with
both sexes of *oleracea;* the differences are more easily to be seen
than described, though the extreme limits of variation of *oleracea*
do by no means permit us to include within its boundaries this
comparatively persistent form; it is more heavily marked than the
extreme of *oleracea*.

Eastern Labrador.

SCUDDER.

In order the better to compare together some of our species of
Pieris, I introduce here descriptions of some new species of this
genus from our western coast.

9. P. venosa *Scudder.* Pr. Bost. Soc. N. H. VIII, Sept. 1861, 181.

Above, white tinted with very pale greenish-yellow; base of all the wings black, and costal border of primaries with a black band, extending about half its length; extremities of upper nervules of primaries broadly margined with black scales, with a spot of the same color in the middle of the space between first and second inferior nervules; a black dot at the tips of the nervules of secondaries. The female differs from the male in having nearly all the nervures on upper side of primaries somewhat bordered with grayish scales, and the extremities of the lower nervules almost equally with the upper; but most characteristically by the presence of a band of grayish scales along the posterior border of primaries, which is bent abruptly upwards in the direction of the spot in the space between first and second inferior nervules, and continues to third inferior nervule, sometimes interrupted at the angle.

Beneath, as in the darker forms of *P. oleracea*, with the ground color slightly more highly colored than the upper surface, the nervures of the secondaries being heavily, and those of the primaries more narrowly bordered with grayish scales, with a saffron-colored spot at base of costa of secondaries.

Antennæ black, with incomplete white annulations interrupted above; tip of club yellowish; body black, with whitish hairs beneath; the wings expand from 1.75 to 2 inches.

I have examined twenty specimens (5 ♀, 15 ♂), brought to the Museum of Comparative Zoology by Mr. Alexis Agassiz, from San Mateo and Mendocino City, California.

[Doubleday in his Gen. Diurn. Lep. states that *P. callidice* Godt. is found among the Rocky Mountains; Boisduval, in his Lep. de la California, enumerates *P. leucodice* Eversmann among them, remarking that his specimens "do not differ from individuals from Altai;" and lastly, Ménétriés, in his St. Petersburg Catalogue, gives *P. autodice* Hübn. as an inhabitant of California. Since no description has been given in any of these cases, and the insects themselves are so closely allied, one can scarcely doubt that these entomologists had before them specimens of the same Californian species. Among the large number of species from the Pacific coast, which I have examined, I have never seen anything approaching near enough to either of these to warrant the positive assertion that it was the species referred to by them. *P. venosa* is the most nearly allied for which I cannot but think they have mistaken it, and as the blunder may be. *P. callidice, leucodice,* and *autodice* are represented by *P. protodice,* belonging to an entirely different section of the genus from *P. venosa.*]

SCUDDER.

10. P. marginalis *Scudder*. Pr. Bost. Soc. N. H. VIII, Sept. 1861, 183.

This species is most closely allied to the preceding *P. venosa*. The ground color is as in *venosa*, but almost devoid of markings; base of all the wings black; costal border of primaries with a narrow black band, extending about half its length; a few grayish scales at the tip of wings; outer edge of primaries, and posterior edge of secondaries with a very fine black line, slightly swollen at the tips of the nervures; fringe white; beneath as in *P. venosa*, with the secondaries and apex of primaries more yellowish; males and females alike in their markings.

Body black, with some white hairs above, and a considerable number of yellowish white ones beneath; antennæ as in *P. venosa*. The wings expand two inches.

I have seen only two specimens (1 ♀, 1 ♂) which are in the Museum of Comparative Zoology. The female came from the Gulf of Georgia, and the male from Crescent City, California. They were obtained by Mr. Agassiz.

Scudder.

11. P. pallida *Scudder*. Pr. Bost. Soc. N. H. VIII, Sept. 1861, 183.

Above, very pale-yellowish, nearly white; base of both wings and basal half of costal border of primaries dotted with grayish scales; whole costal edge of primaries black; the male has, in addition, a band of grayish scales on the posterior border of primaries as in the male of *P. venosa*, turned abruptly towards, and sometimes interrupted at the angle, extending to the third inferior nervule; and in the middle of the space between the first and second inferior nervules, as in both sexes of *P. venosa*, a cluster of grayish scales.

Beneath, secondaries and apex of primaries yellowish, with sometimes a few indistinct grayish scales scattered along the nervures, otherwise quite immaculate.

Body, above black, with scattered yellowish hairs; beneath yellow; antennæ as in *P. venosa*. The wings expand two inches.

This species was obtained by Mr. Alex. Agassiz, at the Gulf of Georgia. I have had before me five specimens (3 ♀, 2 ♂), which are in the Museum of Comparative Zoology.

Scudder.

91

12. P. tau *Scudder.* Pr. Bost. Soc. N. H. VIII, Sept. 1861, 183.

Above, pure white; costal border of primaries with a broad black band, suddenly bending downwards and ontwards, and following the discal nervule to its uttermost extremity, forming, with the black body, an elegantly formed T; this band has a white streak in it at the base; beyond the costal band, and connected with it by the black edge of the costal border, is a large apical spot, the inner edge of which runs parallel to the outer edge of the extension of the costal band, till it reaches the first inferior nervule, when it curves towards the base a short way, and again extending downwards, with an incurved border, reaches the second inferior nervule, where it is rather abruptly broken; this spot has three or four, sometimes five white, unequal, oval, sometimes round spots, the largest nearest the apex; some blackish scales follow the principal nervures of the secondaries for a short distance, and the tips of the nervures are sometimes black, otherwise there are no markings on the secondaries of the male, except the dusky reflection of the markings of the lower surface, which the transparency of the wing allows; the female, however, repeats slightly at the outer angle the markings of the lower surface.

Beneath, pure white; the markings of the upper surface of the primaries are repeated, with the white spots and streaks slightly enlarged and increased; the nervures of the secondaries are all narrowly bordered with blackish scales, which expand at the tips; commencing at the termination of the first superior nervule, a submarginal narrow band approximately follows the curve of the margin, is bent at the third superior nervule, and extends to the inner angle.

Labial palpi with mingled black and white hairs; antennæ black, with white scales scattered irregularly over the sides and under surface, as far as the club. Body black, with whitish hairs, especially below. The wings expand two inches.

It represents in Washington Territory the *P. sisimbrii* Boisd. of California. A large number of specimens are in the Museum of Comparative Zoology, obtained by Mr. A. Agassiz at the Gulf of Georgia.

The distinction I have made between males and females in the foregoing descriptions, is founded upon characters which I first noticed by comparing together the two sexes of *P. protodice*, a species whose sexes have been known for a long time, and which are easily distinguished by their markings. On placing together, side by side, series of males and females of this species, it was discovered that there was a sexual distinction in the cut of the hind margin of the secondaries; it consists in the female having the outer angle more prominent, and so the whole hind margin less regularly curved, or, as it might be expressed, more flattened— these differences, though slight and requiring a careful examination, hold persistently in all species of *Pieris* I have examined. I have in several cases tested it carefully, by separating, upon this characteristic, the specimens of those species which exhibit two classes of individuals with distinct markings, and have in all cases found the markings to be coincident unequivocally with the cut of the wing. It will be seen, however, that in all the species it does not hold, as in *P. protodice*, that the female is the darkest.

Two of the species I have described from Western America, *P. venosa* and *P. pallida*, represent respectively the *P. napi* and *P. rapæ* of Europe. It will be noticed in the European species that each has the same plan of ornamentation upon the upper surface of primaries, namely, a large apical and small submarginal central spot, and that the peculiar distinction between the two is found in the presence or absence of the dark scales bordering the nervures of the secondaries. Just so is it in the Western American species, separated most characteristically from one another by the same distinction in the under surface of the secondaries, and linked together in the same way by certain characters of ornamentation (which, however, are not borrowed from its European congeners), that is, by the presence in the males of the bent band of the inner margin of primaries, and a small submarginal central spot. But when we turn to Eastern America we find this striking circumstance, that *P. oleracea*, within its own wide range of variation represents both *P. rapæ* and *napi* of Europe, and both, *P. pallida* and *venosa* of the Pacific coast;—and what do we discover here, but that, discarding the strict lines of demarcation which separate alike *P. rapæ* and *napi* and *P. pallida* and *venosa*, it follows instead, with remarkable similarity, the range of variation discoverable in *P. protodice*, as before described, a species much farther removed from it in the genus than are they, thus simulating rather its *geographical neighbor* than its *nearest congeners*.

P. frigida and *P. marginalis* appear to have no true representatives.

SCUDDER.

FAM. V. NYMPHALIDAE, p. 40.

By W. H. EDWARDS (in Pr. Acad. Nat. Sci. Philad. 1861).

MELITAEA FAM. p. 50.

7. M. mylitta *Edwards.*

Male. Upper side fulvous; fringe of primaries alternately black
and white, of secondaries white; on hind margin of primaries a
broad black border, in which is a series of fulvous lunules, the
middle one largest and projecting, preceded by a sinuous row of
round fulvous spots which increase in size towards the inner margin; next, a fulvous band, the upper half of which intersects the
preceding row at the fifth spot, making it appear blind on the costal
margin; this band is edged anteriorly by a black line which is
dilated on costal and on inner margin; on the distal arc a fulvous
streak entirely edged with black; base of both wings covered by
wavy confluent black lines, as in Thoros.

Secondaries have a narrow black marginal border, on the anterior edge of which is a row of fulvous lunules, the one next the
anal angle bisected longitudinally by a black line; above these a
row of black dots, the one in the anal angle oblong; on the costal
margin near the outer angle a black patch, from which an interrupted dark line crosses the wing to near the abdominal margin.

Under side: primaries pale fulvous, clouded with yellowish on
the apex and hind margin; the black markings on the disk of
upper side indicated below from the transparency of the wing; a
black patch near the inner angle, a faint black streak on costal
margin, and another on inner margin corresponding with the
dilated extremities of the line above; both wings bordered by
lunules.

Secondaries yellowish, clouded with brown on the disk and on
the hind margin; the middle lunule white and arrow-shaped, those
next the angles yellowish, the others dark brown; a row of brown
points corresponding with the spots above; across the middle of
the wing an irregular band of yellowish white edged with ferruginous; next the base several white or yellow-white spots edged with
ferruginous.

Female. One third larger than the male, which it resembles;
the marginal spots and transverse band on primaries are of lighter

color, the latter tawny; the marginal lunules on secondaries are
tawny; beneath, the lunules next the inner angles of secondaries
are silver white, as are the band and the spots next the base; near
the apex of primaries are four or five small silver spots. Expands
1.9 inch.

Texas, Kansas, California.

This species appears to vary widely in color. Individuals are
found blackish instead of fulvous, the wavy lines near the base lost
in the uniform shade. The marginal spots and band are light
colored, nearly yellow, but disposed as in the type above described;
the under side exhibits little variation.

EDWARDS.

8. M. minuta *Edwards*. Pr. Acad. Nat. Sci. Philad. 1861.

Upper side orange fulvous; a narrow black border upon the
hind margin of both wings, within which is a series of fulvous
lunules; preceding the black border a narrow common fulvous
band edged anteriorly with black, and inclosing on costal margin
of primaries a transverse row of four obsolete white spots; from
this band to the base both wings are marked by transverse, undulated black lines; base clouded with brown; costa of primaries
brown; fringe white, cut with black at the intersection of the
nervures.

Under side orange, brighter on secondaries; a narrow white
border on the hind margin of both wings; anterior to this a series
of white lunules, each edged with black; on costal margin of primaries a transverse row of four white spots; beyond this to the
base black markings as on upper side; on secondaries the lunules
are preceded by an immaculate orange band, beyond which is a
broad transverse white band, containing three rows of black spots,
somewhat irregularly placed, and mostly oblong; some of the
middle row circular; another irregular white band crosses the
wing towards the base, edged with black spots; at the base a
white spot edged with black. Expands 1.4 inch.

Texas.

EDWARDS.

9. M. nyoteis *Doubleday*. Figured in Doubl. & Hewitson, pl. 23.

Male.—Upper side tawny; fringe long, with alternate bars of
black and white; primaries next the base crossed by black undulated lines edged without by a zigzag black band which is dilated
on the costal and on the inner margin; a broad black border on

blnd margin and apex, within which, along the margin is an interrupted series of points, the middle one lunular, the two next the
apex white, the others tawny; preceding these a transverse sinuous row of small spots, nearly round, tawny, except the two on
the costal margin, which are white and minute; between the black
border and the zigzag band a broad sinuous tawny band common
to both wings.

Secondaries next the base greenish-black, lightly sprinkled with
tawny atoms, and marked by two or three patches of same color,
the outline less irregular than on primaries; on hind margin a
narrow black border, which extends also along the costal margin
to the common tawny band; from its anterior edge on the costa,
a wavy black line crosses the disk and terminates inside the abdominal margin; upon the hind margin a series of yellow lunules,
the third from the anal angle largest and projected; above these a
broad tawny band, edged anteriorly by the wavy black line, incloses a row of six black spots, the middle one largest, the one in
the anal angle long; abdominal margin paler than disk.

Under side: primaries tawny, next the base showing faintly the
black markings of the upper side; a small patch of black on inner
margin; hind margin and apex pale brown, clouded and spotted
on the apex with white; a marginal series of arrow-shaped spots
of yellowish-white, the third from the inner angle and two next
the apex largest; anterior to these, the transverse row of spots on
upper side is reproduced faintly; secondaries pale brown, clouded
in the disk and on hind margin with black; a marginal series of
unequal silver lunules; above these a row of six black spots edged
with yellow, the first next the costa nearly obsolete, the second
and third round, the fourth and fifth semi-oval, and the sixth long;
the fourth faintly papilled with white; across the middle of the
wing an irregular silver band, and between this and the base several silver spots, all edged with dark brown; within the cell two
small yellow spots; body above greenish-black, beneath white;
antennæ brown, annulated with white; club reddish-brown.

Female. One-third larger than male, which it closely resembles;
the marginal spots on primaries beneath are long and attenuated;
the silver lunules of secondaries take the form of a deeply crenated
band; a distinct silver pupil in the fourth black spot. Expands
1.4 inch.

Illinois, Missouri.

ROWANA.

LIMENITIS Fab. *Nymphalis* Latr. p. 64.

5. **L. weidemeyerii** *Edwards.* Pr. Acad. Nat. Sci. Philad. 1861.

Male. Upper side brownish-black, with a broad common white band a little beyond the middle, making an obtuse angle within on the primaries and tapering towards the abdominal margin of secondaries, divided into long spots by the nervures; posterior to this band on secondaries an obsolete row of fulvous spots; within the hind margin of both wings a series of small white spots, minute on secondaries; between these and the band on costal margin of primaries a short transverse row of four white spots, the second largest, the fourth minute; crenations white.

Under side paler, with a common white band and four white spots on primaries as above; on secondaries a row of fulvous spots posterior to the band; a little within the hind margin of both wings a series of large lunules cut transversely and unequally by a crenated black line parallel to the margin; these lunules are bluish-white except towards apex of primaries, where the inner row is white; on primaries a narrow ferruginous band upon the discal arc, followed within the cell successively by blue atoms, a bluish-white band and a ferruginous band, both narrow, transverse, and oblique; next the base blue atoms; costa ferruginous; on secondaries the broad abdominal margin is bluish-white; the entire space between the band and the base is striped transversely with white and bluish-white, divided into spots by the nervures, with ferruginous lines between the stripes; costa white; body above black; beneath white, with a black stripe along the side of abdomen; palpi and legs white; antennae and club brownish-black. Expands 2.6 inch.

Rocky Mountains.

Edwards.

Fam. SATYRIDAE, p. 70.

SATYRUS Fab. p. 76.

5. **S. sylvestris** *Edwards.* Pr. Acad. Nat. Sci. Philad. 1861.

Male. Upper side brown; fringe same color; behind and along the discal cell of primaries a dark patch extending from the base half way to the apex; near the apex a small round black spot with a faint iris; a black point near the inner angle. Under side paler; primaries with a tinge of yellow; two ocelli corresponding to the spots above, the larger next the apex, each with white pupils and yellow iris; the disks of both wings finely streaked with dark brown; a dark line parallel to and near the hind margin of primaries; on secondaries are two dots—a white one in the anal angle, a dark one near the apex.

Female. Same size as the male, a little lighter color; near the apex of primaries a single spot; the dark patch as in the male; on the under side two dots near the anal angle of secondaries. Expands 1.9 inch.

California.

EDWARDS.

COENONYMPHA, p. 80.

3. C. inornata *Edwards.* Pr. Acad. Nat. Sci. Philad. 1861.

Male. Upper side ochrey brown, lighter in the disk of all the wings; costal margin of primaries and abdominal margin of secondaries grayish; no spots above or below; fringe gray, crossed by a darker line.

Under side : primaries same color as above from the base to beyond the middle ; then a transverse sinuous ray of paler color, and beyond this to hind margin grayish; sometimes this ray disappears, the basal color extending nearly to the apex ; secondaries gray, with a slight greenish tinge, darker from base to middle, and this shade separated from the paler margin by a transverse, tortuous, interrupted ray, the course of which is parallel to the hind margin.

Female. Wholly dull ochrey yellow, marked as the male. Expands 1.4 inch.

Lake Winnipeg.

EDWARDS.

4. C. ochracea *Edwards.* Pr. Acad. Nat. Sci. Philad. 1861.

Male. Upper side entirely of a bright, glossy ochre yellow, without any spot or mark, except what is caused by the transparency of the wings ; base of both wings dark gray; abdominal margin of secondaries pale gray ; fringe pale gray, crossed by a darker line.

Under side : primaries same color as above; costal margin, apex and base grayish ; near the apex a round, sometimes rounded-oblong, black spot with white pupil and pale yellow iris; this is preceded by an abbreviated, pale yellow, transverse ray.

Secondaries light reddish-brown, grayish along the hind margin; abdominal margin and base dark gray; near the hind margin and parallel to it is a series of six black dots, sometimes obsolete, usually with white pupil and broad yellow iris; near the base two irregular pale brown spots, and midway between the base and the hind margin a sinuous, interrupted ray of same color, extending nearly across the wing.

Female. Like the male. Expands 1.4 to 1.6 inch.

Lake Winnipeg; Kansas; California.

EDWARDS.

FAM. VIII. LYCÆNIDAE, p. 81.

LYCÆNA Ochs.   (*Thecla* Fab.) p. 11.

26. L. anna *Edwards.* Pr. Acad. Nat. Sci. Philad. 1861.

Male. Upper side violet-blue with a pink tinge, brighter at the base and on costal margin of primaries; hind margin of both wings narrowly edged with black, which in the primaries extends slightly along the nervures and the costal margin; fringe white.

Under side grayish-white with a tinge of blue at the base; primaries with a discal streak, followed by a transverse series of six small black spots, the one next the inner angle double, and the fifth largest; both wings bordered by rusty spots surmounted by black crescents, the four or five nearest the anal angle powdered posteriorly with silver atoms; secondaries have three small spots near the base, an obsolete discal spot, and a transverse series of eight small spots in a double unequal curve.

Female. Upper side light brown, with an obsolete discal spot on primaries; hind margin of both wings bordered by a series of fulvous crescents, which in the secondaries partly inclose spots of dark brown. Under side fawn-colored, marked as in the male. Expands 1.3 inch.

California.

EDWARDS.

27. L. scudderii *Edwards.* Pr. Acad. Nat. Sci. Philad. 1861.

Male. In size, form and color, resembles *ægon* of Europe. Upper side dark violet blue; hind margin of both wings and costal margin of secondaries edged with black; costal margin of primaries has a fine black border; fringe white.

Under side dark gray; primaries have an oval black discal spot, a transverse, tortuous series of six black spots, all edged with white, the one next the inner angle double, the fifth twice as long as the others; on the hind margin a double series of faint spots; secondaries with four black spots near the base, one being very close to the inner margin, and minute; a discal streak and a series of eight spots in a double unequal curve, all of which, as well as the basal spots, are edged with white; a marginal series of six or seven metallic spots, each surmounted by a spot of fulvous, which is bordered anteriorly by a dark crescent; these metallic spots are edged posteriorly and sometimes replaced by black; ends of nervures expanded into small black spots.

Female. Upper side brown, with a black discal spot on primaries; secondaries with a marginal row of obsolete spots surmounted by grayish crescents. Under side pale buff; primaries as in the male, except that the discal spot is preceded by a small double spot, and all the spots are larger; on the secondaries the spots are less distinct, and some of them wanting; the transverse series is set in a band of white; marginal spots without the metallic gloss. Expands 1.1 inch.

Lake Winnipeg.

EDWARDS.

28. L. fuliginosa *Edwards.* Pr. Acad. Nat. Sci. Philad. 1861.

Male. Upper side entirely blackish-brown; fringe lighter. Under side light brown, with a dark discal spot and a double row of rusty points parallel to the hind margin of both wings, the outer row on primaries obsolete.

Female. A little larger, of lighter color both above and below, but similarly marked. Expands 1.8 inch.

California.

EDWARDS.

FAM. VI. ÆGERIADAE, HARRIS, p. 137.

TROCHILIUM, p. 137.

13. T. acerni *Clemens.* Proc. A. N. S. for 1860, p. 14.

Both wings transparent. Antennæ little thickened at the tips.

Abdomen sessile, tufted at the tip. Hind tarsi very slender and smooth, as long as the tibiæ.

Head and labial palpi deep reddish-orange, the former white in front of the eyes. Antennæ bluish-black, the basal joint reddish-orange in front. Thorax ochreous yellow, with the tegulæ in front touched with pale bluish-black. Abdomen bluish-black, varied with ochreous yellow; terminal tuft deep reddish-orange. Fore wings with the margins and median nervure bluish-black, dusted with yellowish; a large diseal, bluish-black patch; terminal portion of the wing ochreous yellow, with a blackish subterminal band, and the nervules blackish; the hinder margin bluish-black and the cilia deep fuscous. Hind wings with a black discal patch; nervules blackish, and hinder margin blackish. Under surface of the body ochreous yellow, with a bluish-black patch on each side of the second abdominal segment. The middle and posterior tibiæ annulated with bluish-black at their ends; the anterior blackish, with the coxæ touched with reddish-orange. All the tarsi touched with blackish above. The larva bores the trunk of the maple.

Northern States.

CLEMENS.

Group **Paranthrene.**

14. **T. basaiformis** *Walker.* C. B. M. VIII. 39.

Male. Black. Head with red hairs behind. Palpi red, with some black hairs beneath. Antennæ red, minutely pectinated, very slightly thickened towards the tips, very much longer than the thorax. Thorax with two testaceous (?) stripes. Abdomen with testaceous (?) dorsal spots, much narrower than that of P. *respiformis.* Posterior tibiæ with a single testaceous band; fore tibiæ and anterior tarsi red; hind tibiæ and hind tarsi much longer than those of *Æ. respiformis*; hind tarsi testaceous. Fore wings purplish, with a limpid basal stripe, and with a reddish streak in front. Hind wings limpid, with a lurid tinge; ciliæ cupreous. Length of the body 6½ lines; of the wings 12 lines.

United States.

WALKER.

15. **T. pyramidalis** *Walker.* C. B. M. VIII. 40.

Male. Black. Head with yellow hairs about the eyes. Palpi yellow beneath; third joint elongate-conical, much less than half the length of the second. Antennæ rather stout, almost filiform, slightly pectinated, ferruginous beneath, very much longer than the thorax. Thorax with two yellow spots on each side, one at the base of the fore-wing and one in front. Abdominal segments with yellow bands, which are broadest and most distinct beneath. Legs with whitish stripes. Wings limpid with blackish cupreous ciliæ. Fore wings blackish cupreous along the costa and at the tips, and with a blackish cupreous band, which is slightly bordered with red; a red line along the hind border. Length of the body 5½—6 lines; of the wings 9—11 lines.

St. Martin's Falls, Albany River, Hudson's Bay.

WALKER.

Group Hembecia.

16. T. odyneripennis *Walker.* C. B. M. VIII. 42.

Female. Dark brown, slightly cupreous. Head whitish about the eyes. Palpi yellow, obliquely ascending, not long. Antennæ bluish-black, simple, subfiliform, rather stout, very little longer than the thorax. Thorax with three yellow spots on each side. Abdomen with a yellow band on the hind border of each segment. Legs yellow; femora striped with brown. Wings limpid, with cupreous ciliæ. Fore wings cupreous along the costa and at the tips, and with the usual band of the same hue. Length of the body 5½—6½ lines; of the wings 11—13 lines.

Nova Scotia.

WALKER.

17. T. emphytiformis *Walker.* C. B. M. VIII. 43.

Male. Purplish black. Head with white hairs in front. Palpi thickly clothed beneath with rather long brown and tawny hairs. Antennæ ferruginous. Thorax with a yellow band in front, and with a yellow spot at the base of each fore wing, and one at the tip of the scutellum. Abdomen with a yellow band on each segment; apical tuft black, with a few yellow hairs. Legs red, partly yellow; femora black; tibiæ with black stripes. Wings purplish cupreous. Fore wings yellow and partly red in the disk, which is interrupted by the usual band. Hind wings slightly streaked with red, limpid towards the base. Length of the body 5 lines; of the wings 10 lines. *Female.* Head yellow in front and along the hind border. Palpi yellow, clothed beneath with reddish hairs. Antennæ red, blackish towards the tips. Apical tuft of the abdomen luteous, with a few black hairs on each side. Tibiæ wholly red. Fore wings with red disks. Hind wings mostly red along the borders.

In this species and in the Æ. Odyneripennis the antennæ of the male are more deeply pectinated than in the European species of the group Bembecia.

United States.

WALKER.

18. **T. pyralidiformis** *Walker.* C. B. M. VIII. 44.

Female. Cupreous brown. Head with yellow hairs about the eyes. Palpi yellow, slender. Antennæ slender, subclavate, very much longer than the thorax. Pectus with a yellow stripe on each side. Abdomen with a yellow band at the middle of its length. Hind tibiæ mostly yellow; hind tarsi whitish. Fore wings cupreous-brown, with a yellowish basal streak on the under side. Hind wings limpid, with cupreous-brown ciliæ. Length of the body 4 lines; of the wings 8 lines.

United States.

WALKER.

Group Conopia.

19. **T. eupygæformis** *Walker.* C. B. M. VIII. 45.

Male. Bluish-black. Head with red hairs behind. Palpi red, black above towards the base. Antennæ serrated and pubescent beneath, very much shorter than those of the European Conopiæ. Abdomen with a slight red band at the base; segments from the 6th to the eighth red; apical tuft blue. Anterior tibiæ tawny; hind tibiæ with red tips; tarsi mostly testaceous. Wings with cupreous cilæ. Fore wings blue, purple towards the tips, with a red discal streak, behind which there is a limpid streak. Hind wings limpid. Length of the body 4 lines; of the wings 8 lines.

This species differs much from the typical form of Conopia, and somewhat approaches Pyropteron.

United States.

WALKER.

20. **T. gelliformis** *Walker.* C. B. M. VIII. 46.

Male. Black. Head white on each side in front. Palpi almost bare; third joint lanceolate, rather less than half the length of the second. Antennæ bluish-black, simple, ferruginous beneath and slightly thicker towards the tips, about twice the length of the thorax. Abdomen red, black at the base; apical tuft bluish-black; red towards the base. Fore wings bluish-black. Hind wings limpid, with blackish tips and hind borders. Length of the body 3 lines; of the wings 6 lines.

United States.

WALKER.

SANNINA WALKER.

Male. Body rather stout. Proboscis almost obsolete. Palpi slender, curved, acuminated, obliquely ascending, almost bare; third joint very slender, just half the length of the second. Antennæ filiform, simple, rather slender, acuminated at the tips, nearly twice the length of the thorax. Abdomen about twice the length of the thorax. Legs slender; hind tibiæ long and stout, somewhat pilose, as is also the hind metatarsus. Wings narrow, opaque, squamous. Hind wings limpid at the base. *Female?* Palpi a little stouter than those of the male; third joint shorter and stouter. Antennæ like those of the male. Abdomen about twice the length of the thorax. Hind tibiæ more slender and much shorter than those of the male; hind metatarsus slender, not pilose. Fore wings opaque. Hind wings limpid, opaque at the base.

1. S. urocerlformis *Walker.* C. B. M. VIII. 64.

Male. Bluish-black. Head reddish behind. Palpi reddish, black towards the tips above. Thorax somewhat ferruginous. Abdomen with a broad orange band on the fourth segment. Wings metallic green, mingled with blue and purple; cilia cupreous. Hind wings limpid at the base. Length of the body 7 lines; of the wings 14 lines. *Female?* Head and palpi black. Antennæ whitish at the base. Abdomen with a red band. Wings with black cilia. Hind wings limpid, bluish-black at the base. Length of the body 9 lines; of the wings 14 lines.

United States.

WALKER.

MELITTIA Walker.

Body rather stout. Proboscis elongated. Palpi moderately long, slightly pilose; third joint lanceolate, hardly half the length of the second. Antennæ subclavate or clavate, rather longer than the thorax. Abdomen oblanceolate, much longer than the thorax. Legs stout; hind legs most densely pilose, with long hairs, which extend nearly to the tips of the tarsi. Wings hyaline, rather narrow. Fore wings occasionally opaque; fourth inferior vein not very remote from the third, which is near to the first and to the second.

North America.

1. M. ceto *Walker.* C. B. M. VIII. 66.

Aurato-viridis; caput antice et apud oculos album; palpi lutei, basi albi; abdomen rufum maculis dorsalibus nigris, subtus luteum; pedes rufi, nigro albo que varii; alæ anticæ aurato-virides; posticæ limpidæ.

United States.

Walker.

Var.? Olivacea; palpi pallide flavi, fasiculo subapicali nigro; antennæ viridi-nigræ; abdomen ochraceum, fascia basali maculis que dorsalibus nigris; pedes postici pilis extus ochraceis intus nigris dense horti; alæ anticæ olivaceo-fuscæ opacæ, posticæ limpidæ fusco marginatæ.

Massachusetts.

Walker.

2. M? flavitibia *Walker.* C. B. M. VIII. *Trochilium tibiale* Harris. Am. Journ. Sci. XXXVI.

Fuscescens; caput apud oculos flavum; antennæ nigræ; thorax flavo bivittatus; abdominis segmenta flavo marginata; tibiæ flavæ, posticæ pilis flavis dense vestitæ; alæ limpidæ, anticæ marginibus fascia que abbreviata pallide fuscis.

New Hampshire.

Walker.

FAM. XI. NOTODONTIDAE, p. 238.

HUTEROCAMPA.

3. H. semiplaga *Walker.* Canadian Naturalist, 1861.

Male and Female. Cinereous, thickly pilose, with a slight olive-green tinge, whitish-cinereous beneath. Palpi distinct, obliquely ascending, not extending beyond the frontal tuft. Thorax by the hind border and abdomen at the base black. Wings partly clouded with black, adorned with three indistinct irregular denticulated black lines; marginal line black; fringe with black points. Fore wings somewhat rounded at the tips, with a submarginal line of black dots. *Male.* Antennæ tawny, moderately pectinated to three-fourths of the length. *Female.* Antennæ simple. Length of the body 9 lines; of the wings 20 lines.

Township of Montcalm, Canada.

WALKER.

FAM. XII. ARCTIADAE, p. 243.

ARCTIA Schr.

Stature robust. Head and thorax with long hairs. Tongue usually very short. Palpi porrect, short, very hairy; first article longer than the second; the third subacute. Antennæ slender, rather long. Thorax not crested. Abdomen annulate, robust. *Male.* Antennæ pectinate. *Female.* Antennæ serrate, sometimes pectinate. Hind tibiæ with four spurs; fore tibiæ simple. Colors and markings different; primaries dark, sometimes white, gray, or yellow, or with bright spots or streaks; secondaries with dark spots on a lighter ground. Secondaries with eight veins. Flight nocturnal. *Larvæ* solitary.

1. A. americana *Harris.* Figured in Agassiz' Lake Superior, pl. 7, fig. 3.

Head brown; antennæ white above, with brown pectinations. Thorax brown above, margined before with an arcuated yellowish-white band, which is continued on the outer edge of the shoulder covers; upper edge of the collar crimson-red. Primaries coffee-brown, with three yellowish-white spots on the outer edge, and crossed by irregular anastomosing yellowish-white lines. Secondaries bright ochre-yellow, with a large reniform central black spot, two round black spots behind, a third smaller spot near the anal angle, and a black dot between the middle and inner margin. Abdomen tawny, with four blackish dorsal spots. Legs dusky; thighs and anterior tibiæ fringed with red hairs; hindmost tarsi whitish, annulated with black.

Lake Superior.

HARRIS.

2. **A. parthenos** *Harris.* Figured in Agassiz' Lake Superior, pl. 7.

Head brown, with a crimson fringe above and between the black antennæ. Thorax brown above, margined before with an arcuated cream-colored band, which is continued on each side of the outer edge of the shoulder covers; upper edge of the collar crimson red. Primaries dusky brown, with three small cream-colored spots on the outer edge; four spots of the same color in a line near the inner margin, and several more scattered on the disk. Secondaries deep ochre-yellow, with the base, the basal edge of the inner margin, a triangular spot in the middle, adjoining the basal spot and a broad indented band behind, black. Abdomen dusky above, tawny at the tip and beneath. Legs dusky, thighs and tibiæ fringed with crimson hairs.

Lake Superior.

HARRIS.

3. **A. placentia** *Abbot.* Figured in Sm. Abb. pl. 65.

Fuscous; primaries with one or three pale testaceous spots; secondaries reddish, margin and some submarginal spots fuscous; abdomen above reddish, with the dorsal spots and apex fuscous.

Var. a. Fore wings with the outer fringe partly pale testaceous; and with several spots and dots of the same color in the disk.

Var. b. Fore wings with the outer fringe wholly blackish-brown, unspotted, except two very minute testaceous dots.

North America.

4. **A. virginalis** *Boisd.* Ann. Soc. Ent. 2me sér. X, 321.

Upper side black, with about twenty yellow spots on the primaries. Secondaries fulvous, with three bands and the principal nerves black; the band of the extremity incomplete, ending before reaching the anal angle; sometimes all the bands are united by

22

the nerves, the ground is then black, with fulvous squares. Head fulvous; thorax black, with the shoulders yellow; scutellum fulvous; body fulvous above, with black rings, bluish-black below. Under side of the secondaries as above. Under side of the primaries with the spots at the base and of the middle fulvous.

San Francisco.

Boisd.

5. A. virgo *Sm. Abb.* Var. *Callimorpha parthenice* Kirby. Figured in Sm. Abb. pl. 62; Naturalist's Lib. vol. 38, pl. 10. Var. in Faun. Bor. Amer. IV, pl. 5.

Primaries carneous, fading to reddish buff, and covered with many stripes and lance-shaped spots of black; secondaries vermilion-red, with several large angular spots towards the posterior margin. Antennæ ferruginous; thorax fulvous, with three broad black stripes and two small black spots over the eyes. Under side of the abdomen black; upper side vermilion red, with a row of black spots close together along the top of the back. *Larva* brown, rather thickly covered with tufts of brown hair.

Var.? Thorax carneous with five black spots; primaries black, with pale carneous streaks; secondaries reddish, with five black spots.

United States.

Nat. Library.

6. A. virgnncula *Kirby.* Figured in Faun. Bor. Amer. IV, pl. 4.

Head pallid; orbit of the eyes and mouth black; antennæ black, serrato-pennate; thorax pallid with five lanceolate black spots; the posterior ones being the largest; primaries black with pallid rivulets, which are formed by the scales that clothe the nervures, and produce the rays at the apex of these wings, when the lines are traversed by a transverse, angulated band; underneath they are pale, with the black points less distinct, except at the apex; a black spot in the disk near the costal margin; the secondaries are orange-tawny, spotted at the apex with black; abdomen tawny above, below pale, with a dorsal and on each side a double lateral black macular stripe; trunk underneath black, with pale hairs, intermixed; legs black; tibiæ pale above; thighs with a pale spot at the base and apex.

Canada.

Kirby.

7. A. nais *Drury*. Figured in Drury, pl. 7.

Antennæ black and pectinated. Head and body light yellowish-brown. Thorax with three black longitudinal marks, and several spots on the abdomen. Primaries black, with broad ochre stripes, the second farcate; ciliæ light yellowish-brown; secondaries light yellowish or ochre brown, with a faint black spot on each and a broad irregular border of a dusky-black running along the external edges, but narrow in the middle. Wings entire. Under side paler.

Var. a. Male. Fore stripe of the primaries not joining the costa.

Var. b. Male. Inner border of the secondaries reddish.

Var. c. Male. Primaries with no pale oblique band towards the tips.

Var. d. Female. Like *Var. c.* Secondaries red, with broad blackish borders. Abdomen wholly brown, except on each side above towards the base.

Var. e. Female. Primaries with testaceous veins; fore stripe and part of the middle stripe almost obsolete.

United States.

WESTWOOD.

8. A. phyllira *Drury*. Figured in Drury I, pl. 7; Sm. Abb. II, pl. 64.

Primaries black, ciliæ cream-color; margin next the body cream-color; one longitudinal line, two transverse lines and near the tip two zigzag lines, forming a W of buff. Secondaries red, with four black spots. Margins black.

United States.

HARRIS.

9. A. parthenice *Kirby*. Var. A. virgo.

Antennæ black pectinated; thorax flesh-colored, with two anterior and three posterior oblong black spots, the latter being the largest; primaries black, with the so-called rivulets pale, with a slight pinkish tint; the main streams, especially towards the apex, form several islets, most of which are divided by slender ones which do not appear on the under side; the secondaries are of the color of red lead, with five black spots towards the posterior margin, the intermediate three forming a macular band above which is one smaller, and below it another. Underneath, also, a small spot at the costal margin above the other.

Canada.

KIRBY.

10. **A. dione** *Hübn.* Fab., Sm. Abb. *Arge* Drury. Figured in Drury, I, pl. 18; Sm. Abb. pl. 63; Naturalist's Library, vol. 36, pl. 19.

Ground color of primaries and thorax cream-color, sometimes delicate pink; surface variegated with numerous black lines and angular spots. Secondaries cream-color or tinged with red, with a fulvous marginal line and many oblong black spots behind. Antennæ black at the extremities; neck red, with two small black streaks above it; thorax with a black stripe in the centre and another on each side; abdomen with three rows of black spots, those along the back being largest. Anterior femors red, with two black spots close to the head.

Var. a. Primaries reddish-white, with cuneiform black spots. Secondaries red, with black yellow bordered spots.

Var. b. Spots of the primaries much larger and forming a stripe toward the hind border.

Var. c. Spots of the primaries still larger and more inclined to form stripes. Spots of the secondaries without yellow borders.

Var. d. Secondaries whitish, spots small and without yellow borders.

Larva dark brown, with five pale or yellow longitudinal stripes, each segment bearing a transverse row of fulvous tubercles, from which spring a dense tuft of brown hairs.

United States.

NAT. LIBRARY.

11. **A. hyperborea** *Curtis.* C. R. M. 611.

Fuscous; primaries with a costal spot and posterior villa interrupted with rust-red; secondaries fuscous, with a band unimaculate and margin ochry.

Arctic America.

WALKER.

12. **A. isabella** *Hübn.* Figured in Sm. Abb. II, pl. 68.

Antennæ filiform, tawny-yellow. Thorax tawny and brownish. Abdomen tawny, deeper color beneath; three rows of black spots, six or seven in each row. Primaries tawny, with a few black scattering spots. Secondaries nearly transparent, slightly tawny, with six spots; legs black or dark brown.

United States.

SM. ABBOT.

13. A. gelida *Mœsch.* C. B. M. 611.

Black, thorax bivittate with yellow; sides of the abdomen yellow, spotted with black; primaries yellowish, with black angular spots; secondaries subcinereous.

Labrador.

WALKER.

14. A. rubricosa *Harris.* Ins. Mass. 233.

Primaries reddish-brown, almost transparent, with a small black spot near the middle; secondaries dusky, becoming blacker behind (more rarely red with a broad blackish border behind), with two black dots near the middle; the inner margin next to the body and the fringe, reddish; thorax reddish-brown; abdomen cinnabar red, with a row of black dots on the top and another row on each side. Expands an inch and a quarter.

Massachusetts.

HARRIS.

15. A. dahurica *Boisd.* Ann. Soc. Ent. 2me sér. X, 321. Figured in Boisd. Icon. Hist. Lep. 126, 2, pl. 60.

Carneous; head, three streaks of the primaries black; secondaries yellowish, base and cilia yellow, with black spots.

California, Siberia.

BOISD.

16. A. figurata *Drury,* II, pl. 12.

Upper side. Antennæ dark brown and pectinated. Thorax cream-color and black. Abdomen black, sides red. Primaries black, a cream-colored line running from the shoulders parallel to and at a small distance from the posterior edge, towards the lower corner, stopping at about one-third from the external edge, from whence, near the end of this line, arise two others, which run almost to the anterior edges. Secondaries, red in the middle, surrounded, except on the abdominal edges, by a broad black margin. Sometimes only with a small red spot on the secondaries.

Under side. Palpi hairy and black; wings as on the other side, with the colors less distinct.

Southern States.

WESTWOOD.

SPILOSOMA Steph.

White, gray or yellow, with black dots or vittæ; abdomen with five rows of black dots, one above and two rows on each side; sometimes the points indistinct.

1. S. acrea *Drury.* *Caprotina* Cram.; *persterninea* Peck. Figured in Drury, I, pl. 3; Cram. Pap. Exot. III, pl. 287; Sm. Abb. pl. 67.

Head, thorax and primaries of the male cream-color or deep ochre-yellow; the surface of the latter with numerous black spots, five of which are placed in a regular row along the anterior border and six on the external one; secondaries entirely yellow, with a few black spots near the external edge and middle. Abdomen yellow, with a row of black spots down the centre and another on each side; apex cream-colored; under side of wings and thighs deep yellow. *Female.* All the wings white, with numerous black spots, variable in their distribution, but there is a marginal row on the inferiors which is wanting in the male. Eyes and antennæ in both sexes, black.

Larva white, when young; nearly black, when full grown; intermediate stage, reddish-brown; two yellow lines along the sides, and a transverse series of orange spots on each segment. From the back of each segment arises a tuft of blackish hairs.

2. S. soho *Sm. Abb.* Figured in Sm. Abb. II, pl. 63.

Wings white, veins on both sides margined with black; abdomen luteous, with black spots.
Georgia.

Sm. Abbot.

3. S. virginica *Fab.* Supp. Ent. a. 437. C. B. M. 668. *Epicauis* Drury, III, pl. 23.

White, with a black point on the middle of the primaries, and two black dots on the inferiors; one in the middle and the other near the posterior angle, much more distinct on the under side; a row of black dots on the back; another on each side and between these a longitudinal deep yellow stripe; femora and tibiæ of the fore legs ochre-yellow.

Larva varies in color; often of a pale yellow or straw color, with a black line along each side of the body, and a transverse line of the same color between each of the segments, and it is covered with long pale yellow hairs. Others are of a brownish-yellow or foxy red. Head and ends of the feet ochre-yellow; body below blackish.

Var. a. Wings wholly white.

Var. b. Primaries with one black dot.

Var. c. Primaries with one black dot; secondaries with two black dots.

Var. d. Primaries with two black dots; secondaries the same.

Var. e. Primaries with three black dots; secondaries the same.

North America.

WALKER.

4. S. cunea *Drury.* *Punctatissima* Sm. Abb. Figured in Drury, I, pl. 18; Sm. Abb. pl. 70.

Antennæ black, pectinate; head white; back and abdomen ash-color. Primaries white; spots numerous, of many forms, and sooty black; external margin with five spots; those nearest the tips triangular. Secondaries with a dark spot near the external edge, and faintly marked near the external angle. Length of the body 5—6 lines; of the wings 13—18 lines.

WALKER.

5. S. congrua *Walk.* C. B. M. 669.

White. Tarsi with black bands. Fore coxæ and fore femora luteous, with black spots on the inner side; fore tibiæ striped with black on the inner side. *Male.* Head and fore part of the thorax with a slight testaceous tinge. Primaries with four oblique very imperfect and irregular bands, composed of pale brown dots. Length of the body 6—7 lines; of the wings 16—20 lines.

Georgia.

WALKER.

6. S. egle *Drury.* Figured in Drury, II, pl. 20.

Wings rather long, thin, delicate, of a bluish-gray color, paler on the front edge and without spots; head, thorax, under side of the body and legs, gray; neck cream-color; top of abdomen bright yellow, with a row of black spots and two rows on each side. Expands from one inch and three-quarters to nearly two inches.

Larva black; a whitish line on each side, covered with short tufts of hairs proceeding from tubercles.

United States.

WALKER.

7. **B. textor** *Harris.* Ins. Mass. p. 275, 2d ed.

White, without spots; fore femora tawny-yellow; feet blackish. Expands from one inch and a quarter to one and three-eighths.

Larva greenish, dotted with black; a broad blackish stripe along the top of the back, and a bright yellow stripe on each side. The warts from which the thin bundles of spreading, silky hairs proceed, are black on the back and rust-yellow or orange on the sides. Head and feet black. Spin large webs and live in communities.

Northern States.

HARRIS.

8. **B. collaris** *Fitch,* 3d Report, 265.

Milk-white and glossy; head, neck, base of the outer edge of the fore wings and anterior hips pale ochre-yellow; feet pale brown. Width 1.35.

Mississippi.

FITCH.

9. **B. punotata** *Fitch,* 3d Report, 265.

White; a continuous black stripe on the fore side of the anterior feet and shanks, their thighs and hips being yellow in front and the fore wings having a black central dot, and in the males a row of small blackish spots extending from the middle of the inner margin to the tip.

New York.

FITCH.

CALLIMORPHA Latr. *Hypercompa* Hübn.

Palpi very short, pilose, scales appressed; tongue much longer than the head; antennæ in both sexes simple, ciliated, with two strong *setæ* at each joint. Body slender. Wings densely squamose. Feet robust, squamose; anterior tibiæ much shorter than the femora.

1. C. clymene *Esper.* *Colona* Hübn. *Carolina?* Harris. Figured in Esper Schmett. IV, 22, 10, pl. 163; Noct. 103, f. 1.

Luteous; antennæ black; palpi black at the apex; prothorax biguttate with fuscous; disk of thorax white, quivittate with fuscous; abdomen often with fuscous dorsal spots; primaries with an angulate basal fuscous vitta, three anterior spots and one posterior subapical divided, white; secondaries often with two fuscous spots.

Var. a. Secondaries with three submarginal spots and a marginal streak.

Var. b. Secondaries with two submarginal spots.

Var. c. Secondaries with one submarginal spot.

Var. d. Secondaries immaculate.

United States.

WALKER.

2. C. militaris *Harris.* Ins. Mass. 2d ed. p. 264.

Primaries white, almost entirely bordered with brown; with an oblique brown band from the inner margin to the tip; the brown border on the front margin generally has two short angular projections, extending backwards on the surface of the wing. Secondaries white, without spots. Body white; head, thorax and femora yellow; a longitudinal brown stripe along the top of the back from the thorax to the tail.

Var. a. Primaries with four white spots; second nearly round.

Var. b. Second spot forked; fourth interrupted.

Var. c. Third spot nearly divided.

Var. d. Second and third spots divided.

United States.

HARRIS.

4. C. confinis *Walker.* C. B. M. 681.

White. Head, prothorax, fore coxæ and abdomen at the base luteous. Proboscis tawny. Palpi with black tips. Antennæ black. Thorax and abdomen with a brown stripe. Primaries brown, with a discal slightly angular white stripe, and an elongate triangular oblique subapical white band. Length of the body six lines; of the wings eighteen lines.

United States.

WALKER.

5. C. contigua *Walker*. C. B. M. 650.

White. Head, prothorax and fore coxæ luteous. Proboscis
tawny. Palpi black, luteous at the base. Antennæ black. Thorax
and abdomen with a brown stripe. Primaries brown, with a white
discal stripe which widens from the base to a little beyond the
middle, and with two large subapical white spots. Secondaries
with a small brown spot near the hind border. Body 6 lines long;
wings 18.

United States.

WALKER.

6. C. comma *Walker*. C. B. M. 652.

Luteous, partly testaceous. Proboscis tawny. Palpi with black
tips. Antennæ black. Thorax and abdomen with a brown stripe.
Primaries above with a brown border, which is interrupted at the
tips and by the hind angle, near which there is a curved brown
streak. Secondaries occasionally with a small round brown spot
near the hind border. Body 7 lines long; wings 20.

United States.

WALKER.

PHRAGMATOBIA Steph.

Head and thorax with long hairs. Palpi short, scarcely distinct,
very pilose. Proboscis subspiral. Antennæ short, ciliate—*of the
male*, serrate; *of the female*, simple. Thorax thick. Abdomen
maculate. Anterior tibiæ unarmed; posterior tibiæ with four
spurs. Wings subdiaphanous.

1. P. vagans *Boisd.* Ann. Soc. Ent. 2me sér. X, 322.

Monæ-color; primaries immaculate; secondaries black, fringe
cinereous; all the wings cinereous below, with a black lunule.

North California.

BOISD.

2. P. assimilans *Walker*. C. B. M. 630.

Male. Red. Antennæ testaceous. Thorax with brown hairs.
Wings red; veins darker. Primaries slightly brown along the
costa, and elsewhere indistinctly sprinkled with pale brown, with
two blackish dots. Secondaries brighter red, with three black
dots, two in the disk and one near the hind border towards the
inner angle. Length of the body 6 lines; of the wings 16 lines.

Var. Primaries almost wholly brown. Secondaries with a broad blackish submarginal stripe.

United States.

ECPANTHERIA Walker.

Body stout. Proboscis moderately long. Palpi very short; third joint acuminated, small. Abdomen extending more or less beyond the hind wings. Legs stout; hind tibiæ with minute apical spurs. Wings moderately broad. Primaries much longer than secondaries. *Male.* Antennæ serrated; secondaries short. *Female.* Antennæ simple, not serrated.

1. **E. scribonia** *Stoll. Macularia* Fab., Cram. *Oculatissima* Sm. Abb. *Chrysis,* Gott. Figured in Stoll. Supp. Cram. V, pl. 41 ; Sm. Abb. pl. 69 ; Nat. Lib. vol. 37.

Antennæ black; head white, with a black point on each side near the antennæ. Thorax with ten or twelve black spots, with a pale bluish-white centre, making them appear annular; the two hinder spots largest and somewhat curved. Ground color of the wings white, the surface of the superiors variegated with black spots, most of which are ocular, placed irregularly towards the base, but having a tendency to form transverse rows externally; inferiors white, with a few faint black spots behind. Abdomen blue-black, variegated on the back and sides with orange-yellow ; legs white, the extremities with black rings.

Larva brownish-black, with an orange-red band along each side. The hairs are placed on tubercles alternately nearer the anterior edges of each segment, so that they form a pretty broad band and leave the rest of the body naked.

United States.

HALESIDOTA Walker. *Lophocampa* Har.

Body stout. Proboscis long. Palpi stout, porrect, not long ; second joint much longer than the first ; third conical, very minute. Abdomen extending for about one-third of its length beyond the secondaries. Legs stout; hind tibiæ with four moderately long spore. Wings long, narrow. *Male.* Antennæ slightly pectinated. *Female.* Antennæ serrated.

1. **H. caryae** *Harris.* Ins. Mass. 2d ed. p. 279.

Color, light yellow-ochre; the fore wings are long, rather narrow, and almost pointed, are thickly and finely sprinkled with little brown dots, and have two oblique brownish streaks passing backwards from the front edge, with three rows of white semitransparent spots parallel to the outer hind margin; the hind wings are very thin, semitransparent, and without spots; and the shoulder-covers are edged within with light brown. They expand from one inch and seven-eighths to two inches and a quarter or more. The wings are roofed when at rest; the antennæ are long, with a double, narrow, feathery edging, in the males, and a double row of short, slender teeth on the under side, in the females; the feelers are longer than in the other Arctians, and not at all hairy; and the tongue is short, but spirally curved.

Larva covered with short spreading tufts of white hairs, with a row of eight black tufts on the back, and two long, slender, black pencils on the fourth and on the tenth ring. The tufts along the top of the back converge on each side, so as to form a kind of ridge or crest; and the warts, from which these tufts proceed, are oblong-oval and transverse, while the other warts on the body are round. The hairs on the forepart of the body are much longer than the rest, and hang over the head; the others are short as if sheared off, and spreading. The head, feet, and belly are black; the upper side of the body is white, sprinkled with black dots, and with black transverse lines between the rings.

United States.

HARRIS.

2. **H. tessellaris** *Sm. Abb.* Figured in Sm. Abb. pl. 75.

Faintly tinged with ochre-yellow; their long, narrow, delicate, and semitransparent wings lie almost flatly on the top of the back; the upper pair are checkered with dusky spots, arranged so as to form five irregular transverse bands; the hind edge of the collar, and the inner edges of the shoulder-covers are greenish-blue, and between the latter are two short and narrow deep yellow stripes; the upper side of the abdomen and of the legs are deep ochre-yellow.

The tufts on the *larva* are light yellow or straw-colored, the crest being very little darker; on the second and third rings are two orange-colored pencils, which are stretched over the head when the insect is at rest, and before these are several long tufts of white hairs; on each side of the third ring is a white pencil, and there are two pencils, of the same color, directed backwards, on the eleventh ring. The body is yellowish-white, with dusky warts, and the head is brownish-yellow.

United States.

HARRIS.

3. H. fulvo-flava *Wall.* C. B, M. 733.

Testaceous, paler beneath. Proboscis tawny. Thorax with two tawny stripes, which converge hindward, and with two tawny spots in front between the stripes. Femora and tibiæ hairy; fore femora and fore tibiæ tawny above. Primaries yellow, with a tawny spot at the base, with two oblique tawny bands, with darker borders; these bands are partly connected, and the inner one is especially irregular and ramose, being forked in front and dilated in the disk towards the base, and emitting a branch to each border. Secondaries whitish, with a slight testaceous tinge. Length of the body 6—7 lines; of the wings 16—18 lines.

Var. Primaries tawny, with yellow spots at the base, at the tips, along the costa, and forming an oblique band beyond the middle.

North America.

WALKER.

4. H. annulifascia *Walker.* C. B. M. 734.

Pale testaceous. Proboscis and antennæ tawny. Thorax with two tawny stripes, which converge hindward. Primaries with tawny punctures, which are most numerous, and partly confluent on the disk beyond the middle, and with four oblique bands of whitish tawny bordered spots; veins tawny. Secondaries whitish, with a slight testaceous tinge. Length of the body 6—8 lines; of the wings 18—22 lines.

United States.

WALKER.

5. H. maculata *Harris.* Ins. Mass. 258.

Light ochre-yellow, with large irregular light brown spots on the primaries, arranged almost in transverse bands. It expands nearly one inch and three-quarters.

HARRIS.

DASYCHIRA, p. 256.

3. D. clandestina *Walker.* Canadian Naturalist, 1861, p. 36.

Male. Cinereous, varied with black, thickly pilose. Antennæ short, broadly pectinated. Legs short, very pilose. Wings partly shaded with black, with four irregular undulated black lines which are dilated on the costa of the fore wings; under side paler, with the lines obsolete except by the costa. Length of body 8 lines; of wings 14 lines.

Devins Lake, Montcalm, July 7.

WALKER.

For the following notes of synonymy, geographical distribution, etc., I am indebted to Mr. W. H. Edwards.   J. G. M.

OBSERVATIONS BY W. H. EDWARDS.

The following species are known to be resident in Texas, &c., by me:—

Papilio pilumnus. Texas.
   "   *aristodemus.* Texas.
   "   *cresphontes.* This has been confounded with *Thoas*, but is restored by Doubleday. Ménétriés, in Cat., notes the difference between these two species.
Leptalis melite. New Mexico. Boisd. Spec. Gen. 472.
Callidryas cipris. Texas. Boisd. Spec. Gen.
   "   *orbis.* Texas. Boisd. Spec. Gen.
   "   *philea.* Florida and Texas. Boisd. Spec. Gen.
   "   *ar_ante.* Texas. Boisd. Spec. Gen.
Terias mider. California, according to Ménétriés in Cat. Boisd. Spec. Gen.
   "   *palmira.* Poey in Memorias. Florida and Georgia.
   "   *elathea.* Georgia. Boisd. Spec. Gen.
Colias eurytheme. Boisd. Ann. Ent. Soc. X, 256. This is the species usually taken for *Edusa*, I believe. Boisduval had doubts of *Edusa* being found in this country. I have never seen the European *Edusa* here, and do not believe in it.
Synchloe janais. Texas. Drury, III, 17.
Catagramma clymene. Florida. Described and figured in Lucas.
Cystineura amymone. Texas. Ménétriés, in Cat. and figured.
Eumæia atala. Florida. Figured and described in Poey's Cent.
Rhodocera clorinde. Texas. Boisd. Spec. Gen.
Morpenia serganthia. Texas. Hübner.
Ageronia feronia. Texas. } One or both of these is figured in Drury.
   "   *fornax.* Texas. }

Timetes chiron. Texas. Herbst. 62.
Limenitis eulalia. California. Doubleday & Howitson.
Sayrna karsinali. Texas.
Victorina steneles. Figured and described in Lucas.
Megistanis coduus. Texas. Cramer.
Cybdelis hyperepte. Florida. Hübner.

Besides them, I find mentioned in authors—

Parnassius Smintheus. Rocky Mountains. Doubleday & Howitson.
Colias rauxlans. California. Boisd.
Argynnis Boisducalli. Labrador. Sommer.
    "   *thais.* Figured in Godart, and described in Herbst.
    "   *frigga.* Herbst. 273.
Chionobas chryxus. U. S. Doubleday & Howitson.
    "   *bore.*
Mycalesis antita. Georgia. Hübner.
Thecla melinua. California. Boisd. Ann. Soc. Ent. X.
Lycaena Franklinii. Polar Amer. Curtis in Ross Exp.
Polyommatus anthelie. Newfoundland. In C. R. M.
    "   *amicetus.* Albany River.
Thanaos tristis. California and Texas. Boisd. Ann. X.
    "   *Cervantes.* California. Graslin, Ann. Ent. Soc.
Anthocaris crousa. California.
    "   *lanceolata.* California.
    "   *eusania.* California.
Paphia glycerium. Texas; Illinois.

P. rutulus is said by Gray to be *eurymedon.*

P. solicaon is said by Ménétriès, in Cat., to be same as *machaon.*

P. ajax I do not believe to be same as *marcellus.* All my *ajax* came from Savannah, ♂ and ♀, and all my *marcellus* from West Virginia, ♂ and ♀. All of each were taken in the Spring.

Nathalis irene Fitch, is simply *iole*, with a trifling variation.

C. Vossarowski of Ménétriès, is *C. eurydice* of Boisd. in Ann.

Melitaea serene should have been *Argynnis.*

M. palla is not a synonym for *nycteis* of Doubleday, as given on page 52. The latter is found in Illinois and vicinity.

On page 70, *orion* has a vast distribution.. It comes from Brazil, Grenada, Central America, and West Indies. It is as likely to be in Florida as any other species common to Cuba.

Debis andromacha and *portlandia* are the same.

Cosmogyphia s midea, page 80. This species is a *Chionobas.* Is same as *C. also* of Boisd., but Say should have the preference.

Page 101. *T. aubuniaea* is *smilacis.*

Page 111. *H. alatea* is *cenes.*

CORRECTIONS BY DR. B. CLEMENS.

Page 340. *Arctia imbella* is *Spilosoma imbella*.
" " *A. rubricosa* is *A.? rubricosa*, probably identical with the genus *Crocota*.
" 342. *Spilosoma echo* is *Hypantria echo*.
" " *S. cunea* is *Hypantria cunea*.
" 343. *S. textor* is *Hypantria textor* (type gen.).
" " *S. egle* is (*Euchætes*) *egle*.
" " *S. collaris* and *S. punctata* probably likewise belong to the genus *Hypantria*.
" 344. Gen. *Callimorpha* should be *Hypercompa*; the latter is a generic group created from the former.
" 345. *C. cunea* is *Hypercompa interrupto-marginata* Beauv.
" 349. *H. fulvo-flava* synon. *H. maculata?*
" " *H. annulifascia* synon. *H. caryæ?*

ERRATA.

In the description of *A. aphrodite*, on p. 43, after "marginal," add, "triangles surmounted with black, and above them, near the costa, two others; the secondaries have a marginal series of black crescents."
P. 62, 5th line from bottom, read "secondaries," instead of "primaries."
P. 65, 21st " " " "often," " "after."
UROTA, p. 248, should be put into Fam. LIPARIDÆ.
DASYCHIRA, p. 256, " " " "
LAGOA, p. 257, " " " LIMACODIÆ.
MICRA, p. 253, read MIKRA.
P. 329, 3d line from bottom, read "*L. Speyderii.*"

INDEX OF GENERA

INDEX OF SPECIES.[1]

[1] Synonyms are in italics.

www.ingramcontent.com/pod-product-compliance
Lightning Source LLC
Chambersburg PA
CBHW030902270326
41929CB00008B/538